Contraband Cultures

MODERN AMERICAS

Modern Americas is a series for books discussing the culture, politics and history of the Americas from the nineteenth century to the present day. It aims to foster national, international, transnational and comparative approaches to topics in the region, including those that bridge geographical and/or disciplinary divides, such as between the disparate parts of the hemisphere covered by the series (the US, Latin America, Canada and the Caribbean) or between the humanities and social/natural sciences.

Series Editors

Claire Lindsay is Reader in Latin American Literature and Culture, UCL.

Tony McCulloch is Senior Fellow in North American Studies at the Institute of the Americas, UCL.

Maxine Molyneux is Professor of Sociology at the Institute of the Americas, UCL.

Kate Quinn is Senior Lecturer in Caribbean History at the Institute of the Americas, UCL.

OTHER TITLES IN THE SERIES

Early Civilization and the American Modern
Eva Miller
https://doi.org/10.14324/111.9781800087200

Decolonising Andean Identities
Edited by Rebecca Irons and Phoebe Martin
https://doi.org/10.14324/111.9781787354968

American Cities in Post-Apocalyptic Science Fiction
Robert Yeates
https://doi.org/10.14324/111.9781800080980

Decolonizing Science in Latin American Art
Joanna Page
https://doi.org/10.14324/111.9781787359765

Comics Beyond the Page in Latin America
Edited by James Scorer
https://doi.org/10.14324/111.9781787357549

Canada in the Frame
Philip J. Hatfield
https://doi.org/10.14324/111.9781787352995

Contraband Cultures

Reframing smuggling across Latin America and the Caribbean

Edited by Jennifer Cearns and Charles Beach

UCLPRESS

First published in 2024 by
UCL Press
University College London
Gower Street
London WC1E 6BT

Available to download free: www.uclpress.co.uk

A CIP catalogue record for this book is available from The British Library.

ISBN: 978-1-80008-724-8 (Hbk)
ISBN: 978-1-80008-725-5 (Pbk)
ISBN: 978-1-80008-726-2 (PDF)
ISBN: 978-1-80008-728-6 (epub)
DOI: https://doi.org/10.14324/111.9781800087262

Contents

List of figures

List of contributors

Charles Beach is a social anthropologist with a PhD from UCL. His doctoral research looked at petrol smugglers on the Colombian–Venezuelan border of Norte de Santander and their successful attempts to unionize and gain government support for vocational retraining programmes. He currently lectures in political anthropology at King's College London's Department of European and International Studies.

Jennifer Cearns is an anthropologist based at UCL and previously held the Leach Fellowship in Public Anthropology at the Royal Anthropological Institute of Great Britain and Ireland. She has conducted ethnographic research in Brazil, Cuba, the US, Guyana, Panama, Mexico, Spain and the UK. Her monograph, *Circulating Culture* (University Press of Florida 2023) presents networks of circulation between socialist Cuba and the capitalist Cuban diaspora, following *mulas* (smugglers) back and forth as they navigate all the complexities the geopolitical borders present.

Olivier Allard is Associate Professor at The School for Advanced Studies in the Social Sciences and a member of the Social Anthropology Laboratory, Paris. He has published on kinship and emotion, on bureaucracy and politics, and currently studies the Venezuelan Orinoco Delta and the Guyanese Northwest as an Indigenous borderland.

Luis Javier Cintrón-Gutiérrez is Assistant Professor of General Education at the University of Sagrado Corazón in San Juan, Puerto Rico, and a PhD candidate of Latin American Studies at University at Albany, State University of New York. His current research focuses on narcoculture, marginality, and the inner city in the contemporary transnational Hispanic Caribbean.

Joseph M. H. Clark is Assistant Professor of History at University of Kentucky. He is a social and cultural historian of the early modern Atlantic world, with interest in African diaspora, contraband trade, and environmental history. His first monograph, *Veracruz and the Caribbean in the Seventeenth Century*, was published by Cambridge University Press in 2023.

Charles Dolph is Research Fellow in the Anthropology department at UCL, where he is currently part of the project 'The Sociality of Tax: A multiperspective study of fiscal relations'. He received his PhD in Anthropology from the Graduate Center of the City University of New York in 2022. He works broadly at the intersections of economic and political and legal anthropology, with research interests including agrarian transformations, resource governance, state formation, monetary policies and taxation in Latin America.

Rebecca Galemba is Associate Professor at the Josef Korbel School of International Studies at the University of Denver (DU) and Co-Director of the DU Center for Immigration Policy & Research. Her first book, *Contraband Corridor: Making a living at the Mexico–Guatemala border* (Stanford University Press 2017) details the livelihood strategies of border residents and petty smugglers in times of heightened border securitization and regional trade integration. Her most recent, award-winning book, *Laboring for Justice: The fight against wage theft in an American city* (Stanford University Press 2023), is a community-engaged ethnography of immigrant day labourers, their advocates and the struggle to combat wage theft in Colorado.

Mélanie Montinard is Postdoctoral Research Fellow in the Department of Communication at FAPERJ, the Carlos Chagas Filho Foundation for Research Support in the State of Rio de Janeiro, and holds a PhD in social anthropology from the National Museum of Brazil, UFRJ. Mélanie's research centres on dynamics of Haitian networks and mobility in the Americas. Her current research turns towards remittances as drivers of international migration. By analyzing the volume of remittances, cross-referenced with ethnographic material, her research provides an understanding of how remittances strengthen networks and consolidate transnational social and economic ties, as well as vulnerabilities.

Silvia Posocco, Reader in Social Anthropology at Birkbeck, University of London, works at the intersections of anthropology and gender and sexuality studies. Silvia has a long-term commitment to ethnographic research in Guatemala and is the author of *Secrecy and Insurgency: Socialities and knowledge practices in Guatemala* (2014), and co-editor of five volumes, including *The Cambridge Handbook for the Anthropology of Gender and Sexuality* (2023). Current projects include the book, *Traces, Remnants, Genocide: Transnational adoption in Guatemala*, and new research into forensic biorepositories, bioinformation and evidence.

David C. Thompson is Postdoctoral Research Fellow in the School for International Studies at the Simons Foundation Canada, Simon Fraser University, and holds a PhD in Sociocultural Anthropology from the University of California, Berkeley. David's research centres on prisons and incarceration in Brazil. Drawing on ethnographic fieldwork, he examines the social and political futures that have emerged in the wake of mass incarceration. His current research turns towards Brazil's decarceration movement, the growing network of actors that seek to end mass imprisonment and address its harms.

Cari Tusing is Assistant Professor at the Institute of Anthropological Studies, Austral University of Chile and Postdoctoral Fellow at the Department of Anthropology, University of Copenhagen. She has carried out research in Paraguay and Chile, on property regimes, collective land titling, rural livelihoods, violence, and political memory. She has two current research projects, one studying Mapuche Lafkenche foodways with seaweed pedlars in southern Chile and the other studying the relationship between fire and agribusiness in Brazil.

Eva van Roekel is Assistant Professor at the Department of Social and Cultural Anthropology at Vrije University Amsterdam. Her research and teaching expertise is in violence, economic crisis, human rights, morality and natural resources in Venezuela and Argentina. She is the author of various articles and short stories in anthropological and regional journals and the awarded monograph *Phenomenal Justice: Violence and morality in Argentina*, published by Rutgers University Press (2020). Eva is also an independent filmmaker and cofounder of the Creative Anthropologies Network.

Sophie Villérs was born in Coatepeque, Guatemala, and adopted by a Belgian family at the age of five months. Despite a happy childhood, Sophie grew up with a feeling of something missing and had an irrepressible desire to understand her story and, most importantly, her mother's story. Originally studying psychology, she changed direction and became a social worker and undertook research into her family in Guatemala with the support of the Guatemalan League of Mental Hygiene (LGHM). In 2022, Sophie reunited with her family and discovered the truth about her adoption. Since then, Sophie has been a member of the LGHM, to support people adopted in Europe.

Acknowledgements

This volume materialized from a set of online workshops organized by the editors at the outset of the COVID-19 pandemic in 2020. The editors would like to thank all the contributing authors, as well as Gloria C. Pérez-Rivera and Vikram Tamboli for their input and engagement. The editors would also like to express their gratitude to the editorial team, peer reviewers and copyeditors at UCL Press for their support and careful attention throughout the publishing process.

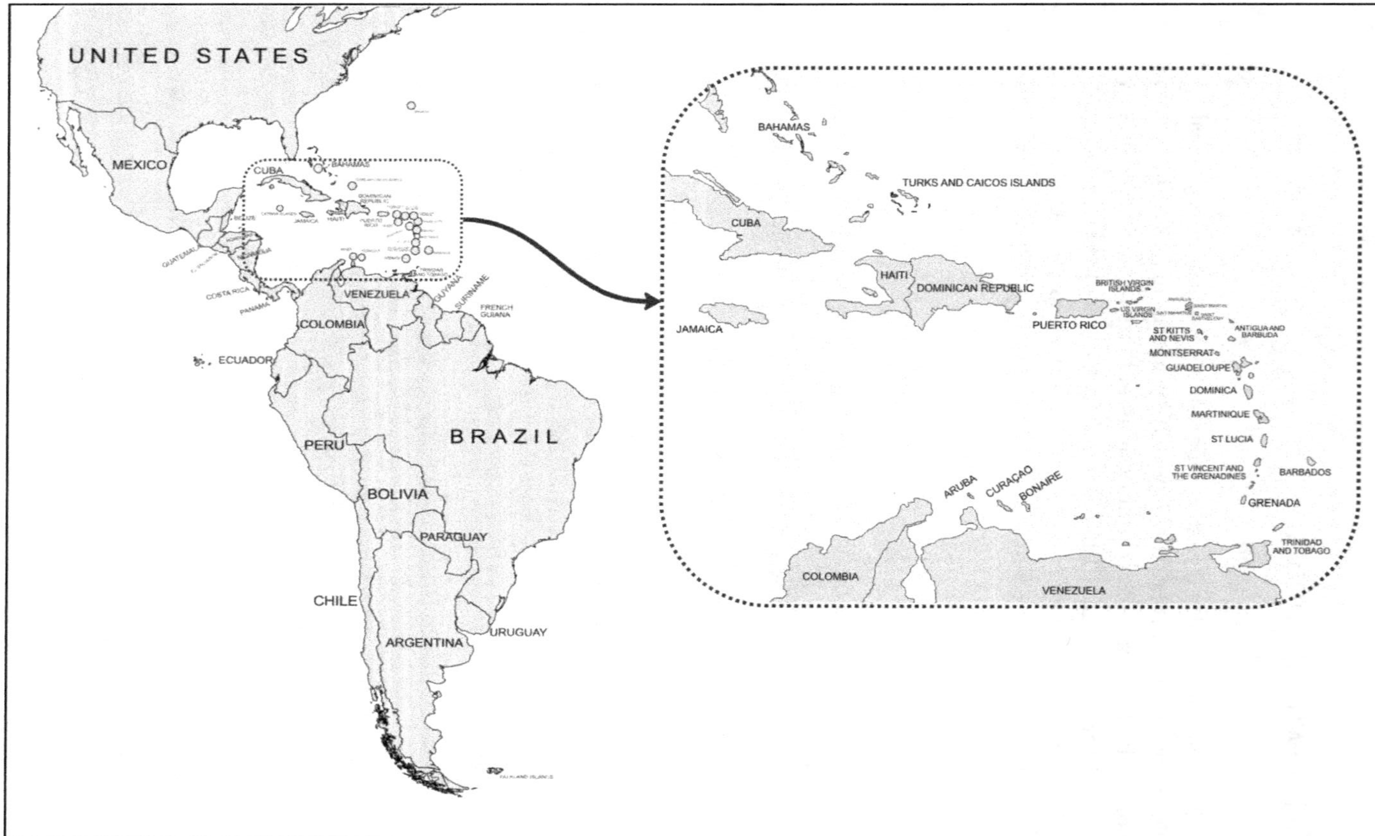

Figure 0.1 Map of the Americas, including expanded view of the Caribbean. © Jennifer Cearns.

Introduction: contraband as culture, culture as contraband

Jennifer Cearns and Charles Beach

It's early on a Sunday morning in the small Colombian border town of Ragonvalia and the central road slopes down into a thick mist at the border. Only the mountain peaks of Venezuela jut out from the top of the clouds. A hunched figure slowly lurches up the hill. The person approaches from out of the mist and nods as he trudges by. As he passes on upwards towards the central town square, his hunched shape again comes into view: it is really formed by huge bundles of spring onions loaded onto his back. More people appear out of the mist, equally loaded with different kinds of vegetables. A motorbike throttles up the road and screeches to a halt, facing toward the sizeable procession coming out of the mist. 'They're Venezuelan farmers bringing goods to sell at campesino market', the rider explains. 'Acá no lo llamos contrabando, lo llamamos comercio' – here we don't call it smuggling, we call it commerce – he says, smiling.

In the popular imagination, contraband and Latin America go hand-in-hand. Most of us are familiar by now with common depictions of the 'smuggler' or *contrabandista*, as portrayed in hit shows like *Narcos* (Netflix), or suggested through media headlines such as: 'Human trafficking second only to drugs in Mexico' (Brice 2010). Such depictions build on a longstanding portrayal of the Latin American and Caribbean region as beyond legality, 'out of control', and somehow subversive. Yet scholarly approaches to the region, by those working within the social sciences and humanities, reveal far more nuanced practices of consumption, circulation and cultural generation at play, interacting in complex ways.

This edited volume presents narratives, representations, practices and imaginaries of smuggling and extralegal or informal circulation, across and between the Latin American region (including the Caribbean) and its diasporas. In so doing, this book seeks to reclaim the term 'contraband' as not merely belonging to a sensationalized and fetishized 'narco' culture, but also as part of the fabric of communal life: looking at phenomena as wide-ranging as the 'art of making do', non-state sovereignty, political resistance, national pride, the fluidity of borders and the socio-economic strategies asserted within and across families and households. Countering a fetishizing and hegemonic imaginary (typically originating from the Global North) of smuggling activity in Latin America as chaotic, lawless, violent and somehow exotic, this book reframes such activities through the lenses of kinship and gender, political movements, cultural and economic exchange, and resistance to capitalist state hegemony.

The volume is predominantly ethnographic in its framing, but comprises a broad range of papers, from historians, cultural theorists and anthropologists, that use various methodological techniques, theoretical traditions and analytic approaches to explore the efficacy and valence of 'smuggling', or 'contraband', as a window onto modes of personhood, materiality, statehood and political (dis)connection across Latin America, broadly construed.

From onions to culture: what is contraband?

This volume is in dialogue with (and often in opposition to) several of the distinct fetishized imaginaries that pervade vernacular discourse about smuggling and contraband. There are four key imaginaries that we consider problematic, and which we suggest quickly disintegrate through an ethnographic lens of enquiry.

Firstly, smugglers are typically seen as armed and inherently violent; romanticizing (and often stigmatizing) discourses generally depict *contrabandistas* as charismatic and aggressive gun-toting figures. Secondly, they are usually seen as inextricably linked to borders and borderlands, relegated to the literal margins or hinterlands of the nation state. Thirdly, smugglers are also typically positioned at the margins of law and order and viewed as divergent from the model or upstanding citizen. Lastly, they are associated most heavily in the popular imagination with drugs, immorality and a general material or symbolic dirtiness that is wrapped up with illicit narcotics or other troublesome or compromised goods.

The Venezuelan *campesinos* (peasants) carrying onions, that introduced the beginning of this chapter, weren't armed or violent, yet through these top-down portrayals of contraband, their quotidian practices also become swept up in these larger, moralizing discourses. While Venezuela and Colombia may observe a formal border, drawn in ink across a map, the Indigenous Wayuu peoples of the Guajira region still regularly cross the open desert of their ancestral land to trade their crops. To state bureaucrats, the region may be a marginal territory that is home to smuggling and contraband activity, but for many of its inhabitants, they are simply living at the centre of their ancestral land.

In Chapter 3 of this collection, Olivier Allard explores how the Warao people of Venezuela and Guyana actively smuggle as a claim over land sovereignty and as a means of resisting both the colonial assertion of a border and the label of 'contraband'. This does not make them violent or armed insurgents, but perhaps rather freedom fighters, or a community of resistance mobilizing their 'weapons of the weak' (Scott 1985). The Warao may be in the hinterlands of the formal states of Venezuela and Guyana, but this is also the heartland of their ancestral territory, to which they are central, not marginal, actors. In Chapter 2, meanwhile, Luis Javier Cintrón-Gutiérrez explores how the violent and perhaps even taboo imaginaries of narcoculture, made so famous through Puerto Rican reggaeton music and broadly associated with global imaginaries of the illicit or deviant, can also be reframed as a cultural product directly stemming from a dying aspirational middle class; such imaginaries in fact proffer a direct response to hegemonic formulations of the 'model citizen'. To similar effect, Jennifer Cearns shows us in Chapter 10 how contraband media piracy in socialist Cuba and its diaspora forms a response (or perhaps a retort) to a global capitalism that is perceived as colonizing in its insistence upon individual profit and ownership. Again, contraband activity is shown to be a symbiotic response to shifting class systems, and in this way, we see how some of the cultural associations of a *contrabandista* are not divergent from concepts of 'the model citizen' but perhaps even products of – or reactions to – such ideas, albeit within different ideological frameworks.

This volume comes out of a desire to challenge these classic imaginaries of contraband, created by the often voyeuristic media gaze or through states' own ideological discourses. If something as simple and as necessary as onion crops (this chapter) or food products (Chapter 6), basic fuel (Chapter 5), medicine (Chapter 7) or even birth certificates (Chapter 11) can be seen as contraband, then what valence can this term even have analytically? We set out to address this question, by expanding upon contraband activities not only as top-down categories, but also as bottom-up lived practices that shape and are shaped by communities and cultures.

Nonetheless, terms such as 'contraband', 'illicit' and 'smuggling' are frequently used, both in popular and academic literature, and these words have historical, moral and legal weight. It is therefore important to delineate a range of terms that are often used by scholars when discussing some of the cultures and communities of exchange that are the central topic of this volume. Lively debates have developed, particularly since the 1980s in the social and political sciences, around terms such as 'informality', 'licit' or 'illicit' economies, and so on, and each belies a particular way of 'slicing and dicing' data. Given the substantial interest over the years in the significant presence of informal economies across Latin America and the Caribbean region, these different analyses of existing data on informality have also typically belied shifting normative ideologies about the region as well, which can be charted alongside various theoretical schools of thought.

In the 1960s, US social scientists began to characterize the supposed 'underdevelopment' of the so-called 'Third World' as a predominantly social problem, caused by internal challenges within largely 'traditional' societies (Rostow 1960). Economic theories of modernization posited the informality typical to regions such as Latin America and sub-Saharan Africa as essentially remnants of 'traditional' or 'pre-capitalist' modes of production and subsistence. Informality was likened to 'traditional' (used here as a synonym for 'backward') in opposition to 'modern', which sat alongside 'capitalist' on a spectrum of economic development.

In the 1970s, Keith Hart introduced the idea of unregulated or informal labour activities as a phenomenon unto itself, which he labelled the 'informal sector' (1973). Hart's work describing the transactions of 'petty entrepreneurs' in Ghana sparked a wider interest among social scientists in economic sectors that evade – by will or by default – the oversight of government and the institutionalization of major capital. In what has been dubbed by some as the 'dependency approach' to informality (Ebenau 2012), the condition of informal economic actors is one of 'disarticulation from the dominant economy and of autonomous attempts at survival through a myriad of interstitial economic activities' (Portes and Walton 2013, 78). The term encompasses a broad target of economic activities, referring to everything from drug trafficking to working 'under the table', to household economies, and for a long time has been considered by economists a phenomenon most typical of so-called 'underdeveloped' countries. Such 'informal' activities were generally interpreted as survival strategies employed by informal workers to navigate the challenges of working in 'Third World' cities.

In the 1980s, sociologist Alejandro Portes and his colleagues challenged this formulation, arguing that informal labour markets exist (and indeed flourish) in the so-called 'advanced' capitalist economies of the West, as well as in the centrally planned socialist economies under the Soviet bloc at the time (Portes and Böröcz 1988; Portes et al. 1989). Peruvian economist Hernando de Soto also took a starkly different view as to why 'informality' abounded to such a visible extent across Latin America. De Soto characterized the informal sector within Latin America as a popular (or perhaps populist), bottom-up reaction to an overbearing and largely corrupt state apparatus that sought to overregulate everything. Unlike earlier schools of thought, viewing informality as absence of the state, de Soto's arguments advocate for the individual entrepreneurs and their initiatives to operate across and despite top-down structures that stand in their way (De Soto 1989). Essentially, de Soto views the informal sector in Latin America as a revolutionary front of the masses, united not as proletarians against capitalist exploitation, but instead as 'extra-legal, micro-entrepreneurs against a bureaucratic, state-directed economy that excludes them from becoming full capitalists themselves' (see Henken 2005, 363). Quite the opposite to the positioning of informal labourers as 'traditional' or 'pre-capitalist' in the modernization theories set out above, de Soto's conceptualization of informal workers in Latin America positions them within a neoliberal, late capitalist landscape where each person must exploit their own labour through entrepreneurialism.

This is in some ways complementary to, but also distinct from, the structuralist approach to informality, which also dominated discussions in the 1980s and 1990s. This position argues that informality only came into existence as a distinct category in the production process after its antithesis, the formal, relatively protected worker, was created through years of struggle by labour unions. In other words, deep and necessary connections exist between the informal sector and the larger 'formal' economy, whereby 'formal and informal activities are simply alternative facets of the same economy and their articulation adopts a "variable geometry" depending on the scope of state regulations, the requirements of capitalist firms, and the size and characteristics of the labor force' (Portes and Schauffler 1993, 25).

All these top-down theories of informality have one thing in common, however, which is an objective to explain *why* such strategies are employed. This is perhaps because much of the scholarly attention on such phenomena has sought to measure the size of the problem, as a step towards mitigating it. From a state top-down perspective, informality is a problem: this is all economic activity that avoids scrutiny and consequently also evades tax. This may be one reason why so many terms have coalesced around the border between 'licit' and 'illicit', 'formal' and 'informal', 'legal' and 'illegal'. Fewer scholarly accounts address the nuances of *how* these activities take place on the ground, and if, indeed, they can and should all be lumped together in one category. Combined with the more moralistic overtones that terms such as 'smuggling' or 'piracy' typically convey (at least in English), it can be challenging to represent and discuss some of the narratives explored throughout this volume without falling into using hierarchical or hegemonic language.

In an effort to counter this, we have opted to refer to 'contraband' in this volume (although of course individual contributors also engage with other parallel terms within their discussions). *Contrabando* (in Spanish and Portuguese, *contrabande* in French) is a term heard frequently in much of Latin America, the Caribbean and its diasporas, and stems etymologically from the Latin *contra* ('against' or 'across') and *bannum* (of Germanic origin, meaning 'to command'). The term contains the sense of illicit or illegal activity, but also perhaps a sense of resistance or belligerence to top-down or normative stances. It also helps us to steer away from the more moralizing or romanticizing discourses that often follow terminology such as 'smuggling', 'piracy' or 'trafficking'. Most of the chapters that follow engage with the term ethnographically, which is to say, the contributors define such terminology through the perspective of their interlocutors, and where necessary, explain what it does and does not mean within specific sociocultural, economic and historical contexts.

The invention of contraband

The whole region of Latin America (from the US–Mexico border all the way down to the southernmost tip of Chile) and the Caribbean, as we recognize it today, is a relatively modern invention. Moreover, in its current guise, the region was (re)invented through specifically capitalistic concerns which centred around discourses of freedom to profit and trade without limit. From the late fifteenth century onwards, the entire region was swept up in increasingly extractivist and aggressively profit-oriented machinations by the Spanish and Portuguese crowns, joined in the seventeenth and eighteenth centuries by the French, the Dutch and the British. To look at a modern-day map of the region, and to note the hard lines delineating nation states (languages, currencies, and so on) is to peer back at centuries-old colonial and commercial projects which from the outset sought to impose 'order' upon the movement of people and things across geographical space, for explicitly economic motives (see Figure 0.1).

Colonial powers rapidly established commercial hubs around the region, particularly in the Caribbean and along the Atlantic coast of South America, and latterly further inland as trading posts and stopping points for missionaries. Yet for many inhabitants of the region, life (and trade) continued to operate across and along boundaries, despite shifting political and imperial allegiances. In the eighteenth-century Iberian world, the Real Academia's *Diccionario de la lengua castellana* of 1729 defined contraband as acts contrary to the law (literally, *contra bando*) and then discussed the term's most common meaning as merchandise, clothing, goods and 'all that is prohibited from entering these kingdoms as it comes from enemy nations barred from our trade', namely any items that had not been examined and approved by port and customs officials (Klooster 2009, 141). But for most people across the region, and especially along the coast, contraband practices:

> constituted more a normative state of commerce than an exotic indulgence for early modern inhabitants of Spanish America and the larger circumCaribbean … These areas found connection and community through illicit exchange. The practice brought subjects of rival early modern empires into daily contact with one another. Their interaction contravened and contorted official statutes promoting imperial separation. (Cromwell 2018, 30)

Moreover, legal pluralism in the early modern world made for different meanings for the socially constructed term (Cromwell 2018).

Contraband as a practice conceived of legally was thus an invention of imperial powers to demarcate their sovereignty (in opposition to rival colonial powers), and archival research suggests that preoccupations with contraband or smuggling activity centred around concerns with controlling the local populations' mobility. The imposition of laws, around who (and what) could move where, represented attempts by the ruling state powers to 'make a society legible', or rather, to arrange the population in ways that simplified taxation and conscription functions and prevented rebellion (see also Scott 2020). As a vocation and a state of market consciousness, therefore, contraband practices, from the outset of the colonial period, created a 'mobility and mutability across the Atlantic that imperial bureaucrats found subversive', which broke up the 'cultural homogeneity and economic rationality [that] officials had worked so hard to cultivate ... contrabandists in peripheral regions deeply influenced the development of these territories' commercial independence from colonial mercantile systems' (Cromwell 2018, 42).

For residents of areas that had been subsumed as relatively peripheral parts of expanding empires, moreover, contraband practices became ways of recentring their own location at the heart of commercial connections. Historians have demonstrated how, through careful cultivation of their own patronage networks (which sometimes resisted wider hegemonic hierarchies of race and gender), local inhabitants 'actively negotiated and transformed the meaning and reach of imperial bureaucracies and institutions for their own benefit', and 'illicit commercial exchanges played a crucial role in reshaping the Atlantic' region (Ponce Vázquez 2020, 5, 16; Hauser and Kelly 2011). Indeed, in many cases the processes involved in evading the law sometimes became more institutionalized (or conceived of as moral) than the structure of the law itself (Conrad 1969, 617); something which remains the case to the present day, and which is explored in several chapters in this volume. In a sense, the prevalence of such local contraband strategies may have begun the process of establishing the region as both transnational and 'locally American' in its own post-colonial right (Pérotin-Dumon 1991, 60). Several historians have argued that the revolutions of the long eighteenth century (the American, the French, the Bolívarian) would not have occurred without the precondition of communities actively collaborating to resist mercantile regulations and heavy taxation.[1]

The sovereign centre and the contraband margins

The study of contraband through historical and ethnographic lenses inevitably engages (and challenges) literatures on borders, sovereignty and the state. As discussed in the previous section, many states in Latin America and the Caribbean have, historically, mobilized the idea of a margin, outside of the state's own power and reach, as a justification for their own existence, and, arguably, continue to do so to the present day. In Colombia, for example, state officials often draw 'a distinct boundary between the central state and the local state as separate, often competing entities', yet united through their common goal to control the wider population, which is broadly characterized as a 'population [of] criminals and guerrilla supporters, existing outside the law' (Tate 2015, 242). The concept of a state's margin – 'the other side of the nation' – here is used to justify the expenditure of heavy force and facilitate the abuse of human rights. In her modern classic of Colombian anthropology, *El Revés de la Nación* (*The Other Side of the Nation*), Margarita Serje argues that Colombia's 'savage' territories, internal and external frontiers, and its supposed no man's lands, are actually 'part of a global stage that generates a certain type of political geographies that cannot be considered as "physical geographies" nor as "natural regions", but as spaces of projection that are the object of a process of mystification ... They have been turned into virtual spaces inhabited by the myths, dreams and nightmares of the modern world' (2011, 23, our translation). In other words, the very idea of the nation and state sovereignty relies upon this constant creation and mobilization of an 'other', across from which it sits in dialogue. This 'other', across the region of Latin America and the Caribbean, has long been framed as the domain of contraband: wild, uncontrollable, 'primitive' even, lurking at the margins. As we will see in several of the chapters to come, this in turn is often mapped onto other characteristics, of ethnicity, gender, religion and language, that further reflect such marginalization.

It is important to hold in mind that constructions such as margin-versus-centre and state-versus-informality (or contraband) are socio-political discourses, which in lived reality are altogether more difficult to pin down. As anthropologist and border theorist Anastasia Piliavsky notes: 'smugglers know all too well that national border crossing is only one part of business whose impulse lies beyond border regions' (2013, 26); the borderline itself is only a tiny part of the story for those involved in the social creation of contraband. This point is also accentuated in many of the chapters that follow, which take borders and margins as social constructions more than topographical or geopolitical lines. Piliavsky calls on us not to fixate on 'defining the limits of borderlands as substantive entities – as territorially, socially, linguistically and politically discrete zones' (Piliavsky 2013, 26). In so doing, she argues, we end up merely reifying these as new regions, 'drawing them on maps with thicker felt pens over and over again. As territorial entities with a distinctive political, economic, and sociocultural life, borderlands appear like replicas of the nation states they circumscribe' (Piliavsky 2013, 40). Contraband is a set of sociocultural practices, as this volume will demonstrate, that reach far beyond borders and even can challenge the idea of what a border is. When theorists and scholars deliberately seek out the limits of state's power, through looking for objective frontiers, borders and margins, we often end up replicating the very state ideology and language we were trying to avoid.

In this light, contraband and illegal networks more generally can themselves be a constituent part of state formation. Illegal networks are usually seen as pointing to the limits of the state, yet there are numerous 'social context[s] in which illegal political networks, far from indicating the external boundaries of the state, [are] creations of state power, and [act] as key mechanisms by means of which state organisation [is] brought into being and reproduced' (Nugent 1999, 92; see also Beach 2018). As Talal Asad argues: 'the entirety of the state is a margin. Or rather, the sovereign force of the law is expressed in the state's continual attempts to overcome the margin' (2004, 287). The chapters in this book collectively challenge the presumption that the state has an objective existence which can be traced into social fields outside the state, where it is taken to be an a priori objective category and unit of analysis, or what Christopher Krupa and David Nugent call the 'realist ontology' of the state. They ask us instead to 'take as a central problem to be solved the very productions of realness and the aura of objectivity that may surround the state' (2015, 10). In Chapter 10, for example, Jennifer Cearns discusses how media piracy is wielded by the Cuban state itself, as a declarative act of resistance against 'colonialist' and/or capitalist discourse from beyond its borders: as a state, Cuba sets itself up as a pirate decentring hegemonic notions of private ownership. By looking beyond the realist ontology of the state, the chapters of this volume together dispel some of these fetishized imaginaries of contraband, namely that contraband is inextricably linked to borders and borderlands and that smugglers are inherently on the margins of law and order.

Countering contraband

As historian Ernst Pijning notes: 'the case of the United States combining smuggling with national heroism is instructive' in linking the realms of economic subterfuge with social and political action (2005, 67). The idea that the Boston Tea Party was an act of liberation against British oppression is deeply ingrained in United States history, as is, implicitly at least, the formulation of smuggling (at the centre of Bostonian merchants' complaints) as not contradictory to the ideal of 'liberty'. Several of the chapters in this volume address this recurring theme of contraband as a site of resistance, albeit in different ways, contexts and points in time. In chapters 6, 7 and 8, in particular, we see how the state's inability to provide core resources (fuel, food and medicine) to its citizens is met with informal entrepreneurial strategies to furnish people with the necessities of life. According to James Scott: 'when such acts are rare and isolated, they are of little interest; but when they become a consistent pattern (even though uncoordinated, let alone organized) we are dealing with resistance' (1986, 27). In this way, contraband practices become political acts countering top-down hegemonies, contributing to the ways that resources are controlled, allocated, produced and used (Tria Kerkvliet 2009).

Yet an ethnographic view of the contextual specificities also reveals that things are not always so straightforward. In Chapter 10, Jennifer Cearns's ethnography of digital-media piracy in Cuba and the Cuban diaspora in Miami reveals that while informal media sharing is a common workaround for the lack of digital connectivity provided by the state, this is also in line with a wider socialist construction of common ownership, which challenges copyright and intellectual private property, in line with wider counter-colonial and counter-capitalist ideologies in Cuba. In this light, contraband might be interpreted as both a local strategy to circumvent top-down policies on the island, and a national strategy in answer to the perceived colonializing projects of international corporations.

Similar contradictions materialize in Chapter 5, where Charles Beach describes how a social movement based on a strong cultural identity of smuggling negotiates a state-provided vocational retraining programme geared to 'resocializing' the participants into non-smugglers. While a contraband culture is central to their strategy to negotiate with the state, the state also capitulates to their demands with benefits that in fact dismantle the very culture that made the demands possible in the first place. In a similarly contradictory vein, David Thompson shows us in Chapter 7 how medicine smuggled into the Rio de Janeiro prison system is officially contraband, but also unofficially permitted to such a degree it has integrated itself into the prison medical system. In this case contraband does not exist as a parallel, illicit market, but as an integral part of the prison medicine system itself; an infrastructure upon which the superstructure relies.

Such ethnographic accounts muddy the waters of the old binaries of state–individual, local–global (and so on) upon which commentaries on informal economies and contraband practices so often rely. The ethnographic focus of this volume therefore reveals that while individual actors are far from apolitical – indeed they may often wield considerable political and economic power – they also may do so in ways that seem to distort some of the theoretical categories that scholars so often use to interpret economic action. Much of the entrepreneurial action, exchange, sharing and material relation-building discussed in this volume points to more of a 'push-and-pull' arrangement that alters 'processes of negotiation, co-optation and realignment' (Fernández-Kelly et al. 2006, 19).

Care must also be taken in distinguishing what is (and is not) contraband in the first place, given that such nomenclature evokes a colonial past that sought to delineate 'unwanted' economic activity from 'acceptable' economic activity (such as, at one point, the trafficking of human slaves). The borders that bring about cross-border contraband trade and the laws that make it illegal are social and political constructs, deeply entwined with the processes of border-making, colonialism and the territorial expansion of states. Through history, different goods and trade corridors have been criminalized and decriminalized, while borders have been drawn, erased and redrawn. As Gallien and Weigand point out in their recent volume on smuggling, a focus on borders themselves also 'risks over-emphasizing one particular aspect of smuggling activities – the logistics of movement – at the expense of dynamics of production, consumption and in particular financing, which are more frequently located in the political and economic centres' (Gallien and Weigand 2022, 5).

Inevitably then, this volume also engages with the substantial literature on borderlands and frontiers, but also seeks to move beyond this somewhat, to reconceptualize what borders, and therefore 'contraband', might mean outside of a colonial state apparatus. One need not (necessarily) cross a nation state border to be involved in contraband practices, as David Thompson reminds us, in Chapter 7, in his work on kinship systems and the smuggling of medicines into prisons in Brazil. If borders represent the operational assertion of power and control at a national level, so too do institutions (such as prisons and hospitals) assert themselves as spaces of 'governmentality' and surveillance (Foucault 1991). Borders, both internal and external, are in this sense everywhere (Van Houtum and Van Naerssen 2002; Lyon 2013). Thus, in this volume we do not take the border spaces of contraband to be understood as material, static, homogenous or binary in nature, delineating 'in' from 'out'. Rather, we understand borders and spaces of contraband as social products, which is to say, 'heterogenous, polysemic, and dynamic where multiple actors are engaged in the process of creating meaning and symbolism' (Peña 2022, 108). In this vein, contraband becomes akin to a Geertzian model of culture itself, forming 'webs of significance' in which people are suspended in activities of spinning and respinning threads and ultimately whole structures of meaning (Geertz 1973, 5).

Communities through contraband

A central argument made cumulatively throughout the chapters in this volume is that what might be loosely described as 'contraband activity' (although it goes by numerous other local names in different examples) permeates all aspects of lived experience in Latin America and the Caribbean. While the delineation of what constitutes 'contraband' may typically be top-down, drawing upon a colonial and imperial history of rule-making and political strategies to 'modernize' and control local populations, the enactment of contraband, when set within its ethnographic and historical context, reveals how intricately contraband is entwined with other local formulations of identity. In this vein, many of the chapters in this volume depict a social landscape whereby communities are formed, held together and refashioned *through* contraband: contraband acts as a binding force within the social fabric of life, touching all other domains of experience, from language and gender to ethnicity and socioeconomic class.

Historically, the definition of contraband activity often corresponded to the ethnicity of the perpetrators; 'creolization and contraband were intertwined' (Rupert 2012, 7). Contraband trade was far more than merely an economic sphere of life, it enabled interaction between a variety of people from different social classes, ethnicities, linguistic backgrounds, political or religious affinities, and gender identities (see Clark, Chapter 1). 'Economic interactions required and facilitated social interactions' (Clark, Chapter 1), creating alternative channels for cultural exchange and the formation of dynamic new communities across the region. This remains the case to the present day, and several of the chapters that follow describe at length how new communities emerge by necessity as a way of facilitating such activity.

Through the lens of contraband, we see how common assumptions of what constitutes 'kinship' and 'relatedness' come into question, giving way to a myriad of other assemblages of human kinship. As Dianne Otto notes: 'relational ties that invoke human solidarities that are inconsistent with the national story of belonging are demonized, criminalized or pathologized' (2017, 257) as such kin networks operate across formal or legally recognized notions of family. Montinard's work (Chapter 8) among Haitian migrants, and Posocco and Villérs's work (Chapter 11) with Guatemalan adopted children, both highlight the central role that contraband activities have in the creation and maintenance of kinship forms within the region and the diaspora. The language of kinship is of course often used within a nationalist political discourse as a means of defining who is 'in' and 'out', separating the centre from the periphery, as does the delineation of what constitutes contraband (Orsini Aarón 2007). For those dislocated from the official structures of the state, a sense of community through contraband creates a very real belonging within an alternative sort of family, the likes of which can be just as politically and economically powerful (Goldstein 2005). After all, it is often the expansive kinship ties invoked through the informal circulation of remittances from diaspora abroad that underwrites the building of local infrastructure, within Latin America, that is not provided by the state (Fouratt 2017; Cearns 2023; Kahn 2019).

As others have pointed out (Gallien and Weigand 2022), the colonial and imperial history of delineating contraband through border-making also disproportionately affects those at the margins of the state, often pointing to racialized (Schwartz 2021; see also chapters 3, 4 and 7, this volume; Tassi 2010) and gendered (Cearns 2023; Sasunkevich 2016) power structures at work. Indeed, by focusing on contraband practices and the communities formed through and sustained by them, we also bring our ethnographic lens towards groups of people typically marginalized by the state, and consequently also by much of the top-down research apparatus used to measure issues of economic 'development'. As Caroline Schuster points out, much of the everyday informal trade (similar to the activities described in many chapters of this volume) works 'because women do not fit the expected template of a smuggler, and can thus slip past border guards and checkpoints' (2022, 173). Frequently the gendered roles of caregiving, social-network maintenance, and household-budget management leave women in Latin America and the Caribbean well-positioned to also manage informal exchanges of goods within their networks (Freeman 2001; Smith 2005; Ulysse 1999). Meanwhile in Beach's Chapter 5, we see how a strong working-class cultural identity forms around the act of smuggling, and how this becomes key to social mobilization and creation of community among an otherwise dispersed population, in their attempts to leverage resources from the state.

This book explores how contraband activities help to form communities with a distinct culture, but it also opens up the idea of culture itself as contraband. Joseph Clark's Chapter 1 positions this idea historically, considering how culture is deemed by state forces to be contraband, due to its perceived threat to law and order or stability of the colonial state. Culture itself becomes something that can be smuggled intentionally across borders by dissidents, pirates or smugglers, or unintentionally alongside the successive waves of migration that have also become typical of the region. Allard, in Chapter 3, alludes to something similar, in his account of how, alongside the smuggling of essential goods, the Warao smuggle political claims to sovereignty and citizenship: through cross-border movement, culture and contraband become potent counter-political flows of local agency. In breaking open contraband as an analytical category, we also break open culture as a discrete unit authorized or prescribed by actors claiming sovereign legitimacy. We start to see the 'systems of inherited conceptions' (Geertz 1973, 89) or 'webs of significance' (Geertz 1973, 5) that get carried across borders as they are spun, unspun and respun with every illicit crossing or stamping of a document.

Overview of the volume

This volume explores contraband across Latin America, the Caribbean and their diasporas, but also quite explicitly seeks to decentre and respond to local definitions, boundaries and frontiers as well. The wider world may divide the region into nation states, but there are also powerful internal borders and cultural regions across the continent: Andean and upland regions are sometimes positioned in opposition to the lowlands (rainforest or coastal areas), urban centres set themselves apart from rural domains, and this in turn is often mapped (at least through informal discourses) onto the age-old binary of modern versus 'primitive'. In Colombia one might hear reference to *tierra caliente y tierra fría* – hot land and cold land – by way of suggesting altitude; in Brazil many people will talk of *litoral* (coastal) versus *interior* (inland).

Some of these regions stretch across the entire Latin American region and are ratified as trading blocs, such as the Pacific Alliance that includes the countries of Chile, Peru, Colombia and Mexico, or the political and economic union of the Caribbean Association, which links the countries of South America with Mexico and most Caribbean island nations. The term *Cono Sur* (Southern Cone) is a cartographical description referring to Chile, Argentina, Uruguay and Paraguay that together form a cone shape on the map, but they are just as frequently linked together through a shared history of Falangist-style dictatorships in the twentieth century, which also links 'the cone' with Brazil and its 21 years of military dictatorship (1964–85).

Other cohorts of countries in the region share colonial or ideological trajectories that still evoke discourses of commonality to the present day. The former members of mega-republic Gran Colombia (nowadays Colombia, Venezuela, Ecuador and Panama) are often framed as sister countries, united by their founder Simón Bolívar 'The Liberator', for example. The election of socialist governments in Venezuela, Bolivia and Cuba have likewise produced cultural synergies between those countries. Bolivia and Peru draw solidarity from and through their large Indigenous populations, lending a pre-Columbian dynamic to state and politics. These regions can of course also be imbued with a racialized discourse, with different regions also referring to a particular ethnicity. The Pacific region in Colombia is synonymous with an Afro-descended population, whereas the Cono Sur is often said to be more European, with its large waves of migration from western Europe up until the middle of the twentieth century. Syncretic Afro-Latin-American religions, such as *candomblé* in Brazil, *vodou* in Haiti and *santería* or *palo* in Cuba, also draw on specific shared histories of colonialism, as do various dialects and creoles of Spanish, Portuguese, French, Dutch and English, across the broader region.

Many of the chapters in this volume engage with these local dynamics, underpinned by internal regional borders asserted along lines of topography, ethnicity, religion, language, colonial history, political ideology and so on. We see how contraband moves not only across official state borders, but also responds to subtler shifts along less tangible internal boundaries that are often made more apparent through these material exchanges. This volume attempts to represent some of that broader diversity of the region, as such dynamics also give life to the instances of contraband explored throughout the chapters presented here.

This work also raises methodological issues when conducting ethnographic fieldwork across the region: inevitably, conducting ethnographic research on activities that are deemed illegal or illicit can introduce methodological challenges. When the main research interest cannot be inquired about directly, research becomes like trying to look at the sun: something that has a structuring effect on social life but cannot be focused on directly. Yet as Cari Tusing explores in Chapter 4, when the researcher tries not to look directly, every interaction seems to relate to contraband, such is its embeddedness in the fabric of social life. Tusing proposes 'lateral' ethnography in response to these challenges, and similar themes emerge in chapters here by Montinard, Cearns, Beach and Allard.

The volume begins with a historical chapter, to lay the foundations for the chapters that follow. In Chapter 1 Joseph Clark examines how colonial forces began to construct the region around capitalist concerns, and how local approaches to trade and exchange began to resist the legal structures imposed by the state. In this way, the opening chapter of the book establishes how the very idea of contraband – which the volume aims to open up as an ethnographic field of inquiry – developed as a set of practices within the region. This chapter also provides crucial context for arguments that are developed through the other chapters in the book; primarily, that 'contraband' itself is a normative term imposed upon an assortment of local practices, many of which either predate or are responses to marginalization and colonization over several centuries across the region. Chapter 2 then looks to the present, re-examining the ever-familiar media representations of contraband in popular culture, to argue that Puerto Rican narcoculture is as much a product of a dwindling middle-class sensibility as it is of extreme criminality.

The following chapters then ethnographically explore the local manifestations and practices of contraband in different economic, political and cultural settings across Latin America, to show how local communities employ contraband strategies in response to the marginalization and ruptures they face. These four central chapters all present disparate ethnographic examples of local responses to political crisis and bottom-up repair strategies to top-down rupture. All four focus on the supposedly 'hard borders' of the nation state to interrogate the practices that enable the movements of people and material commodities across and between political states.

In the first two of these chapters, we hear first from Indigenous groups in the northeast and southwest of the continent, who live across state borders in a way of life often ignored, or considered peripheral by state actors. These two chapters thematically deal with the margins of the state, its national borders, and those who traverse borders regularly as a means of subsistence. The next two chapters (5 and 6) then explore borders of a nation state as sites of crisis, civil unrest, and historically situated economic rupture, that must be navigated on two different geographical sides of the Venezuelan territory. How does crisis and economic strife affect those who live or work across those territories, and how might these ruptures account for the normative categories of smuggler and smuggled? While in chapters 3 and 4, borders are seen as the hard lines between nation states, in chapters 5 and 6, economic crisis starts to destabilize these conceptual categories.

This then sets up the final chapters of the book, which stretch these conceptual limits, and even challenge the theoretical validity of these categories. From seeing contraband as semiformal prison healthcare, to digital media piracy and even the movement of children as state-led acts of contraband, chapters 7 to 11 move us towards reframing what contraband can even mean, focusing on the more mundane everyday facets of lived experience within Latin America and its diasporas. Through looking at these social and cultural aspects of smuggling, they ask what is contraband, and what is a border? When smuggling is integrated into the social fabric of being, can we even still call it contraband? The themes of these chapters range from contraband as delivery of healthcare in prisons, to strategies for diasporic mobility and kinship maintenance, from the immaterial exchanges of digital data to the highly material concerns of the movement of the human body itself.

In this regard, each chapter makes its own individual argument about the valence of 'contraband' as a lens onto local strategies of cultural expansion, economic survival and political resistance, and in combination all the chapters offer ethnographic or historical cases which cumulatively speak to the multiple ways in which contraband activities constitute everyday life across Latin America. One person's contraband can be another person's commerce, but it can equally politically subvert the meaning of commerce and challenge Eurocentric ideas of value and economy. Moreover, the volume as a whole demonstrates that 'contraband' itself is a top-down and potentially colonializing lens onto what is more of an improvised assemblage of practices informed by local customs and communities. In their totality, the chapters of the volume successively paint a broader picture of how 'contraband' is not just a peripheral, illegal, and illicit practice, demonstrating the political turmoil of Latin America so often depicted in global media, but rather, contraband is a locally defined culture, or a mode of being, which has developed from centuries of economic and political rupture as a locally situated response.

Note

1 See, for example: Breen, T. H. 2005. *The Marketplace of Revolution: How consumer politics shaped American Independence*. Oxford University Press; Grahn, L. R. 1997. *The Political Economy of Smuggling: Regional informal economies in early Bourbon New Granada*. Westview; Lane, K. E. 1998. *Pillaging the Empire: Piracy in the Americas, 1500–1750*. Sharpe; Pérotin-Dumon,

A. 1991. 'The pirate and the emperor: power and the law on the seas, 1450–1850'. In *Bandits at Sea: A pirates reader*, edited by C. R. Pennell, 25–54. New York University Press.

References

Asad, Talal. 2004. 'Where are the margins of the state?'. In *Anthropology in the Margins of the State*, edited by V. Das and D. Poole, 279–88. Santa Fe, NM: School of American Research Press.

Beach, Charles. 2018. 'Frontera combustible: Conceptualising the state through the experiences of petrol smugglers in the Colombian/Venezuelan borderlands of Norte de Santander/Táchira', *Journal of Extreme Anthropology* 2(2). Accessed 29 February 2024. https://doi.org/10.5617/jea.6257.

Brice, Arthur. 2010. 'Human trafficking second only to drugs in Mexico', *CNN World*, 26 August. Accessed 29 February 2024. https://edition.cnn.com/2010/WORLD/americas/08/26/mexico.human.trafficking/index.html.

Cearns, Jennifer. 2023. *Circulating Culture: Transnational Cuban networks of exchange*. Gainesville: University Press of Florida.

Conrad, Robert. 1969. 'The contraband slave trade to Brazil, 1831–1845', *Hispanic American Historical Review* 49(4): 617–38.

Cromwell, Jesse. 2018. *The Smugglers' World: Illicit trade and Atlantic communities in eighteenth-century Venezuela*. Williamsburg: Omohundro Institute of Early American History and Culture.

De Soto, Hernando. 1989. *The Other Path: The invisible revolution in the Third World*. New York: Harper & Row.

Ebenau, Matthias. 2012. 'Varieties of capitalism or dependency? A critique of the VOC approach for Latin America', *Competition & Change* 16(3): 206–23.

Fernández-Kelly, María Patricia and Jon Shefner (eds). 2006. *Out of the Shadows: Political action and the informal economy in Latin America*. University Park: Pennsylvania State University Press.

Foucault, Michel. 1991. 'Governmentality'. In *The Foucault Effect: Studies in governmentality*, edited by Graham Burchell, Colin Gordon and Peter Miller, 87–104. Chicago: University of Chicago Press.

Fouratt, Caitlin. 2017. 'Love for the land: Remittances and care in a Nicaraguan transnational community', *Latin American Research Review* 52(5): 792–806.

Freeman, Carla. 2001. 'Is local: global as feminine: masculine? Rethinking the gender of globalization', *Signs: Journal of Women in Culture and Society* 26(4): 1007–37.

Gallien, Max and Florian Weigand (eds). 2022. *The Routledge Handbook of Smuggling*. Abingdon: Routledge.

Geertz, Clifford. 1973. *The Interpretation of Cultures*. New York: Basic Books.

Goldstein, Daniel M. 2005. 'Orphans of the state: Conceptualizing citizenship, space, and kinship in Bolivian municipal politics', *Cultural Dynamics* 17(1): 5–31.

Hart, Keith. 1973. 'Informal income opportunities and urban employment in Ghana', *Journal of Modern African Studies* 11(1): 61–89.

Hauser, Mark W. and Kenneth G. Kelly. 2011. 'Colonies without frontiers: Inter-island trade in the eighteenth- and nineteenth-century Caribbean'. In *Islands at the Crossroads: Migration, seafaring, and interaction in the Caribbean*, edited by L. Antonio Curet and Mark W. Hauser, 41–57. Tuscaloosa: University of Alabama Press.

Henken, Ted A. 2005. 'Entrepreneurship, informality, and the second economy: Cuba's underground economy in comparative perspective'. In *Cuba in Transition*, vol. 15, 360–75. Washington, DC: Association for the Study of the Cuban Economy.

Kahn, Jeffrey S. 2019. 'Smugglers, migrants, and demons: Cosmographies of mobility in the northern Caribbean', *American Ethnologist* 46(4): 470–81.

Klooster, Wim. 2009. 'Inter-imperial smuggling in the Americas, 1600–1800'. In *Soundings in Atlantic History: Latent structures and intellectual currents, 1500–1830*, edited by Bernard Bailyn and Patricia L. Denault, 141–80. Cambridge, MA: Harvard University Press.

Krupa, Christopher and David Nugent (eds). 2015. *State Theory and Andean Politics: New approaches to the study of rule*. Philadelphia: University of Pennsylvania Press.

Lyon, David. 2013. 'The border is everywhere: ID cards, surveillance and the other'. In *Global Surveillance and Policing: Borders, security, identity*, edited by Elia Zureik and Mark B. Salter, 78–94. Cullompton: Willan.

Nugent, David. 1999. 'State and shadow state in northern Peru circa 1900: Illegal political networks and the problem of state boundaries'. In *States and Illegal Practices*, edited by J. M. Heyman, 63–98. Oxford: Berg.

Orsini Aarón, Giangina. 2007. *Poligamia y Contrabando: Nociones de legalidad y legitimidad en la frontera Guajira, siglo XX*. Bogotá: University of the Andes.

Otto, Dianne. 2017. 'Resisting the heteronormative imaginary of the nation-state: Rethinking kinship and border protection'. In *Queering International Law: Possibilities, alliances, complicities, risks*, edited by Dianne Otto, 236–57. London and New York: Routledge.

Peña, Sergio. 2022. 'Borderlands, frontiers, and borders: Changing meanings and the intersection with smuggling practices'. In *The Routledge Handbook of Smuggling*, edited by Max Gallien and Florian Weigand, 107–17. Abingdon: Routledge.

Pérotin-Dumon, Anne. 1991. 'Cabotage, contraband, and corsairs: The port cities of Guadeloupe and their inhabitants, 1650–1800'. In *Atlantic Port Cities: Economy, culture, and society in the Atlantic World, 1650–1850*, edited by F. W. Knight and P. K. Liss, 58–86. Knoxville: University of Tennessee Press.

Pijning, Ernst. 2005. 'Sources and historiography: Conceptualizations of contraband trade in colonial Brazil', *América Latina en la Historia Económica* 24: 67–84.

Piliavsky, Anastasia. 2013. 'Borders without borderlands: On the social reproduction of state demarcation in Rajasthan'. In *Borderland Lives in Northern South Asia: Non-state perspectives*, edited by David N. Gellner, 24–46. Durham, NC: Duke University Press.

Ponce Vázquez, Juan Josè. 2020. *Islanders and Empire: Smuggling and political defiance in Hispaniola, 1580–1690*. Cambridge: Cambridge University Press.

Portes, Alejandro and József Böröcz. 1988. 'The informal sector under capitalism and state socialism: A preliminary comparison', *Social Justice* 15(3): 17–28.

Portes, Alejandro, Manuel Castells and Lauren A. Benton (eds). 1989. *The Informal Economy: Studies in advanced and less developed countries*. Baltimore, MD: Johns Hopkins University Press.

Portes, Alejandro and Richard Schauffler. 1993. 'The informal economy in Latin America: Definition, measurement, and policies'. In *Work Without Protections: Case studies of the informal sector in developing countries*, edited by Gregory K. Schoepfle and Jorge F. Perez-Lopez, 3–39. Washington, DC: US Department of Labor.

Portes, Alejandro and John Walton. 2013. *Labor, Class, and the International System*. London: Academic Press.

Rostow, Walt Whitman. 1960. *The Stages of Economic Growth: A non-communist manifesto*. Cambridge: Cambridge University Press.

Rupert, Linda Marguerite. 2012. *Creolization and Contraband: Curaçao in the early modern Atlantic World*. Athens: University of Georgia Press.

Sasunkevich, Olga. 2016. *Informal Trade, Gender and the Border Experience: From political borders to social boundaries*. London: Routledge.

Schuster, Caroline E. 2022. 'Gender and smuggling'. In *Borderlands, Frontiers, and Borders: Changing meanings and the intersection with smuggling practices*, edited by Max Gallien and Florian Weigand, 168–79. Abingdon: Routledge.

Schwartz, Steven. 2021. 'The politics of bachaqueo', *American Ethnologist* 48(4): 504–19. Accessed 29 February 2024. https://doi.org/10.1111/amet.13036.

Scott, James C. 1985. *Weapons of the Weak: Everyday forms of peasant resistance*. New Haven, CT and London: Yale University Press.

Scott, James C. 1986. 'Everyday forms of peasant resistance', *Journal of Peasant Studies* 13(2): 5–35. Accessed 29 February 2024. https://doi.org/10.1080/03066158608438289.

Scott, James C. 2020. *Seeing Like a State: How certain schemes to improve the human condition have failed*. New Haven, CT and London: Yale University Press.

Serje, Margarita. 2011. *El Revés de la Nación: Territorios salvajes, fronteras y tierras de nadie*. Bogotá: Ediciones Uniandes.

Smith, Cheryl A. 2005. *Market Women: Black women entrepreneurs, past, present, and future.* Westport, CT: Praeger Publishers.

Tassi, Nico. 2010. 'The "postulate of abundance": Cholo market and religion in La Paz, Bolivia', *Social Anthropology* 18(2): 191–209. Accessed 29 February 2024. https://doi.org/10.1111/j.1469-8676.2010.00104.x.

Tate, Winifred. 2015. 'The aspirational state: State effects in Putumayo'. In *State Theory and Andean Politics: New approaches to the study of rule*, edited by C. Krupa and D. Nugent, 235–53. Philadelphia: University of Pennsylvania Press.

Tria Kerkvliet, Benedict J. 2009. 'Everyday politics in peasant societies (and ours)', *Journal of Peasant Studies* 36(1): 227–43.

Ulysse, Gina. 1999. *Uptown Ladies and Downtown Women: Informal commercial importing and the social/symbolic politics of identities in Jamaica*. Ann Arbor: University of Michigan Press.

Van Houtum, Henk and Ton Van Naerssen. 2002. 'Bordering, ordering and othering', *Tijdschrift voor Economische en Sociale Geografie* 93(2): 125–36.

1
'Born in this abominable sin': contraband trade in colonial Spanish America

Joseph M. H. Clark

Informal trade, smuggling and contraband – as well as the social and cultural relationships built up around these activities – have played a prominent role in Latin American and Caribbean history since the early colonial period (Klooster 2011).[1] It would be a mistake, however, to think of contraband as an undifferentiated throughline in Latin American history. Not only have the commodities, networks and geographies of contraband changed over time, but so have the political and cultural meanings of informal trade. While scholars of the recent past and of the Latin American present have examined the illicit exchanges of gasoline, medicine, media and other commodities (see Chapters 5, 7 and 10, this volume) to reveal the creative and entrepreneurial tendencies of submerged and grassroots networks, for the colonial period, studies of contraband trade have typically focused on interimperial rivalries and competitions between colonies and metropoles. Within the colonial period, the culture-forming effects of contraband were not static. As we will see, in the early colonial period contraband relationships were loosely structured. By the eighteenth century, the decline of Spanish commercial power led to the formalization and quasi-legality of transimperial relationships. However, in both the early colonial period and in the eighteenth century, contraband did not simply respond to changing political and commercial realties but was often the force behind these transformations.

Recently, scholars of the colonial period have taken renewed interest in contraband and quasi-licit trade across imperial borders. In particular, they have examined how transimperial relationships – and attempts at regulating informal trade during the Bourbon Reform period (c.1750–1810) – may have informed early movements for colonial sovereignty and, ultimately, independence in the late eighteenth and nineteenth centuries (Rupert 2012; Reichert 2012; Venegoni 2013; Prado 2015; Schmitt 2015; Bassi 2017; Cromwell 2018; Soriano 2018). Building on the foundational scholarship of Ramón Aizpurua (1993; 2011), Johanna von Grafenstein (1997), and Wim Klooster (1998; 2002; 2011), these scholars have shown how a '*de facto* right to trade' (Cromwell 2018, 11) basic goods like hides, linen and tallow – as well as more valuable commodities like gold and silver – across legal boundaries produced not only strong economic relationships and interdependency, but also social and cultural ties that could spark political rebellion when challenged.

While there is little doubt that transimperial trade expanded in the late seventeenth and eighteenth centuries, as English, French and Dutch American colonies grew in commercial power, a close examination of the early colonial period demonstrates that this growth was, in some sense, a formalization of a long-established pattern of exchange. As Juan José Ponce Vázquez, Isabelo Macías Domínguez and others have shown, colonial officials throughout the Spanish Americas had complained of rampant smuggling since the sixteenth century. While their accounts must be read cautiously, they leave an unmistakable impression of the centrality of contraband in early colonial society and culture (Ponce Vázquez 2020; Macías Domínguez 1978; Moutoukias 1988; Lane 2015). According to some accounts, as many as forty or fifty smuggling ships might be off the coast of northern Hispaniola or southern Cuba at any time. As one colonial official in Caracas put it in 1612, transimperial trade was so frequent that '[Dutch and English ships] pass this port as if it were the English Channel' (Newson 1979, 134). As Ponce Vázquez has described for Hispaniola, the effect of this trade on colonial culture was extensive, allowing colonists latitude to build local autonomy under conditions of salutary neglect. Notwithstanding Ponce Vázquez's much-needed interventions, however, the narrative of colonial contraband remains tilted toward the eighteenth century, as if early contraband was a precursor to larger, more important transimperial relationships in the late colonial period. In this chapter, I argue for a narrower periodization of colonial contraband and the careful differentiation of its social and cultural meanings through different stages of development.

Among the distinctive cultural consequences of informal trade in the early colonial era was the centrality of religion in both its execution and its suppression. Informed by the ascendance of religious intolerance in Iberia – both its anti-Jewish and anti-Protestant politics – local officials in the Americas and metropolitan authorities routinely described the spiritual turpitude of trade that took place outside a narrowly defined Catholic realm. For administrators, contraband posed a risk not only to the colonies' commercial integrity, but to their spiritual integrity and, consequently, their political loyalty. Beginning in the early seventeenth century, they responded to this risk with increasingly drastic measures that left a lasting impact on colonial society. The measures included large-scale forced migration; prohibitions on particular commodities; indiscriminate expulsion of non-Spanish residents; draconian, often extra-judicial, penalties; and the imposition of strict ecclesiastical controls, including excommunication, denial of absolution, and the establishment of inquisitorial tribunals in Mexico City, Lima, and Cartagena.

Although state- and church-generated accounts may have overstated the pervasiveness of informal trade – as well as its capacity for religious contagion – civil and religious officials also used it to conduct bureaucratic politics among themselves and between rival Spanish colonies. For example, in 1606, the president of the audiencia of Santo Domingo, Antonio de Osorio, sent a peninsular auditor to Santiago de Cuba to pursue alleged smugglers who had fled there, much to the chagrin of local officials, who did not welcome the auditor's presence, per a letter of November the following year (AGI-Santo Domingo 52). In such cases, we are left to question whether the auditor really was 'odious', as officials in Cuba alleged, or whether his presence imperilled their own interests in informal trade. Not only did officials use allegations of contraband against rival colonies, they also frequently used them against their predecessors in the same colony, as a foil against which they demonstrated their own efficiency and service. The use of contraband as an issue that could strengthen one's own institutional power, or weaken that of a rival, troubles the veracity of reports of contraband, while simultaneously highlighting its political importance. Even if claims of contraband were exaggerated, it nonetheless structured the early colonial state.

Although the suppression of contraband and the bureaucratic infighting influenced the development of the early colonial state and church, it remains unclear how contraband informed the beliefs and practices of alleged practitioners. As is often the case, we are forced to assess early colonial contraband culture as it was seen and described by the people who sought, or claimed to seek, its eradication. At the same time, however, by contextualizing archival records in a landscape dominated by administrative discourse on smuggling, we can begin to imagine how 'illicit' economies informed the construction of social networks and, consequently, of social and cultural affinities, the likes of which are ethnographically explored in the other chapters of this volume. For example, inquisitorial proceedings against alleged witches and 'crypto-Jews', ostensibly born of religious motives, could serve as proxies for the elimination of contraband. Cases like that of the accused witch Antonia Bello, which this chapter will examine in detail, rarely betray explicit allegations of contraband, but, when read in the context of contraband, can illuminate the beliefs, practices, and networks entwined with contraband cultures. In other words, the communities and practices these cases reveal can be read as a product of informal trade, allowing us to see interimperial trade not as part of an inexorable march to sovereignty in the nineteenth century, but synchronically, as part of a decentralized social system whose other constitutive elements included incorporative, popular religious belief, multiethnic corporatism, and commons exploitation.

As non-Spanish colonies grew in number and commercial power, in the late seventeenth century, the nature of contraband trade in the Americas changed. It did not end – in fact, it expanded – but it was increasingly controlled and centralized as English, French and Dutch state power became established in newly-won colonies. This was part of a process of enclosure; territorial growth necessitated clearer demarcation and enforcement of borders, gradually reining in and formalizing informal economic activity. As Klooster and others have noted, contraband trade took a 'quantitative leap' at the end of the seventeenth century, but it also became more customary, turning the bound waters of the Americas into what Ernesto Bassi has called a 'de facto free trade area' (Bassi 2017, 24). It was in this context that state attempts to formalize and regulate transimperial trade in the eighteenth century provoked political resistance and demands for local autonomy. In the broad sweep of the colonial period, the social and cultural meanings of contraband changed significantly, as informal exchanges gave way to forms of trade that, while still illicit, were increasingly commonplace.

'A crime of treason, divine and human': religion and contraband to 1660

Non-Spanish trading ships first began arriving in the Americas in significant numbers in the middle of the sixteenth century, driven largely by the European wars of religion. As contraband grew in the late sixteenth century, particularly during the Anglo-Spanish War (1585–1604) and with the increased sponsorship of the Dutch States-General, Spanish administrators in the Americas and the metropole pursued increasingly creative and draconian measures to suppress it. In 1604, the Crown ordered governors across the Americas to take a census of all non-Spanish Europeans living in the Americas and to exile any who had resided in the colonies less than ten years. The move provoked equivocation from local officials, who responded that such residents not only constituted a large population, but also provided necessary services (see Keith 1969; Hanke 1961). Two years later, in February 1606, the Council of the Indies issued an injunction against the growing of tobacco along the coast of South America and in the Leeward Antilles, citing the tendency of 'foreigners and transients' to cruise the coast in search of the crop. Here, the Council sought to regulate the production of commodities deemed an inducement to smuggling. In July 1606 local officials objected, claiming that smuggling along the coast was not the product of tobacco growing but 'laxity in punishing smuggling' and arguing that the prohibition of a profitable enterprise would impoverish the colony and deprive the royal treasury of its revenue (AGI-Santo Domingo 201).

While metropolitan officials sought to contain contraband by establishing controls on migration and production, local officials in the Americas used it to conduct institutional politics. For example, in the Mexican port of Veracruz, local treasury officials complained repeatedly (in December 1576, August 1598, November 1625 and January 1629) that the castellan of the fortress San Juan de Ulúa and the admiral of the transatlantic fleet denied them access to ships to inspect incoming cargo, suggesting that they may have been either transporting goods across imperial borders or evading taxes (AGI-México 351). Meanwhile, in 1607, Pedro de Valdés, governor of Cuba, sought to have the metropolitan auditor Manso de Contreras removed from the island, alleging that he was lazy and that 'his presence is odious for reasons touching his personal decency', noting that many people who Contreras had investigated for smuggling complained about him (AGI-Santo Domingo 52). Newly appointed officials also routinely cited the laxity of their predecessors, hoping to fare well in comparison.

Perhaps the most drastic measure to reduce smuggling was the forced depopulation of the towns of Puerto Plata, Bayahá, Monte Cristi and La Yaguana on the northern coast of Hispaniola. First proposed by Baltasar López de Castro in 1598 and carried out under governor Antonio de Osorio in 1605–6, the 'Osorio devastations' forcibly relocated residents of the island's northern coast to the interior (Lugo 1947; Ponce Vázquez 2020, 107–18). Those who refused to comply, after extended notice, were to be arrested and summarily executed. Meanwhile, all cattle on the northern coast were also to be rounded up, and all buildings, docks, ships or other structures, were to be destroyed, 'so that not a sign remains to encourage enemies to settle or fortify' the abandoned settlements (Rodríguez Demorizi 1945, 213–15). Osorio, for his part, justified his tactics in October 1605 by citing 'the slight fear of God and of your Majesty, the enormous offenses they were committing against both' (AGI-Santo Domingo 52). In this, he voiced a recurrent aspersion: smuggling was not only a threat to Spanish commerce in the Americas, but to its religious integrity. As we will see, the particular concern that smuggling led to apostasy played a key role in Spanish efforts to suppress contraband, which in turn suggests its centrality to religion and culture, not just colonial economies.

The eradication of smuggling required religious remedies as well as civil and political ones. For example, in 1607, the Bishop of Santiago de Cuba, Juan de las Cabezas Altamirano, resolved to withhold absolution for parishioners who engaged in smuggling. Instead, he instructed them to 'satisfy the royal treasury' (AGI-Santo Domingo 116). Possibly the most lasting religious remedy for smuggling was the establishment and development of three permanent tribunals of the Inquisition in the Americas: in Mexico and Peru in 1571 and in Cartagena in 1610. The Mexican Inquisition was a specific response to the encroachment of Elizabethan Sea Dogs and French corsairs, such as John Hawkins, Francis Drake, and Jacques de Sores, culminating in Hawkins's battle with Spain's transatlantic fleet in Veracruz in 1568. Hawkins's defeat in Veracruz precipitated the formal establishment of the Inquisition's tribunal and provided many of the tribunal's first victims. After his defeat, Hawkins abandoned about one hundred English sailors on the Mexican coast near Panúco, where they were eventually apprehended and sent to Mexico City, coming before the tribunal in 1572 (Barnadas 1984, 530). For the next thirty years, although the tribunal was headquartered in Mexico City, its operations were disproportionately concentrated at the coast, where inquisitors inspected incoming ships to prevent Protestant books and passengers from entering the colony (Nesvig 2009, 134–63). Similarly, the Lima Inquisition got its start inspecting arriving ships for Protestant literature and prosecuting northern European sailors, including, prominently, John Drake, cousin to Francis, who was tried in Lima in 1584 and condemned to the galleys (Liebman 1971; Carvacho 1983; Quiroz 1986; AGI-Patronato Real 266; Fischer 1972, 153; Prien 2012, 206).

When the Cartagena Inquisition was established, forty years after the Lima and Mexico City tribunals, it was likewise intended to exclude Protestant interlopers from the Americas. In 1607, the Council of the

Indies first proposed the establishment of a new Inquisition in Santo Domingo because 'enemies and foreigners – Lutherans and heretics of other sects – in the course of their smuggling and trade procure and propagate their false and heretical ideas, books, and passengers' (Toribio Medina 1899, 42 n1, 434; AGI-Santo Domingo 51; Sluiter 1948, 174). Although the Mexico City office already had jurisdiction over the Caribbean, the Council argued it was 'too far to keep up' with the frequency of foreign incursions (AGI-Santo Domingo 1). The Crown agreed to send two inquisitors from Spain to found a new office, but two years later the location of the court was changed to Cartagena (Toribio Medina 1899, 42–8).

Once established, the Cartagena tribunal, like its predecessors, undertook the investigation and arrest of English and Dutch sailors in the city, who were alleged to be smugglers (Klooster 2006). In one illustrative case from 1620, Cartagena's civil authorities arrested five English sailors who attempted to land outside the city's walls, presumably to conduct small-scale contraband. Rather than be tried by civil courts, however, the Cartagena Holy Office demanded the prisoners be released to the Inquisition 'for reasons touching the Faith'. Cartagena's governor, García Girón de Loaysa, was reluctant to do so, but wrote to the Crown that although he questioned the Inquisition's 'power or jurisdiction to issue such orders, I knew that with such a reply they would be determined to excommunicate me'. Girón went on to request the Crown issue a formal decree determining whether his authority outranked that of the tribunal (AGI-Santa Fe 38).

Girón's request indicates one of the rationales for establishing American Inquisitions in the first place: to establish an authority outside of the chain of civil government, one presumably less corruptible, to quash non-Catholic intrusion in the Americas. Importantly, peninsular officials understood Spanish subjects born in the Americas – including priests and local administrators – to be more susceptible to crimes of smuggling and heresy. Consequently, the colonies needed more peninsular oversight. For example, in 1604, an *oidor* (judge) in Santo Domingo, Marcos Nuñez de Toledo, reported to the Crown that '[the suppression of smuggling] appears to me to be a deed worthy of the zeal, Christianity, and greatness of a King so Catholic … from people [of this land], nothing good is to be expected, for all love smuggling, being born in this abominable sin' (AGI-Santo Domingo 52). Similarly, in 1606, Juan de las Cabezas, the aforementioned Bishop of Cuba, lamented that 'this island is so ruined by smuggling that licentiousness, I am informed, has gone so far that a person living outside of Havana would not baptize a son until a smuggler could act as godfather', connecting the baptismal sacrament to illicit trade. People of the Americas, he suggested, were welcomed not into the true faith, but into the sin of smuggling (AGI-Santo Domingo 116). Others saw people of non-Spanish ancestry as particularly threatening, complaining especially about '*tangomãos*', Luso-African merchants, usually born in Cape Verde, who came to the Americas as slave traders and proceeded to act as agents for Dutch, English and French merchants (AGI-Santo Domingo 155; Deive 1996; Wheat 2016, 104–41). Meanwhile, people of Portuguese descent in the Americas were often believed to be secret Jews. In 1606, a Spanish judge sent to Cuba and Hispaniola to investigate reports of smuggling claimed that, for all the Dutch, French and English trading illegally in the Americas, 'all other foreign nations together have not been as injurious nor prejudicial as the Portuguese ... the majority [of whom] are New Christians and are subtly ingenious [with money]' (AGI-Santo Domingo 100; Hamm 2019).

As early as 1603, the Council of the Indies expressed concern that 'heavy penalties and excommunication by the prelates' had not stopped Spanish subjects in the Americas trading 'with heretics ... [who] bring their books into the area' (AGI-Santo Domingo 1). The particular concern that illicit commerce would become an avenue for the introduction of Protestant ideas was not unfounded. For example, when Spanish colonizers expelled the English settler Henry Colt from Trinidad in 1633, they catalogued his library of 77 books, 42 of which they deemed heretical and sent to the Cartagena Inquisition (Adams 1955). In some cases, political motives probably did underly the introduction of Protestant literature in the Americas. Between the 1590s and 1610s, the Dutch-Portuguese merchant Jan Aventroot regularly conducted contraband trade between the Netherlands and the Spanish Americas, using the Canary Islands as a transshipment point where Dutch goods could be loaded onto Portuguese ships bound for the Americas, and where returning ships could transfer American goods for the Netherlands (AGI-Santo Domingo 100; Thomas 2018). A Protestant zealot who was later executed by the Inquisition in Madrid in 1633, Aventroot filled his Indies-bound ships with Protestant books and pamphlets, hoping to spark a revolt against the Catholic Church and the Crown (AGI-Santo Domingo 1, 54; Schmidt 2001, 201–5).

Colonial governments' concern, that smuggling and cross-confessional trade might lead to religious degradation, was informed by the intolerance that followed Spain's *Reconquista* and the politics of the Protestant and Catholic Reformations. It was also informed by a legal rationale: Spain's claim on exclusive right to control American commerce extended from the papal bull *Inter caetera* of 1493, which granted this control on the condition that the Crown would oversee the catholicization of American territories. For colonial officials, the proliferation of Protestant and Jewish merchants, travellers, or ideas in the Americas threatened to violate this promise and to provide rival European states legal ground for ignoring Spanish claims of exclusivity (Kagan 2009, 1–15; Benton and Straumann 2010). Contraband therefore both challenged Spanish commerce and the legal basis on which commerce was predicated. While informal trade may not have functioned as a conduit for heretical and rebellious ideas in the way Spanish administrators feared, as we will see in the following section, it did support American communities that adhered to a diversity of religious and social practices that ran afoul of Baroque Catholic orthodoxy.

Circum-Caribbean witchcraft: a contraband culture

On 26 March 1611, the governor of Santo Domingo, Diego Gómez de Sandoval, interrogated the French sailor, Guillermo Pereira. In testimony, Pereira, a native of Le Havre, recounted how he had come to the Americas six years earlier on a smuggling mission to Cuba. Before the French vessel could reach its destination, however, it was captured by an English privateer. After a year in captivity, the English ship abandoned Pereira in Cabo Tiburon, in western Hispaniola, where he was discovered by an African maroon community. According to Pereira, the maroons numbered about 50, whom he described as 'very *ladino*', suggesting that they spoke Spanish and may have practised Catholicism. Their captain, a 'very old' African of 'the Zape nation', allowed Pereira to remain with them for four years, during which time two English and one Dutch ship arrived to trade. As he described it, when a trading ship spotted the maroons, they would enter the harbour and fire one cannon shot, at which point seven or eight maroons armed with muskets, arquebuses and arrows would reconnoitre to determine if the ship was Spanish or not. If it was not, then all of the maroons would come to the coast and exchange hides and meat for any goods the smugglers had to offer: cloth, thread, canvas, small arms, and, on one occasion, 23 enslaved Africans the smugglers had captured from a Portuguese slave ship (AGI-Santo Domingo 54).

If colonial officials saw smuggling as a threat to the religious and political fidelity of the Americas, did those who participated in it also see it as subversive? While official responses to contraband – prohibitions, expulsions, forced migrations, harsh penalties and inquisition – played an important role in shaping the social and economic landscape of the early Spanish Americas, the extent to which contraband itself – and not only its suppression – informed cultural practices and political loyalties remains uncertain. Historians interested in the cultural consequences of informal trade are typically obliged to view contraband through the eyes of the people tasked with suppressing it. To elucidate the beliefs and practices of people whom the state considered its opponents, historians have employed a range of methods: from the quantitative methods of social history to discursive readings of state- and church-produced sources, including analyses of archival silences, fragments and lacunae; readings 'with' or 'against' the grain or 'along the bias grain'; and critical fabulation (Trouillot 1995; Stoler 2010; Fuentes 2016, 78; Hartman 2008). While these methods have allowed us to tell more detailed and empathic narratives, even when they are skilfully employed, we still see most historical subjects in confrontation with the state and not as people whose diverse motives did not depend on the state's ascriptive power. How can we begin to understand contraband cultures if we see practitioners of contraband only in instances of confrontation?

In Spanish colonial sources, people accused of smuggling – often non-Spanish nationals, religious minorities, people of African descent, or unmarried women – do sometimes seem to be engaged in political resistance. Many undoubtedly harboured political and religious beliefs at odds with Spanish colonial order, and some probably did smuggle in pursuit of those beliefs. Most Spanish American subjects who engaged in informal trade, however, likely did not act out of specific political or religious motives, but out of self-interest – an interest that must be read not only in opposition to the state, but on its own terms. The maroons of Cabo de Tiburon, for example, may have sought to protect their autonomy against the state by purchasing weapons from English and Dutch traders. But Pereira offers scant insight into the maroons' political or religious beliefs, beyond autonomy. While we must treat his description sceptically as that of an outsider, his testimony suggests that the maroons were Hispanicized, possibly Catholic, and worked mainly as cattle ranchers with the aid of enslaved labour, and occasionally engaged smugglers, not unlike Spanish colonists throughout the island. If we treat them only as a challenge to the Spanish empire, as the state did, we might forgo the opportunity to imagine what else their lives may have meant to themselves.

Not all Spanish officials viewed Spanish subjects who smuggled as inherently rebellious, though most did see smuggling as tacit support for Spain's foreign enemies. For example, Antonio de Osorio's depopulation of Hispaniola's northern coast was controversial among Spanish administrators. In 1601, when the tactic was still being considered, the archbishop of Santo Domingo, a Mexican-born Dominican priest named Agustín Dávila y Padilla, offered his opinion to the Crown: instead of suppressing smuggling directly, the Crown should send legal trading ships directly to the northern coast, providing coastal residents with an alternative to smuggling (Hernández Tapia 1974). Dávila y Padilla's opposition to depopulation was powerful enough that Osorio did not begin to clear the coast until after the archbishop's death in 1604. Once the depopulations began, some Hispaniolans – not limited to those of the northern coast – bemoaned Osorio's tactics. In June 1605, a *licenciado* (lawyer) in Santo Domingo named Gonzalo de Valcárcel wrote that the depopulations risked transforming coastal residents from simple smugglers into decisive allies of the Dutch, drawing a distinction between smuggling and outright rebellion (Hernández Tapia 1974; Peña Pérez 1980).

Other descriptions of smuggling portray those who participated in it less as rebellious and more as naive. In January 1612, as the newly appointed governor of Trinidad, Sancho de Alquiza, reported on his investigation of smuggling on the island, concluding that 'I find everyone generally guilty, without a single exception, and for this reason no one has been arrested'. Alquiza related how, after attending mass, the island's parishioners accompanied him to his home, where the procurator presented him with a petition affirming that all Trinidadians 'from the least to the greatest' were guilty of smuggling. '[After] the petition was read', Alquiza wrote, 'all the *vecinos* [neighbours] and the women with them knelt down on their knees, confessing their sin and begging mercy, which was a very pitiable act'. Comforting the penitent and observing that he 'did not have sufficient men or jails' to carry out the law, he resolved to grant a general pardon, 'for not doing so, everyone there ten years and older might be hanged' (AGI-Santo Domingo 54; Norton and Studnicki-Gizbert 2018, 270–3; Ferry 1989, 34–5).

Alquiza was not one to portray himself as lenient. Six years earlier, after he had assumed his first colonial governorship in Caracas, he described at length how his predecessor had failed to enforce prohibitions on transimperial trade, observing that before his arrival the city's residents 'smuggled with great openness with rebel ships … as if they were not rebels'. He noted, however, that upon his arrival smuggling ceased because residents waited to see whether he would be as permissive as the former governor. Alquiza soon gave them an answer when his spies captured a *mestizo* (mixed-race) man who allegedly entered a Dutch ship in Puerto de Arrecifes and exchanged 'a few trivialities of little value'. Noting that this was the unfortunate man's second offence (the first had been pardoned), Alquiza ordered him to be hanged, a punishment that, in his view, 'served as an example for many who deserve the same' (AGI-Santo Domingo 193).

Reflected in Alquiza's accounts is not only the pervasiveness of contraband, but its banality. Although Alquiza, like his contemporaries, believed transimperial trade to be a threat to Spain's commercial, political and religious interests and advocated for the use of force to eradicate it, he also acknowledged that its practice was not the work of hardened rebels set on resistance. As he noted in Caracas, transimperial trade was so common, people engaged in it 'as if' foreign merchants 'were *not* rebels' (my emphasis), besides which the things they traded were 'trivialities of little value'. To this end, he advised the Crown to rescind peremptory measures against contraband, like the prohibition on tobacco growing, and to instead double down on punitive measures and exemplary violence. Later, when he arrived in Trinidad, he described his new charges as pitiful and ignorant rather than rebellious.

While Alquiza's reports downplayed the political motives of Spanish subjects who dealt in contraband, his paternalistic tendencies do not allow us a better understanding of their motives. To consider this, we turn to an unlikely source: inquisitorial investigations against women accused of witchcraft. Between roughly 1610 and 1636, the Inquisitions of Mexico and Cartagena focused increasingly on witchcraft, just as tribunals had concentrated on Protestantism in the late sixteenth century and Judaism after the revolt in 1640 that began the Portuguese Restoration of Independence. According to Ana María Silva Campo, the Cartagena tribunal prosecuted 51 witchcraft cases in these years, substantially more prosecutions than for any other crime (Silva Campo 2018, appendix A). In Mexico, witchcraft cases represented a smaller number of inquisitions overall, but were especially prominent in the port of Veracruz, where multiple groups of women were prosecuted in the 1620s and 1630s (Campos Moreno 2012; García de León Griego 2017). In Havana, too, church officials and lay clergy remarked on the scourge of witchcraft. The Holy Office's power in the third major node of Spain's transatlantic trade was weaker than it was in Cartagena and Veracruz, but in 1622, the bishop of Havana complained to inquisitors in Cartagena about the 'rampant' plague of witchcraft and the failure of the island's governor to support its suppression. Two years later, an informant of the Inquisition based in Havana, Francisco de Bonilla, reiterated this point, claiming the civilian government in Havana had thwarted his attempts to discover and report supposed witches (Alonso López 2005).

What can we make of the sudden spike in witchcraft cases in the Caribbean? Some scholars have understandably drawn comparisons with European 'witch crazes' of the late medieval and early modern periods, sometimes suggesting that inquisitors mistook unfamiliar traditions of Indigenous and African religious practice and healing for more recognizable manifestations of immorality (Behar 2001; Germeten 2013, 31–44). Others have emphasized the ways witchcraft threatened patriarchal systems in colonies where Baroque Catholic orthodoxy was not firmly established (Silva Campo 2021). However, by synchronizing the rise in witchcraft cases with the political and commercial evolution of the Spanish Americas – and especially with the expansion of transimperial trade – we can arrive at another explanation.

To begin, we might consider the people who were most often accused of witchcraft and what they had in common. Almost all were women, and the majority were either unmarried, widowed, or separated from their husbands. Many were Afro-descended, but most were unenslaved. They hailed from many places, but especially large numbers of accused witches were concentrated in the ports and coasts of the Caribbean and Gulf of Mexico – Veracruz, Cartagena, Santo Domingo, Havana, and Campeche – where they worked in nascent service economies, as innkeepers, tavern owners, healers, food vendors, and sex workers (Germeten 2013; 2020; Silva Campo 2021; 2018; Alonso López 2005; McKnight 2016; Díaz Burgos 2020; Mannarelli 1998; Molina-Bautista 2022; Miranda Ojeda 1999; Ceballos Gómez 1995). Importantly, too, many were mobile and had lived in more than one Gulf-Caribbean port.

Having characterized the people who tended to be accused of witchcraft, we can place them within the context of transimperial trade. While colonial governments attempted to suppress smuggling – efforts in which the Inquisition was involved, though not always to the liking of civil officials – inquisitorial tribunals in Cartagena and Mexico initiated a series of witchcraft cases against property-owning single women in the service economies of major ports. What does the suppression of smuggling have to do with the suppression of witchcraft? Viewed at a distance, the simultaneous surge of witchcraft cases and smuggling leads to one theory: smugglers need fences to receive smuggled goods. Independent women operating in a port city's service economy would appear to be well placed to provide such services.

While it seems plausible, if not likely, that substantially the same group of women who were potential targets of witch hunts may have also had a prominent role in the operation of informal economies, individual cases of witchcraft (at least those I have seen) rarely bear out an explicit connection. Details of those cases, however, when read in the context of contraband, can be surprisingly suggestive. Consider the case of Antonia Bello, a widowed, 37-year-old native of the Andalusian village of Alcia Alcaçar, who, in March 1627, was arrested in Veracruz. Like other women accused of witchcraft, Bello had lived a mobile life to that point, having come to Havana in 1609 at the age of 20, where she met and married a tile maker named Gaspar Esteves (AGI-Contratación 5310). When he died in 1614, she returned to Seville, where she remained for eight years. Prior to her arrest, she had been four years in the city of Veracruz where, according to an informer of the Inquisition named Santiago de Estrada, she lived scandalously (Trial of Antonia Bello, f. 2r).

Between May and August 1626, 12 of Bello's associates in Veracruz denounced her, collectively accusing her of 45 acts of superstition and witchcraft (Trial of Antonia Bello, f. 3r–35r). Most of the allegations centred on her possession and use of magical objects to attract men and secure their fidelity, either for herself or her clients: male and female lodestones to compel a man; three enchanted oranges to arouse him; amulets prepared with a special oil to detect if he had been unfaithful (f. 52v–61r). Others included more malicious actions, such as surreptitiously introducing magical powders into the food of people she wished to control (f. 64r). Notably, Bello's wrongdoing accrued not only to her time in New Spain, but in Spain and Havana as well, where, deponents 'heard it said', she had learned enchantments and kept transgressive contacts.

If we consider cases like Antonia Bello's within the institutional and political context of the early American inquisitions, we can begin to see a connection between witchcraft and contraband. Bello was not explicitly accused of handling stolen goods, smuggling, or suborning Spain's foreign enemies. The testimony in her trial is, however, suggestive, reminding us that she lived in a world where such things were possible. For example, the deponent Leonor de Yslas described Bello in an act of favomancy (divination with beans). He claimed that in December 1625 he walked in on a fortune-telling session in which Bello offered another woman (her neighbour, Beatriz de Valdés) advice on how to find 'a group of Portuguese slave traders' who, with a little supernatural persuasion, would agree to sell to Valdés a captive on credit, with Bello as her guarantor (Trial of Antonia Bello, f. 22r–23r, 52v–53v). According to Yslas, Bello then led Valdés to a house of Portuguese slave traders who were breaking the Nativity fast. When she was presented with these charges against her, Bello responded by disclaiming association not only with the named slave traders but with '*any* Portuguese men' (my emphasis). The accusation – and Bello's strenuous denial – is laden with the suggestion that she associated with a class of non-Spanish merchants who were secretly Jewish, particularly given the detail about the merchants breaking the Nativity fast. A similar suggestion was embedded in the accusation that she had conjured not only Satan but the biblical villain Barabbas, a central figure in anti-Jewish mythology surrounding the crucifixion.

While inquisitors questioned Bello's clandestine association with non-Spanish merchants, other superstitious and magical practices implicated Spain's maritime trade. For example, in her own testimony, Bello admitted to instructing an associate of hers, Luisa García Yslena, in the use of the oration of 'niños perdidos'. García Yslena was anxious that the man she intended to marry, the sailor Blas García, might be 'taken by enemies' while on a trading mission to Cartagena (Trial of Antonia Bello, f. 65v). Bello claimed to have learned the prayer from a woman she knew in Triana, Francisca de Miranda, whose husband was the captain of a ship in the transatlantic fleet (f. 65r). In another instance, the accuser Marianna de Berdesia, a free Black woman from Jamaica, described how Bello made and sold '*cintas de atacar*', ligaments 'made in the sea' to bind a male lover and secure his fidelity while overseas (f. 3r–4v; 55r–55v). As Nicole von Germeten and others have observed, women in port cities likely had more use for this kind of binding, specifically because their partners tended to be mariners (Germeten 2013, 131). Another target of Bello's love magic was a sailor from Cartagena named Gaspar Garcia, to whom Bello had fed magical powders while the fleet was in port (Trial of Antonia Bello, f. 25r–29v). Both in prayers to protect Spanish sailors from 'enemies' and in magical objects to control their behaviour, there is the suggestion of more than a casual association with maritime commerce, and with the women's attempts to control aspects of it. While the taming of men may have threatened notions of Spanish patriarchy, the supernatural control of men *of the sea* may have threatened Spanish commercial integrity.

Another accusation involved Bello's alleged use of a *carta de tocar*, a paper talisman that could be worn under clothes to bring good luck or, if touched to a man's shoulders and loins during a carnal act, discover his infidelity (Trial of Antonia Bello, f. 16r–24v, 55r). The touch letter is one of the most disputed accusations in Bello's *proceso* (trial). Two of Bello's accusers – Yslas and Valdés – both accused Bello of keeping a touch letter. Bello in turn accused Valdés and a third woman, Ynes de Miranda (whose testimony is not part of the investigation), of bringing a touch letter with them when they came to Veracruz from Havana in 1621. She further claimed she had heard that the touch letter had been made in Havana by a specialist named Polanco and that Valdés and Miranda both had returned to Havana multiple times since coming to Veracruz, to transport magical ingredients, spells and objects (f. 61v). That the women may have moved between the cities with frequency is in itself notable, and while the objects they carried are not the same as the merchandise surreptitiously introduced by Dutch, English and French traders, Bello's testimony is in its way direct evidence of contraband smuggling.

More than any specific crime, Bello's threat to Spain's commercial system might be evident in her associates, like Valdés and Miranda, who were not only unmarried but also surprisingly mobile. The amount of biographical detail available for deponents in Bello's case is variable. For most, inquisitors noted name, caste, age, birthplace, residency, and, for women, marital status. They did not usually record previous residences, as they did for the accused. In some cases, however, previous residences were mentioned in testimony. Because of this, we know that of 12 denouncers, only three were natives of New Spain and five had previously lived in Havana, like Bello herself. Additionally, Bello named three people in her testimony whom she claimed had lived in Cartagena before coming to Veracruz, and one other (Ynes de Miranda) who had lived in Havana. A fourth person named in Bello's testimony, Catalina Mendoza, Bello referred to as '*hogar en la flota*' or 'domiciled in the fleet'. In fact, Mendoza, alias 'La Pilota', was arrested and tried by the Inquisition in Veracruz for acts of witchcraft allegedly committed both at sea and in the port. According to her denouncer, a ship captain named Hernando Guerra, she was romantically involved with the fleet's admiral, Fernando de Sosa, again implicating the association of unmarried women with corruptible Spanish sailors (García de León Griego 2017, 9; 2011, 595–6).

Because the testimony in Bello's case, like most witchcraft cases, was coerced and contentious, it is difficult to say, with confidence, what was the precise nature of her relationships with other witnesses. Consider, however, that inquisitors, like later historians, were also trying to disentangle complex webs of affiliation. Perhaps if we draw back from fine-grained examination of which of the women may have been allies, competitors or rivals, we can begin to view cases like Bello's as inquisitors might have: not knowing whose testimony to trust, but seeing the broad outline of a large group of independent women of mixed backgrounds, who moved in and between the port cities of the Iberian Atlantic with relative freedom; had regular access to sailors, traders and transients; and who may have used supernatural methods to affect control over both their own and their male associates' mobility. As much as their marital status and economic independence may have threatened colonial social hierarchies, or their methods approximated Old World definitions of witchcraft, their ability to navigate maritime networks in vulnerable ports suggests another reason for inquisitorial interest.

Inquisitors in American ports were not the only ones who prosecuted cases of witchcraft in the early seventeenth century and, ultimately, if there is evidence to implicate Bello (or other alleged witches) in commercial – rather than spiritual – wrongdoing, it is not enumerated explicitly in her trial (*proceso*). Inquisitors eventually deemed Bello's crimes to be severe enough to merit punishment both by an *auto-da-fé* (public penance) in Veracruz's main square – she was sentenced to be paraded with a white conical hat, a rope around her neck and a candle in her hand, after which she would be subject to one hundred lashes – and by permanent exile from the Americas. Whether the Inquisition viewed her unmarried status, uncertain background and involvement in Veracruz's maritime service economy as a potential vulnerability to smuggling or other forms of commercial heresy, we do not know. By placing Bello's case within the context of contraband, however, we can begin to see aspects of it in a new light. If we think of the Inquisition's crackdown on witchcraft not only as mechanism for articulating social hierarchies in the Americas, but as part of the suppression of a potentially more far-reaching challenge to Spain's commercial and imperial power, we can begin to imagine the women targeted not only as locally powerful, but regionally powerful. In elaborating cases like Bello's, and the networks they suggest, we can find ways of connecting the people accused, across space, to understand how they navigated overlapping jurisdictions, shared ideas and practices, and created communities that did not conform with strict colonial categories. In this, we can begin to map a kind of contraband culture – one in which the people accused are not defined either as political subversives or as naive children, but as resourceful agents and practitioners who built long-distance networks in the uncontrolled spaces of the Gulf-Caribbean world.

Although inquisitions of witchcraft continued well into the eighteenth century, by the middle of the seventeenth century, their relative prevalence began to decline as American inquisitors increasingly focused on other perceived threats to the religious and commercial integrity of the Spanish Americas, beginning with a renewed interest in Portuguese New Christians. Following the revolt of Portuguese nobility against the Spanish Crown, in December 1640, Spanish officials throughout the Americas translated long-held suspicion of Portuguese nationals residing in the colonies into a far-reaching campaign to arrest and expel them. The primary institutional apparatus through which this was achieved was the Inquisition, which, as Stanley Hordes (1982), Rodrigo Escobar Quevedo (2008), Robert Ferry (2006), and Antonio García de León (2007) have shown, used the 'loose ties' of far-flung mercantile networks to identify targets. As these scholars have demonstrated, the Inquisition prosecuted the Portuguese on the premise of crypto-Judaism, but what it targeted was loosely controlled commercial networks.

The American inquisitions began in the 1570s to protect Spain's commercial monopoly against the contraband of northern European sailors, accused of 'Lutheranism' and, in the 1640s, sought to expel Portuguese merchants suspected of crypto-Judaism. In between these two periods, the Inquisition disproportionately prosecuted, for witchcraft, a multiethnic, economically independent group of unmarried women, in Spanish American ports. While it is not possible to say how much these prosecutions extended from concerns over commercial orthodoxy, if we consider the community they uncovered to be an artefact of informal trade, we can begin to see the folk-healing, gendered relationships, spiritual practices and mobility these cases reveal as a form of contraband culture.

While an interest in suppressing contraband may be a throughline connecting these three inquisitorial stages, the Portuguese revolt of the 1640s also signalled a major breaking point in transimperial trade itself. Whether or not Portuguese merchants in the Americas sustained contraband, as Spanish officials alleged, they did sustain legitimate commerce. As the commercial infrastructure built during the Iberian Union – everything from credit networks to shipbuilding – was transformed, non-Iberian traders realized new opportunities to enter Spanish American markets. It is to this transformation we turn by way of conclusion.

Conclusion

In her 1627 trial for witchcraft, Antonia Bello's formal occupation is left ambiguous, but some details about her means and status do emerge. Though she was not wealthy, she owned a stone-and-thatch house in the port of Veracruz – a major crossroad of Spain's Atlantic and Pacific commerce – and had acquired a modest collection of gold and silver jewellery, mahogany furniture and silks. Forced to bear the cost of her imprisonment, these possessions were auctioned. Referring to the property she had sacrificed to pay the tribunal, she pleaded forgiveness for the balance of her debt 'for I am a woman and do not have any other fortune nor estate (*hacienda*) than that which has been sold' (Trial of Antonia Bello, f. 106r–106v, bis). As a widow living independently in Veracruz for four years, Bello's inquisition impoverished her and deprived her of her home. Significantly, the same fate befell at least two of the women whom Bello accused (and who had accused her), Leonor de Yslas and Beatriz de Valdés (whose house shared a wall with Bello's). In a self-propagating series of trials, then, Veracruz's local landscape was remade as at least three free, single women – all of whom lived in the same neighbourhood – were forced to sell their homes. As Ana María Silva Campos has shown for Cartagena, inquisitions targeting witchcraft thus resulted in a transfer of wealth from upwardly mobile women to men of higher station.

In the late seventeenth century, American colonial landscapes underwent a gradual process of enclosure. As the number and commercial power of non-Spanish colonies grew, the 'masterlessness' of maroonage, privateering, commons exploitation and informal trade, ceased to provide a competitive advantage and instead came to threaten the colonial order those things had helped establish. This did not happen all at once. Importantly, although a late-seventeenth-century explosion in sugar cultivation – supported by an equally terrible expansion of the transatlantic slave trade – made English, French and Dutch American colonies extraordinarily profitable, Spain still controlled the largest sources of metal wealth in the Atlantic World, in the mines of Mexico and South America. Shortages of specie encouraged the continuation of illicit trade across imperial boundaries well into the eighteenth century.

As non-Spanish governments sought the formalization of transimperial trade, they and their agents made increasingly bold attempts to access American specie. This included both efforts to find their own competing mines in the North- and South-American mainland and unfulfilled plans to invade and occupy mining areas claimed by Spain in Texas, New Mexico, and Northern Mexico (Laprise 2007). When they came up short, they redoubled their efforts to gain legitimate access to Spanish American markets, which they did in the resolution of the War of the Spanish Succession, which marked the end of the Spanish Habsburg monarchy. In the 1713 Treaty of Utrecht, Spain agreed to allow one British ship per year (known as the annual ship or the *navío de permiso*) to trade at select Spanish-American ports (Finucane 2016). This concession gave cover for the expansion of illicit and quasi-licit interimperial trade while simultaneously committing non-Spanish governments to the suppression of more brazen contraband that might threaten legitimate commerce.

Informal trade was commonplace in the Spanish Americas throughout the colonial period. By the late eighteenth century, a long legacy of unconstrained trade catalysed potent social and cultural relationships that sat in tension with a colonial state that had been shaped by an equally long legacy of efforts to suppress contraband. As Spanish colonial officials began to recognize the futility of trying to eliminate interimperial trade and instead sought to control and regulate it, they imperilled an established order in which informal trade thrived, even as state power officially opposed it. In response to this new threat, Spanish Americans who had become accustomed to de facto free trade mobilized against the state. What they sought to protect, however, was not the informal trade of the sixteenth and seventeenth centuries, but something else entirely. In the early colonial period, informal commerce took place in a world of fluid and poorly defined borders, between people who often existed outside centralized state power or on the margins of it – religious minorities, enslaved and unenslaved Africans, maroons, and unmarried women. By the eighteenth century, this world was increasingly delineated and while colonial states had not succeeded in eradicating contraband, they had eradicated many of the communities that previously sustained it, just as inquisitors imprisoned, deprived and exiled women like Antonia Bello and her contemporaries. By the end of the colonial period, informal trade no longer bore the symbols of the early modern period, but those of the nation-states that would come to dominate the commercial relationships of the nineteenth and twentieth centuries.

Note

1 Following Wim Klooster, I use 'contraband' and 'smuggling' interchangeably and define them as transimperial exchanges in which at least one party to the exchange was the subject of a colonial state that considered that exchange to be illegal.

References

Primary materials

Archivo General de Indias (AGI)
Contratación
5310, n. 42, 20 March 1609
México
351, 23 December 1576; 1 August 1598; 18 November 1625; 20 January 1629
Patronato Real
266, r. 54
Santa Fe
38, 28 July 1620
Santo Domingo
1, 31 December 1596; 22 April 1603; 10 November 1607
51, 28 March 1596
52, 24 August 1604; 20 October 1605; 21 November 1607
54, 6 April 1597; 26 March 1611; 13 January 1612
100, 6 October 1606
100, r. 2, n. 66; 20 November 1608
116, September 1603; 28 June 1607
155, 10 September 1597
193, 20 July 1606
201, 19 July 1606

'Processo criminal contra Antonia Bello muger soltera vezina de la Çiudad de Nueva Veracruz y natural de Sevilla Acialcaçar' – Trial of Antonia Bello, single, resident of Nueva Veracruz. 1627. Mexican Inquisition Papers, HM 35115, The Huntington Library, San Marino, CA.

Secondary materials

Adams, Eleanor B. 1955. 'An English library at Trinidad, 1633', *The Americas* 12(1): 25–41.

Aizpurua, Ramón. 1993. *Curazao y la costa de Caracas: Introducción al studio del contrabando en la provincia de Venezuela en tiempos de la Compania guipuzcoana, 1730–1780*. Caracas: Academia Nacional de la Historia.

Aizpurua, Ramón. 2011. 'Revolution and politics in Venezuela and Curaçao, 1795–1800'. In *Curaçao in the Age of Revolutions, 1795–1800*, edited by Wim Klooster and Gert Oostindie, translated by Susan Greenblatt, 97–122. Leiden: KITLV Press.

Alonso López, Eugenio A. 2005. 'Mohínas de la Inquisición'. Accessed 5 March 2024. https://www.academia.edu/11054817/Mohínas_de_la_Inquisición.

Barnadas, Josep M. 1984. 'The Catholic Church in colonial Spanish America'. In *The Cambridge History of Latin America*, vol. 1, edited by Leslie Bethell, 511–40. Cambridge: Cambridge University Press.

Bassi, Ernesto. 2017. *An Aqueous Territory: Sailor geographies and New Granada's transimperial greater Caribbean world*. Durham, NC: Duke University Press.

Behar, Ruth. 2001. 'Sexual witchcraft, colonialism, and women's powers: Views from the Mexican Inquisition'. In *Gender and Witchcraft: New perspectives on witchcraft, magic, and demonology*, edited by Brian P. Levack, 218–46. New York: Routledge.

Benton, Lauren and Benjamin Straumann. 2010. 'Acquiring empire by law: From Roman doctrine to early modern European practice', *Law and History Review* 28(1): 1–38.
Campos Moreno, Arceli. 2012. 'Un tipo popular en la Nueva Esapaña: La hechicera mulata. Análisis de un proceso inquisitorial', *Revista de Literaturas Populares* 12(2): 401–35.
Carvacho, Rene Millar. 1983. 'Las confiscaciones de la Inquisición de Lima a los comerciantes de origen judío-portugués de la "gran complicidad" de 1635', *Revista de Indias* 43: 27–58.
Ceballos Gómez, Diana Luz. 1995. *Hechicería, brujería e inquisición en el Nuevo Reino de Granada: Un duelo de imaginarios*. Medellín: Universidad Nacional.
Cromwell, Jesse. 2018. *The Smugglers' World: Illicit trade and Atlantic communities in eighteenth-century Venezuela*. Chapel Hill: University of North Carolina Press.
Deive, Carlos Esteban. 1996. *Tangomangos: Contrabando y piratería en Santo Domingo, 1522–1606*. Santo Domingo: Fundación Cultural Dominicana.
Díaz Burgos, Ana María. 2020. *Tráfico de saberes: Agencia femenina, hechicería e Inquisición en Cartagena de Indias (1610–1614)*. Madrid: Iberoamericana.
Escobar Quevedo, Ricardo. 2008. *Inquisición y judaizantes en América española (siglos XVI–XVII)*. Bogotá: Universidad del Rosario.
Ferry, Robert J. 1989. *The Colonial Elite of Caracas: Formation and crisis, 1567–1767*. Berkeley: University of California Press.
Ferry, Robert J. 2006. 'Trading cacao: A view from Veracruz, 1629–1645', *Nuevo Mundo Mundos Nuevos*: 1–65. https://journals.openedition.org/nuevomundo/1430.
Finucane, Adrian. 2016. *The Temptations of Trade: Britain, Spain, and the struggle for empire*. Philadelphia: University of Pennsylvania Press.
Fischer, Martin. 1972. 'Die Inquisition im spanischen und portugiesischen Kolonialreich Amerikas', *Brasilianisches Jahrbuch* 51: 147–60.
Fuentes, Marissa. 2016. *Dispossessed Lives: Enslaved women, violence, and the archive*. Philadelphia: Pennsylvania University Press.
García de León Griego, Antonio. 2007. 'La Malla Inconclusa: Veracruz y los circuitos comerciales Lusitanos en la primera mitad del siglo XVII'. In *Redes sociales e instituciones comerciales en el imperio español siglos XVII a XIX*, edited by Antonio Ibarra and Guillermina del Valle, 41–83. Mexico City: Instituto Mora, UNAM.
García de León Griego, Antonio. 2011. *Tierra Adentro, Mar en Fuera*. Mexico City: FCE.
García de León Griego, Antonio. 2017. 'Comercio, amor y buena fortuna: Vínculos mercantiles y amorosos entre las Canarias y la Nueva España', *XXII Coloquio de Historia Canario-Americana* XXII–077: 1–12.
Germeten, Nicole von. 2013. *Violent Delights, Violent Ends: Sex, race, and honor in colonial Cartagena de Indias*. Albuquerque: University of New Mexico Press.
Germeten, Nicole von. 2020. 'Paula de Eguiluz, seventeenth-century Puerto Rico, Cuba, and New Granada (Colombia)'. In *As if She Were Free: A collective biography of women and emancipation in the Americas*, edited by Erica Ball, Tatiana Seijas and Terri L. Snyder, 43–57. New York: Cambridge University Press.
Grafenstein, Johanna von. 1997. *Nueva España en el Circuncaribe, 1779–1808: Revolución, competencia imperial, y vínculos intercoloniales*. Mexico City: UNAM.
Hamm, Brian. 2019. 'Between acceptance and exclusion: Spanish responses to Portuguese immigrants in the sixteenth-century Spanish Caribbean'. In *The Spanish Caribbean and the Atlantic World in the Long Sixteenth Century*, edited by Ida Altman and David Wheat, 113–35. Lincoln: University of Nebraska Press.
Hanke, Lewis. 1961. 'The Portuguese in Spanish America, with special reference to the Villa Imperial de Potosi', *Revista de Historia de América* 51: 1–48.
Hartman, Saidiya. 2008. 'Venus in Two Acts', *Small Axe* 26(2): 1–14.
Hernández Tapia, Concepción. 1974. 'Despoblaciones de la isla de Santo Domingo en el Siglo XVII', *Revista AULA*: 129–61.
Hordes, Stanley M. 1982. 'The Inquisition as economic and political agent: The campaign of the Mexican Holy Office against the crypto-Jews in the mid-seventeenth century', *The Americas* 39(1): 23–38.
Kagan, Richard L. 2009. *Clio and the Crown: The politics of history in medieval and early modern Spain*. Baltimore, MD: Johns Hopkins University Press.
Keith, Henry H. 1969. 'New World interlopers: The Portuguese in the Spanish West Indies, from the discovery to 1640', *The Americas* 25(4): 360–71.

Klooster, Wim. 1998. *Illicit Riches: Dutch trade in the Caribbean, 1648–1795*. Leiden: KITLV Press.

Klooster, Wim. 2002. 'Between Habsburg neglect and Bourbon assertiveness: Hispano-Dutch relations in the New World, 1650–1750'. In *España y las 17 provincias del Países Bajos: Una revisión historiográfica (XVI–XVIII)*, vol. 2, edited by Manuel Herrero Sánchez and Ana Crespo Solana, 703–18. Córdoba: Universidad de Córdoba.

Klooster, Wim. 2006. 'Communities of port Jews and their contacts in the Dutch Atlantic world', *Jewish History* 20(2): 129–45.

Klooster, Wim. 2011. 'Inter-imperial smuggling in the Americas, 1600–1800'. In *Soundings in Atlantic History: Latent structures and intellectual currents, 1500–1830*, edited by Bernard Bailyn and Patricia L. Denault, 141–80. Cambridge, MA: Harvard University Press.

Lane, Kris E. 2015. *Pillaging the Empire: Piracy in the Americas, 1500–1750*. 2nd ed. New York: Taylor and Francis.

Laprise, Raynald. 2007. 'The privateers of Saint-Domingue and Louis XVI's designs on Spanish America, 1683–1685', *Terrae Incognitae* 39(1): 68–82.

Liebman, Seymour. 1971. 'The great conspiracy in Peru', *The Americas* 28: 176–90.

Lugo, Américo. 1947. 'Baltasar López de Castro y la despoblacion del norte de La Española', *Revista de Historia de América* 24 (1947): 281–301.

Macías Domínguez, Isabelo. 1978. *Cuba en la primer mitad del siglo xvii*. Seville: EEHA.

Mannarelli, María Emma. 1998. *Hechiceras, Beatas y Expósitas: Mujeres y poder inquisitorial en Lima*. Lima: Ediciones del Congreso del Perú.

McKnight, Kathryn Joy. 2016. 'Performing double-edged stories: The three trials of Paula de Eguiluz', *Colonial Latin American Review* 25(2): 154–74.

Miranda Ojeda, Pedro. 1999. 'Hechicería amorosa en Yucatán durante el siglo XVII', *Revista Científica de Estudios Regionales* 21(2): 307–27.

Molina-Bautista, Angélica-María. 2022. '"Yo te conjuro por san Pedro …": Prácticas mágicas y vida cotidiana en mujeres de origen africano en la Inquisición de Cartagena durante el siglo XVII', *Historia y Sociedad* 43: 250–77.

Moutoukias, Zacarías. 1988. *Contrabando y control colonial en el siglo XVII: Buenos Aires, el Atlántico y el espacio peruano*. Buenos Aires: CEAL.

Nesvig, Martin A. 2009. *Ideology and Inquisition: The world of censors in early Mexico*. New Haven, CT: Yale University Press.

Newson, Linda. 1979. 'Foreign immigrants in Spanish America: Trinidad's colonisation experiment', *Caribbean Studies* 19(1/2): 133–51.

Norton, Marcy and Daviken Studnicki-Gizbert. 2018. 'The multinational commodification of tobacco, 1492–1650: An Iberian perspective'. In *The Atlantic World and Virginia, 1550–1624*, edited by Peter C. Mancall, 251–73. Chapel Hill: University of North Carolina Press.

Peña Pérez, Frank. 1980. *Antonio Osorio, monopolio, contrabando y despoblación*. Santo Domingo: UCMM.

Ponce Vázquez, Juan José. 2020. *Islanders and Empire: Smuggling and political defiance in Hispaniola, 1580–1690*. New York: Cambridge University Press.

Prado, Fabrício. 2015. *Edge of Empire: Atlantic networks and revolution in Bourbon Río de la Plata*. Berkeley: University of California Press.

Prien, Hans-Jürgen. 2012. 'The Inquisition and the "extirpation of idolatry": Defending the Iberian colonization and commerce monopoly and the Catholic confessional monopoly against the Protestant seaborne powers and the persistence of traditional Indigenous religions'. In *Christianity in Latin America*, edited by Hans-Jürgen Prien, 199–222. Leiden: Brill.

Quiroz, Alfonso W. 1986. 'La expropriación inquisitorial de cristianos nuevos portugueses en Los Reyes, Cartagena, y México (1635–1649)', *Histórica* 10: 237–303.

Reichert, Rafał B. 2012. 'Navegación, comercio y guerra: Rivalidad por el dominio colonial en la región del Golfo de Honduras, 1713–1763', *Peninsula* 7(1): 13–37.

Rodríguez Demorizi, Emilio (ed.). 1945. *Relaciones históricas de Santo Domingo*, vol. 2. Trujillo: Montalvo.

Rupert, Linda M. 2012. *Creolization and Contraband: Curaçao in the early modern Atlantic world*. Athens: University of Georgia Press.

Schmidt, Benjamin. 2001. *Innocence Abroad: The Dutch imagination and the New World, 1570–1670*. New York: Cambridge University Press.

Schmitt, Casey. 2015. 'Virtue in corruption: Privateers, smugglers, and the shape of empire in the eighteenth-century Caribbean', *Early American Studies* 13(1): 80–110.

Silva Campo, Ana María. 2018. 'Roots in Stone and Slavery: Permanence, mobility, and empire in seventeenth-century Cartagena de Indias', PhD thesis, University of Michigan, Ann Arbor.

Silva Campo, Ana María. 2021. 'Fragile fortunes: Afrodescendant women, witchcraft, and the remaking of urban Cartagena', *Colonial Latin American Review* 30(2): 197–213.

Sluiter, Engel. 1948. 'Dutch–Spanish rivalry in the Caribbean area, 1594–1609', *Hispanic American Historical Review* 28(2): 165–96.

Soriano, Cristina. 2018. *Tides of Revolution: Information, insurgencies, and the crisis of colonial rule in Venezuela*. Albuquerque: University of New Mexico Press.

Stoler, Anne Laura. 2010. *Along the Archival Grain: Epistemic anxieties and colonial common sense*. Princeton: Princeton University Press.

Thomas, Werner. 2018. 'The Inquisition, trade, and tolerance in early modern Spain'. In *Entrepeneurs, Institutions, and Government Intervention in Europe (13th–20th Centuries): Essays in honor of Erik Aerts*, edited by Brecht Dewilde and Johan Poukens, 279–91. Leuven: Katholieke Universiteit.

Toribio Medina, José. 1899. *Historia del Tribunal del Santo Oficio de la Inquisición de Cartagena de las Indias*. Santiago de Chile: Imprenta Elzeviriana.

Trouillot, Michel-Rolph. 1995. *Silencing the Past: Power and the production of history*. Boston, MA: Beacon Press.

Venegoni, Giovanni. 2013. 'La contrebande caraïbe et la première "américanisation" de l'empire (1723–1763)', *Cahiers d'Histoire* 32(2): 41–59.

Wheat, David. 2016. *Atlantic Africa and the Spanish Caribbean, 1570–1640*. Chapel Hill: University of North Carolina Press.

2

'Yo siempre quise ser bichote' in 'P FKN R': Bad Bunny and the representation of Puerto Rican narcoculture in the gore capitalism era

Luis Javier Cintrón-Gutiérrez

Capitalism in Latin America and the Caribbean has triggered profound social rifts. This dichotomy has translated into a discussion around 'the narcos' (drug dealers) and their everyday narratives and aesthetics as an object of study. Our common regional history is rooted in the institutionalization of poverty, resulting from standard policies on privatizing essential services and the articulations of governments and states that assume less responsibility for the care of their constituents. This dispossession has given way to the institutionalization of informal economies that have become the invisible engine of markets and the insertion of marginalized citizens into the consumer society. Some elements that have precipitated social inequality in Puerto Rico are the end of the industrialization project, following the repeal of Section 936 of the US Internal Revenue Code,[1] together with the consolidation of a global economy within free trade agreements in which the Caribbean nation cannot participate, due to its territorial relationship with the United States. As explained by the sociologist Miriam Muñiz Varela, Puerto Rico is currently challenging the collapse of the 'reformist populism' government model, that had once managed to neutralize class-based exclusion, through a 'welfare state' solidified in US federal assistance programmes and an economic model that relies on individual indebtedness (2013, 101–2).

In many parts of the world, the drug trafficking economy also found parallels among legitimate business organizations. Drug trafficking has adopted capitalist logics and has become an industry that generates many jobs outside of 'legitimate' industries. The economic panorama of contemporary Puerto Rico faces high unemployment and poverty rates. Economist José Alameda estimates that the drug trafficking surplus value is over US$366.8 million annually, distributed among some 542 illicit *puntos* or points of sale of drugs (see Torres Gotay 2016). This sum is three times the size of the consolidated budget of the municipality of Ponce, the second largest and second most important city in Puerto Rico. Ponce's budget was approximately US$130.7 million for the 2017–18 fiscal year (Rodríguez Grafal 2017). This occurs in the context of deindustrialization and privatization of goods and services that had historically been part of the social contract between the colonial government and its citizens. According to the Puerto Rico Institute of Statistics (2019), 44.5 per cent of the population and 40.9 per cent of families in the archipelago live below the poverty line.

According to the United Nations Office on Drugs and Crime (UNODC 2012), illicit drug trafficking activities profited from sales of some US$400 billion in 1995. As discussed in an interview with José María Ramos on BBC Mundo (Nájar 2010), drug trafficking revenue sustains daily life in cities and spaces marginalized by capitalism. Much of the drug money also goes into highly visible expenditures such as prestige cars and luxury goods. This represents a much higher economic return than the steel, motor vehicle, tourism or textile industries (UNODC 1998, 4). The emergence of new players and social actors, responding to contexts of exclusion and failed states, is nothing new for the Latin American and Caribbean context. Authors such as Fernando Picó (1999) point to figures like privateers and pirates as responses to exclusion and marginalization in places such as Puerto Rico. According to Picó, governments in Puerto Rico have rarely been able to meet the population's needs (1999, 33). This disconnection between the state and the people has led to a long history of the law being ignored in daily life. In the case of Puerto Rico, there have been various manifestations of state weakness since the sixteenth century. An example of this is the pirates and privateers.

An extensive collection of essays and academic works developed by scholars such as Omar Rincón (2009; 2013), Sayak Valencia (2016), Miguel Cabañas (2008; 2014), Ainhoa Vázquez Mejias (2018), and others, have pointed to the development of a cultural production left over from savage capitalism, where, to escape poverty, 'anything goes'. Other works from anthropology, sociology and philosophy have pointed out that cultural artefacts serve as a kind of ethnography to narrate the social events of an era. Many of these authors have pointed to the development of a narcoculture and the penetration of drug trafficking into the different cultural artefacts of our everyday life. Social scientists such as Howard Becker (2015) and Ernesto Castro (2019) point in this direction. Becker highlights that just as a map represents the cartographic notion of a city, narrative and cultural products such as theatre, film and fiction can give us a sociological representation of a specific historical and social moment, with the same validity as an ethnography or a mathematical model (2015, 25–7). Media and cultural production are mirrors that reflect the social, political and cultural dynamics of their respective localities and historical periods. David Beer argues that popular culture serves as a register with analytical dimensions where it cannot be ignored by the social sciences (2014, 678). He also mentions that the products of popular culture capture and communicate the local realities of everyday life and expose the differences, inequalities and tensions of local communities. In this way, Jaffe (2014) presents cultural products, such as hip-hop, as an ethnographic product that can help us understand sociospatial divides and urban inequalities. In other words, from the social sciences, we can understand cultural products as a contemporary ethnography.

Cultural products related to drug trafficking as an alternative engine of the economy, such as narco-literature, are the visible part of a conflict of economic and social destruction. These products reflect a normalization of violence and a break with hegemonic narratives. The literature suggests that this lived experience of drug trafficking, a product of economic harshness, has created a 'narco-aesthetics' (Rincón 2009) and a language that has permeated our way of narrating everyday life (Reguillo 2011). It has also been resignifying aspirational notions of class (Valencia 2016). More recently, and with the development of digital social networks, we can see how narcoculture has been analysed through the internet and digital consumption. In this field, the work of Alejandra León Olvera and Virginia Villaplana Ruiz (2022) tells us about the different forms of articulation from social networks as a space of representation and self-representation of some aesthetics related to narcoculture. Many of these manifestations point to the pollution of the violence of drug trafficking and other forms of violence in pop culture and everyday life.

With the issue of the construction of citizenship as a function of consumption, narcoculture presents us with the ostentation of luxury cars, high-fashion brands, jewellery, and weapons. In other words, the person exists if they consume luxury goods, but in a vulgar manner, according to the most conservative views within public opinion in Colombia (Urgelles Latorre 2022). It is worth noting that narcoculture has penetrated different social groups and exerts influence beyond the realm of drug trafficking. In this sense, authors such as Omar Rincón (2013) and Manuel Valenzuela Arce (2019) highlight that individuals can immerse in narcoculture and consume its narratives without necessarily being involved in narcotics trafficking.

Recent academic work has emerged to call attention to Puerto Rican narcoculture. Some literature reviews and fieldwork point towards reggaeton and other products close to the artists of this genre baptized by the mainstream media as 'urban music'. In this direction is the research developed by Rafael Ponce-Cordero (2016) and Omar Ruiz Vega (2018), where they subtract the narratives of the *bichotes*[2] ('drug lord' or 'the head of the streets') and contextualize them as articulations of a social bandit, or a heroic and humanized criminal.

The main objects of analysis in this paper are two songs by Puerto Rican artist Benito Ocasio, known as Bad Bunny. The songs selected for this initial dialogue are 'Ser Bichote' (from the album *X 100pre*, 2018) and 'P FKN R' (*YHLQMDLG*, 2020). Both songs have been selected because they make reference to elements of the violence constitutive of a particular period wherein drug trafficking has become an alternative engine for some social sectors in Puerto Rico, and which is portrayed by mainstream news media in a highly theatricalized manner. In this chapter, I seek to initiate an analysis exploring how levels of exaltation of criminal life are articulated in a country where the middle class has been in decline and has been forced to emigrate to the United States.

In an opinion column in *Metro Puerto Rico* (January 2022), Puerto Rican sociologist Emilio Pantojas-García emphasizes that Puerto Rico is facing a third great social transformation. Pantojas-García points out that each previous transformation has had its cultural product, with 'Lamento Borincano' being the song that reflects the era of the coffee plantation and the sugar-cane fields, while during *Operación Manos a la obra* (Operation Bootstrap),[3] 'Verde Luz' and 'En mi Viejo San Juan' are the anthems of the transition of the Puerto Rican economy and society, from agrarian to industrial lifestyles. The Puerto Rican sociologist and researcher highlights that the song 'P FKN R', by the urban performer Bad Bunny, is emblematic of the third transformation that Puerto Rico is beginning to undergo. While Pantojas-García articulates this perspective from the issue of the establishment of elites 'without a homeland', who are displacing Puerto Ricans from their land, we can also articulate that 'P FKN R' shows another reality, that has also been reflected in a continental manner, the emergence of drug trafficking as an economic activity and a contemporary form of socialization.

Cultural artefacts in general can be used as a chain of testimonies and narratives of sectors on the margins of state power, that seek to document how drug trafficking and the war on drugs in Puerto Rico has become part of everyday life. In the case of reggaeton, underground music or 'rap en español' was criminalized in Puerto Rico, making the narratives of this musical genre clandestinely available outside mainstream culture (Negrón-Muntaner and Rivera 2007). Enrique Díaz Álvarez stresses that contemporary artistic production becomes living testimony to violent events (2021, 20). In the field of literary criticism and cultural studies, we can understand products such as *narconovelas* (dramatizations) and the *narcocorrido* (narrative ballad) musical genre as an opportunity to rewrite the 'official' and 'global' history of the war on drugs, and as a reflection of the violence that is a product of the capitalist system and globalization (Cabañas 2008, 519–20). Many cultural critics, sociologists and intellectuals point out that cultural artefacts should be seen as the record and narrative of a particular generation and place (Servigne and Stevens 2020, 165). In the same way that a map represents the cartographic notion of a city, the American sociologist Howard Becker argues that narrative and cultural products such as theatre, film and fiction provide a sociological representation of a particular historical and social moment, with the same validity as an ethnography or a mathematical model (2015, 25–7). Media and cultural production become mirrors that reflect the social, political and cultural dynamics of their respective regions and times. Scholars such as David Beer contend that popular culture is a register with analytical dimensions that the social sciences cannot overlook (2014, 678). His work explores how products of popular culture capture and communicate the local realities of everyday life and expose the differences, inequalities and tensions of local communities. For her part, Rivke Jaffe (2014) presents cultural products – in her case study, hip-hop – as an ethnographic product that can help us understand sociospatial divides and urban inequalities. In other words, we can understand cultural products as texts that describe contemporary ethnographies.

Although they are cultural products with different historical developments, we can compare reggaeton and other musical genres that the music industry has placed within the 'urban genre' with *narcocorridos* in the Mexican context. In that direction, Alejandra León Olvera (2019) tells us that the narrative of the *corrido* in the present time reflects the dynamics of consumption and normalizing violent deaths. This type of cultural product exposes discourses that intermingle violence and the consumption of certain luxury brands, which seem to make violence a brand to consume (2019, 42). In what has become known as 'gore capitalism' (Valencia 2016), violence becomes a vehicle to satisfy consumer needs (León Olvera 2019, 69). Violence becomes decorative and an item of consumption. Within these logics, and with a shrinking middle class, the subjects of illegal enterprises become increasingly a reference point for both society and pop culture. With an increasingly gore-based development, we move from the reference and consumption of dramas about rich men, portrayals such as by Fernando Colunga in the popular 1990s *telenovela* (soap opera) *María la del Barrio,* to uber-macho and (narco) sex symbols, like Rafael Amaya in *El Señor de los Cielos* (2013–present).

Sayak Valencia (2016) highlights drug trafficking and narcoculture as a result of the crises of modernity and the state. In Valencia's case, we can see narcoculture as an issue linked to capitalism in its 'gore' phase. Within gore capitalism, drug trafficking and narcoculture are a response to the current economic order, anchored in precarization, inequality and problems of access to citizen legitimation through consumption, that creates dystopian subjects and actions (2016, 67). Valencia points out that gore capitalism is the citizens' response to a state that fails in its role of preserving life and human rights, as we find in the Puerto Rican context, where the state does not attend to the needs of large sectors of the country and in addition exercises violence with 'foundational myths' that erase diverse physical populations, as well as racial and gender identities (Casanova-Vizcaíno 2021, 43). The concept of gore capitalism, according to Valencia, is a way of extreme (re)colonization through consumption and self-affirmation (2016, 67). In this sense, the construction of the subject derives from its capacity to acquire products and goods within a context of exclusion, poverty and failed states, as García Canclini argues in *Consumidores y Ciudadanos* ('Consumers and Citizens') (1995). The quickest way to acquire those goods that legitimize citizenship, and its agency, is through dystopian activities such as informal business (Valencia 2016, 67).

In this way, we can see reggaeton as the manifestation of a rupture in Puerto Rican society caused by economic disparity (Pérez 2008, 5). Social problems are articulated by representing poverty through the use of catchy phrases, accompanied by danceable rhythms which originated in Puerto Rico, inspired by Panamanian reggae (Fugellie Videla 2014, 9), hip-hop, and the rap style of the United States, which since its origins has addressed social problems and themes such as 'street, sex and struggle' (Dinzey-Flores 2008, 36). Jesús Martín-Barbero (2010), anchored in Appadurai's theoretical framework, suggests that within the very media and cultural artefacts of the capitalist system and the dominant class, there are spaces where collective dissents and questions about issues imposed in everyday life are narrated. In the narratives of reggaeton songs, at least in their origins, the hostilities of social inequality, routinely spotlighted by the traditional media, are emphasized. This turned this genre into the mouthpiece and spokesperson of the experiences of the *caserío* (Puerto Rican term used to refer to public housing projects managed by federal and local agencies), the neighbourhood and the 'street', very similar to what the *nueva canción* (new song) was for the Latin American left, or in the past in Puerto Rico the *bomba* and the *plena* were for the Black and working classes. Prior to reggaeton, salsa had been another musical genre where social and class asperities were reflected. The academic work of Puerto Rican sociologist Ángel G. Quintero Rivera, on salsa, anchored in the sociology of music studies, highlights that music is a cultural artefact with which we can express and feel time, as well as sociocultural identities and their interactions (2020, 152). In an essay published in the digital magazine *80grados*, Iván Chaar López (2010) makes an exercise of linking the salsa of artists such as Willie Colón with the representations and imaginaries of some reggaeton artists.

Drug trafficking, narcoculture and gore capitalism as an everyday occurrence

Drug trafficking is an illicit global economic activity with high profitability, and centred in capitalist logics. The 2012 United Nations Office on Drugs and Crime (UNODC) World Drugs Report highlights that between 3.4 and 6.6 per cent of the world's population uses illicit drugs. The Organization of American States (2014)[4] estimates the economic impact of total retail sales at approximately US$320 billion. This would be equivalent to 0.9 per cent of gross world product (GWP), more than the operating budget of the government of Puerto Rico, or that of New York City. In the Mexican context, illicit economic activities related to drug trafficking represent a monetary impact of close to US$991 million dollars per year (Ríos 2008, 2). Unlike the legal capitalist system, where companies listed on stock markets claim to have transparency and regulation by the state, drug trafficking is a closed neoliberal activity, of which little is known about its internal operations.

The social asperities and inequalities between social classes have meant that, from these informal economies, drug trafficking has become a non-state actor that influences the decision-making of many governments. Work by Jorge Domínguez (1998), and by Jennifer Holmes, Sheila Gutiérrez de Piñeres and Kevin Curtin (2008), goes in this direction. Domínguez suggests that drug trafficking has many parallels with the behaviour of piracy in the sixteenth century. On the other hand, Holmes, Gutiérrez de Piñeres and Curtin argue that in the long run, drug trafficking is a problem that alters the functions of the state, leaving essential services orphaned by the pursuit of an almost invisible enemy, as seen in the Colombian experience.

As highlighted at the outset of this volume in the introduction, drug trafficking is a recurring topic in Latin America, and one which gains a great deal of scholarly and journalistic attention. In Puerto Rico, drug trafficking – and its aftermath in the form of murders, police operations and associated images that could fit into a gangster movie – is increasingly gaining notoriety in the press. The recent economic order in the region has been linked to the growth of drug trafficking as a mode of social integration with capitalist logic. This is because huge sectors of the population have not been able to join with the promise of consumption and modernity. With this comes the 'deployment of corruption, impunity, violence and death that accompanies it and the complicit condition of an "adulterated state"' (Valenzuela Arce 2015, 13). In this sense, the 'narco-world' has been introduced into various everyday life practices. On the one hand, this issue has been fundamental in the development of political relations on the American continent. It is an issue that transcends the imagination and imposition of borders (Valencia 2016, 135). It has also been an issue addressed by the media in different ways, ranging from journalistic chronicles to the fictional representations in *narconovelas*. Some of the themes that draw attention to this illicit activity are the high levels of violence, militarization and a torn social fabric. The latter is a metaphor used by Claudio Lomnitz (2021) to describe how extralegal outlets, the 'good guys–bad guys' binary, and the violent control of fragmented territories are part of contemporary everyday life at a time when sovereignty and the state are being recomposed. In this sense, Lomnitz understands that beyond a 'failed state', a new type of state is emerging (in the Mexican context) where sovereignty is enjoyed, but the administration of it remains lacking. In the Puerto Rican context, we might see things a little differently, insofar as many of the policies are imposed from the colonial relationship with the United States.[5] Despite the colonial context with the US, the literature analysing the Mexican context could serve as a frame of reference to understand some of the dynamics of living in a space where local political power encounters similar elements of violence and fragmentation. In the Puerto Rican context, we can find many parallels with this analysis in the writings of Fernando Picó in his book *De la Mano Dura a la Cordura* (1999).

Mexican anthropologist Rossana Reguillo starts from the premise that narco-trafficking is the most latent symptom of a rupture in social fabric as we know it, which opens up a world for 'the growth of authoritarianism, the erosion of civil society, the deterioration of human rights, the transformation of cities and towns into ghost regions or theatres of war, and the rise (or return) of "expressive violence" – lethal violence with no utilitarian end other than to represent its own power' (in Braham 2016, 130). Around this social erosion resulting from drug trafficking, various theories have emerged. The concept of narcoculture, one of the most widespread concepts related to drug trafficking in everyday life, is a very broad one in which there is not necessarily a hegemonic notion. Apart from the criminal aspect, according to Howard Campbell (2009, 19), narcoculture is a contemporary element of cultural hybridization that rests on nationalist, neocolonial and postcolonial elements, based on the existence of the United States as an empire, and Latin America as a periphery. It interweaves local notions and practices with global visions. An example given by Omar Rincón (2009, 151) in this direction is the formation of the idea of narcoculture in Colombia and its aesthetics mixed with practices and aesthetics of the nouveau riche Americans and the Colombian and Antioquian highlanders.

According to Miguel Cabañas (2008, 537), narcoculture is a cultural representation of the drug industry that in turn serves as a vehicle of resistance to globalization on the part of the popular classes. For Cabañas, this comes with the significant paradox of incorporating these marginalized sectors into the processes of globalization. Cabañas points out that narcoculture is a vehicle for narrating the experiences of marginalized sectors in globalization, outside the official narrative of the 'war on drugs' (2008, 520). This could well go hand in hand with the work of Ana Wortman (2003), which posits the emergence of a middle class as a product of Fordism and modern industrialization that created a different lifestyle. This new middle-class lifestyle provoked several transformations in the consumption of cultural products.

Sayak Valencia (2016) points out that narcoculture reflects a social and economic shift in which the middle class is disappearing, and figures related to drug trafficking are increasingly becoming a social and cultural reference. This is due to the fact that the logic of work has been reconfigured and socialization has been based on consumption. The anthropologist Néstor García Canclini also pointed in this direction in his book *Consumidores y Ciudadanos* ('Consumers and Citizens') (1995). Valencia tells us that within a logic of hyperconsumption, values and levels of things that we are willing to accept are being (re)articulated. In an economic system where opportunities within legality are increasingly scarce, drug trafficking has been reinterpreting the market and work (2016, 69). In this sense, in the face of the increasingly difficult articulation of the middle class, Valencia points out that criminal life has become an identity affiliation which in turn has become an aspirational category and an object of consumption in the mass media (81). In a very peculiar context, Sayak Valencia defines the category of gore capitalism to explain a contemporary reality, particularly in border spaces where the subaltern subject is developing under the transnationalizing forces of the First World (26). Valencia points to the emergence of *necro-empowerment* within the concept of gore capitalism. That is, the systematic and uncontrolled use of violence.

Within this logic that Sayak Valencia describes, the work of Rafael Ponce-Cordero tells us about the articulation of figures close to drug trafficking as bandits, but who become mythical figures within subalternities. In this direction, we can see figures such as the *bichote* becoming contesting entities. Analysing the film *Talento de Barrio* (2008), starring rapper Daddy Yankee, Rafael Ponce-Cordero sees the *bichote* as a social bandit who at times can be narrated as someone 'outside the law' but with 'virtues' and 'heroic' deeds (2016, 147).

A brief context of recent Puerto Rico

This chapter seeks to initiate a conversation about the most recent economic and social transformations, between the end of the twentieth century and the beginning of the twenty-first. That said, I dare to assert that one cannot speak of Puerto Rico without referencing elements such as death, exclusion and violence. Some of the more painful and traumatic events in the last decade include the period of Luis Fortuño's administration, when homicides reached historic figures of over 1,000 per year, and the passage of Hurricane María, during Ricardo Rosselló's administration. If we try to narrate the Puerto Rico of the 1990s, we cannot avoid including extremely bloody events such as the *mano dura contra el crimen* – iron fist against crime. As Sayak Valencia highlights, the history of the twenty-first century is no longer told from the point of view of the survivors, but from the point of view of the number of dead, in a situation where the movement of people is more limited than the flow of contraband drugs, violence and the capital generated by these elements (2016, 30).

To put the social and economic framework of the Puerto Rico that Bad Bunny narrates into context, economist Orlando Sotomayor explains that poverty and precariousness in Puerto Rico is the inability to satisfy basic needs such as housing, health, nutrition and access to participation in the political process, and the formation of cultural or national identity established by the hegemonic culture (Sotomayor 2002, 2). Based on this premise, Eduardo Kicinski and Orlando Sotomayor argue that, despite the country's great economic progress, poverty and inequality have continued to be serious problems in Puerto Rico since the 1960s (1997, 18). This is due to the inability of the current system to incorporate the population into the world of work, and the absence of an alternative or complementary development model that promotes self-management outside of social assistance programmes.

Although Puerto Rico's political situation is colonial and subject to the powers of the US Congress, the archipelago is still a place that is culturally disconnected from globalization and neoliberalism. Indeed, the colonial relationship makes Puerto Rico part of what Juan Bosch (2009) calls 'the imperial frontier of the Caribbean'. In recent years, Puerto Rico has become a bridge for cocaine trafficking to the United States. This problem prompted the US federal government, beginning with the George H. W. Bush Administration, to promote the Caribbean Third Border Initiative. This interagency initiative was also a central focus of the administration of former governor Luis Fortuño (2009–12). The issue of Puerto Rico as a springboard for cocaine to the north was taking place in a context of industrial slowdown in the archipelago and a significant increase in poverty levels. In this sense, in the face of the collapse of the colonial economic model in legality, drug trafficking as an illicit economic engine becomes a painful alternative, without making a break with capitalism. In general, we can understand that the historical development of the Caribbean has been anchored in a permanent crisis in which the state is unable to satisfy the needs of the population. Fernando Picó (1999) highlights this in his work on the *mano dura* period.

An overview of Bad Bunny

The Puerto Rican artist and influencer Bad Bunny is the self-proclaimed leader of *La nueva religión* ('new religion', a reference to reggaeton as a cultural movement). Bad Bunny, or Benito Martinez Ocasio, is one of the most prominent Puerto Rican urban artists on the international scene. He was born in 1994 in Vega Baja, a town located in the northern part of Puerto Rico's main island. According to *Up Close & Personal: Bad Bunny*, a magazine special issue published by A360 Media LLC in 2023, Benito was raised in a Catholic, working/lower-middle-class, suburban home, where his father was a truck driver and his mother a schoolteacher.

In addition to being an internationally known 'urban' musician and performer, Bad Bunny has collaborated in the design of some models of Adidas, a multinational sports footwear brand. He was guest editor of the newspaper *Metro PR*, has three flavours of ice cream at the San Juan ice cream parlour, Señor Paleta, and participated as a wrestler in the WWE (World Wrestling Entertainment). As an object of study, Bad Bunny has been analysed mainly for his music, performance, and masculinities. In the work of Mónica Lugo-Vélez and Megan Gargiulo (2020) and Sarah Platt (2018), for example, the queer performance of his aesthetics and music are highlighted.

Benito was born and raised in the Puerto Rico of the 1990s, the period of *mano dura contra el crimen*. While it is true that Benito, unlike many urban artists, did not grow up within a space of conflict, Jesús Martín-Barbero (2001; 2004) points out that with the media today, we all live certain realities without being physically there. Some of Bad Bunny's musical hits aim to narrate themes of essentially urban violence. Mónica Lugo-Vélez and Megan Gargiulo (2020) point out that in an interview, Bad Bunny mentioned that he had never held a gun until it was time to act in the Netflix series *Narcos Mexico*. Still, many of his songs echo armed self-defence. He also makes constant allusions to a mystification of criminal life. This can be understood in terms coined by Jesús Martín-Barbero (2004, 81) when he talks about the media being the vehicle that generates proximity with the '*cosa pública*' (public thing). Within this logic, we can understand that one does not have to be part of a group or a subculture to experience it. In this sense, Bad Bunny, without living within the 'frontal battlefield' of *mano dura contra el crimen,* but with its media repercussions and its influence on our everyday life, can assume a performance of what Luis Figueroa Rivera calls the stereotypes associated with street violence, 'pimps' and '*bichotes*' or 'druglords' (2020, 102).

'Being a critter' in P FKN R: an ethnography of Puerto Rico in gore capitalism

Within the 'poetics of Benito'[6] I have selected two songs that I believe are essential in situating Puerto Rico within gore capitalism. I selected 'P FKN R' from the album *YHLQMDLG* (2020). Throughout the song, Bad Bunny and collaborators make onomatopoeias that allude to gunshots and 'Los maliante'[7] – the bad guys – with the 'Prr-prr-prr-prr-prr-prr-prr'. Several observations are also made about Puerto Rico and the San Juan metropolitan area. For example, Bad Bunny claims that in Puerto Rico 'even babies *maliantean*'.[8] While Bad Bunny doesn't assume in this song that he is a direct child of the marginalized areas and the conflict of the local drug war, he does give a forum to several people who were born into that social environment. The other lyric that I analyse in this chapter is 'Ser Bichote', from the album *X100pre* (2018). In this song, the *bichote* is represented as an authority figure in marginalized spaces, with an intervention, two minutes into the song, that reads:

> *¿Cómo que què me pasó a mí, papi?*
> *Que yo mando aquí en el caserío*
> *Y yo digo que te tienes que ir pal' carajo ¡Tírala!*
>
> What do you mean, what happened to me, Daddy?
> That I am in charge here in the block
> And I say you've got to get the fuck out of here!

Similarly, Benito mentions in the song[9] an inversely proportional relationship, wishing death on his critics and observing that *puntos* (drug sale spots) open while schools close. The local newsletter *Primera Hora*, in its digital version of 6 April 2019 ('Keleher sobre el cierre de escuelas'), mentions that Julia Keleher (former Secretary of Education under the unfinished term as governor of Ricardo Rosselló) said at a forum at Yale University that, in Puerto Rico, she was the 'responsible adult', who undertook the reorganization of the public education system, that resulted in the closure of 255 schools. In 2015, police authorities were talking about the existence of more than 500 drug points distributed throughout Puerto Rico. In 2018 they were talking about more than 600. About 90 of these illicit sales spots, according to the *El Vocero*, are located in San Juan, with an estimated profit of over US$50 million (Rivera Puig 2018).

In the song 'Ser Bichote', Bad Bunny talks about several issues that can be analysed under the conceptual framework of gore capitalism. In the first part of the song, he says his mother, father and teacher all wanted better things for him – to be a teacher, a baseball player, a firefighter … but, no: he's going to do what he wants. This passage comes after many repeats of: '*yo siempre quise ser bichote*' – I always wanted to be the head of the streets. In this part, we can stumble upon a dichotomy that Valencia (2016) introduces by saying that the aspirational figures of the middle class are fading away, due to the various economic crises, and are succumbing to the myth of the 'criminal life'.

In the same song, reference is made to the ostentation of luxury items. Bad Bunny, in 'Ser Bichote', says he liked working, he liked parties, but that wasn't it. Now he's a millionaire, doing things his way, and if he wants a Ferrari or 'Lambo', he can buy it.

In these verses we can find two constituent elements of the social and cultural turn that gore capitalism is taking.

Conclusion

Through content analysis of these two songs, we see how Bad Bunny weaves a narrative of the dichotomies that Sayak Valencia (2016) identifies as central to gore capitalism. On the one hand, we see how the figure of the *bichote* is privileged and mythologized, over other legally acceptable professions. We see how the two songs provide a diagnosis of how Puerto Rican society has been rearticulating its aspirational models. While it is true that we cannot be sure that there is a tendency for Puerto Ricans to aspire to be *bichotes*, we can see that within capitalist logics, there is a desire to insert themselves into consumer society, but one anchored in that which is defined as 'distasteful' by dominant and conservative classes.

In Bad Bunny's songs the drug dealer, specifically the *bichote*, is seen as a successful figure, constructed as a social outlaw defying authority, and as a heroic character who can insert himself into consumer society by buying luxury vehicles. In 'P FKN R', Bad Bunny mentions that he as an artist has made millions, and is respected in the *barrios* (neighbourhoods) and *caseríos*. In other words, he equates his personal success with the stereotypical *bichote*. This can be understood within the logic of the legitimization of citizenship through ostentation, presented by Néstor García Canclini (1995). The two songs analysed, as well as others by Bad Bunny, give us a framework for examining the 'aftermath' of the 'iron fist against crime' (*mano dura*) and its echoes in pop culture, as well as the landscape and idiom used to talk about the emergence of new 'social bandits' within Puerto Rican popular culture. The genres in which Bad Bunny moves, as Ernesto Castro (2019) defines them, are the 'metamusic' of periods of crisis. In the words of Cristina Rivera Garza (2019), the 'poetics of Benito' could serve as textual production against the processes of material and cultural devastation unleashed by current capitalism, exemplifying what Sayak Valencia (2016) defines as gore capitalism.

Acknowledgements

My gratitude to Dr Jossianna Arroyo (University of Texas at Austin), Dr Alejandra Bronfman (University at Albany, State University of New York), Aníbal López Correa (Universidad de Puerto Rico, Recinto de Río Piedras), and Yashira Santana Rivera for their support, insights and comments.

Notes

1 Section '936' of the US Internal Revenue Code was a system of federal tax exemptions for US possessions. The '936' exemptions allowed remitting profits without paying federal taxes to US subsidiaries operating in the possessions and making investments in the territories (US General Accounting Office 1993). This system of tax exclusions was born in the 1970s thanks to the administration of Rafael Hernández Colón (Popular Democratic Party) and the US Congress (Ayala and Bernabe 2009, 379).

2 '*Bichote*' is the popular Puerto Rican name for the owner of a drug point or '*capo*', from the Spanishization of the term 'big shot'. It is also a play on words that uses the term '*bicho*', which is the popular name for the penis in Puerto Rico (Bourgois et al. 2013), having a specific connotation and charge of masculinity, insofar as it highlights a phallic image.

3 As explained by Déborah Berman Santana (1998), *Manos a la obra*, or 'Operation Bootstrap', was the world's first programme of 'third world' economic development via export-led industrialization. *Manos a la obra*, in conjunction with Estado Libre Asociado (or commonwealth), the new status formula created by the US Congress, was to meet the challenge of keeping the strategically vital archipelago loyal to the US as a hegemonic empire in the western hemisphere in times of the Cold War.

4 The OAS study is based on 2003 data (Organization of American States 2014).

5 We can define *mano dura contra el crimen* as the local version of the 'war on drugs' in the Puerto Rican context. The debate on the war on drugs in Puerto Rico gained notoriety in the 1992 general elections when Pedro Rosselló and the Partido Nuevo Progresista (PNP – New Progressive Party, a local party that supports the incorporation of Puerto Rico as a state

of the US) adopted this social problem as a campaign banner, highlighting the 'failure' of Governor Hernández Colón's administration to deal with it. From the perspective of Jesús Martín-Barbero (2001), we can understand this as a period of intersection between a crisis of authority and legitimacy of state institutions and the construction of citizenship. According to Fernando Picó, governmental institutions in Puerto Rico have rarely been able to meet the population's needs (1999, 33). This disconnection between the state and the people has led to a long history of omissions of the law as an element of everyday life. In the case of Puerto Rico, there have been various manifestations of state weakness since the sixteenth century. Pirates and privateers are a case in point. Picó stresses that the iron fist against crime responds to the need of rulers to demonstrate that they do not tolerate illegality (1999, 36). In this period, *mano dura* against crime sought to confront drug trafficking and murders in a punitive manner, under the logic of the US-led Global War on Drugs (LeBrón 2019, 5; 2016, 115). *Mano dura* represented the militarization of poor sectors of the country's *barrios* and *caseríos* (2016, 114).

6 The term 'Benito's poetics' was coined by several colleagues from my doctoral stay at Albany. Thanks to Marina Bonilla and Nerisha Padilla Cruz, both from the Department of Languages, Literature and Culture in the University at Albany, State University of New York.

7 *Maliante* (*maleante* or *maleantes/maliante* in plural) can be translated as 'villain' or 'delinquent'. In the context of recent Puerto Rico, *maleante* is used to refer to 'naughty guys' or people with a bad attitude. In some cultural products such as 'urban music', this noun is conjugated as '*maliantear*' or '*malianteo*'.

8 'Baby' or 'babies' is used in Puerto Rican Spanish as a 'cute' or 'pretty' person. Sometimes it is used to refer to a friend or closer family.

9 The song's complete lyrics can be found online, https://lyrics.lyricfind.com/lyrics/bad-bunny-ser-bichote. Accessed 4 April 2024.

References

A360 Media LLC. 2023. *Up Close & Personal: Bad Bunny*. 7 April. Accessed 10 March 2024. https://rivershare.overdrivee.com/rivershare-scottcounty/content/media/9794709.

Ayala, César J. and Rafael Bernabe. 2009. *Puerto Rico in the American Century: A history since 1898*. Chapel Hill: University of North Carolina Press.

Becker, Howard. 2015. *Para hablar de la sociedad la sociología no basta*. Buenos Aires: Siglo XXI Editores.

Beer, David. 2014. 'Hip-hop as urban and regional research: Encountering an insider's ethnography of city life', *International Journal of Urban and Regional Research* 38(2): 677–85.

Berman Santana, Déborah. 1998. 'Puerto Rico's Operation Bootstrap: Colonial roots of a persistent model for "Third World" development', *Revista Geográfica* 124: 87–116.

Bosch, Juan. 2009. *De Cristóbal Colón a Fidel Castro: El Caribe frontera imperial*. México City: Editorial Miguel Ángel Porrúa.

Bourgois, Philippe, Fernando Montero Castrillo, Laurie Hart and George Karandinos. 2013. 'The habit of rage in a United States ghetto', *Open Space* 22(2): 201–13. Accessed 10 March 2024. https://europepmc.org/articles/pmc3924749.

Braham, Persephone. 2016. 'True-crime, crime fiction, and journalism in Mexico'. In *Globalization and the State in Contemporary Crime Fiction: A world of crime,* edited by Andrew Pepper and David Schmid, 119–39. London: Palgrave Macmillan.

Cabañas, Miguel. 2008. 'El narcocorrido global y las identidades transnacionales', *Revista de Estudios Hispánicos* 42(3): 519–42.

Cabañas, Miguel. 2014. 'Imagined narcoscapes: Narcoculture and the politics of representation', *Latin American Perspective* 41(2): 3–17.

Campbell, Howard. 2009. *Drug War Sone: Frontline dispatches from the streets of El Paso and Juárez*. Austin: University of Texas Press.

Casanova-Vizcaíno, Sandra. 2021. *El gótico transmigrado: Narrativa puertorriqueña de horror, nisterio y terror en el siglo XXI*. Buenos Aires: Ediciones Corregidor.

Castro, Ernesto. 2019. *El Trap: Filosofía millennial para la crisis en España*. Madrid: Errata Naturae.

Chaar López, Iván. 2010. 'Ética y participación en la narcocultura de Puerto Rico', *80 grados*, 12 November. Accessed 10 March 2024. https://www.80grados.net/etica-y-participacion-en-la-narcocultura-de-puerto-rico/.

Díaz Álvarez, Enrique. 2021. *La palabra que aparece: El testimonio como acto de supervivencia*. Barcelona: Editorial Anagrama.

Dinzey-Flores, Zaire. 2008. 'De la disco al caserío: Urban spatial aesthetics and policy to the beat of reggaetón', *Centro Journal* 20(2): 35–69.

Domínguez, Jorge. 1998. 'The powers, the pirates, and international norms and institutions in the American Mediterranean'. In *From Pirates to Drug Lords: The post-Cold War Caribbean security environment*, edited by M. C. Desch, J. Domínguez and A. Serbin, 79–96. Albany, NY: SUNY Press.

Figueroa Rivera, Luis Enrique. 2020. 'Bad Bunny's transgressive gender performativity: Camp aesthetics and hegemonic masculinities in early Latin trap', *Journal of Latin American Communication Research* 8(1–2): 86–108.

Fugellie Videla, Ema. 2014. 'Nadie nos puede pasar a llevar construcción de masculinidades en jóvenes Reggaetoneros de Conchalí' (Master's Thesis). Santiago: Universidad de Chile. Accessed 10 March 2024. https://repositorio.uchile.cl/handle/2250/130029.

García Canclini, Néstor. 1995. *Consumidores y Ciudadanos*. México City: Grijalbo.

Holmes, Jennifer S., Sheila Amin Gutiérrez de Piñeres and Kevin M. Curtin. 2008. *Guns, Drugs, and Development in Colombia*. Austin: University of Texas Press.

Jaffe, Rivke. 2014. 'Hip-hop and urban studies', *International Journal of Urban and Regional Research* 2: 695–9.

Kicinski, Eduardo and Orlando Sotomayor. 1997. 'Pobreza y desigualdad en Puerto Rico: Problemas y alternativas', *Boletín de Economía* 2(3): 18–19.

LeBrón, Marisol. 2016. 'People before debt: Puerto Ricans confront the island's debt crisis "from below"', *NACLA Report on the Americas* 48(2): 115–17.

LeBrón, Marisol. 2019. *Policing Life and Death: Race, violence, and resistance in Puerto Rico*. Berkeley: University of California Press.

León Olvera, Alejandra. 2019. 'La feminidad buchona: Performatividad, corporalidad y relaciones de poder en la narcocultura mexicana', Doctoral thesis. Tijuana: El Colegio de la Frontera Norte.

Lomnitz, Claudio. 2021. *Interpretación del Tejido Social Rasgado*. México City: El Colegio Nacional.

Lugo-Vélez, Mónica E. and Megan Gargiulo. 2020. 'Queer Bunny: La performatividad de género de Bad Bunny a través de su música y su (auto)representación visual'. International Congress of the Latin American Studies Association: LASA 2020.

Martín-Barbero, Jesús. 2001. 'Reconfiguraciones comunicativas de lo público', *Anàlisi: Quaderns de comunicació i cultura* 26: 71–88.

Martín-Barbero, Jesús. 2004. 'Mediaciones urbanas y nuevos escenarios de comunicación'. In *Las ciudades latinoamcricanas en el nuevo [des]orden mundial*, edited by P. Navia and M. Zimmerman, 73–84. México City: Siglo XXI Editores.

Martín-Barbero, Jesús. 2010. 'Comunicación y cultura mundo: Nuevas dinámicas mundiales de lo cultural', *Signo y Pensamiento* 29(57): 20–34. https://www.redalyc.org/articulo.oa?id=86020052002.

Muñiz Varela, Miriam. 2013. *Adios a la Economía*. San Juan: Ediciones Callejón.

Nájar, Alberto. 2010. 'Dónde están las ganancias del narcotráfico mexicano', BBC Mundo, 15 December. Accessed 10 March 2024. https://www.bbc.com/mundo/noticias/2010/12/101214_mexico_dinero_narcotrafico_lavado_dinero_fp.

Negrón-Muntaner, Frances and Raquel Z. Rivera. 2007. 'Reggaeton nation', *NACLA Report on the Americas* 40(6): 35–9.

Organization of American States. 2014. 'The OAS Drug Report', OEA/Ser.D/XXV.4.1. Accessed 10 March 2024. https://www.oas.org/docs/publications/layoutpubgagdrogas-eng-29-9.pdf.

Pantojas-García, Emilio. 2022. 'Dos Puerto Rico, un papelón', *Metro Puerto Rico*, 3 January. Accessed 10 March 2024. https://www.metro.pr/pr/opinion/2022/01/03/dos-puerto-rico-un-papelon1.html.

Pérez, Luz Adriana. 2008. 'Reggeatón: Manifestación artística de los marginados' (Master's Thesis). San Antonio: The University of Texas at San Antonio. Accessed 27 March 2024. https://www.proquest.com/dissertations-theses/reggeatón-manifestación-artística-de-los/docview/276005182/se-2.

Picó, Fernando. 1999. *De la Mano Dura a la Cordura: Ensayos sobre el estado ausente, la sociabilidad y los imaginarios puertorriqueños*. Río Piedras: Ediciones Huracán.

Platt, Sarah. 2018. 'Nociones de género, música urbana y cultura popular: Cómo el fenómeno Bad Bunny está redefiniendo la masculinidad', *Primer Coloquio sobre hombres y masculinidades*, Universidad de Puerto Rico, Recinto de Río Piedras. Accessed 27 March 2024. https://www.academia.edu/38419902/Nociones_de_género_música_urbana_y_cultura_popular_Cómo_el_fenómeno_Bad_Bunny_está_redefiniendo_la_masculinidad.

Ponce-Cordero, Rafael. 2016. 'Reguetón, narcocultura y bandidaje social en el filme puertorriqueño "Talento de barrio"', *Mitologías hoy* 14: 135–49.

Primera Hora. 2019. 'Keleher sobre el cierre de escuelas: "Alguien tenía que ser el adulto responsable"', 7 April. Accessed 10 March 2024. https://www.primerahora.com/noticias/gobierno-politica/notas/keleher-sobre-el-cierre-de-escuelas-alguien-tenia-que-ser-el-adulto-responsable/.

Puerto Rico Institute of Statistics. 2019. 'En pobreza el 50% o más de la población en 36 Municipios de Puerto Rico. Así lo indican los estimados más recientes de la Encuesta sobre la Comunidad'. Accessed 10 March 2024. https://censo.estadisticas.pr/Comunicado-de-prensa/2019-12-19t145558.

Quintero Rivera, Ángel G. 2020. *La Danza de la Insurrección: Para una sociología de la música latinoamericana; Textos reunidos de Ángel G. Quintero Rivera (1978–2017)*. Buenos Aires: Consejo Latinoamericano de Ciencias Sociales.

Reguillo, Rossana. 2011. 'La narcomáquina y el trabajo de la violencia apuntes para su decodificación', *E-misférica* 8(2). Accessed 10 March 2024. https://hemisphericinstitute.org/es/emisferica-82.html.

Rincón, Omar. 2009. 'Narco.aesthetics and narco.culture in narco.lombia', *Nueva Sociedad* 222: 147–63. Accessed 10 March 2024. https://nuso.org/articulo/narcoestetica-y-narcocultura-en-narcolombia/.

Rincón, Omar. 2013. 'Todos llevamos un narco adentro-un ensayo sobre la narco/cultura/telenovela como modo de entrada a la modernidad', *Matrizes* 7(2): 1–33. Accessed 27 March 2024. https://doi.org/10.11606/issn.1982-8160.v7i2p193-219.

Ríos, Viridiana. 2008. '¿Quién se vuelve narco y por qué? El perfil del narcotraficante mexicano', *Este País: Tendencias y Opiniones*. Accessed 27 March 2024. https://silo.tips/download/quien-se-vuelve-narco-y-por-que-el-perfil-del-narcotraficante-mexicano-viridiana.

Rivera Garza, Cristina. 2019. *Los Muertos Indociles: Necroescritura y despropiación*. Mexico City: Debolsillo.

Rivera Puig, Miguel. 2018. 'Suman más de 600 los puntos de drogas', *El Vocero*, 28 February. Accessed 10 March 2024. https://www.elvocero.com/ley-y-orden/suman-m-s-de-600-los-puntos-de-drogas/article_ef76c26e-1c30-11e8-ae3f-23640cedd0a4.html.

Rodríguez Grafal, Jason. 2017. 'Nuevo presupuesto de Ponce resta millones en servicios a los ciudadanos', *La Perla del Sur*, 31 May. Accessed 10 March 2024. https://www.periodicolaperla.com/actualidad/alcalde-de-ponce-presenta-nuevo-presupuesto-de-96-4-millones/.

Ruiz Vega, Omar. 2018. 'Representando al caserío: Narcocultura y el diario vivir en los videos musicales de reggaetón', *Latin American Music Review* 39(2): 229–65.

Servigne, Pablo and Raphaël Stevens. 2020. *Colaposología*. Barcelona: Arpa.

Sotomayor, Orlando. 2002. 'La pobreza en Puerto Rico'. In *Ensayos Sobre la Pobreza en Puerto Rico*, edited by F. Martínez and F. Catalá, 1–18. San Juan: Centro de Investigaciones Económicas & Publicaciones Puertorriqueñas.

Torres Gotay, Benjamín. 2016. 'El mapa de la droga en Puerto Rico', *El Nuevo Día*, 9 December. Accessed 10 March 2024. https://www.elnuevodia.com/noticias/seguridad/notas/el-mapa-de-la-droga-en-puerto-rico/.

UNODC (United Nations Office on Drugs and Crime). 1998. 'Economic and social consequences of drug abuse and illicit trafficking'. Accessed 27 March 2024. http://css.unodc.org/pdf/technical_series_1998-01-01_1.pdf.

UNODC (United Nations Office on Drugs and Crime). 2012. 'World drugs report'. Accessed 10 March 2024. https://www.unodc.org/unodc/en/data-and-analysis/WDR-2012.html.

United States General Accounting Office (GAO). 1993. 'Puerto Rico and the section 936 tax credit'. Accessed 27 March 2024. https://www.gao.gov/assets/ggd-93-109.pdf.

Urgelles Latorre, Ingrid. 2022. 'Prólogo'. In *#NetNarcocultura: Estudios de género y juventud en la sociedad red*, edited by V. Villaplana Ruiz and A. León Olvera, 7–14. Barcelona: Institut de la Comunicació, Universitat Autònoma de Barcelona.

Valencia, Sayak. 2016. *Capitalismo Gore: Control económico, violencia y narcopoder*. Mexico City: Editorial Paidós.

Valenzuela Arce, José Manuel (ed.). 2015. *Juvenicidio: Ayotzinapa y las vidas precarias en Amèrica Latina*. Barcelona: Ned Ediciones, El Colegio de la Frontera Norte & ITESO.

Valenzuela Arce, José Manuel. 2019. *Trazos de Sangre y Fuego: Bio-necropolítica y juvenicidio en América Latina*. San José: Editorial Universidad de Costa Rica & Bielefeld University Press.

Vázquez Mejias, Ainhoa. 2018. 'Narco series: A new narco-ethics?', *Voices of Mexico*. Accessed 10 March 2024. https://ru.micisan.unam.mx/bitstream/handle/123456789/19508/VOM_2015_0100_0056.pdf?sequence=1.

Villaplana Ruiz, Virginia and Alejandra León Olvera. 2022. 'Net-narcocultura: Tendencias discursivas sobre violencia feminicida y cultura joven en el consumo de la estética narcorap frente a las resistencias feministas del rap'. In *#NetNarcocultura: Estudios de género y juventud en la sociedad red*, edited by V. Villaplana Ruiz and A. León Olvera, 19–38. Barcelona: Institut de la Comunicació, Universitat Autònoma de Barcelona.

Wortman, Ana. 2003. *Pensar las Clases Medias: Consumo culturales y estilos de vida urbanos en la Argentina de los noventa*. Buenos Aires: La Crujía Editores.

3

Entitled to contraband: citizenship and sovereignty in an Indigenous borderland (Guyana–Venezuela)

Olivier Allard

In Guyanese localities close to the (contested) border with Venezuela, I witnessed in late 2018 numerous Venezuelans smuggling fuel, which they had bought for almost nothing in their country and sold in Guyana for about US$100 per drum, so they could go back with food and manufactured goods. Venezuela had been suffering a deep crisis for several years, characterized by high inflation and shortages of basic products, but fuel was still available at the time. In previous years, the country had also known another widespread form of small-scale illicit trade, the sale of subsidized food on the interior black market, commonly known as *bachaqueo* (after *bachaco*, a term for leafcutter ants, which are known for carrying heavy loads). In both cases, trade was illegal because people were not allowed to resell subsidized goods, intended for domestic consumption only, and certainly not at a price set above the official one and therefore deemed 'speculative'. Venezuelans were not selling goods that were illicit per se (such as drugs), but rather infringing trade regulations: it therefore represents 'contraband' in a broad sense, even though only fuel was exported across an international border.[1] In the context of twenty-first century Venezuela, it would not be meaningful to deal separately with the smuggling of fuel to neighbouring countries and the sale of food on the black market. Both activities are practised and justified in similar ways, and they are profitable because those items are heavily subsidized by the Venezuelan state (see also Van Roekel, Chapter 6 in this volume). They represent a way of diverting public spending that depletes the treasury, as much as instances of smuggling that more traditionally shrink public revenue by evading tariffs and customs (see Beccaria 1872 [1764], 127).

The Guyanese–Venezuelan borderland, which includes the Orinoco Delta and the area south of the Orinoco River, is a forested region where most traffic uses river transportation and whose inhabitants are largely – but not only – Indigenous people. On the Venezuelan side of the border, the state of Delta Amacuro, the people mostly identify as 'Warao' and live alongside a handful of Spanish-speaking, nonindigenous Venezuelans, who represent the majority only in cities. Venezuelan Warao numbered about 50,000 in the last official census (2011), most of them speaking their own Indigenous language, with widely varying degrees of fluency in Spanish. On the Guyanese side, Region 1, also known as Barima-Waini, there are a few thousand Warao, and also Indigenous people who identify as 'Amerindians' if they speak only English, as well as nonindigenous English-speaking Guyanese, who may be of African or South Asian descent. While I tend to foreground the experience of Warao Indigenous people, with whom I have done most of my field research since 2007, it is important to note that all of these people were to some extent involved in smuggling and illicit trade.

The condition of Warao people is representative of the ambivalent citizenship of the underprivileged in general in twenty-first century Venezuela. On the one hand, they have been prime targets of manifold policies of social and political inclusion – the motto of the Bolivarian regime, instituted by Hugo Chávez and continued by Nicolás Maduro, being '*Venezuela ahora es de todos*', Venezuela now belongs to everyone – whereas they used to be treated as national subjects whose rights were conditioned on their progressive integration, especially at the hand of Catholic missionaries since the beginning of the twentieth century. Warao and other Indigenous people have eagerly seized these new opportunities, which notably included the right to vote and to receive social benefits. On the other hand, they have been 'unruly', often accused of causing the failure of policies meant to improve their condition. While subsidized food is presented as a way of giving poor families access to a balanced diet, Warao and nonindigenous Venezuelans who sell such products are, according to widespread narratives, causing the shortages that plague the country, and therefore bring about their own suffering.[2] Well-intentioned outsiders dealing with Warao people in Venezuela or Guyana, for instance humanitarian agents or missionaries, often remark that they are particularly difficult to help.

The study of small-scale contraband therefore offers a way of understanding the complex relationship that exists between subaltern people who conduct most of this activity in defiance of official injunctions, and states which attempt to regulate trade but also take care of their population, often through different and sometimes rival administrations (Li 2007, 12–14). In this chapter, I want to thematize less this ambivalence of states – care provided in coercive ways and control exercised to the point of violence – than Indigenous people's transgressions, which raise problems of their own. In order to do so, I will draw on the insights of the anthropology of illegality, which has especially challenged the opposition between legality and illegality, and with it, the assumption that smuggling could simply be explained by the weakness or remoteness of state centres (see Heyman 1999; Abraham and Van Schendel 2005; Thomas and Galemba 2013).

One way of correcting official statist views relies on the concept of sovereignty. The challenge to state or imperial authorities that smuggling represents may be seen as the expression of a competing sovereignty – and, in particular, an Indigenous one. This may result from an effort to see things from the perspective of the borderlands themselves, as advocated by Hämäläinen and Truett (2011). In the Guajira Peninsula at the northern tip of South America, for instance, Wayuu people preserved their economic and political autonomy by refusing colonial Spanish claims of trade monopoly, and dealing with other European powers present in the Caribbean (Polo Acuña 2005). Even today, Indigenous sovereignty has not disappeared, although it is often 'nested' in that of modern states: according to Audra Simpson (2014), Mohawk people who carry cigarettes across the border between Canada and the United States, while often denounced as smugglers, are in fact exercising their ancient right to freely move on and across their land. The context of lowland South America is, however, vastly different. Is it enough to qualify sovereignty, paradoxically making it 'nested' (Simpson 2014) or 'layered' (Burbank and Cooper 2010)? Such expressions underscore the spatial dimension of sovereignty, which has been especially theorized to address colonization.[3] I will argue that it is useful to understand processes on the Guyanese side of the border, and especially how illicit trade relates to local territorial control (see Galemba 2012). However, this notion of sovereignty also carries the idea that Indigenous people are politically constituted as 'people', in the sense of a political community, which would be a mistaken assumption regarding the Venezuelan Warao.

In fact, Warao Indigenous people engaged in illicit trade in the Guyanese–Venezuelan borderland are not merely asserting their independence with respect to states; they resist but also depend on them, evidencing the thorough imbrication between state centres and margins that has been underscored by many anthropologists since the volume edited by Das and Poole (2004). In Venezuela, the contraband of subsidized goods represents a way of appropriating the subsidies themselves, that is to say, of accessing public resources. It represents a form of resistance against the state, but also a claim *on* the state – a complex imbrication that might best be understood through the concept of citizenship.

Indigenous sovereignty and national citizenship are often contrasted as contradictory political orientations in the literature on North American Indigenous people: they lose their own sovereignty when they become US or Canadian citizens (see Biolsi 2005; Simpson 2014). In South America, the opposition does not hold in such a way, and citizenship and autonomy have been joint goals of Indigenous movements. The meaning of citizenship should nonetheless not be taken for granted. We need to move beyond its characterization as a clearly defined legal status, in order to approach it through the experience of ordinary citizens and highlight dimensions that are ignored in official texts (Lazar and Nuijten 2013). Citizenship might then be considered 'insurgent' when people challenge the terms of their inclusion, the legitimate definition of their participation and belonging (Holston 2009). Warao and nonindigenous Venezuelans who engage in contraband do so in order to tap into state resources and, while such direct appropriation might be illegal (because it undermines public policies), it also relies on the assumption that citizens have a fundamental right to the country's wealth, which derives from its subsoil, a view that Coronil (1997) has shown to be widely shared in Venezuela. Could smuggling therefore appear as a subversive way, for some Venezuelans, of claiming their rights as citizens, and specifically as a means for Indigenous people of becoming full national citizens (Allard 2019a; Schwartz 2021)? This is my central argument, but I also argue here that such a concept mostly holds on the Venezuelan side of the border, so that Warao people who cross into Guyana are sometimes confronted with fundamentally different assumptions about state resources and political communities.

The claims made by Warao people and other Venezuelans are not articulated collectively, and there is therefore always a form of ambiguity or indecision that remains. These claims must be read into their speakers' practices and deduced from side-comments, and there are important variations. To summon an overused concept, those claims are mostly 'infrapolitical' (Scott 1990), which does not mean that they are lacking in political elaboration, but rather that they are effective only insofar as they remain covert. This is precisely why they escape the dichotomy between (liberal) individual citizenship and (Indigenous) collective sovereignty. However, while contraband may be read as a matter of 'resistance' to control (a common corollary of infrapolitics), it also represents a form of 'refusal' of what is presented as a gift or a good (to borrow a concept from Simpson 2014). By selling subsidized fuel or food, Warao people reject expectations or stereotypes regarding the proper behaviour of authentic Indigenous people: they are not 'original socialists' (*socialistas originarios*), supposed to set an example for everyone else, but rather people who could profit from illicit trade and decide autonomously how they should consume and spend, even in ways considered morally wrong or politically deficient by others. In non-coordinated ways, they not only resist control, but also refuse others' definition of how they should behave for their own good.

I will set out this argument in five steps. I start by discussing the separation of legality and illegality, which we find, for instance, in the idea that 'outlaws' are apart from the law: while it is well-known that illegal trade is often locally legitimate, especially in border areas and during times of crisis, it is equally accepted that contraband is also an unwanted consequence of the legislation – it is both distanced from and of the centre. I then move to the Venezuelan context, where contraband is more directly a means of accessing national wealth, even for (or especially for?) Indigenous people such as Warao villagers, who thus claim full citizenship. The implicit ideology that it belies, according to which everyone has an equal right to a share of the country's wealth, should however not hide their highly variable involvement in illicit trade, that is, that the democracy of small-scale smuggling is highly relative. Such variations can partly be accounted for by the danger and uncertainty that affected Venezuela at the time of my fieldwork, and I will show that the blurring of boundaries that characterizes contraband was so pervasive that it affected social reality itself. Finally, I argue that many local residents also fight this uncertainty by engaging in the never-ending work of restoring boundaries, especially on the Guyanese side of the border where Indigenous people (some of whom identify as Warao) defend the (limited) sovereignty of their recognized villages.

Between local legitimacy and state legislation

Let us start with a simple and well-established fact: illegal activities are often locally considered perfectly legitimate or licit (Abraham and Van Schendel 2005, 4; Scheele 2009, 88). Although the smuggling of fuel and the *bachaqueo* for food were frequently denounced as criminal activities[4] which, as I mentioned in the introduction, were said to exacerbate the shortages suffered in Venezuela, most of my interlocutors considered it acceptable and even natural to take part in them. It had nothing to do with, for instance, robbery, which many Warao people condemned as a typically nonindigenous behaviour.

To my interlocutors, contraband represented a way of making a living, of accessing needed goods in a time of crisis, when consumption habits and expectations had suddenly been disrupted. The severe economic and political crisis that has affected Venezuela since the mid-2010s is crucial to understanding how illicit trade is justified. The public allowances that poor families had been increasingly receiving since the beginning of the century became practically worthless because of the high rate of inflation. Sometimes, as I witnessed when I conducted fieldwork in the Delta in early 2017, transportation costs that Warao villagers from the lower Delta had to pay, to go to get their allowances in the regional capital, Tucupita, were more than the actual amount people received, and they joked about the weakness of the 'hard Bolivar' (*Bolivar fuerte* or BsF) that was the currency at the time. However, unlike financial assistance, the real value of subsidized goods remained constant, and it therefore became crucial for most people to get some of them – either food or fuel.

Venezuelans received subsidized food through various state-controlled distribution circuits, and I will mention only one: Mercal – for *Mercado de Alimentos S.A.* – a chain of state supermarkets that had been established throughout the country in the 2000s. Warao people had to wait until 2014 to get a store in the lower Delta, however, which was precisely when shelves started to be empty in the rest of the country. The store was opened in Guayo (short for San Francisco de Guayo), a main locality of the lower Delta originally founded by missionaries in the 1940s. I stayed for long periods of time in a village in the vicinity, which I will call Burojo,[5] whose members I accompanied during their weekly visits to Mercal. They could acquire basic food products at a low price – a price that inflation[6] rendered comparatively even cheaper – and it was a privileged way of getting sugar or rice, which other stores in Guayo did not have anymore: it therefore offered a valued complement for people who essentially lived off fishing and slash-and-burn agriculture. Mercal also gave them a crucial opportunity, however: at least for a while, they could buy a pack of milk powder, whose consumption was not in their habit, but which fetched a high price on the interior black market. With the money they earned in such a way (Bs.F 6,000 for a kilo of milk powder that had cost them Bs.F 350),[7] they could shop at Mercal the following week and often buy other goods that they actually wanted, without being limited by government assumptions regarding their basic necessities. My host José and his wife Candida, in Burojo, were often very anxious about the products they would find during their next trip to Mercal: had it been resupplied, and would there be pasta, cooking oil and milk powder? Or merely rice and sugar? Conversely, they knew that selling the food was not the difficult part, and they answered my doubts by saying that government officials understood that the state of the country left them no other choice.

Fuel was the other subsidized commodity: distribution was entirely in the hands of state-owned *Petróleos de Venezuela S.A.* (PDVSA), and its price had not been raised for years. Everyone considered that a low price was crucial to individual mobility and to the transport of goods, especially in the Delta where motor-powered boats required people to get at least a couple of 200 litre drums whenever they went to the fluvial service station. The almost null price of fuel naturally made it very tempting to smuggle into neighbouring countries. It has been well documented at the border with Colombia, where land transportation allows very small quantities to be sold with profit (hence a *bachaqueo* of fuel, see Schwartz 2021; Beach 2018 and Chapter 5, this volume). In the Delta, on the other hand, people would pool their resources and transport up to a few dozen drums into Guyana, often using the long iron canoes that they had received through government-sponsored schemes in previous years. While I only occasionally visited the service stations when they acquired fuel, I conducted fieldwork in 2018 in a Guyanese area where they would land: Mabaruma, the capital of Region 1, and a neighbouring Amerindian village that I name Deepwatta (see Figure 3.1). The contraband of fuel had always been profitable, and each drum was sold for more than US$100 (the currency used to discuss such deals in the border area). It became a vital activity, however, when the crisis struck Venezuela, since so many things were impossible to find there, smugglers would often come back with goods that they had bought in Guyana, rather than with money.

While contraband here cannot be understood without taking the crisis into account, it must also be contextualized in the longer history of the borderland, where, as a Guyanese Amerindian shop-owner from Deepwatta, grown slightly exasperated with my naive questions, put it: 'smuggling is a way of life'. He meant that most business opportunities in the area had always been related to contraband, even if they had changed over time. While the smuggling that took place in colonial times was largely forgotten, everyone remembered that, in the 1980s, Guyanese were deprived of food products such as wheat flour

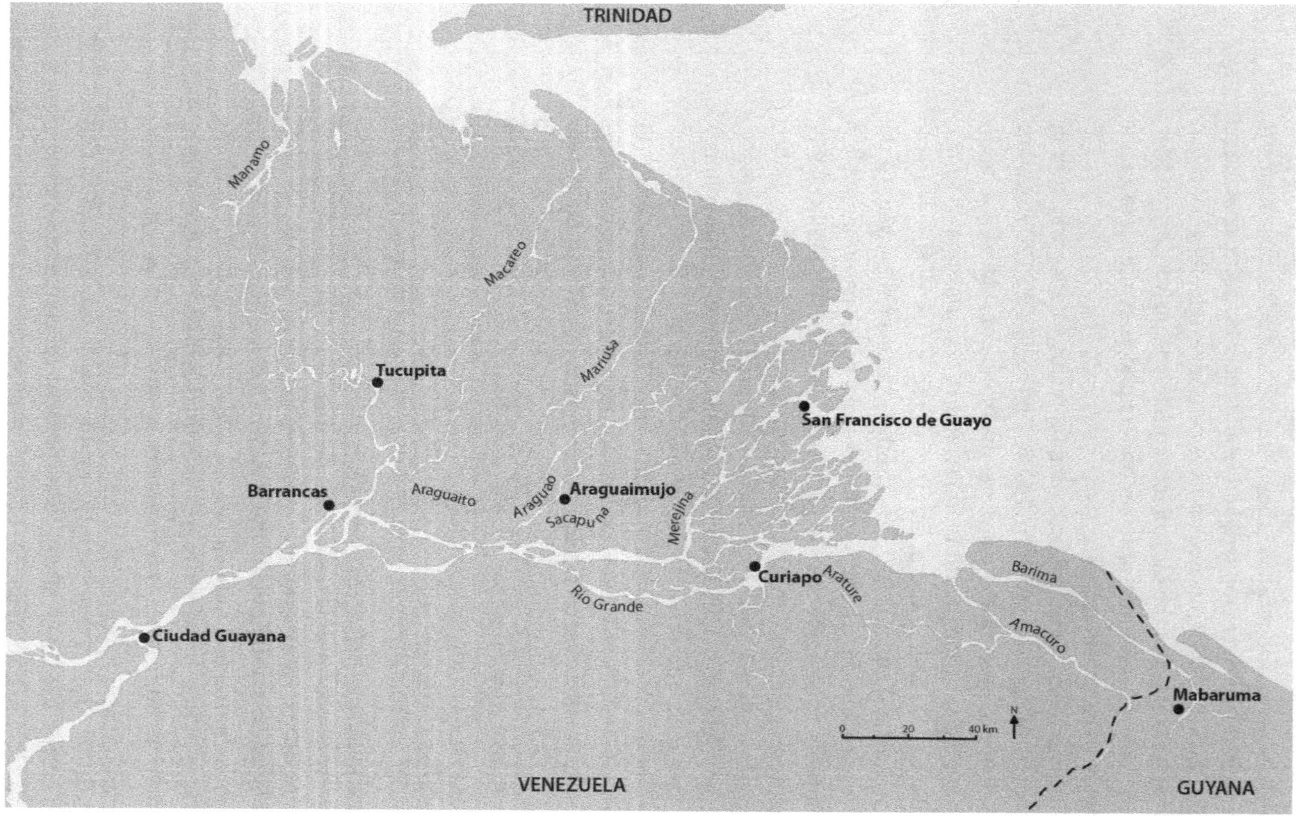

Figure 3.1 Map of the Orinoco Delta and the Guyanese–Venezuelan borderland, omitting the locations of 'Burojo' and 'Deepwatta' to protect their anonymity. © Olivier Allard and Nicolas Verdier.

or canned sardines ('banned items') by the self-sufficiency policies of then-President Forbes Burnham, and people had to get them illegally from Venezuela. They knew that the political or economic tide could change again, and that smuggling would remain central to the region. The special character of borderlands is sometimes acknowledged by authorities, which often tolerate contraband because they are aware that local economy and administration require it (Grahn 1997, 29). On the Venezuelan side of the border, border posts were poorly provisioned: although the military knew that people needed smuggled goods for their own consumption, they were themselves desperately reliant on them, sometimes handing smugglers on their way out a list of things to bring them on their way back – extortion could be disguised as care. On the Guyanese side, a measure was taken in 2014 to legalize the smuggling in of fuel from Venezuela, on the condition that a tax of GY$5,000 (about US$25) per drum was paid and that it was consumed in Region 1. It was so distant from the rest of Guyana that it was expensive to supply, and border contestation implied that legal trade with Venezuela was virtually nonexistent. By adopting such a measure, Guyanese authorities quite explicitly recognized that the prosperity of the region – and particularly of its mining industry – depended on smuggling (Tamboli 2019, 427).

While it is necessary to highlight the specificity of a crisis affecting a border area, it would be wrong to imagine that local morality simply exists 'outside the law', as if it constituted a kind of parallel world, anterior to and independent from official legislation. Various anthropologists such as Bocarejo (2018) have already challenged this implicit spatialization of legality and illegality. Indeed, since Beccaria's treatise *On Crimes and Punishments* it has been recognized that: 'The crime [of smuggling] is owing to the laws themselves; for the higher the duties, the greater is the advantage, and, consequently, the temptation' (1872, 127). It is not merely that the law creates a crime (which would not be a crime if it were not forbidden), but more precisely that state regulation generates the incentives for contraband. In Venezuela in the late 2010s, when shortages of basic products started to occur and prices were rising, the government reacted by instituting regulated prices, which it called 'fair' (*justos*), so that shopkeepers who did not respect them were accused of being profiteers who sold at 'speculative prices'. In order to monitor demand, those products were also rationed, so that it was, for instance, impossible to buy more than one bag of milk powder at a time – and, in Guayo in 2017, people were allowed to come to Mercal only once a week, and their shopping cart had been filled in advance. While fixed prices and rationing are a common answer to scarcity, they generate the price differential and unfulfilled demand that make a black market possible and lucrative. Similarly, smuggling is caused by the border and the difference in legislation it creates (see Peraldi 2007), whether we consider the controlled sale of subsidized fuel in 2010s Venezuela or the ban on some food items in 1980s Guyana. The Guyanese Amerindian village where I conducted fieldwork used to be 'high bush' until the 1970s and only became populated, according to older residents, when people settled there to smuggle foodstuff from Venezuela – its territory goes up to the border and offers discreet routes between both countries. It is already well-known that a border is at once both a division and a bridge (Heyman 2009), and here it has a power of attraction precisely because it creates a differential: the village would be a ghost town if the border was totally closed, as a young sergeant posted there told me, and he agreed that it would also be the case if there were no border at all (for instance, imagining that Venezuela's territorial claims were satisfied and that the whole region became part of its territory, see Allard 2020). Both the smuggling of fuel and the black market for food are therefore direct, even though unwanted, effects of state legislation – but was it only that?

A claim on national resources

In early twenty-first century Venezuela, and in the Delta in particular, contraband was also a way of accessing state resources, and more precisely the oil-wealth of the country. This is highly specific to that time and place, and, for instance, it was not at stake when Guyanese used to smuggle food into their country in the 1980s. As already mentioned, illicit trade concerned products that were heavily subsidized by the state thanks to its oil production: people already benefited from the subsidies by consuming those products, but trading them was a way of converting the subsidies back into monetary form, that is to say to realize (in the financial sense) the value of what they had received, without suffering the consequences of inflation. As Guyer (2004) has argued, it is crucial to pay attention to what happens at thresholds of conversion, which are often highly contested.

Once again, it is necessary to highlight the significance of the crisis that has affected Venezuela since the mid 2010s. At that time, contraband became the only means through which Warao and nonindigenous Venezuelans could continue accessing the resources that they had been promised and that the government failed to deliver. This was actually the latest twist in a longer history. In the preceding years, after Hugo Chávez was elected president of Venezuela in 1998 and launched his 'Bolivarian revolution', underprivileged Venezuelans had benefited from manifold generous social policies, from grants enabling adults to pursue their education (*Misión Robinson*) to collective productive projects run by 'communal councils'. Special attention was given to Indigenous people who, maybe for the first time in the history of the country, had the same rights as others, and even some advantages, in order to redress social inequalities (for instance being able to receive the old-age pension five years younger). In the Delta, it produced a radical change: within a few years, most Warao received cash transfers and goods to which they had scarce access previously, since they usually had to go into debt with local fishing bosses in order to obtain commodities – and they did not imagine it would stop so brutally. Those generous policies probably had their own roots in an earlier concept of the relation between Venezuelans and the country's rich subsoil. Coronil (1997) has shown the emergence, since the beginning of the twentieth century, of the idea that Venezuela is made of a social body (its citizens) and a physical body (its subsoil), which should ideally be made to coincide – so that political conflicts have often focused on the uses and (mis)appropriations of oil wealth. From that perspective, Chávez's Bolivarian revolution can be (partly) understood as the promise that everyone would share the resources (and power) that were previously monopolized by a minority, and this 'petro-citizenship' has been particularly meaningful for Indigenous people, as also described by Penfield (2019) for the Amazonian Sanema (see also Lauer 2006). In this context, *bachaqueo* and smuggling represent an insurgent way of demanding this promise to be fulfilled (Allard 2019a).

It is, indeed, as Venezuelan citizens that Warao people have claimed a right to this wealth. Although there had been some exploration in the past, no underground resource has been found in the Delta. Oil has historically been extracted from the western end of the country, while attention has more recently been drawn to the 'Orinoco Oil Belt' and the 'Orinoco Mining Arc', neither of which includes the Orinoco Delta itself.[8] Most of my Warao interlocutors, in villages of the lower Delta, talked about the government's money or Venezuela's wealth, without ever mentioning its origin in oil. They might have been aware of it, but it was not of particular concern to them. When I discussed Venezuela's crisis with Burojo's headman, in 2017, he argued that it was caused by politicians stealing the country's wealth, which he deemed inexhaustible: there was nothing else to add. Although some of their practices and discourses were similar to those of the Añú, as recorded by Steven

Schwartz (2021), they have a very different meaning. Añú people live in La Guajira, in western Venezuela, which is the region of major oil extraction, and they have suffered its environmental consequences, so that their smuggling of fuel across the border with Colombia could be understood as a claim to control the resources of their own territory, a nascent sovereignty claim. However, it is difficult to argue anything of the sort about the Warao or inhabitants of the Delta in general: while some conflicts may have arisen regarding resource extraction (fishing in particular), what they obtained through contraband was access to Venezuelan national wealth.

I heard a very explicit – if somewhat surprising – formulation of such a view when I met, in 2018, a Warao man who had come to Guyana to sell a boatload of drums of fuel, as so many people were doing at the time. Speaking forcefully in Warao, while incorporating many Spanish words and sometimes sentences, he granted me a few minutes, although he was busy conducting business. He presented himself as the headman of a community of Warao who had settled outside of the Delta itself, in the garbage heap of one of the largest Venezuelan cities, Ciudad Guyana, which many Warao have visited to scavenge for clothes and other things over the past decades (Ayala-Lafée and Wilbert 2008; Sørhaug 2014). It gave them an easier access to fuel (whereas inhabitants of the lower Delta had to travel far to reach a service station), but they still had to deal with the authorities. My interlocutor assertively brushed the problem aside: they had reached an agreement with a General from the powerful Bolivarian National Guard, who agreed that it was their only source of income and that they were protected by 'the law of the late president'. If some members of his community were arrested while conveying fuel, he could therefore confront the authorities and demand their release from prison. With this seemingly made-up or naive reference (to which I will return in the following sections), he stated that their involvement in activities usually denounced as illegal was in fact lawful: it was more than a mere question of local legitimacy.

I believe that this view was at least implicitly shared by state agents, even though they were often denouncing contraband, and Warao people knew not to take official discourses at face value. For instance, when they made their weekly visit to Guayo, the Mercal supervisor often reminded them that milk powder was for themselves and their children to drink, a valuable complement to their diet, otherwise the government would stop supplying it. But they never paid much attention to those admonishments: José and Candida joked that they were not stupid '*indios*' anymore – a derogatory word they sometimes use themselves in such a way – who did not know the real worth of milk. Paradoxically, following official guidance would not turn them into good citizens. And, although anthropologists of Amazonia have highlighted the importance of alimentary diet in defining identity (see Renard-Casevitz 1991), drinking milk – a nonindigenous food in Amazonia – would here make them more Indigenous. It appears that Warao people, even when they lived in villages of the lower Delta and spoke little Spanish, knew how to critically appraise official statements and policies.

Although many officials denounced *bachaqueo* and smuggling in their speeches, their behaviour, that is to say, the actual logic of the institution, said otherwise. In Guayo, I was struck by the very elaborate controls implemented at Mercal. When people came to shop, they had to show their ID cards, an employee would check that they were on the list of authorized customers, they would be called and given a token they had to hand to the cashier, the cashier also did a biometric control, ensuring that their fingerprints matched those registered in the computer; and a security guard would check their receipt when they left. I was impressed that people who came by canoe, usually paddling or sailing, had to go through such elaborate and technically advanced procedures. There was a stark contrast between such controls and the fact that, as soon as they left, they would sell the milk powder and cooking oil they had just legitimately acquired: the border guards did not prevent contraband at all – but were they really meant to? In practice, controls rather served to ensure that no one could buy twice, that no one got more than their share: everyone received exactly the same basket of food.

A similar interpretation can be made of the centrality of the (waiting) 'list' at fluvial service stations: '*la lista*' was the focus of much anxiety, as among the Sanema of Southern Venezuela (Penfield 2016), and suspicions of favouritism sometimes triggered violent quarrels. Fairness meant that people got fuel when their turn came, even though emergencies were in theory justifiable, for instance for medical reasons. Local authorities therefore made efforts to preserve peace by making sure that everyone got their share, rather than controlling what they did with it. Admittedly, the importance of fuel smuggling played a part in the decision not to reopen the fluvial service station of Tucupita, after it accidently burned down in 2018. Was it really part of an effort to curb smuggling? Or rather that the place had become too disorderly because of the rivalry between buyers? Indeed, while controls served to ensure that everyone had an equal access to goods that could be smuggled, the fairness of the distribution was always contested.

The relative democracy of contraband

Small-scale smuggling is often described as 'democratic' by its very actors, for instance Añú people at the border between Colombia and Venezuela (Schwartz 2021, 511) or inhabitants of the Chad Basin (Roitman 2005, 29). Sometimes explicitly, people contrast it to large-scale smuggling practised by real criminals who have contacts well-placed within state administration and the military (or the other way around) (see Nordstrom 2007). This was a widespread view in Venezuela. The real thieves, those who were really plundering the country's resources, were members of the emerging *Boliburguesía* (Bolivarian bourgeoisie). On the one hand, they could move huge cargos that dwarfed the tiny shipments managed by Warao or local nonindigenous people: the few drums sold by the latter could not have any noticeable impact. On the other hand, large-scale smugglers were in no way a model to emulate: they were thieves because, contrary to ordinary citizens, they appropriated more than their share. The opposition was certainly exaggerated – since there were also connections between small- and large-scale smugglers (Schwartz 2021, 510) and even Warao people would cultivate their contacts with the military – but it is undeniable that *bachaqueo* was a resource for the poor.

However, democracy is always relative, and we should be aware that such claims may hide major differences. Let us start with the example of Mercal. In Burojo, where I conducted most of my fieldwork, all permanent residents were allowed to shop at Mercal, men as well as women – if they had enough children, both parents were entitled to a basket, and single adults could also claim one. However, only members of communities located in a restricted area around Guayo had that right, which therefore amounted to a privilege. Soon after the opening of that branch of Mercal in 2014, customers started coming from further and further away, including nonindigenous people living in cities, because it kept on being supplied while other public and private supermarkets were struck by severe shortages. I was told that one had to come well in advance, and queue sometimes for an entire day and night on a stilted platform that was not made for such a purpose. The answer to this problem was to restrict access to Mercal to a limited number of communities whose permanent residents were recorded in a census. In a way, this restriction made *bachaqueo* possible (city residents could only buy milk powder from Warao from the lower Delta), but it also fuelled local tensions. Indeed, where was the line to be drawn, between communities considered as belonging to the vicinity of Guayo and others deemed too distant? It caused strife with residents of villages that were as distant as Guayo from urban centres, and were equally Indigenous, and therefore complained that their exclusion was an unfair political decision.

Differences were even more marked with respect to fuel, since one theoretically needed an outboard motor, a boat, documents and money, as well as connections, in order to buy some. Community leaders and their families were privileged from this point of view, as well as larger communities that had attracted most of the governmental attention. Since distant river navigation is a gendered activity, in particular among the Warao (see Wilbert 1993), it is not surprising that most smugglers were men. Women therefore had less access to the benefits of fuel contraband, but it does not mean that they were systematically excluded. Indeed, gender equality had been a significant goal of the Bolivarian revolution, so that motors and boats had sometimes been granted to Warao women – in an effort to promote their political leadership and economic autonomy. And it was a success, at least with respect to contraband: at the river port of Tucupita, some of them were deeply involved in the smuggling of fuel, employing their male relatives as hands, managing the money and dealing directly with state officials.

Many Warao people nonetheless considered that smuggling was too dangerous. In Burojo, my host José was appalled when I mentioned that some other villagers had offered me to join them on their trip to Guyana: the canoe could capsize, the military could arrest us, and we could be attacked by criminals. There was indeed a growing insecurity in the Delta, and while subsidized food and fuel had become highly valued products, it also meant that they were targeted by criminal groups: smugglers could be robbed by those who did not have 'legal' access to subsidized goods, thieves who were violent and therefore unambiguously condemned. Even a trip to Tucupita, which they had made countless times, could be judged too risky: while some people took there the bags of milk powder and bottles of cooking oil that they had acquired at Mercal, knowing they could get a better deal just by offering them on the street, most preferred to sell to the itinerant traders who regularly visited their villages. The calls of '*wabimo*' – 'sellers' in Warao, which refers to pedlars carrying all sorts of things – had been replaced by those of '*nisamo*' ('buyers') or '*lecheros*' ('milkmen', in Spanish), even though they were often the same people. Villagers had to negotiate hard: Candida for instance argued with a buyer that she knew quite well how much he would get for the bag of milk powder in Tucupita.

However, even though the price would be lower, selling to such intermediaries reduced uncertainty and risk.

Some Warao were even reluctant to go that far. In March 2017, while most villagers were eager to go to Mercal every week, anxious to know whether it had been resupplied, some older couples were avoiding it altogether, preferring instead to go in the forest to extract moriche palm sago. This is a resource associated with the Warao's past, which has also remained an emergency food, available when they flee potential danger by dispersing in the forest. If the Orinoco Delta in general is a zone of refuge that has hardly been colonized, the swampy islands of the lower Delta, where moriche palm groves are concentrated, constitute a refuge within a refuge (Allard 2019b). In a context of increased uncertainty, even going to Mercal was dangerous: the congregation of people coming from many different villages made sorcery attacks more likely. Teenagers found the gatherings exciting, because it gave them an occasion to flirt; but adults often complained that they had fallen ill after going shopping. Moriche palm sago extraction represented a way of procuring food while limiting social interactions and their dangers. Such a possibility is probably available to Indigenous people more than others, since they often still have the knowledge of a variety of forest uses, but it does not mean that they were stuck in the past. Candida's father, who had built a temporary shelter in the forest during my visit, was frequently visited by his son and sons-in-law: they were thus learning or recalling how to extract palm sago, but they also went to Mercal and had experiences of the nonindigenous world. As analysed by Gow (2018), Indigenous Amazonian sociality is often characterized by an oscillation between opposite movements of emergence and hiding (see also Kelly Luciani 2016), so that even those who favoured forest resources over contraband could reverse their priorities at a later date. The unequal involvement of Warao people in illicit activities is however largely explained by the increased violence that affected the Delta at the time, and I want to describe how it produced generalized uncertainty.

Boundaries blurred

Warao people and other Venezuelans have suffered violence at the hands of criminal bands, which multiplied in the late 2010s and are simply called *sindicato* in the Delta (short for 'crime syndicate'), but also at the hands of Venezuelan police and military, whose principal body is the Bolivarian National Guard, usually referred to as *guardias*. Indeed, legislation adopted with the stated aim of fighting smuggling and the black market had criminalized ordinary activities: those who carried small quantities of food or fuel could be doing so for personal use, but any traveller caught with some food or fuel might be accused of illicit trade. While mutual support between kin was crucial to survival at the time, I heard many people complain that they could not take food to their relatives living in another Venezuelan state, or could not travel with a motor borrowed from someone else (since its documents would not bear their own name). What was the limit between personal consumption and commercial activity? In Guyana, a custom officer let a couple of Warao men pass with two drums of fuel without asking them to pay any duty because, as he commented, such a small quantity was for 'personal use' – even though they had only paddles and no motor, and were obviously intending to sell the fuel. Conversely, Venezuelan authorities were much more likely than Guyanese officials to harass people carrying small quantities, and they were barely disguising their threats of violence. Indeed, this is one reason why I often heard in Guyana that people were not 'free' anymore in Venezuela: they could not do as they wanted with their possessions, and their mobility was restrained by both *guardias* and *sindicato*.

The military were however not trying to prevent contraband, since, as I mentioned, it was often a source of their own supplies. They were mostly extorting a bribe or levying informal taxes on any cargo, warning they could seize all of it, or sometimes threatening to arrest people. In Guyana, I often overheard some Venezuelans comparing the number of *alcabalas* (checkpoints or tollgates) they had had to go through, and the number could be up to ten, between the *sindicato*, the army, the navy, the *guardias*, and the Guyanese customs. Their concern was that it reduced their earnings – sometimes to the point of making their activity barely profitable, according to some – but it did not matter who or what institution had stopped them: there was little difference between officials and criminals, between tax and racket. One of them commented, partly in irony, that Warao people who supplied smugglers with fuel in Ciudad Guyana had to pay US$2 per drum to the local *sindicato*, since 'it makes it more legal for people in the community' – as if criminals enforced a law of their own.

The legitimacy of state agents may therefore always be called into question, to the point of making visible its very contingent nature: as Bourdieu (2012, 220–1) notes, taxation is merely legitimate extortion, and he stressed the need to investigate how it has become so entrenched that its origin is forgotten. But anthropologists often witness moments of crisis, when such a violent and arbitrary origin becomes palpable again. Roitman (2005, 32) has explored how the power to seize wealth, in the Chad Basin in Africa, has been experienced as a 'right of state' that may also be resisted by ordinary citizens or enacted by non-state armed actors: distinctions are always being reconfigured. It is not merely whether a tax is legitimate or not, but whether it is actually tax or racket. Roitman describes how travellers who pass through official checkpoints may successively be asked to pay a toll by various people wearing a uniform or waiving a professional ID: among them, who is the true customs officer (Roitman 2003, 99–100)? Such uncertainty is however not limited to state agents and institutions. On the Guyana–Venezuela border, smugglers often justified their buying relatively large quantities of fuel with fishing permits, and it is said that they received authentic permits through their contacts in the administration, which led some local journalists to title a piece: 'The smuggling of fuel is now legal in Delta Amacuro'.[9] It however implied that such permits were denied to others, so that officials in league with the smugglers 'have questioned the truthfulness of true fishermen', and the article concludes by reiterating its anxious question: 'who are the true fishermen? … who are the fishermen?' – a repercussion of the doubt regarding the true military officials. Reality itself becomes uncertain when the legitimacy of state agents is thrown into doubt, since they do not guarantee its univocal existence anymore (see Boltanski 2012).

This pervasive blurring of boundaries explains how a Warao headman could refer to 'the law of the late president' to justify his involvement in the smuggling of fuel, even though he would probably have had trouble citing a particular act or decree. He was not being naive or ignorant, as could be imagined by contrast with Indigenous people in other countries who possess relevant legal knowledge (see, for instance, Colliaux 2019). I argue that he rather showed his good understanding that it was not always possible to distinguish between right and might, in early twenty-first century Venezuela, and that armed actors could bring up legal dispositions in arbitrary ways. He was in fact referring to general principles that reflected the balance of power: Indigenous people were now full citizens who did not have lesser rights than nonindigenous Venezuelans. They had always been loyal supporters of Chávez's Bolivarian regime, and those elements gave the Warao headman leverage in his negotiations with the military. Only some Warao people were however attempting to engage in this uncertain process. Others, as I mentioned, turned to forest resources, and many decided to settle permanently in Guyana to enjoy a more stable social environment, a goal that, I will attempt to show, required their active involvement.

Boundaries restored

Guyanese officials were unsurprisingly working to maintain or restore boundaries that were blurred on the other side of the border by the crumbling of Venezuela. The head of regional customs, for instance, reminded his subordinates that they had to give a receipt to traders who paid the tax on fuel imported from Venezuela – it was an official tax, not a bribe, even though I doubt that smugglers themselves cared about the distinction. Yet, more importantly, other local residents were also engaged in similar projects. Many people who had crossed the border from Venezuela as 'refugees' or 'migrants' (as they were sometimes called) wanted criminals to be prevented from entering after them: they wanted the border to be selectively permeable, but not to be nonexistent (a statement that also applies to smugglers), since they wished to move to a different state where they would be safer. As Reeves (2011, 920) notes with respect to Kyrgyzstan: 'being bordered often *matters* intensely to those living at the border'.

In Deepwatta, people were often anxious about the possibility that *sindicato* members would pass undetected, since little distinguished them from other Venezuelans, and only those who had witnessed their participation in criminal activities could eventually identify them. One morning in 2018, I learned that the village had been deeply disturbed by the rumour that *sindicato* people had come in to attack and rob residents: those settled near the river connecting the village to Venezuela rushed towards its opposite end, which leads to the regional capital. The commotion was such that soldiers were sent to patrol at night, and even people in the national capital apparently heard about it on social media. The next day, the situation was calm again. The soldiers, frustrated by a sleepless night on the border, tried to investigate but could not reach any definitive conclusion: was it a false alarm? Or had they thwarted a dangerous attempt to infiltrate the village and the country? The border is a place of rumours and fragmentary information, impossible to check for people who, like the Guyanese soldiers (or me), could not cross to the other side. Yet, it is important to observe that many ordinary residents had expectations regarding the border and its workings: they wanted to be able to differentiate between Venezuelan and Guyanese territories, between lawful soldiers they could call on for help and corrupt ones who would extort them, between ordinary migrants that could cross and *sindicato* that should be stopped.

Contraband between Venezuela and Guyana was flourishing partly because there were many possible routes. Smugglers (and migrants) could for instance reach the regional capital, Mabaruma, directly, but they could also enter an Amerindian village such as Deepwatta. In the latter case, they were getting into a different national territory but also into a recognized Indigenous territory. The route was less practical, since fuel that arrived by boat from Venezuela had to be carried across a swamp before being loaded onto trucks, but it had one major advantage. While there were soldiers stationed in the village, it escaped the attention of custom officers, and smugglers could therefore avoid paying the GY$5,000 (US$25) official tax. Village authorities however quickly reacted to the increased passage of smugglers by levying their own tax of GY$500 per drum: it was decided by the village council and a councillor was appointed to check the entry point and collect the 'contribution' or 'donation', as they called it. It is strikingly similar to the situation, described by Galemba (2012), at the Mexico–Guatemala border, although the members of the community she studied built an actual chain to block the transit of trucks through their village. In Deepwatta, conversely, the appointed councillor was alone and unarmed, and the terms of 'contribution' and 'donation' have connotations of voluntariness, but the decision may be read as an act of territorial sovereignty (exercised not through smuggling itself, as among the Mohawk, but rather through its control, see Simpson 2014). The village has a right to control who and what passes through its territory, as much as the state controls the national territory – it makes democratic decisions through its elected council, and such contributions ensure that smuggling benefits the village as a whole and not some of its members only.

To be used in such a context, the notion of sovereignty must however be qualified in two ways. On the one hand, it is markedly 'nested' or embedded. Indeed, contrary to the Mohawk case analysed by Simpson (2014), from whom I borrow the expression 'nested sovereignty', it does not cut across states but rather is entirely encompassed within Guyana, so that boundaries are hierarchically organized in a statist way (Rubenstein 2001). The territory under consideration is not that of, for instance, 'the Warao' (who do not consider themselves a unified polity), but rather that of a specific Guyanese Amerindian village (in contrast to other Amerindian villages). Even more strikingly, a boundary stone, erected in 1901 to mark the border between then British Guiana and Venezuela, is located within the territory of Deepwatta. While the border has been contested by Venezuela since 1962, Guyanese Amerindian villagers saw it as their duty to look after the boundary stone and national flag: their being encompassed by and included in a national state certainly mattered.

On the other hand, expressions of local sovereignty relied on Guyanese legal tools and institutions: while residents of Deepwatta often described to me a rather absolute view of village sovereignty, arguing that the village council and headperson could even legally forbid government people from entering (which might be an exaggeration), they were justifying it with the 2006 Amerindian Act, that is to say national legislation. The idea of the village council being an elected 'body corporate' acting in the collective interest of the village, and of a territory that is strictly demarcated and held collectively, have been instituted by the legislation – so that, for some of my interlocutors, being Amerindian represented a legal status as much as a personal identity. Such institutions were, conversely, totally absent on the Venezuelan side of the border. Deepwatta therefore levied its own tax on fuel that was smuggled through its territory, but did so within Guyanese territory and through Guyanese legislation: in spite of some verbal affirmations to the contrary, local sovereignty was nested and limited. This is certainly why Guyanese state actors were tolerating it and not cracking down on smugglers who avoided paying the official duty by meeting the local contribution, or on village councillors who were collecting it. Those processes were negotiated because villagers needed to convince smugglers and travellers to respect their decisions, without regional officials or the military seeing local autonomy as a threat to their own authority.

Conclusion

An ethnographic perspective on contraband reveals how statist and official concepts may be challenged in various ways by ordinary activities, and especially how illegal activities may be pursued for legitimate ends. The differential created by an international border represented the main resource used by smugglers, but here it also introduced an asymmetry in the meaning of contraband. While I have started by stressing the legitimate character of smuggling in a borderland area, especially in a time of crisis, the notion of borderland should not mask the fact that there were some crucial differences between each side of the border. In Venezuela, Warao and nonindigenous people sold subsidized food on the black market and exported fuel to Guyana in order to reap the benefits associated with full Venezuelan citizenship, rather than wait for the goodwill of the authorities. They exploited side-effects of the legislation, as is always the case with contraband, but above all attempted to access their share of national wealth – although the fairness of this distribution was hotly contested. In Guyana, conversely, there were no such connotation since the state only had, until the recent discovery of offshore oil fields, rather limited resources. But Guyanese Indigenous communities are also recognized entities, which enabled them to assert a collective control on smuggling that passed through their territory: on the one hand, it contrasted to the blurring of boundaries that happened in Venezuela; on the other hand, it could be read as a form of nested sovereignty.

In both cases, claims of citizenship or sovereignty are 'smuggled in', so to speak: they are mostly made in an implicit or covert way, which is, I believe, a condition for their success. This infrapolitical dimension enables them to avoid direct political opposition or repression, but it should not be understood as strategic manipulation. This is also how Indigenous people may express political claims when they are not constituted as 'peoples' in the sense of forming real 'nations'. As Schwartz (2021, 516–17) argues, we should pay attention to the broad scope of their responses to state control, beyond those that belong to the repertoire of recognized political action, such as legal activism or direct confrontation, without assuming what Indigenous people are or should be. On the Venezuelan side at least, in the lower Delta, the political life of Warao people is characterized by dispersion, as is common in lowland South America (see Viveiros de Castro 2010), and contraband offered them an opportunity to make their claims in such a way. It is all the more important in highlighting the meaning of their acts that they were criticized both by state officials, who saw them as lacking civic sense, and by Indigenous activists, who denigrated them as incapable of organizing themselves. And yet, many Warao people refused to let others define how they should behave, and it is worth trying to recover the positive signification of those so-called deficiencies.

Notes

1 Merriam-Webster Dictionary, for instance, defines contraband as: '1. Illegal or prohibited traffic in goods. 2. Goods or merchandise whose importation, exportation, or possession is forbidden'. See https://www.merriam-webster.com/dictionary/contraband. Accessed 14 March 2024.

2 See, for instance, 'En claves: Las consecuencias del bachaqueo', 25 May 2015. https://www.telesurtv.net/news/En-claves-Las-consecuencias-del-bachaqueo-en-Venezuela--20150525-0023.html. Accessed 14 March 2024.

3 Such approaches are largely distinct from those that focus on 'emergent' sovereignties and their exercise of violence on bodies (see Hansen and Stepputat 2006) – whereas Indigenous sovereignties are often considered legitimate because they are said to predate colonization.

4 The *Ley Orgánica de Precios Justos* (21 November 2013, Gaceta Oficial no. 40.340, 23 January 2014) punishes the 're-sale of first necessity items', with a lucrative aim, with a fine and the seizure of said items, 'extractive smuggling' with a sentence of ten to fourteen years of imprisonment, 'speculation' (sale of goods and services at a price above that fixed by the authorities) with a sentence of eight to ten years of imprisonment, and so on.

5 *Burojo* means 'island' in Warao; I use made-up names for this community, for the village where I stayed in Guyana, as well as for all my interlocutors, in order to protect their anonymity.

6 Inflation estimates were above 250 per cent for 2016 and 2017, before hyperinflation in 2018 which peaked at 130,000 per cent. See IMF figures: https://www.imf.org/external/datamapper/PCPIEPCH@WEO/VEN?zoom=VEN&highlight=VEN. Accessed 20 March 2024.

7 Bs.F6,000 represented about US$600 at the official rate of exchange and US$2 at the parallel rate of the time. I however only want to give an idea of the relative price at which Warao villagers would buy and sell bags of milk powder. The differential between the official and parallel exchange rates was not really relevant in the area at the time, because no one could access US$ at the official rate (except, according to rumours, high government officials).

8 There is, admittedly, small-scale gold mining in the Sierra Imataca, south of the Orinoco Delta, and Warao people who live in the area may either benefit from it (for instance selling food or carrying fuel) or, being threatened by gold miners, be forced to flee.

9 'El contrabando de combustible ya es legal en Delta Amacuro', http://tanetanae.com/contrabando-combustible-ya-legal-delta-amacuro/, 3 April 2017. Accessed 4 May 2017. The article is unfortunately not accessible anymore. I therefore give here the original formulations: the accomplices 'han cuestionado la veracidad de los verdaderos pescadores … ¿Quienes son verdaderos pescadores? … ¿Quienes son los pescadores?'.

References

Abraham, Itty and Willem van Schendel. 2005. 'Introduction: The making of illicitness'. In *Illicit Flows and Criminal Things: States, borders, and the other side of globalization*, edited by Willem van Schendel and Itty Abraham, 1–37. Bloomington: Indiana University Press.

Allard, Olivier. 2019a. 'Trafics citoyens aux marges de l'État: Les Warao dans la crise du chavisme (Venezuela)', *Terrain*, 1 July. Accessed 14 March 2024. https://doi.org/10.4000/terrain.18541.

Allard, Olivier. 2019b. 'Le palmier des marais: Remarques sur les usages d'un environnement inhabitable'. In *Au Seuil de la Forêt: Hommage à Philippe Descola, l'anthropologue de la nature*, edited by Geremia Cometti, Pierre Le Roux, Tiziana Manicone and Nastassja Martin, 52–64. Mirebeau-sur-Bèze: Éditions Tautem.

Allard, Olivier. 2020. 'Fuites frontalières entre le Guyana et le Venezuela: Migrations et contrebande dans un Village Amérindien', *Cahiers des Amériques Latines* 93: 35–54.

Ayala-Lafée, Cecilia and Werner Wilbert. 2008. *La Mujer Warao: De recolectadora deltana a recolectadora urbana*. Caracas: Fundación La Salle de Ciencias Naturales.

Beach, Charles. 2018. 'Frontera combustible: Conceptualising the state through the experiences of petrol smugglers in the Colombian/Venezuelan borderlands of Norte de Santander/Táchira', *Journal of Extreme Anthropology* 2(2): 1–19. Accessed 14 March 2024. https://doi.org/10.5617/jea.6257.

Beccaria, Cesare. 1872 [1764]. *An Essay on Crimes and Punishment*. Albany, NY: Hackett Publishing.

Biolsi, Thomas. 2005. 'Imagined geographies: Sovereignty, indigenous space, and American Indian struggle', *American Ethnologist* 32(2): 239–59.

Bocarejo, Diana. 2018. 'Thinking with (il)legality: The ethics of living with bonanzas', *Current Anthropology* 59(S18): 48–59.

Boltanski, Luc. 2012. *Énigmes et Complots: Une enquête à propos d'enquêtes*. Paris: Gallimard.

Bourdieu, Pierre. 2012. *Sur l'État: Cours au Collège de France (1989–1991)*. Paris: Éditions Raisons d'Agir.

Burbank, Jane and Frederick Cooper. 2010. *Empires in World History: Power and the politics of difference*. Princeton: Princeton University Press.

Colliaux, Raphaël. 2019. 'Ciudadanos de la comunidad: Appropriation de la bureaucratie et expérience de la "communauté" chez les Matsigenka (Amazonie Péruvienne)', *Journal de la Société des Américanistes* 105(2): 69–90.
Coronil, Fernando. 1997. *The Magical State: Nature, money, and modernity in Venezuela*. Chicago: University of Chicago Press.
Das, Veena and Deborah Poole. 2004. 'State and its margins: Comparative ethnographies'. In *Anthropology in the Margins of the State*, edited by Veena Das and Deborah Poole, 3–34. Santa Fe, NM: School of American Research Press.
Galemba, Rebecca. 2012. 'Remapping the border: Taxation, territory, and (trans) national identity at the Mexico–Guatemala border', *Environment and Planning D: Society and Space* 30: 822–41.
Gow, Peter. 2018. '"Who are these wild Indians": On the foreign policies of some voluntarily isolated peoples in Amazonia', *Tipiti: Journal of the Society for the Anthropology of Lowland South America* 16(1): 6–20.
Grahn, Lance. 1997. *The Political Economy of Smuggling: Regional informal economies in Early Bourbon New Granada*. Boulder, CO: Westview Press.
Guyer, Jane. 2004. *Marginal Gains. Monetary transactions in Atlantic Africa*. Chicago: University of Chicago Press.
Hämäläinen, Pekka and Samuel Truett. 2011. 'On borderlands', *Journal of American History* 98(2): 338–61.
Hansen, Thomas Blom and Finn Stepputat. 2006. 'Sovereignty revisited', *Annual Review of Anthropology* 35: 295–315.
Heyman, Josiah M. (ed.). 1999. *States and Illegal Practices*. Oxford: Berg.
Heyman, Josiah M. 2009. 'A border that divides. A border that joins', *Anthropology Now* 1(3): 79–85.
Holston, James. 2009. *Insurgent Citizenship: Disjunctions of democracy and modernity in Brazil*. Princeton: Princeton University Press.
Kelly Luciani, José Antonio. 2016. *About Anti-Mestizaje*. Florianópolis: Cultura e Barbárie.
Lauer, Matthew. 2006. 'State-led democratic politics and emerging forms of indigenous leadership among the Ye'kwana of the Upper Orinoco', *Journal of Latin American Anthropology* 11(1): 51–86.
Lazar, Sian and Monique Nuijten. 2013. 'Citizenship, the self, and political agency', *Critique of Anthropology* 33(1): 3–7.
Li, Tania Murray. 2007. *The Will to Improve: Governmentality, development, and the practice of politics*. Durham, NC: Duke University Press.
Nordstrom, Carolyn. 2007. *Global Outlaws: Crime, money, and power in the contemporary world*. Berkeley: University of California Press.
Penfield, Amy. 2016. 'Maneuvering for paper: Physical and social experiences of bureaucracy in Venezuelan Amazonia', *Journal of Latin American and Caribbean Anthropology* 21(3): 457–77.
Penfield, Amy. 2019. 'Extractive pluralities: The intersection of oil wealth and informal gold mining in Venezuelan Amazonia'. In *Indigenous Life Projects and Extractivism: Ethnographies from South America*, edited by Cecilie Vindal Ødegaard and Juan Javier Rivera Andía, 75–93. Cham: Palgrave Macmillan.
Peraldi, Michel. 2007. 'Économies criminelles et mondes d'affaire à Tanger', *Cultures et Conflits* 68: 111–25.
Polo Acuña, José. 2005. *Etnicidad, Conflicto Social y Cultura Fronteriza en la Guajira (1700–1850)*. Bogotá: Ediciones Uniandes.
Reeves, Madeleine. 2011. 'Fixing the border: On the affective life of the state in Southern Kyrgyzstan', *Environment and Planning D: Society and Space* 29: 905–23.
Renard-Casevitz, France-Marie. 1991. *Le Banquet Masqué: Une mythologie de l'étranger*. Paris: Lierre et Coudrier.
Roitman, Janet. 2003. 'La garnison-entrepôt: Une manière de gouverner dans le bassin du lac Tchad', *Critique Internationale* 19: 93–115.
Roitman, Janet. 2005. *Fiscal Disobedience: An anthropology of economic regulation in Central Africa*. Princeton: Princeton University Press.
Rubenstein, Steven. 2001. 'Colonialism, the Shuar federation, and the Ecuadorian state', *Environment and Planning D: Society and Space* 19: 263–93.

Scheele, Judith. 2009. 'Tribus, États et fraude: La région frontalière algéro-malienne', *Études Rurales* 184: 79–94.

Schwartz, Steven. 2021. 'The politics of *bachaqueo*: Gasoline black markets and indigeneity in Venezuela', *American Ethnologist* 48(4): 504–19.

Scott, James C. 1990. *Domination and the Arts of Resistance: Hidden transcripts*. New Haven, CT and London: Yale University Press.

Simpson, Audra. 2014. *Mohawk Interruptus: Political life across the borders of settler states*. Durham, NC: Duke University Press.

Sørhaug, Christian. 2014. 'Foraging for love'. In *Breaching Borders: Art, migrants, and the metaphor of waste*, edited by Juliet Steyn and Nadja Stamselberg, 257–75. London: I.B. Tauris.

Tamboli, Vikram. 2019. 'Hustling fuel, striking gold: Smuggling in the Guyanese–Venezuelan Borderlands', *NACLA Report on the Americas* 51(4): 422–32.

Thomas, Kendron and Rebecca Galemba. 2013. 'Illegal anthropology: An introduction', *PoLAR: Political and Legal Anthropology Review* 36(2): 211–14.

Viveiros de Castro, Eduardo. 2010. 'The untimely, again'. Introduction to *Archaeology of Violence*, by Pierre Clastres, 9–51. Los Angeles: Semiotext(e).

Wilbert, Johannes. 1993. *Mystic Endowment: Religious ethnography of the Warao Indians*. Cambridge, MA: Harvard University Center for the Study of World Religions.

4

Ranching, rustling and wage work: navigating the entangled smuggling economy in northern Paraguay

Cari Tusing

At once a frontier of the expanding drug trade, a border region of Brazil, and an area of contested land and property lines, the region of northern Paraguay under discussion in this chapter demonstrates the livelihood challenges different people face during struggles over land. I carried out my ethnographic research with a focus on land titling and property claims in an area with diverse and contested livelihoods such as large-scale cattle ranching, industrial soy farming, and both peasant[1] and Indigenous[2] subsistence farming. Yet beyond my focus on these struggles over land, the ethnographic data about the drug trade and cultivation I present in this chapter leaked into my ethnography and focus, despite my attempt to draw boundaries otherwise. As illicit information arrived unsolicited and was difficult to ignore, I began to understand it was entangled in struggles over land. This chapter, then, argues that the illicit permeates land-and-livelihood relationships in northern Paraguay, and thus constitutes an important, unavoidable aspect of ethnographic research in the region. From my fieldwork experiences, I propose 'lateral ethnography' as a method to study this 'leaky'[3] information, where the licit and illicit are entangled in everyday ways of life, borders and livelihoods.

Smuggling (goods) and struggling (over land)

Studies on smuggling in Paraguay often focus on its more southern tri-border region with Brazil and Argentina, with its nexus of contraband, smuggling, trafficking and alleged links to funding terrorism. Ciudad del Este has been called the 'largest illicit economy in the Western

Hemisphere' (Brown 2009; Tucker 2016), and it is the region's top producer of contraband cigarettes, through the TABESA company (Gomis et al. 2018), owned by a former president. All kinds of goods are smuggled across the triple frontier, including contraband cars, that instantiate a series of snarls in Paraguay's attempts to regulate the concentrated flow of goods to the area (Schuster 2019).

The Paraguayan state itself is often accused of rampant corruption and pilfering of public money, carried out by politicians of both the governing Colorado and opposition Liberal parties. For example, despite a 2020 emergency spending package of US$945 million (2.5 per cent of the GDP) to address the COVID-19 crisis, doctors and nurses took to the streets just one year later to protest the complete lack of basic medicine and supplies in state hospitals (Carneri and Politi 2021). Turner (1993) has shown that the Colorados and Liberals, Paraguay's two major political parties, both run the government as patronage networks, all the way down to the local level, where political loyalty and favours are key to the everyday functioning of the state. These patronage politics and state–*campesino* (smallholder peasant) relations are organized through political relationships called *correlí* or *correligionarios* (literally 'co-religionaries' or sharing the same religion), as people are expected to maintain quasi-religious party loyalty, and political affiliation is handed down through families.

Overall, contraband is an enormous part of the economy. Paraguay is one of the largest marijuana producers in the world, sending much of its harvest to neighbouring Brazil, and it is illegal in both countries. The northern region around the Paraguayan city of Pedro Juan Caballero, which shares an open land border with the Brazilian city of Ponta Porã (in the state of Mato Grosso do Sul), produces up to three harvests in a season as its temperatures and soil are well-suited for cannabis (Mendoza and Bevilaqua Marin 2014). Due to intense conflicts over the drug trade, the northern city of Pedro Juan Caballero has been called 'the city of blood' (Desantis and Stargardter 2020). The murder rate in Pedro Juan Caballero was 107 per 100,000 inhabitants in 2016, with 80 per cent of crime in 2015 linked to murders for hire (Todo Noticias 2018; Ultima Hora 2016). This is on par with the highest urban murder rates around the world, including that of much larger cities.

Because Pedro Juan Caballero and Brazil's Ponta Porã are contiguous, without any physical divisions or checkpoints, *sicarios* (hired killers or hitmen) often move back and forth between countries to avoid police dragnets. The open border allows for a constant flow of goods, services and people, which is only haphazardly checked. The first checkpoint is usually at Cruce Bella Vista, a crossroads where both roads from the north and from the west connect Paraguay and Brazil. Police and/or military from the Joint Task Force (*Fuerza de Tarea Conjunta/* FTC in Spanish), charged with guarding against possible terrorist attacks from a small extremist peasant group, run the checkpoint while chatting, drinking *terere* (a cold, yerba mate typical in Paraguay) and scanning their mobile phones. In this area of lax control, and with infrequent raids, anywhere between 9,000 to 55,000 metric tonnes of cannabis are grown each year (Tegel 2016). This accounts for some 2–15 per cent of the world's production (Garat 2016).

In turn, Brazilian criminal groups such as Comando Vermelho and Primeiro Comando da Capital have expanded into the Paraguayan market. Disputes over the Paraguayan market exploded spectacularly during my fieldwork, with the murder of Jorge Rafaat in 2016, killed in a four-hour shoot-out around the city centre, involving military-grade anti-aircraft and machine guns, as the *sicarios* attempted to flee across the border. The stakes are high as Brazilian gangs move into the Paraguayan market; estimates of marijuana production in northern Paraguay show its value to be approximately equal to that generated in the formal sector of soybean production, where Paraguay is one of the world's top exporters. That is, an estimated US$650 million is generated per year in Paraguay through marijuana production (IELA 2016). As Moriconi and Peris (2019, 2211) observe, northern Paraguay, with Pedro Juan Caballero as its hub, is a site of hybrid legality and illegality, where drug smuggling and politics have created an 'ecosystem of legality and criminality'.

These headline-grabbing events are serious, but they also obscure other dramatic changes in the economy and landscape in Northern Paraguay, where the industrial agro-ranching frontier is transforming the rural sphere. During 20 months of research in northern Paraguay, 2016–18, on the relationship between land titling and livelihoods, I carried out ethnographic fieldwork in the region of Amambay, Pedro Juan Caballero its capital, as well as the neighbouring region of Concepción. My research focused on the relationships between land titling, property and livelihoods between Indigenous Guarani communities, *campesino* (smallholder peasant) communities, and Paraguayan and Brazilian cattle ranchers.

Beginning in the 1980s, the Paraguayan state declared an Indigenous collective land title law, creating a shift in the property regime of the day, under which *campesinos* had been able to homestead and gain smallholdings since the 1960s, and large-scale cattle ranchers had continued to hold the majority of land titles and land itself. What would happen when Indigenous Guarani were able to collectively title the land they had lost to colonization? Studying its impacts required a multisited approach. Therefore, my research considered different groups and actors: Indigenous Guarani communities who carried out agroforestry and wage work, *campesino* homesteads with their mix of subsistence farming and wage work, and Paraguayan and Brazilian cattle ranchers, with their large-scale ranches and holdings. By gathering together the viewpoints of the diverse actors, often competing over land and livelihoods, I was able to document a changing economy, as the Atlantic Forest was cut down, cattle ranching expanded, and *campesinos* and Indigenous Guarani were pushed off land. Thus, attempts at *campesino* colonization, intensification of ranching, and an attempt to safeguard Indigenous communities through collective land title, came together in a fraught landscape of both competition and collaboration between interlocutors who became neighbours through the emerging property regime.

Lateral ethnography of the il/licit

It was in this context I decided that I would set up my base in the city of Concepción, instead of Pedro Juan Caballero, though I spent many months in the countryside in the Amambay region. And while there is admirable anthropological fieldwork focusing on the drug trade, corruption and everyday violence (Taussig 1992; Dunlap and Johnson 1999; Bourgois 2003; Scheper-Hughes and Bourgois 2004), I chose not to focus directly on the illicit market, for pragmatic, safety reasons. My research focused on land conflicts and resolutions, as different groups found ways to carry out land control and gain land title. A focus on this contested property regime was tense enough, with conflicts over land claims, accusations of squatting, falsified records, racialized insults and violent evictions in the context of the *campesino* and Guarani fight for land.

As a safety strategy, then, I made it clear that I was not researching anything to do with the drug trade and trafficking whenever I spoke about my research focus. I often made a specific gesture of crossing my hands and sweeping them away, to show that I even physically rejected the topic. I said I was not interested in making any trouble or hearing about trouble or causing trouble anywhere. Additionally, Paraguayan researchers who were better informed, equipped, and with longer-standing relationships, had worked carefully and anonymously with Guarani and *campesino* communities, to establish what they saw as the impacts of the marijuana trade (see Quiroga and Ayala Amarilla 2014; Cardozo et al. 2016).

In choosing this stance, I decided to not pursue direct research on a major factor in the local, regional and transnational economy. I do believe that it was the correct choice, to delineate my lack of research interest in illicit cultivations in an already contested landscape. I was willing to sacrifice access to certain data, to leave my research incomplete, in order to prioritize not just my own safety but also, more specifically, the safety of my host families.

I quickly found, however, that the topics of narcotrafficking and drug cultivation would find me, again and again. My attempt to separate land conflicts from the illegal or informal economy was not possible, because the smuggling economy was part and parcel of the land conflicts. Even as I did not focus on the illicit, it was present in different parts and pieces of my research, as a constitutive facet of the struggle over land. As I will show in this chapter, the regional political economy was entangled with narcotrafficking, from large-scale cultivation to cattle ranching and wage work in marijuana fields. Rather than finding my research incomplete, I was entrusted with fragments of sensitive information, as it was clear I was not interested in gathering information on major players, routes, producers, nor retaining information about them.

I find it useful to understand this repeated interruption of narcotrafficking into my research on land conflicts as a kind of 'lateral ethnography', where the illicit and informal presented themselves in different places and fragments, no matter my intended focus elsewhere. Nyiri (2013) has explored the idea of 'lateral vision' in his ethnography on child migrants, suggesting that seemingly insignificant events become clear in juxtaposition with larger, structural issues. Xiang and Toyota define Nyiri's lateral ethnography as 'ethnography that provides illuminating views "from the side" through juxtaposition' (2013, 280). Rather than juxtaposition, I propose that my experience with lateral ethnography was an exercise in finding relationships between different ethnographic fragments as they seeped into my research. Therefore, in this chapter I explore how different ethnographic materials became relevant over time and in relation to each other, as I was able to put together the story of a rancher's death, as the story came to me, piecemeal, through different sources at different times during my fieldwork. I also build on Nyiri's definition of lateral ethnography, to suggest that field sites with illegal or illicit activities are particularly apt for the method of lateral ethnography, as partial, encoded or incomplete information about these activities filter in through our fieldwork, and we make sense of them over time.

The illicit in the everyday

As usually happens during long-term ethnographic fieldwork, stories and incidents of illicit activities filtered into my field notes as I stayed longer and longer. Not all had to do directly with the drug trade. For instance, the Paraguayan president in office during my fieldwork was accused by the US Embassy of being 'significantly corrupt' (US Embassy in Paraguay 2022). Among other issues, he was accused of being the primary producer and smuggler of counterfeit cigarettes to Brazil. With my interest in land conflicts, I attended one *campesino* meeting where the focus was on a development project. In a parallel conversation, two *campesinas* (peasants) mentioned that then-president Cartes was accused of grabbing land around the tobacco plant, through a proxy buyer with the romantic last name of Romeo. 'How do people know he's linked to the president?' I asked. The answer was: 'We don't, but that's what we've heard. We don't ask too much either'. I did not ask them further, either. In another instance, I accompanied a Guarani leader on a transect to see where her community had filed for an extension to their collective title. During the walk, she told me she refused a rancher's illegal attempt to rent out her community's land, even as renting out Indigenous land was unconstitutional (Tusing 2023b).

In a third example, I went to visit a *campesino* family that was selling land to a woman from Asunción. While I was in transit, a *campesino* was murdered a few kilometres away while he waited to load his *mandioca* (cassava) harvest onto the bus to sell at market. I asked what had happened, when I visited the next community over; a young man told me that he was killed by '*mafia*'. When I exclaimed, 'Oh, I guess I should not ask anything else since it had to do with *narcos*', he thought for a moment and said: 'There is Mafia-with-a-capital M and mafia-with-a-lowercase m. The man was killed by the mafia, lowercase, because he had debts that he hadn't paid to a private lender. His time probably ran out'. The young man's observation astutely aligns with Friggeri's (2021) recent arguments that Paraguay's economy is increasingly organized as 'mafia capitalism', where violence has become a naturalized option to solve financial issues and eliminate competition. Citing Rojas Villagra (2014, 112): 'the accumulation of capital in Paraguay is carried out primarily through exploitation of land, illegal business activity, deals with or made possible by the state, and transnational capital investment'. Sadly, the hitman made the man pay his debt with his life.

Thus, it was impossible to understand land and livelihoods without repeatedly encountering stories about illicit activities. Like other chapters from this volume, my ethnographic research reveals that contraband practices such as smuggling or extralegal lending are pervasive in everyday life in Latin America. Despite an initial attempt to avoid them, or at least not focus on them as a topic of research, they materialized in such quotidian acts as attending *campesino* meetings, walking through Guarani territory, or visiting a homestead.

This constant filtering in of information around illicit activities is evidence of the porous, leaky nature of the licit/illicit divide. There is a rich tradition of work exploring the imbrication of the licit and illicit, where formal and informal practices collide to constitute economies, from the local to the international (Van Schendel and Abraham 2005; Galemba 2008; Hartnett and Dawdy 2013). Not only are the licit and illicit complementary, they often exist together, intimate and intertwined, and cannot be clearly separated – just as I was unable to parse out narcotrafficking from my ethnography in the context of land conflicts in northern Paraguay (see also Allard, Chapter 3, this volume).

In order to explore more extensively the porous boundary between licit and illicit that narcotrafficking breaches, here I present case studies to show the intimate, everyday relationships and power dynamics of the entangled smuggling economy in northern Paraguay. I found that licit and illicit activities, like cattle ranching and marijuana growing, become entangled in unexpected, often tragic ways on the ground. In the coming section, I explore how the regional political economy configured relationships of land and livelihoods towards marijuana smuggling. Yet in keeping with a lateral ethnographic approach, I emphasize that my research focused on the lived experiences of rural landholders in the entangled economy; the networks, routes, players and producers are outside the direct scope of this investigation. As the story unfolds, we will nonetheless see glimpses of how they appeared in fragments and pieces in other stories, highlighting the value of lateral ethnography in understanding the entanglements of an il/licit economy.

Plata he'ẽ, or sweet money

Cattle ranching is a major facet of northern Paraguay's political economy and an important part of Paraguay's national culture. Cattle outnumber people in Paraguay at a ratio of two to one (Ministerio de Agricultura y Ganadería de Paraguay 2008). Complicating the ranching economy is what one Paraguayan rancher, Emilio, called 'sweet money', which I also heard called *plata he'ẽ* in Guarani *jopara* (the local dialect) or *plata dulce* in Spanish. When I visited his ranch for an interview, Emilio explained that he had bought land from a Brazilian neighbour, but it was not until after he had surveyed the land himself that he realized his mistake. The price of the land he purchased was out of sync with the number of cattle the land could support. There was no way he could raise enough cattle within the available space, and with such low soil quality, to justify the purchase price. He had gone along with his neighbour's pricing as he trusted his appraisal, only to later find that it did not make financial sense. The neighbour had invested money in land and cattle not to profit from ranching, but rather to 'clean' his money, laundering it through the ranch. Thus this 'sweet money' is usually linked to illicitly obtained money and narcotrafficking.

Some ranches in the northern regions are bases for organized crime. Five sprawling ranches were finally appropriated by the state in 2019 after their Brazilian owner, alias *Cabeça Branca*, was captured in Brazil in 2017. The narcotrafficker used his ranches to traffic cocaine via not-so-clandestine airstrips and to launder money through cattle (Ultima Hora 2017; 2019). These 'hidden' airstrips pepper the countryside. As they are on private ranches worth millions of dollars, with thousands of hectares, landing strips are often difficult to detect from the ground, but can be clearly seen via satellite. The danger of becoming involved in illicit farming is clear, as they are linked to larger networks of organized crime in Paraguay and Brazil, and the *sicario* business is booming, as is evident from the high murder rate in Amambay, where over the past few years, on average someone is killed every two days (Todo Noticias 2018).

In the case of *Cabeça Branca,* it appears he also was running a *sicario* protection programme in Paraguay through his private security firm. In one meeting I had with a *campesino* organizer from the region, he took my notebook from me to sketch out the cross-border *sicario* relationships. One of his co-organizers had been killed by a *sicario* when attempting to keep sweet money out of his community. According to the surviving organizer's drawing, the *sicario* business worked this way: A *sicario* killed someone in Brazil, and in order to evade the police, he crossed over into Paraguay to work as a private security guard on a ranch. He then patrolled the ranch to make sure Paraguayan police did not enter to search for marijuana planting. The mirror version of this technique was used in Paraguay: when a Brazilian *sicario* killed someone in

Paraguay, he then crossed over to Brazil to work as private security on a money-laundering cattle ranch there. This cross-border *sicario* exchange programme is evidence of the porous border between the two countries, but also of the entangled economy between private security, cattle ranches, marijuana plantations and *matones* (murderers-for-hire).[4]

In order to explore the intimate, on-the-ground entanglements of sweet money, ranching and narcotrafficking, I will now present how I came to hear two different versions of a story about a rancher who was the victim of a murder plot.

Part 1: Ranching and drug trafficking in rural Paraguay

The first part of the story takes place close to the Paraguayan–Brazilian border near the Cruce Bella Vista checkpoint, where an NGO partner and I stayed overnight before heading to an Indigenous Guarani community. Night was quickly falling as we pulled up to the *posta de salud*, a rural health clinic where the attending health worker, Nadia, had her house on the property. Nadia assured us it was a quiet, calm area where not much happened. She said you could walk to the stores in the evenings, and that she'd been there a long time and not much had changed. She told us how much she enjoyed living in the area, that she knew everyone. After dropping our things off in our respective rooms, we walked along a path off the side of the highway to buy cola and bread, to add to dinner. We returned in the quiet cover of the evening, and I thought of the Indigenous and *campesino* communities we were going to visit, out there in the darkness, people around the kitchen fires, lying in hammocks or beds and talking. A sense of community, of knowing people in the area, and the feeling of belonging to a place, might mean that people would feel secure, as Nadia did.

Late in the evening, after dinner, my NGO partner asked after a former classmate who had been killed that year. He had been a successful, large-scale rancher who owned thousands of heads of cattle on a nearby property. 'Did you hear anything about Javier's death?' The health worker looked at the two of us and replied:

'Have you heard of the drug trafficker and *matón* who's in jail?' Nadia named him, and we had.

She continued: 'Well, one time he hid out here behind the clinic. They surprised him in a shootout at a nearby ranch when someone tipped off the Joint Task Force (FTC) about a marijuana shipment. He managed to get away on foot and came here and hid in the dark.

When the police were coming, he called out to me, "Nurse, don't you dare say anything!"' – in Guarani: *Aníke ere mba'eve enfermera*! When the police came to her door to ask if she had heard or seen anything, she said she had not. 'He got away then, but was captured later', Nadia explained.

My NGO partner asked: 'Why, was Javier involved in planting at his ranch? Was that why he was taken out by a *matón*?'

Nadia considered for a moment and responded, 'Javier reported someone growing marijuana on the hills at the far end of his ranch to SENAD [Paraguay's National Drug Secretariat, or *Secretaría Nacional Antidrogas* in Spanish]. He said he was not going to confront them because they might be armed'. She concluded that as long as he reported them once a year, he could say that any marijuana they found had been reported, and that SENAD had not acted.

In reality, she said, trucks came and went while he was there at the ranch, to take out drug shipments. This does not mean that all owners who report marijuana planting on their ranches are actively seeking to cover up their collusion with growers, nor seeking to become growers themselves; it is possible that they are coerced into complying or decline to confront armed groups as traffickers seek to expand in the area. In this way, it is difficult to unravel Javier's participation in marijuana cultivation. Many things were possible – though he denounced marijuana plantations at the edge of his ranch, he could have been involved or he could have been coerced. Either way, his tragic death at the hands of a drug trafficker and murderer-for-hire signalled that his death was entangled in the drug trade.

The tranquillity that the health worker Nadia had earlier described contrasted quite sharply with the story of drug trafficking, theft and murder that she now recounted. The uncertainty of who is linked to narcotrafficking means that one never knows what kind of violent networks are at play. These networks, linked to the international drug trade through the porous land border, create a specific entangled economy where murder-for-hire is always a readily available option on the table.

Part 2: Cattle rustling and hired hands

The second part of this story takes place in an old, colonial style house in Concepción, where my field assistant, David, had arranged for an interview with a rancher. Through his network, he reached out to nine different ranchers all over the regions of Concepción and Amambay.

I interviewed ranchers (*ganaderos*) of Paraguayan and Brazilian descent. Most were about 20–30 years older than my field assistant and me, as they were patriarchs and heads of their ranches. Their adult children would receive parts of the ranch when they married or continue to work with their fathers until they inherited. But this particular rancher was a woman, as my field assistant explained the day before the interview. He had an excellent understanding of my interview motivations: 'I know you're trying to understand the experience of cattle ranchers in general, but also understand different particular cases. So I thought it would be interesting to talk to señora [Mrs] Edelia'. As the vast majority of ranchers were men, señora Edelia's experience was unusual.

We sat in Edelia's comfortable living room on a white sofa and white chairs; apparently none of the deep red earth from her ranch was trekked back into her city home. Over tea, we went through the script of the semi-structured interview I had designed, starting a dynamic, amenable conversation between the three of us – Edelia, David and myself, the anthropologist.

Part of the interview concerned labour relations between local people, as ranches sometimes share a border with a Guarani community or a *campesino* colony. Ranchers may rent out land or hire people from these nearby communities, creating economic ties between neighbours that complicate struggles over land. I asked Edelia about her hired hands and what kinds of gender dynamics she saw as a woman in an industry that is mostly run and worked by men. Edelia considered for a moment and said: 'It's very difficult. I normally take my [adult] sons with me to stay at the ranch. And I always look for hired hands to work for me who have had a *patrona* [woman boss] before, because they have fewer problems working for a woman. Some have left because they can't work for a *patrona*; they're always asking after my sons and talking to them, not me. And they can be impolite and make rude jokes'.[5]

Edelia ventured: 'It's difficult to know who you can trust, because you always need a *capataz* [foreman] you can trust. Since my husband died …' She trailed off. After a pause, I filled in the silence. I said: 'Of course, a *capataz* is like the right-hand man to the rancher. That must be very difficult.' She continued as the volume of her voice raised slightly, 'There is no more honesty. It seems like everyone steals from us, and you have to be on top of them. I've forbidden them to leave when they're working because they make friends with the neighbours, like the *campesinos* or the Guarani, and that can bring problems like marijuana and cocaine'. Along her ranch's forested borders, she said that she sees marijuana cultivators be so bold as to build platforms (*mangrullo*) to keep watch over their illegal plantations on her land, which she registers with SENAD each year. 'There is no more respect for private property', she concluded. 'I hired security from the outside, and they keep up a security border. I closed all of the gates since my husband was killed'. Not wanting to make her retell a traumatic story, we moved on to talk about the pastureland she rented from a neighbouring Guarani community.

After we left, I asked my field assistant how Edelia's husband was killed. David explained that Javier's *capataz* was a cattle rustler who stole over a thousand heads of cattle from the ranch. When it came time to count the cattle during a vaccination campaign that year, the *capataz* knew there was no way he could account for all the cattle that were missing. To inflate numbers, some hired hands paraded the same lot of animals through multiple times, thus vaccinating the cattle multiple times, risking them getting infections and sick from overdosage. But the *capataz* knew that his boss also daubed the cattle with paint as they went through vaccination, so he wouldn't be able to hide his crime. With cattle forming such an important part of the economy, cattle rustling (*abigeato*) is a serious offence and carries a steep sentence of up to ten years if caught. Comparatively, first-degree murder carries a sentence of five to twenty years.[6]

Javier's *capataz* called a friend who was *capataz* at a neighbouring ranch and asked to borrow cattle to cover up his crime. He said he couldn't explain but that it was urgent, and the friend couldn't lend him the cattle because the landowner at his ranch was also coming to take an inventory. He and his friend instead plotted to kill the ranch owner to cover up the loss. They accused him of denouncing marijuana farming on his ranch and spread the news that he was actively collaborating with SENAD to carry out a raid on the illegal plantations on his property. In response, the drug cultivators ordered a hit, and Javier was gunned down at the gates of his ranch by a *matón* who, eventually was convicted of the murder only after being arrested for a different case. It dawned on me that this was the same story I had heard from the nurse, but from a different angle.

Entangled and absorbing: northern Paraguay's smuggling economy

As we drove back through Concepción, I told my field assistant that I had heard the story about Javier's death a few months back while staying at the health clinic, and I was shocked to find out that Edelia was his widow. While I was focused on understanding Edelia's licit relationship to *campesino* and Indigenous communities through wage labour, the illicit, tragic impact of drug trafficking continued to break through. It permeated my fieldwork in the same way as sweet money permeated ranching country. By applying a lateral view, I pieced together the relationships between the licit and illicit, just as the rancher Emilio pieced together the link between his neighbour's ranch and sweet money.

Along the Paraguayan–Brazilian frontier, stories of violence continued to seep through my fieldwork. As mentioned, the *campesino* organizer who drew a map of the *sicario* network knew the process intimately because a *matón* had killed his fellow organizer a few years ago. The mayor (*intendente*) of nearby Bella Vista was murdered only a kilometre away from a Guarani community where I was staying. When visiting the northernmost town of Puentesiño (also called Sargento José Félix López), I met a thin young man who had suffered insomnia for years, after he attended a football match at which the spectator directly next to him was shot and killed by a *matón*.

Frontiers have been conceptualized as porous and expansive areas through the transformation of territories, not to be reduced to the thin strip of leading settlers (Tsing 2011; Campbell 2015). Following Cearns (2023), boundaries and borders signify a lineal divide, whereas frontiers are zones of ambiguity and blurring. As these two regions of northern Paraguay are subsumed into the logics of the drug trade, the violent frontier of the illicit leaks into people's everyday lives in persistent, tragic ways.

Yet I also find it useful to think of the illicit frontier as not only leaking into and permeating the licit economy that makes up the entangled smuggling economy of marijuana and cattle – the illicit frontier is also potentially absorbent. Time and again, people referred to how marijuana plantations and smuggling were growing issues in their everyday life. Guarani leaders spoke of advising young people against growing the crop, despite its cash value, as it put them into direct contact with potentially violent middlemen who held the entire community responsible if anything went wrong. *Campesinos* reflected upon the lack of wage work to complement their subsistence crops, as mechanized soy and feed lots replaced slower modes of production that were more reliant on hired hands. Working in a marijuana plantation was a reliable, if dangerous, way to supplement their subsistence farming with a wage. As the illicit economy booms, it subsumes other, licit options in the Indigenous Guarani and *campesino* fight for land. In this way, Indigenous Guarani, *campesinos* and ranchers alike are all obligated to navigate the entangled smuggling economy in Paraguay, despite the fact that people may not wish to be directly involved, or actively avoid it. Many of the impacts of marijuana plantations and smuggling are unavoidable, reflecting a totalizing aspect of the drug economy, as licit and illicit economies are linked.

With sweet money and a firmly established network of *matones,* there is an easy option to draw on *narco* tactics to 'solve' conflicts. The private loan mafia-with-a-lowercase m depends on the *sicario* network to enforce debt payments through fear of violence, and carries through with its threats. Both Indigenous Guarani and *campesinos* participate in this private loan network, as state subsidies are limited to some farming support. Without a formal banking history, most rural people cannot access loans otherwise, and *sicarios* operate to collect outstanding debts. On the ranch, when Javier's *capataz* was unable to account for the cattle he had rustled, he mobilized the conflict over marijuana plantations to attempt to cover up his own crimes. Inciting the *matón* by spreading the rumour that Javier was collaborating with SENAD, the *capataz* welcomed the violent, illicit alternative (murder), thus merging his cattle-rustling crimes with *narco*-conflicts. As *matones* are hired in non-drug contexts, the illicit drug frontier absorbs other kinds of crimes into its logics. This illicit frontier reworks the land market through sweet money, changing the local landscape as money is laundered through cattle and patches of forest are kept to disguise marijuana plantations.

Despite intentions to focus my fieldwork on land conflicts, the illicit economy nevertheless came up again and again. This is likely due to the violent nature of the illicit crimes I was attempting to avoid studying, because in order to stay safe, paradoxically, I also needed to know where not to tread. As I pieced together señora Edelia's story, I found that the violence of murder-for-hire was utilized as a way to 'solve' or even cover for non-narco crimes, and yet with the murky nature of the illicit, it is often difficult to know who is involved. *Narco* solutions are used to solve non-*narco* issues, merging licit and illicit activities. This is perhaps the soft cover of rural violence that I encountered at the health worker's house. The everyday relationships, close community and seeming quietness of the area might give a false sense of the illicit as *outside* of one's community, but cattle ranching, rustling, and marijuana plantations are all deeply entangled in northern Paraguay's smuggling economy. In tracing a relationship between different fragments and stories about illicit activities over time, I was able to analyse how they were connected through lateral ethnography. Taken in isolation, such data was simply information I might need so as to avoid running into danger while carrying out fieldwork. Taken together, however, the entangled relationships between neighbours, livelihoods and land, bring both the illicit and licit into stark analytical view.

Acknowledgements

Parts of this research were financed by the University of Arizona, Inter-American Foundation, US Department of Education [P022A159946], National Science Foundation [1558558], and P.E.O. Foundation.

Notes

1 Peasants (campesinos in Spanish) are legally considered distinct from Indigenous people in Paraguay. This is reflected in both land title statutes and the state census.
2 In this chapter I follow Indigenous style guides that prefer the capitalized spelling of the term; see Christine Weeber (2020): '[W]hy capitalize "Indigenous"? It articulates and identifies a group of political and historical communities, compared to the lower case 'i' which can refer to anyone'.
3 My use of 'leaky' here is inspired by Krøijer's (2019) study on the 'leaky reality of resource enclaves' (p. 1) that the Sieko-pai (formerly Secoya) navigate in Ecuador; I find it useful to analyse Paraguay's licit and illicit smuggling economy as not only entangled, but also permeable and therefore leaky.
4 In this piece, in addition to the term *sicario*, I also use the term *matón* or *matones*, a noun for a hired killer formed from the verb to kill (*matar*) plus an augmentative suffix (*ón*) used frequently by my Paraguayan interlocutors.
5 This recalls my first interview with a local rancher, who made a rape joke about me being alone with the hired hands and said he'd protect me; see Tusing (2023a).
6 The Civil Code states the punishment for stealing one or more head of cattle is up to 10 years, and for first-degree murder is from 5–10 years.

References

Bourgois, Philippe. 2003. *In Search of Respect: Selling crack in El Barrio*. Cambridge: Cambridge University Press.

Brown, Rachel. 2009. *The Tri-Border Area: A profile of the largest illicit economy in the Western Hemisphere*. Financial Integrity and Economic Development Task Force. Accessed 15 March 2024. https://financialtransparency.org/the-tri-border-area-a-profile-of-the-largest-illicit-economy-in-the-western-hemisphere/.

Campbell, Jeremy M. 2015. *Conjuring Property: Speculation and environmental futures in the Brazilian Amazon*. Seattle: University of Washington Press.

Cardozo, Mario L., Danilo Salas, Isabel Ferreira, Teresa Mereles and Laura Rodríguez. 2016. 'Soy expansion and the absent state: Indigenous and peasant livelihood options in eastern Paraguay', *Journal of Latin American Geography* 15(3): 87–104.

Carneri, Santi and Daniel Politi. 2021. 'Rage spreads in Paraguay as virus surges, exposing corruption', *New York Times*, 11 March. Accessed 15 March 2024. https://www.nytimes.com/2021/03/11/world/americas/paraguay-covid-protests.html.

Cearns, Jennifer. 2023. *Circulating Culture: Transnational Cuban networks of exchange*. Gainesville: University Press of Florida.

Desantis, Daniela and Gabriel Stargardter. 2020. 'Jailbreak in the "city of blood": Brazil's drug gangs overrun Paraguay', Reuters, 3 July. Accessed 15 March 2024. https://www.reuters.com/article/idUSKBN1ZX1H5/.
Dunlap, Eloise and Bruce D. Johnson. 1999. 'Gaining access to hidden populations: Strategies for gaining cooperation of drug sellers/dealers and their families in ethnographic research', *Drugs & Society* 14(1–2): 127–49. Accessed 15 March 2024. https://doi.org/10.1300/J023v14n01_08.
Friggeri, Félix Pablo. 2021. 'Primitive accumulation, mafia capitalism, and the campesino population in Paraguay', *Latin American Perspectives* 48(1): 126–44.
Galemba, Rebecca B. 2008. 'Informal and illicit entrepreneurs: Fighting for a place in the neoliberal economic order', *Anthropology of Work Review* 29: 19–25.
Garat, Guillermo. 2016. *Paraguay: The cannabis breadbasket of the Southern Cone*. Report no. 46, Informes sobre politicas de drogas. Transnational Institute. Accessed 6 September 2023. https://www.tni.org/files/publication-downloads/drug_policy_briefing_46.pdf.
Gomis, Benoît, Kelley Lee, Natalia Carrillo Botero, Philip Shepherd and Roberto Magno Iglesias. 2018. '"We think globally": The rise of Paraguay's Tabacalera del Este as a threat to global tobacco control', *Globalization and Health* 14(1): 1–14.
Hartnett, Alexandra and Sharon L. Dawdy. 2013. 'The archaeology of illegal and illicit economies', *Annual Review of Anthropology* 42: 37–51.
IELA (Instituto de Estudos Latino-Americanos). 2016. 'Paraguay: Narcotráfico gera 650 milhões de dólares ao ano', 25 November. Accessed 15 March 2024. https://iela.ufsc.br/paraguay-narcotrafico-gera-650-milhoes-de-dolares-ao-ano/.
Krøijer, Stine. 2019. 'In the spirit of oil: Unintended flows and leaky lives in northeastern Ecuador'. In *Indigenous Life Projects and Extractivism: Ethnographies from South America*, edited by C. Vindal Ødegaard and J. J. Rivera Andía, 95–118. Cham: Palgrave Macmillan. Accessed 15 March 2024. https://doi.org/10.1007/978-3-319-93435-8_4.
Mendoza, Benito Armando Solis and Joel Orlando Bevilaqua Marin. 2014. 'Produçâo de cannabis em Amambay – Paraguai: O envolvimento de jovens rurais'. In *Plantíos Ilícitos na América Latina*, edited by P. Pontes Fraga, 22–55. Rio de Janeiro: Letra Capital.
Ministerio de Agricultura y Ganadería de Paraguay. 2008. 'Censo Agropecuario Nacional de 2008'. Accessed 15 March 2024. https://www.arp.org.py/images/files/CENSO%20AGROPECUARIO%202008.pdf.
Moriconi, Marcelo and Carlos Aníbal Peris. 2019. 'Merging legality with illegality in Paraguay: The cluster of order in Pedro Juan Caballero', *Third World Quarterly* 40(12): 2210–27. Accessed 15 March 2024. https://doi.org/10.1080/01436597.2019.1636225.
Nyiri, Pál. 2013. 'Lateral vision: Juxtaposition as a method', *Ethnography* 14(3): 369–83. Accessed 15 March 2024. https://doi.org/10.1177/1466138113491677.
Quiroga, Lorna and Oscar Ayala. 2014. *Violencia e Impunidad Hacia el Pueblo Pai Tavytera- Kaiowa: Aproximación a la situación de violaciones de derechos humanos en la frontera paraguayo-brasilena*. Asunción: Tierraviva. Accessed 28 March 2024. https://www.tierraviva.org.py/wp-content/uploads/2014/08/Violencia-e-impundad.pdf.
Rojas Villagra, Luis. 2014. *La metamorfosis del Paraguay: Del esplendor inicial a su traumática descomposición*. Asunción: BASE Investigaciones Sociales. Accessed 15 March 2024. https://biblioteca.clacso.edu.ar/Paraguay/base-is/20170331043524/pdf_1233.pdf.
Scheper-Hughes, Nancy and Philippe I. Bourgois. 2004. 'Introduction: Making sense of violence'. In *Violence in War and Peace: An anthology*, edited by N. Scheper-Hughes and P. Bourgeois, 1–33. Malden, MA: Blackwell Publishing.
Schuster, Caroline. 2019. 'The bottlenecks of free trade: Paraguay's *Mau* cars and contraband markets in the triple frontier', *Journal of Latin American and Caribbean Anthropology* 24: 498–517. Accessed 15 March 2024. https://doi.org/10.1111/jlca.12419.
Taussig, Michael T. 1992. *The Nervous System*. New York: Routledge.
Tegel, Simeon. 2016. 'The front lines of Paraguay's slash-and-burn war on weed', Pulitzer Center, 12 July. Accessed 15 March 2024. https://pulitzercenter.org/stories/front-lines-paraguays-slash-and-burn-war-weed.
Todo Noticias. 2018. 'Pedro Juan Caballero, la capital del miedo: Cómo es el lugar donde mataron a la abogada argentina de narcos brasileños', 13 November. Accessed 15 March 2024. https://tn.com.ar/internacional/pedro-juan-caballero-la-capital-del-miedo-como-es-el-lugar-donde-mataron-la-abogada-argentina-de_915612/.

Tsing, Anna L. 2011. *Friction: An ethnography of global connection*. Princeton: Princeton University Press.

Tucker, Jennifer L. 2016. 'Contraband City: Geographies of extralegal work and life in Paraguay's frontier economy'. PhD thesis, City and Regional Planning. Berkeley: University of California.

Turner, Brian. 1993. *Community Politics and Peasant–State Relations in Paraguay*. Lanham, MD: University Press of America.

Tusing, Cari. 2023a. 'The fieldwork of never alone: Reframing access as relationships of care'. In *The Entanglements of Ethnographic Fieldwork in a Violent World*, edited by N. Weiss, E. Grassiani and L. Green, 48–58. New York: Routledge.

Tusing, Cari. 2023b. 'The New Guarani reductions: Aftermaths of collective land titling in northern Paraguay', *Journal of Peasant Studies* 50(1): 391–410. Accessed 15 March 2024. https://doi.org/10.1080/03066150.2021.1960825.

Ultima Hora. 2016. '80% de los crímenes en Amambay fueron por sicariato', 4 January. Accessed 15 March 2024. http://www.ultimahora.com/80-los-crimenes-2015-amambay-fueron-sicariato-n956642.

Ultima Hora. 2017. 'Cabeza Branca: Cayó capo narco en el Brasil', 1 July. Accessed 15 March 2024. https://www.ultimahora.com/cabeza-branca-cayo-capo-narco-que-operaba-paraguay-y-brasil-n1094105.

Ultima Hora. 2019. 'Organización de Cabeza Branca invertía sus bienes en Paraguay', 10 April. https://www.ultimahora.com/organizacion-cabeza-branca-invertia-sus-bienes-paraguay-n2812888.html.

US Embassy in Paraguay. 2022. 'Designation of former Paraguayan President Horacio Cartes for involvement in significant corruption', 16 August. Accessed 15 March 2024. https://py.usembassy.gov/designation-of-former-paraguayan-president-horacio-manuel-cartes-jara-for-involvement-in-significant-corruption.

Van Schendel, Willem and Itty Abraham (eds). 2005. *Illicit Flows and Criminal Things: States, borders, and the other side of globalization*. Bloomington: Indiana University Press.

Weeber, Christine. 2020. 'Why capitalize "Indigenous"?', *Sapiens*, 19 May. Accessed 15 March 2024. https://www.sapiens.org/language/capitalize-indigenous/.

Xiang, Biao and Mika Toyota. 2013. 'Ethnographic experiments in transnational mobility studies', *Ethnography* 14(3): 277–81. Accessed 15 March 2024. https://doi.org/10.1177/1466138113491655.

5

Emprendedores forzados: ex-smugglers of Venezuelan petrol turned unwilling entrepreneurs in the Colombian border city of Cúcuta

Charles Beach

> Work is a right and a social obligation and enjoys, in all its forms, the special protection of the State. Every individual is entitled to a job under dignified and equitable conditions.
>
> Article 25 of the 1991 Colombian Constitution (translated by Coward, Heller and Torras, 2019)

On May Day 2018, I followed the trade unionists of Cúcuta on their traditional march through the city. Accompanied by brass bands, *vuvuzela* horns and drums, all of the city's trade unions, from teachers and farmworkers to grocers and car mechanics, marched around the city centre, ending up in the central Parque Colón to listen to impassioned speeches. After the national anthem, the socialist anthem *The Internationale* was blasted through the sound system and many in the crowd raised their fists. Among the sea of hands were those from the trade union Sintragasolina. 'SINTRAGASOLINA' stands for *Sindicato de Trabajadores de la Gasolina* – Trade Union of Gasoline Workers. What makes the trade union distinct from trade unions in Colombia is that its members are smugglers of petrol, a class of smuggler among many others that have become iconic in the region.

Cúcuta is Colombia's sixth-largest city and sits on the border with Venezuela. In 1821 the first constitution of Greater Colombia was signed and the city became an important centre for international trade, due to the fast-growing train network connecting it to the Venezuelan port of Maracaibo. After Venezuela's petroleum boom of the twentieth century, Cúcuta continued to maintain a reputation for commerce, even when other parts of Colombia were suffering from economic deprivation and internal armed conflict, as Venezuelans took advantage of their strong currency to cross the border and buy cheap produce. With the global collapse of oil prices in 2014, the Venezuelan economy also collapsed and Cúcuta became a place where Venezuelans, now with a hugely inflated currency, would come to buy essentials no longer produced by their country's failing economy (see also Van Roekel, Chapter 6 and Allard, Chapter 3, in this volume). Sitting between two large sovereign states, the borderland is dynamic, ever-changing with the times and the fickle nature of economies. One thing that remained consistent throughout the pendulum swings of modern history and commerce was Cúcuta's reputation for smuggling, especially the smuggling of petrol. Petrol smugglers, taking advantage of heavily state-subsidized petrol in neighbouring Venezuela, smuggle it over the border, either by road or across the river. They sell it on the streets of Cúcuta, in jerry cans called *pimpinas* and with funnels made from plastic bottles and tubing. Derived from *pimpina,* the informal collective name for petrol smugglers is *pimpineros.* On May Day, among the raised fists, the *pimpineros* of Sintragasolina wore their branded vests and waved their plastic funnels. The funnels were not to signal that there was petrol to sell, like normal, but instead a symbol of identity and protest.

In the centre of the *pimpineros* was Julia, head of the trade union, with her bodyguard and a dozen or so other members of the union. She is in her mid-thirties and used to work as a *pimpinera*. She took on the role of secretary to the director of the union before assuming the role of director herself. The first of May in Colombia, like in many other parts of the world, is *Día de los Trabajadores* – Day of the Workers. It is less politicized than in other countries and is often a general celebration of all lines of work. This is especially the case in right-wing Cúcuta and its wider department of Norte de Santander, where a dim view is held of trade unionists. The public university I was associated with had only a few representatives. 'Most teachers are scared to show up, or disagree with trade unionism', one member told me, 'Cúcuta is where even the public universities are conservative'.

Walking around the periphery of Parque Colón, I overheard a group of middle-aged men talking sneeringly about the congregation. Highlighting the political tensions in Cúcuta, one mimed jokingly the action of throwing a grenade into the centre of the crowd, while laughing. With Colombia's ongoing armed conflict that is, broadly speaking, between left and right, being a trade unionist is dangerous. There is the possible threat from right-wing paramilitaries, who are often involved or aligned with the interests of capital and the state (Civico 2015; Osuna 2015; Madariaga 2006). Among the generally right-wing urban population there is a stigmatization of trade unionism, as being aligned with the left and therefore guerrilla supporting. The trade unions and leftists supposedly demand the economically impossible or do not understand what it is to have a decent work ethic. They want '*todo regalado*' – everything given to them – as is said by right-wing politicians, who constantly point to the economic collapse in Venezuela as a reminder of what will happen if the left wins in Colombia, and what the unions participating in national strikes really aim to achieve (Rojas 2018).

This becomes more complicated in the case of Sintragasolina, as *pimpineros* are often extorted by paramilitaries, who take money from them in exchange for being allowed to sell on the streets or cross the border with contraband. Paramilitaries have an economic interest in smuggling and do not want to see social organizing among the population, especially when that organizing might lead to smugglers moving into formal trades or protecting themselves from extortion. A dim view is taken of mentioning paramilitarism in public. One of Sintragasolina's roles is in making paramilitary extortion visible to the wider public and trying to protect their member base. Thus, Julia is recognized by the state as a defender of human rights and her armed bodyguard is provided by a state entity. The union, over the years, has been building an often-difficult relationship with the state, to get funding for a programme of vocational training and small-business funding. It doesn't have a membership that can withhold its labour in a strike, like a traditional union, nor is there an employer it can negotiate with. But it has a membership across the city that can mobilize for highly visible and disruptive protests. As anthropologist Sian Lazar says in her look at Bolivian unions for informal workers: 'Because many of the organizations, including unions, bring together people who are self-employed, the state (rather than the employer) is the principal interlocutor. Thus, the experience of citizenship for citizens ... is utterly entwined with practices of collective organization on the basis of residence or occupation' (2012, 15).

This is antagonism towards the state. But it is also ultimately the state they are trying to build a relationship with. Many contradictions seem to arise from Sintragasolina's existence. Sintragasolina presents participation in contraband as a legitimate form of work, as a working-class culture that is something to be proud of and facilitates collective action: contraband as a unifying factor for working-class solidarity.

This chapter draws on ethnographic research, undertaken between 2017 and 2019 among unionized and non-unionized *pimpineros,* as well as within small businesses of ex-*pimpineros,* set up through the state-funded vocational retraining programmes, to examine this situation. The chapter will show how, while sharing many attributes of a traditional trade union, Sintragasolina is also forming an 'insurgent citizenship' that makes up for gaps in the modernist liberal citizenship project (Holston 2013). The group takes a step towards the state and demands the programmes and policies they want to see, with 'a range of formal and informal practices employed to claim for missing entitlements' (Butcher and Apsan Frediani 2014, 119).

This chapter is in five parts. The first half of the chapter is made up of two ethnographic sections. The first, 'A trade union for petrol smugglers', introduces Julia as she takes me on a tour of petrol-vending spots in Cúcuta and explains the main functions of their trade union, Sintragasolina. This presents contraband as a culture and as legitimate work. The second section, 'From gasoline to cooking oil', describes the socio-vocational retraining programme that Sintragasolina negotiated from the local government, that helped ex-*pimpineros* create and run co-owned businesses. I meet Carlos, who gives me a tour of his cooperative that collects and sells used cooking oil, which shows the desire of many *pimpineros* to enter into licit, non-precarious work. The second half of the chapter analyses the ethnography. The section '*Emprendedores forzados*' is an analysis of the collapse of several of the businesses, from the practitioners who were involved in the running of the programme and providing support for the ex-*pimpineros* in their business ventures. It explains the ethnographic concept of *emprendedores forzados* (forced entrepreneurs) which is a play on the existing term of forcibly displaced peoples. I use it to highlight the strong emphasis on entrepreneurship in development programmes across Colombia (and the world) as well as using it as a way to show how *pimpineros* are seen, by NGO actors and the state, as nonmodern. In the section 'Creating modern subjects from people without culture', I make this comparison explicit, by using the work of anthropologist Emma Crane to compare the reconversion programme for the *pimpineros* to similar entrepreneurial projects aimed at ex-combatants of FARC, Colombia's now demobilized guerrilla group. The *programa de reconversión sociolaboral* – socio-labour reconversion programme – also, I argue, tries to bring the *pimpineros* into the run of modern life, away from marginality and stigmatization and toward being ideal, productive citizens. In the final section, 'A good *pimpinero* isn't a *pimpinero*', I use the work of anthropologist Roxani Krystalli to compare the *pimpineros* to victims of the armed conflict, who have to perform their victimhood to state bureaucracies to prove that they are deserving and 'good victims', in order to benefit from state help. While those hired to manage the programme blame lack of funding for continued accompaniment and the difficult lived experiences of the *pimpineros*, I use this section to present what I see as an underlying contradiction that inhibits the smooth functioning of the reconversion programme and businesses.

Sintragasolina was able to negotiate such a programme through militant, antagonistic action and strong, collective, *pimpinero* identity. But the programme that they received was about turning them into the opposite: individual, responsible citizens who are no longer *pimpineros*. The *pimpineros* use contraband as identity and culture to support their platform for demanding vocational retraining programmes that negate that very culture.

A trade union for petrol smugglers

A car lurches to a halt outside the house where I am staying. I greet Julia and get in the front. I say hello to the driver, who Julia introduces to me as a *pimpinero* colleague of hers, as well as her bodyguard in the back. We move off and the driver clutches a screwdriver that he uses as a replacement for the gearstick, which is missing. The car breaks down after a few minutes and Julia has to phone another *pimpinero* colleague, with transport, to come and pick us up. 'We used to have a motorbike', she said, but it was stolen. 'The National Protection Unit can supply us with a truck if we can demonstrate a sufficient threat to my life.' As a legally registered human-rights defender, Julia is also supplied with a bodyguard by the *Unidad de Protección Nacional* – the National Protection Unit, or UNP. We head out to the poorer, peripheral parts of town, where we start to see *pimpineros* on the side of the road, waving the makeshift plastic funnels, and pull over to talk to one of them. He has a green bib with Sintragasolina branding and has set up a tarpaulin to keep off the midday sun. A car pulls up and he tanks it up with a *pimpina* of gasoline. The driver pays him through the window and drives off. 'There used to be a *pimpinero* like this on every corner', Julia said with a hint of exasperation. She was saying something that was often said in Cúcuta, but normally positively, by those who approved the removal of the *pimpineros*. 'There was a restructuring of contraband laws that made it more illegal to sell gasoline on the streets – we now have to be far more covert or work in the outskirts where the police pay less attention or have less control. Then Maduro introduced a system that meant you need a chip on your windscreen in order to buy petrol in Venezuela', she said, pointing at a little barcode by the central mirror of the car. 'Then in 2016 the border was shut by Venezuela making it impossible to drive across the border and tank-up.'

'We used to go in big cars, tank-up, then come back. Almost everybody was doing it. Show Charles your ID!', she said to the *pimpinero* as he proceeded to show me an official-looking photo ID card proving membership of Sintragasolina. 'We used to have a *pico y placa* [peak and plate] organized with the police where on certain days a *pimpinero* with Sintragasolina was allowed to sell. It was still technically illegal, but we had negotiated a sort of … decriminalization. It started off with 10 family cooperatives working independently that then formed into Sintragasolina.' *Pico y placa* is a congestion-reduction scheme across Colombian cities, where, based on their licence plate number, cars have alternating days on which they can drive or are banned from driving. 'People were not used to tanking up at a normal petrol station', she told me. 'The day they restructured the laws there were queues around the block to try and get petrol, even now some people are just more comfortable buying off of a *pimpinero* they know. And the Venezuelan petrol is better!'

The driver showed me his card, but instead of *pimpinero* he was registered as a *transportador* (transporter). 'His job was transporting gasoline between the border and vending spots', Julia added. We got back into the car and visited several more sites. We met a woman on the side of a road who I spoke to about smuggling, but she didn't know much more beyond buying petrol from her supplier. She reminded me more of the *minuteros* (people who sell minutes of call time on mobile phones on the streets of Colombia) than a *contrabandista* (smuggler). I realized talking with her about border crossings or the role of the Venezuelan national guard was like asking a *minutero* about telecoms infrastructure. I think it's a point that Julia was trying to make with the tour, that they are not running a large mafia empire, or crossing the border with guns. They are often just the vendors, or transporters, caught up in a more violent border conflict. 'We are the last link in the chain. It's armed gangs who run the *trochas* with complicity of the state. But it's easier to attack the *pimpinero* on the street corner.' In Spanish, *trochas* are off-road paths that in this regional context refer to routes that illegally cross the shallow river into Venezuela.

An example of this chain might be: the Venezuelan National Guard steals gasoline from a truck in Venezuela and sells it to a smuggler, who then pays a member of an armed gang that controls a border crossing, to be able to pass. The smuggler then sells it on the Colombian side, to a wholesaler who buys in bulk and who will then sell it to a Sintragasolina registered transporter, who then sells it to a vendor, again possibly registered as a *pimpinero* with Sintragasolina. There are, as you might imagine, many other permutations of this chain. The person sourcing the petrol in Venezuela may also cross the border, transport and sell it themselves. They may, of course, not even be registered with Sintragasolina.

What is important is the existence of a long supply chain with *pimpineros* at the end of it, earning the least of all, and this is what Sintragasolina is trying to show to the world. Smugglers are not armed. Why would somebody who is armed (and willing to use force) put in the labour to travel, buy, transport and sell, when they could control territory and extort those who do that labour? Julia shows *pimpineros* themselves to be disenfranchised workers who have gone into the only line of work available to them. The formality of a trade union and its material objects, such as a *chaleco* (vest or bib) or ID card, displays a degree of state recognition and draws a powerful symbolic line separating themselves from the criminal gangs that control the border crossings. What they are doing is supposedly legitimate work, even though technically it may be illegal. It is licit work, according to Abraham and Van Schendel, even though it may be illegal. This combination of illegal but licit and socially acceptable is typical of borderlands (Abraham and Van Schendel 2005, 9). 'The right to dignified work is promised to us in both the Colombian constitution and the Declaration of Human Rights', Julia said while in the car. 'It's the responsibility of the state to create an economy and jobs. If they don't want us working informally, make the economy better!'

Through talking to Julia, I learnt that the union uses its status and its symbols to project the legitimacy of its members as real workers, separate from more criminal elements of society. The union then uses human-rights discourse to demand investment that will lead to jobs, either through better management of the economy or in startups. 'Our main focus now is in the *programa de reconversión sociolaboral*', Julia described to me what best translates as: 'programme for vocational retraining' or reconversion. 'For many years now, the state has been investing in small businesses run cooperatively by ex-*pimpineros*. It's important to still work on the street with the vendors, even those who are not members of the union, but the programme can give us an opportunity to get into formal work, to not live in precarity.'

From gasoline to cooking oil

The programme for socio-vocational reconversion had been through several iterations by the time I arrived in the field. The programme was funded by central government's ministry of mining and the local departmental government, as well as the entrepreneurship and innovation agency of the National Government, iNNpulsa.

Each iteration generated a new business, cooperatively run and owned by ex-*pimpineros*. In each case a semiprivate organization or NGO was charged with managing startup funds and hiring the initial staff to accompany the *pimpineros* in the process. This included business managers and psychologists who designed a syllabus of training programmes to help with the specific requirements of this particular vulnerable population. Businesses included a motorbike repair shop, a livery company, a cobbler and a used-oil recycling plant.

While gasoline smuggling can sometimes be highly profitable, it can also be precarious and dangerous. The programme provides an opportunity for the *pimpineros* to work in something legal and legitimate, while giving the state the ability to say that they are providing jobs and protecting the Colombian oil industry, by preventing smuggled imports. In this section I focus on one particular cooperatively owned business and argue that it is one of the many threads in a long process of demanding legitimacy from the state.

'Ahh, you're looking for the club-footed guy with the cooking oil! He's in the next warehouse', the metal worker tells me, taking a break from welding. I'm in an industrial estate on the main ring road outside of town, just near the Venezuelan border. Apart from a half-built shopping centre and gated communities springing up, it is mostly surrounded by shrubland. Stepping over metalwork on the floor, I enter through the large open gate into a sweltering warehouse. There are stacks of *pimpinas* everywhere and a fleet of moto-trike trailers. In the centre, two large cylindrical tanks rise up, about three stories, to the roof of the cavernous warehouse, and are connected to the ground with a series of esoteric looking industrial valves. For a minute I wonder if this is actually all an elaborate way of continuing to sell contraband fuel. Or a vision from an alternate future, where petrol smuggling has continued on its slow path to decriminalization. A man looks up from the back of a trailer and with the help of crutches he swings himself down and hobbles over to me. It's the co-op director James, who it turns out I've met before, when he drove me and Julia around to meet working *pimpineros*. He takes me on a tour of the site.

'The idea is to collect residual oils from restaurants and car workshops. We go out on the moto-trikes and collect the oil that would otherwise be thrown away. There is a lack of recycling in Colombia and this co-op is also meant to fill an ecological need.' Under the right factory conditions, used cooking oil can be converted into biodiesel and there are companies willing to buy the used oil that has been simply filtered and stored. James's organization is a cooperative set up by himself and another colleague as part of the reconversion programme, and is called *Cooperativa de Aceites Residuales Seguridad Industrial de Norte de Santander* or COARSINORTE. We move to the tanks, that loom over us. 'The tank here is for mineral oil and the other tank here is for the cooking oil. We then filter it and sell it to a company in Bucaramanga. The tanks were paid for by the government but they're too big for our needs and we've never been able to fill them. They've just not been necessary for the amount we collect.' I enquire what the problem is – Cúcuta has an official population of half a million and one would think that there would be enough residual oil to supply the enterprise. 'The restaurants have realized that we sell the oil on and are asking us for the money, even though there is now a law saying they have to dispose of their waste oil with us, but it's impossible to enforce.'

He shows me a photocopy of a resolution from the Ministry of Environment and Sustainable Development that aims to encourage businesses to recycle residual oils. 'We're meant to be supporting 100 families but currently only managing to support one.' The idea, James tells me, is that one co-op member earning minimum wage supports one family as well. The discourse is normally framed rhetorically in terms of numbers of families rather than individual members of the co-op. But it's been difficult running a small business, especially with such a unique population, as he explains. 'Our members sometimes have a tough time maintaining relationships with restaurant owners, they get in arguments and don't know how to resolve these problems. You have to understand that most of our members have never had formal work before and maintaining professional relationships isn't easy.' Moving to sit down on plastic chairs outside the small office within the warehouse, James arranges a fan and starts to tell me about the thinking behind the cooperative. 'We wanted to create a cooperative that used the skills that *pimpineros* already had. *Pimpineros* normally haven't even graduated from secondary school, they don't have high rates of literacy and often don't know anything outside of petrol. But they can ride motorbikes and know how to shift liquids between *pimpinas*. We only need to sell 80,000 *pimpinas* of used oil a month to keep running as a business.' I find it a strange inversion of the petrol-smuggling world. They're still measuring profit in terms of *pimpinas.* But really it makes sense, the business has to be a mixture of a financially viable idea along with work that doesn't require a great amount of training and plays to the strengths of the population. But as I saw throughout field work, this is a difficult balance to achieve.

Itty Abraham and Willem van Schendel say that 'both law and crime emerge from historical and ongoing struggles over legitimacy, in the course of which powerful groups succeed in delegitimizing and criminalizing certain practices' (2005, 7). The laws brought in against smuggling and the closure of the border pushed smuggling into the realms of illegal crossing and into the control of armed actors. This oil collection cooperative was trying to regain a legitimacy and licitness through its performance of work and had secured initial state backing in the form of startup capital. As Abraham and Van Schendel say: 'licit and illicit practices coexist in social life and are together imbricated in state processes' (2005, 7). *Pimpineros* are a highly economically productive population that remains untaxed. The state has an interest in bringing this population into the formal economy and the quantifiable and legible legal entity of a trade union.

What came across as slightly surreal about their cooking-oil operation was how closely it resembled petrol smuggling, on a larger, industrial and formal-looking scale, but with many of the characteristics of a smuggler. Instead of ad hoc attachments of *pimpinas* to motorbikes there were brand new trike trailers. Storing the liquid in industrial tanks instead of hiding holes in the patio or kitchen. Part of this was a practical alignment of factors, they wanted a business idea that seemed familiar and appealed to the supposed skillsets of the *pimpineros*. But also, I think there was a slightly ironic performance of work. They were doing similar actions with the same desire to make money and feed their families, but in a different context, as if to say: 'See? What we have always been doing was work!'

Abraham and Van Schendel have their own schema of legitimacy, with their four-way quadrant across double axes of illegal–legal and illicit–licit. Something that is both illegal and illicit is anarchy, legal and licit an ideal state, illegal but licit pertains to borderland or grey areas, and legal but illicit is crony capitalism or a so-called failed state. Licitness here refers to what one might call social acceptability or legitimacy. Underworld or borderland operations and smuggling often fall into a category of something being illegal but licit. This is very much the case of almost all types of smuggling in the Colombian–Venezuelan borderlands.

The *pimpineros*, through their organizing, are trying to form into something both legal and licit, or what forms an ideal state according to Abraham and Van Schendel's schema. In one sense it could be seen that the *pimpineros* and the state are collaborating in constructing the nation state in the borderlands. Yes, they are demanding their right to work with dignity, through a long process of struggle and hostility toward the state. But when the state takes a step towards the *pimpineros*, then their goals also start to align. Sovereignty is also being constructed in these battles, collaborations and performances of legitimacy. As Abraham and Van Schendel say: 'Historically the boundary of illicitness has shifted back and forth as bandits helped make states and states made bandits' (2005, 7). Every NGO, government ministry, charitable foundation and trade union that works 'on the ground' has a branded vest, a *chaleco*. It's the first thing any organization gets made, to appear legitimate. It lends the appearance of a state-sanctioned professionalism, much like putting on a yellow vest to step onto a worksite or football pitch. When many different agencies descend upon a rural area or town it is often called *baile de los chalecos* – dance of the vests. I argue here that sovereignty is being maintained and constructed through this continual dance-off for legitimacy, formality, and state-ness.

Emprendedores forzados

> Among the many solutions to our backwardness, our poverty and the growing unemployment, one of the most frequent proposals of the government is to opt for entrepreneurship, which must be encouraged, promoted and consolidated as an engine of the economy. (Rivas 2014, 44)

I moved between several cooperatives during my fieldwork, as well as spending time in small border towns that wished to start a similar programme but in a rural context. At the start of my fieldwork there were five cooperatively owned businesses, founded and run by ex-*pimpineros*. By the middle of my fieldwork, they had all shut down due to internal complications and financial difficulties. I tracked down some of the original business managers and psychologists, from three of the programme's iterations, who were hired to accompany the *pimpineros*. This section discusses an assortment of complications and difficulties they had with transforming the *pimpineros* into formalized workers.

Psychological accompaniment plays a big part in the discourse around the programme and similar interventions in Colombia, especially among groups that are considered to be vulnerable or from difficult backgrounds. Psychology is the go-to paradigm to smooth the way for potentially problematic social projects. *Cambiar el chip* – changing your chip – is a folk-psychological techno-metaphor that you hear all over Colombia, from schools to social projects. It means to change your way of thinking, to deal with new tasks and situations, like becoming less violent or adapting to a new vocation. In other words, reprogramming, by 'putting a new computer chip into your brain'. With ex-combatants of the armed conflict, it's because they have been in the bush most of their lives and need help adjusting to civilian life. With victims it might be needed because of post-traumatic stress or related problems. With Indigenous people it might be a colonial notion that they don't understand how money works or the concept of employment (Pellegrino Velásquez 2017). With the *pimpineros* it's a mix of various presumed sociological and psychological problems, due to upbringing: a chip that can be changed. The psychologist is the most readily called-upon of the social scientists, as the person who can 'change the chip', and as a result they end up taking on many roles.

Talking with psychologists from various iterations of the programme, they identified several reasons for failure of the ex-*pimpinero* enterprises. Firstly, a lifetime of precarity leads to a unique temperament and attitude to money that makes it difficult to cope with a structured nine-to-five job or make long-term financial projections. There were whole families who have never worked in anything other than illegal petrol. They grow up learning about this world without much access to an education outside of it. The nature of the work leads to precarity and uncertainty. Much of the smuggling work is done at night, for security, and when the petrol is available there is pressure to work as many hours as possible before there could be a shortage or another problem that puts a stop to the income. One *pimpinero* on the programme told me about his 48-hour smuggling shifts, with little rest in-between. He managed to make about a thousand US dollars in a week, which is a huge amount of money, but also an income that was never repeated and which soon ran out. This is a precarity caused by a number of factors: the supply can dry up, due to large geopolitical events between nation-states; the product can be seized, by police or armed gangs; and, the necessary relationships with armed gangs can be highly volatile (Idler and Forest 2015; Idler 2018).

Another problem is that *pimpineros* were too individualistic to work in a team but too collectivist to work a normal nine-to-five job. As one of the psychologists said:

> They like to take a united front, with *pensamiento colectivo* [collective thinking] and there was a clash between the family business model and a structured business model. Chain of command was a difficult concept to teach. They think they're all equal. They were also very, very demanding. Not of me but of the government. The *pimpineros* thought that having all this care and attention around them was a normal part of running a business. They didn't really appreciate what they had been given. A very demanding population.

Another psychologist said that the *pimpineros* are *dueños de su propio dominio* – lords of their own dominion. When in the workplace they had difficulty socializing. They set their own time, in their own space. They were not used to talking with lots of people all day long. They are true 'freelancers', the psychologist said, using the English word. After talking to some of the business managers who would manage the cooperatives for an initial period, before handing over full control to the members of the cooperative, I found out that many of the members would just continue smuggling petrol. After receiving a paycheck there was either little motivation to show up at work or too much temptation to keep smuggling. This jeopardized the public image of the programme, as one of the key outcomes for the major stakeholders was to move many *pimpineros* out of illicit trade. The managers also told me there was a lack of investment in accompaniment. In development interventions in Colombia, emphasis is put on the *acompanamiento* (accompaniment) which refers to the practitioners that follow the beneficiaries and manage projects, programmes and interventions, in this case, psychologists, or business advisers. Almost all of the enterprises had collapsed after the period of third-party accompaniment had ended and many thought that the third-party presence helped prevent arguments and made sure money was managed well. Initial budgeting decisions also had to be made, whether they should have longer periods of accompaniment and more subsidized equipment. I asked one manager why they didn't prioritize accompaniment over machinery. 'They wanted everything! Full accompaniment forever and all the machinery. They are very demanding.' Ultimately, as one manger said: 'The government didn't understand this population's particular needs and situation. The *pimpineros* didn't understand the government and its funding conditions'.

The programme focused on creating small cooperative businesses. At no point did it train people to be employees, or make any other type of development intervention in the population. In terms of government (or development NGO) investment, it's far cheaper to support a programme that sets up a few small businesses or cooperatives than it is to invest in education or infrastructure. Entrepreneurship is also highly valued and linked with histories of colonists conquering the internal frontiers of the early colonies and viceroyalties. Entrepreneurship is tied up with ideas of whiteness, masculinity, colonization, development and the creation of a modern nation (Viveros Vigoya 2013). Many politicians will create policies that appeal to entrepreneurs or present their own entrepreneurial credentials. Entrepreneurship is a cultural and moral value, as well as a skill. In interventions across Colombia there is a general consensus that becoming a business owner is essential to self-empowerment and reintegration into society. The term *proyecto productivo* (productive project), meaning a small business, appears in programmes working with many vulnerable populations, from victims of sexual violence to ex-combatants of FARC. It is also used within the *pimpinero* discourse.

Beneficiaries of development interventions don't really have a choice; they are going to become small-business owners and entrepreneurs. The term I use to describe this phenomenon is *emprendedor forzado*, which means 'forced entrepreneur' and was coined by Carlos Peréz, the director of a social-work foundation in Cúcuta. *Desplacimiento forzado* – forced displacement – is a prevalent socio-judicial term in Colombia, relating to those forcibly displaced during armed conflict. Forced entrepreneurship is a play on this. It points out what is often overlooked: that those working on *proyectos productivos* as part of an empowerment programme might not be in any way naturally inclined towards entrepreneurship. Owning a business is a specialized vocation and not something that everyone takes to naturally.

Carlos Peréz's foundation works with female victims of armed conflict, who use knitting circles as a form of social cohesion and collective income. Unlike similar empowerment projects, Peréz was keenly aware of the fact that being an entrepreneur is not some lofty goal in life, but rather a tool to be used in a less than ideal set of circumstances. It's an apt description that I think highlights two things. One, the emphasis on entrepreneurialism in Colombian development interventions. Two, the way in which interventions are about converting non-modern subjects into entrepreneurial subjects and idealized citizens. The next section will use contemporary anthropological scholarship of Colombia to make the case that the programme for *pimpinero* reconversion is one of many interventions across Colombia that are about creating modern subjects out of a perceived non-modern population.

Creating modern subjects from people without culture

In the peripheral settlements of Bogotá, Colombia's capital, live a large number of ex-combatants of the left-wing guerrilla insurgency, FARC. Many of them, like the *pimpineros*, are involved in state-backed entrepreneurial projects, as a means of reintegration with civil society. Ex-combatants were given startup capital as well as direct cash handouts for personal investment. They were given workshops and training programmes on how to use money wisely and adjust to modern, urban life. As anthropologist Emma Crane describes in her article on this topic: 'In [the reintegration route] the combatant again begins in *el monte* [the bush], and receives healthcare, education, a credit card, a diploma and eventually, an apartment. Through this process the combatant is transformed from an armed group member into an autonomous individual capable of making his or her own choices' (Crane 2020). Crane highlights the importance of financial intelligence and autonomy shown through cartoonified and colourful credit cards on the programme publicity. The title of a report from the International Organization for Migration makes it clear what is expected from ex-combatants: 'From demobilized combatants to business owners with futures!' (Fundación para el Desarrollo Agrícola 2011).

This is clearly relevant to the *pimpineros*, where this othering and infantilizing discourse is also present. Crane quotes an ex-soldier as comparing the process to raising his two-year-old and teaching her to tie her shoes. It's about 'creating a human being', he states, and as her other interlocuters said, the greatest challenge is 'learning to manage behaviour'. The ex-combatant is conceived as a brutish, violent, premodern creature from the bush (Crane 2018). There are many differences between *pimpineros* and ex-combatants of the armed conflict, however two similarities are striking and important. One is how the process is about individualization, a movement from collective action (be that an armed front of FARC or a unionized trade of the *pimpineros*) to an individual model citizen with a bank account and nine-to-five responsibilities. As one former FARC commander explained: 'What the state wants is a negotiation with each individual guerrilla. They want each of us to go home and resolve our problems alone, as best we can' (Crane 2018).

Lesley Gill's historical ethnography of petroleum refinery trade unions, in the Colombian city of Barrancabermeja, deals with this process of individualization. Where a class-conscious, unionized and mobilized proletariat are transformed through the 'neo-liberal' decades, into atomized individuals whose political action can only take place within the framework of 'human rights'. Leftism without its systemic class analysis and potential for collective action (Gill 2016). As Gill says: 'Peasant production systems are in decline; temporary or part-time, nonunionized workers are replacing a relatively small group of people who once had stable union jobs'. I argue that the same process of atomization happens with social retraining programmes across Colombia. All of this paints a picture of a class-conscious, politically active population, that has come to be represented as a vulnerable group with a social problem, and that, through interventions, can be turned into decent subjects of Colombia – individuals that belong to the same political community and project of the modernist state, not premodern, collectively minded people.

This brings us to a second similarity with the FARC interlocutors in Crane's research. An idea that the vulnerable group is somehow 'non-modern' or 'premodern' – maybe not expressed explicitly but often implied. POLFA, the *Policía Fiscal y Aduanera* – Fiscal and Customs Police – always speak about reclaiming public space, about cleaning up the street, about creating a 'culture' of legality and safety. It's common to hear people in Colombia described as '*no tener cultura*' – not having culture – when they don't clean up after their dog, drive badly, do graffiti, lack manners, and so on. It is explicit that the *programa de reconversión sociolaboral* was teaching *pimpineros* to have 'culture', to understand nine-to-five work hours and money management skills.

A previous, left-leaning mayor of Bogotá, Antanas Mockus, tried to encourage civic participation as a means to bring about positive social change in the city (Semana 2016). There was an institutional ideological discourse of 'the good citizen', who is 'capable of complying with the law and the norms instituted by a social order'. The mayor's office intended to 'disseminate the rules and promote their voluntary compliance, highlighting their democratic functioning and the benefits obtained by complying with them' (Acosta et al. 2018). This was a soft approach to governance that encouraged rather than disciplined a citizen into being the right kind of citizen. Explained through a colloquial Colombian vernacular, what is being implied of the *pimpineros* is that they are people without culture, or, at least, have the wrong type of culture. I argue that Sintragasolina through their militant efforts have co-created with the state a development intervention that, rather than just helping to fill a particular social gap, actually produces a neoliberal, entrepreneurial, modern subject. A subject with culture that acts as a citizen should. Sintragasolina and its *pimpinero* members see contraband as a working-class culture to be proud of. The programme saw them as not having the right kind of culture, or no culture at all!

A good *pimpinero* isn't a *pimpinero*

So far in this chapter I have presented the *pimpinero* trade union as an unlikely but effective movement of collective action, with a strong cultural identity that led to smuggling being decriminalized for several years (for discussion of contraband as cultural identity, see also Cintrón-Gutiérrez, Chapter 2 in this volume). I have also presented the reconversion programme that came about after a clampdown on smuggling and a border closure that led the union to militate instead for funding for vocational retraining and startup investment. The cooperatively owned businesses created through the programme all eventually failed. Those involved in accompanying the *pimpineros* in the process gave many reasons relating to the unique, precarious existence of the population. I argued that the programme, like other similar programmes across Colombia, is also about creating a modern, entrepreneurial subject.

In this final section, I propose that a reason for the failure of the cooperatively owned businesses is an inherent contradiction to the programme. In being asked to become modern subjects with even temperament they are expected to become non-*pimpineros*, which was the very collective movement, strong cultural identity and fighting attitude that got them the programme in the first place. The *pimpinero* trade union is looking for, among other things, a good public image and state funding for programmes. I argue that they are not able to present themselves to the state as properly deserving of this continued support, which leads to difficulties with the long-term functioning of the programme.

I want to further this point by making a comparison between the *pimpineros* and victims of Colombia's armed conflict. Being a victim of Colombia's armed conflict is something someone can be recognized as officially, by the state, giving access to various state welfare programmes. There is a large 'bureaucracy of victimhood' that guides and disciplines people through the process, and individuals perform their victimhood in ways that fit with the bureaucracy and create a victim subjectivity.

There is continual labour undertaken by those who want to be recognized as victims by the state.

Anthropologist Roxani Krystalli says that a victim therefore has to perform their trauma correctly, has to be collaborative while not demanding too much, and be humble. This is what she refers to as a 'good victim', in her ethnography of bureaucratic victimhood: 'We are not good victims' (Krystalli 2019). In Colombia there are bureaucratic systems that discipline this behaviour, and NGOs that help them with the bureaucratic process. But with gasoline smuggling more heavily regulated than ever, in the eyes of the state there is no such thing as a good *pimpinero*.

Sintragasolina is trying to get the *pimpineros* seen as victims of economic circumstance, or those whose right to dignified work has been withheld. They are victims in the sense that they are denied the fundamental human right of work, and also in the most literal sense, being victims of violent extortion that their job exposes them to, or victims of the armed conflicts that have pushed them into such lines of work. What they want is a more sympathetic understanding from the public and more resources from the state. But their heavy militating and insurgent nature prevents them from being seen as worthy or 'good' beneficiaries. Their tactics are directed at the people who they then expect to deem them to be worthy victims. However, there are not large infrastructures in place for *pimpinero* reconversion and they have not engaged with the state in a coordinated and systematic way. When they have engaged with the state it has often been combative, militant and politicized. The *pimpineros* have learned to communicate with the state (and everybody) through a politicized discourse that is inherently antagonistic. Relations with the state were opened through collective action and they continue to be prickly.

The trade unionists were regularly described to me as being *peleónes* (quarrelsome fighters), by journalists, policemen and those involved in the current iteration of the programme for reconversion. *Peleón* means an argumentative person or a fighter, but Julia had spoken to me about her poor working-class background and how, through trade unionism, she had learned to speak publicly and defend herself. It is difficult to be a good victim when what you did for a living is stigmatized and illegal and your tactics can be described by the state as disruptive or petulant. The irony is that unionized *pimpineros* have used their cultural identity and militant tactics to fight for a programme of social reconversion that aims to turn them into ex-*pimpineros*. There is no such thing as a good *pimpinero*, in the way there can be a 'good victim'. Their strong identity has helped their political organizing and that political organizing feeds back into their strong identity. This solidifies a proletarian class consciousness, a collectivity that was necessary to negotiate with the state. Being a collective is essential for collective bargaining, as Sian Lazar says of Bolivia: 'State actors will not (or cannot) negotiate with individuals, thus collective organizations become necessary as counterparts, even when they operate at the edges of legality in the informal economy' (Lazar 2012, 20).

Pimpineros are a difficult population to work with, as described by programme practitioners, as well as being physically dispersed across a large city. Sintragasolina's organizing brings them together as a collective that can make them more effective beneficiaries of reconversion programmes. In other words, making themselves less difficult to deal with, but the tactics that have led to that organizing have been deliberately antagonistic and difficult. Now that the trade union's militancy cannot demand further formalization of their trade, due to the clampdown and border closure, they focus their organizational activities on ensuring that the government pays out what it owes to the vocational programmes, and petitioning for further programmes. I argue that the *pimpineros* have shifted from being an organized proletariat with a unique *pimpinero* class consciousness, to a vulnerable population recognized by the state as being deserving of access to benefits. But this role, of good victim and deserving population, is one that they find difficult to play, especially given the empowering nature of their organizational life previously. This is my argument for why the businesses born of the programme failed. The beneficiaries of the programme were a population that gained its class consciousness through antagonism with the state and authority. It wasn't just precarity and psychological issues that led to the businesses failing, but a dynamic integral to the relationship between the members of Sintragasolina and the state. There is no such thing as a good *pimpinero* in the way that there *can* be a good victim.

Conclusion

In this chapter, I have presented an ethnographic account of a trade union for Colombian petrol smugglers, a militant movement characterized by collective action and a resilient cultural identity. Surprisingly, for an extended period this union played a crucial role in the decriminalization of petrol smuggling. This was due to their core belief that they have a constitutional right to dignified work and that their contraband activity is legitimate work. Their success in collective militating came in part from also framing contraband not only as a culture, but a working-class culture. Following that, I delved into the reconversion programme that emerged after the crackdown on smuggling operations and border closure. This ended the period of decriminalized smuggling and prompted the union to advocate for funding directed towards vocational retraining and investment for their own cooperative startups. However, despite the initial optimism surrounding the cooperative businesses established through the reconversion programme, they ultimately failed. Those practitioners involved in assisting the *pimpineros* throughout the process highlighted numerous reasons, tied to the distinctive and precarious nature of the *pimpineros*' previous existence.

I argued that the reconversion programme, along with similar initiatives implemented throughout Colombia, ultimately sought to cultivate a modern and entrepreneurial subjectivity among its participants, to convert them from non-modern to modern subjects. The great irony here is that it is the *pimpineros*' continued exposure to gasoline, the modern material par excellence, that also somehow dirties them and makes them non-modern. Non-modernity and modernity are two sides of the same coin! Through introducing the concept of *emprendedor forzado* (forced entrepreneur), this chapter compared *pimpineros* to other vulnerable populations in Colombia, such as the forcibly displaced, victims of the armed conflict, Indigenous people, campesinos and ex-combatants, all of whom have varying degrees of state or NGO interventions foisted upon them. It also showed how there is a focus on entrepreneurism in Colombia, that means development interventions almost always end up in the creation of small-scale enterprises for the beneficiaries, meaning the beneficiaries are forced to become entrepreneurs.

Finally, this chapter argued that a culture of militancy and agitating trade unionism means the unionized *pimpineros* failed to present themselves as properly vulnerable and their illegality leaves them stigmatized. I posit this as a critical factor contributing to the collapse of the cooperatively owned businesses: an inherent contradiction within the programme itself. The population is seen as difficult, and while they want to show themselves to the state and the general public as victims of both economic failings and direct violence, they fail to perform the role of a 'good victim' (Krystalli 2019; 2021). Their militant nature is what gets them heard and have demands met, but also makes them a too difficult and demanding population to be beneficiaries of state-backed programmes. They were essentially being asked to abandon their identities as *pimpineros* – the very essence of the collective movement, robust cultural identity and resolute fighting spirit that had initially paved the way for their inclusion in the programme.

In seeing their participation in contraband as a working-class culture to be proud of, the *pimpineros* were able to collectivize into a trade union that militated for decriminalization of their trade. Ultimately, however, they had to militate for state programmes that were geared towards giving them a new culture.

References

Abraham, Itty and Willem van Schendel. 2005. 'Introduction: The making of illicitness'. In *Illicit Flows and Criminal Things: States, borders, and the other side of globalization*, edited by Willem van Schendel and Itty Abraham, 1–37. Bloomington: Indiana University Press.

Acosta, Apráez, Claudia Elizabeth, Castro Orjuela, José Ignacio, Neuta Fernández and José Aldemar. 2018. 'La participación ciudadana en Bogotá durante los gobiernos de Antanas Mockus (2001–2003) y Luis Eduardo Garzón (2004–2008): Un análisis crítico del discurso'. Fundación Centro Internacional de Educación y Desarrollo Humano. Accessed 24 February 2024. https://repository.cinde.org.co/handle/20.500.11907/2581.

Butcher, Stephanie and Alexandre Apsan Frediani. 2014. 'Insurgent citizenship practices: The case of Muungano wa Wanavijiji in Nairobi, Kenya', *Analysis of Urban Change, Theory, Action* 18(2): 119–33. Accessed 24 February 2024. https://doi.org/10.1080/13604813.2014.896637.

Civico, Aldo. 2015. *The Para-State: An ethnography of Colombia's death squads*. Oakland: University of California Press.

Coward, Marcia W., Peter B. Heller and Anna I. Vellve Torras (translators). 2019. 'Colombia's constitution of 1991 with amendments through 2005'. Accessed 24 February 2024. https://www.constituteproject.org/constitution/Colombia_2005.

Crane, Emma Shaw. 2018. 'Remaking subjects in the aftermath of war: Colombia's postconflict', *Items*, July. Accessed 24 February 2024. https://items.ssrc.org/from-our-fellows/remaking-subjects-in-the-aftermath-of-war-capitalism-personhood-and-colombias-postconflict/.

Crane, Emma Shaw. 2020. 'Small victories: Urban politics, after war', *PoLAR: Political and Legal Anthropology Review*, 24 November. Accessed 24 February 2024. https://polarjournal.org/2020/11/24/small-victories-urban-politics-after-war/.

Fundación para el Desarrollo Agrícola. 2011. *De desmovilizados a empresarios con futuro: Modelo de fortalecimiento de iniciativas productivas de ex combatientes y sus familias*. Bogotá: Secretaría Distrital de Gobierno (SEGOB), Alcaldía Mayor de Bogotá.

Gill, Lesley. 2016. *A Century of Violence in a Red City: Popular struggle, counterinsurgency, and human rights in Colombia*. Durham, NC: Duke University Press.

Holston, James. 2013. 'Spaces of insurgent citizenship'. In *The Anthropology of Citizenship: A reader*, edited by Sian Lazar, 37–56. Hoboken, NJ: Wiley-Blackwell.

Idler, Annette. 2018. *Borderland Battles: Violence, crime, and governance at the edges of Colombia's war*. New York: Oxford University Press.

Idler, Annette and James J. F. Forest. 2015. 'Behavioral patterns among (violent) non-state actors: A study of complementary governance', *Stability: International Journal of Security & Development* 4(1): 1–19. Accessed 24 February 2024. https://doi.org/10.5334/sta.er.

Krystalli, Roxani. 2019. '"We are not good victims": Hierarchies of suffering and the politics of victimhood in Colombia', *Gender and Intersectional Analysis*. The Fletcher School of Law and Diplomacy. Accessed 24 February 2024. https://www.academia.edu/43060952/_We_are_not_good_victims_Hierarchies_of_Suffering_and_the_Politics_of_Victimhood_in_Colombia.

Krystalli, Roxani. 2021. 'Narrating victimhood: Dilemmas and (in)dignities', *International Feminist Journal of Politics* 23(1): 125–46. Accessed 24 February 2024. https://doi.org/10.1080/14616742.2020.1861961.

Lazar, Sian. 2012. 'A desire to formalize work? Comparing trade union strategies in Bolivia and Argentina', *Anthropology of Work Review* 33(1): 15–24. https://doi.org/10.1111/j.1548-1417.2012.01073.x.

Madariaga, Patricia. 2006. *Matan y Matan y Uno Sigue Ahí: Control paramilitar y vida cotidiana en un pueblo de urabá*. Colección Prometeo. Bogotá: Universidad de los Andes, Facultad de Ciencias Sociales – CESO, Departamento de Antropología.

Osuna, Javier. 2015. *Me hablarás del fuego: Los hornos de la infamia*. Bogotá: EDICIONES B / Penguin Random House.

Pellegrino Velásquez, Silvana Valentina. 2017. 'Incumplir cumpliendo: Una etnografía al papeleo del auto 004'. Bogotá: Universidad de Los Andes. Accessed 24 February 2024. https://repositorio.uniandes.edu.co/handle/1992/61273.

Rivas, Santiago. 2014. *Acaba Colombia: Motivos para apagar e irnos*. Bogotá: Planeta.

Semana. 2016. '¿El regreso de la cultura ciudadana de Mockus?', 8 June. Accessed 24 February 2024. https://www.semana.com/agenda/articulo/cultura-ciudadana-antanas-mockus-enrique-penalosa/49130/.

Viveros Vigoya, Mara. 2013. 'Género, raza y nación: Los réditos políticos de la masculinidad blanca en Colombia', *Maguaré* 27(1): 71–104.

6

Abundance as an ethic: emergency food ingress and moral concern in Venezuela

Eva van Roekel

Bittersweet pineapple

'Here … eat'. It was April 2019 and I had just arrived in Caracas for fieldwork on the complex humanitarian crisis in Venezuela. Upon arrival, the first thing Guillermo Cifuentes offered me was a large chunk of juicy pineapple. Guillermo is my former husband. Different life aspirations and career trajectories had separated us more than ten years ago. I had returned to the Netherlands to obtain my PhD in Cultural Anthropology, while he further developed his now successful software business in Caracas. I could perceive in the way he offered it that he still knew how much I liked pineapple. But this time the fruit tasted less sweet than how I remembered devouring the generous slices during breakfast years ago. Venezuela was now facing the largest economic crisis in its national history. By this point more than 4.5 million Venezuelans had left the country, largely because of hunger and insecurity.[1] The complex humanitarian crisis in the country was of an unprecedented scale. In economic terms, for instance, between 2013 and 2019, the country had lost 62 per cent of its gross domestic product (Bull and Rosales 2020, 2). Statistics also showed that more than 90 per cent of the Venezuelans that remained in the country were having serious trouble purchasing sufficient nutrients.[2] Other numbers stated that the 'average' Venezuelan citizen had lost more than twenty pounds body weight because of inaccessibility to sufficient calories per day due to the rampant food scarcity in the country.[3] And food that did circulate in the country moved through questionable supply chains.

'Eat, I remember how much you like this', Guillermo insisted again. Unconsciously I intuited that rejecting his offer would be somehow a double sin. While back in Venezuela after such a long absence, many people urged me to eat everything I could: *cachapa* (corn pancake), mango, *tequeños* (fried savoury pastries). Someone told me that to eat was to bring back memories of better times. These bittersweet bites were the first signal that prohibited food ingress – in our bodies, but also in the kitchens, bakeries, restaurants, (online) shops and national borders – during my periodic visits to Venezuela became infused with moral concern.

In the media and policy briefs about the crisis in Venezuela, it is argued that in recent years the entire country has turned into a 'black spot' for the trafficking of goods (Ayuso 2018). Not only certain people, places and activities in Venezuela have been targeted as illegal. The country itself is now being purposefully designated as illegal, labelling Venezuela as a 'mafia state', an 'organized crime hub', and the 'Bolivarian Joint Criminal Enterprise' (Farah 2020; *InSight Crime* 2018; Pelcastre 2022). These reports largely focus on the circulation and exchange of drugs and weapons, but also the movements of fuel, food and medication that evade established tax and tariff systems and increasingly operate through irregular resale, in combination with large-scale corruption. I must point out that accurate numbers and the exact whereabouts of trade in Venezuela, like most statistics, are unreliable and largely based on guesswork, but if trafficking is ubiquitous, how then, can our conceptual tools that differentiate contraband from regular trade have any analytical purchase?

The critical food situation in Venezuela and an ad hoc resourcefulness, to live with chronic shortages, modified, to a certain extent, local ethics around food purchase that had little to do with state morality, but more with the changing relationships between suffering, biological need and physical appearance, alongside local notions of justice (Vásquez Lezama 2019, 103). My overall concern in this chapter is therefore with some underlying assumptions that, in my view, continue to dominate our understanding of smuggling and contraband and sit within a new body of anthropological theorizing that is critical about describing these forms of economic activity in terms of legal or illegal, formal or informal, and authorized or unauthorized trade (Galemba 2017; Bocarejo 2018; Bozçali 2020; Donovan 2021; Ødegaard 2019; Schwartz 2021; Yildiz 2020). We seem to be in need of different analytical tools to resolve this binary impasse. This chapter is a move in that direction.

Another way in which this chapter attempts to work within the notion of contraband, albeit uneasily, is to address the unintended politics of state-centred analyses of the circulation and exchange of goods.

Too often our theories overlook ethical behaviour in favour of analyses that emphasize structure, power and interest (Lambek 2010a, 1). Instead, I turn to the emerging debate on ethics in anthropology, to contribute otherwise to an interdisciplinary field of contraband studies and a growing concern that our conceptual tools appear poorly able to make sense of food purchase and ingestion within and across national borders. What does the absence of food and the need to eat during the complex humanitarian crisis in Venezuela, for instance, tell us about what it means to buy and consume in scarcity? More specifically, I am interested in certain ways of thinking, reasoning and moral valuing about natural abundance and infinite potentiality that seem to be inseparable from local experiences of food purchase and consumption in Venezuela and the circulation of goods in general. As such, this chapter draws both on timely discussions within the anthropology of ethics and morality, and recent ethnographic materials from Venezuela. But let me first plunge into another bewildering breakfast with Guillermo Cifuentes in 2019.

Food ingress and moral concern

My short visit to Caracas was just a few weeks after what is now widely known as *el gran apagón*, which was the largest national blackout in Venezuelan history, causing many complications in fundamental services and infrastructure throughout the country, such as essential hospital care and water supplies. The power came back on after a week, in the city, but a general atmosphere of 'being off' remained palpable in Caracas. While almost all of his friends and relatives had left the country, Guillermo and his parents had decided to stay. His software business had become the backbone of the family. They were well-off in comparison to most Venezuelans, yet infrastructural failings and scarcities had also radically changed their everyday life, and Guillermo wanted me to see his normally buoyant city in this somewhat glum state. A ride to the other side of town normally lasted at least one hour, due to the chronic traffic jams, but this time it only took us a few minutes. Guillermo chuckled that at least something positive had come from the recent exodus. The empty streets, without hundreds of cars, small buses, makeshift shops and *buhoneros* (pedlars) mirrored the images, of bare shelves in the supermarkets, I had seen on many reports on the Venezuelan crisis.[4]

I must admit that it was strangely disconcerting to experience Caracas this way. Afterwards, to my surprise, we went for a fancy breakfast at a newly opened bistro near the financial district. We were the only ones being served that morning. While looking at the insane prices on the menu – one Belgian waffle cost more than a monthly minimum wage – I felt my eyes tear up. Eating during a rampant food crisis can become morally bewildering, for multiple reasons. Just a few days before I had assisted in handing out simple breakfasts to thousands of Venezuelans that had illegally crossed the Colombian border to Cúcuta in search of food and care, and to buy essential food items to smuggle back home across the *trochas* (informal border crossings). This omnipresence of 'emergency' smuggling was not new, and like so many things in Venezuela, these movements of goods were both a blessing and a curse. It helped many people to make ends meet, while a few others were making tremendous profits. Various Venezuelans that I met at the soup kitchen confided they were very grateful, while at the same time having a hard time swallowing the food that they were being offered, knowing how their hungry siblings were not able to fill their bellies. Eating became unsettling and crucial at the same time. They seemed also proud to say that they had managed to make some money by reselling some food on the streets – good money they used to buy food and other basic goods to bring back home using the *trochas*. The priest who oversaw the soup kitchen had told me that two meal services had been distributed six days a week, for several years by this point. He did not expect the servings to diminish soon.

Being privileged in so many ways, I must admit that consuming while crying at a fancy bistro in Caracas felt wrong, at least to me, as Guillermo insisted again:

> 'Of course, you can eat and cry, this has been yours as well, Eva.'
> 'Do you cry about it [the food crisis] as well?'
> 'Yes, I do … at night … when I am alone.'

His silences in-between were telling. Then Guillermo ordered an eggs Benedict, and I had scrambled eggs with elaborate wholewheat bread, thick slices of bacon and turkey, all splashed off with a sweet strawberry smoothie and *un marron* (a coffee with milk). Our conversation about the economic crisis continued. We talked about the rampant scarcity that had been ruthlessly aggravated by closed borders, massive bribery and fraud, the implementation of US sanctions, and how all of this had caused a simultaneous expansion of the black market, money laundering, the normalization of widespread smuggling and resale, and the rise of a multicurrency economy due to mindboggling hyperinflation. These drastic economic and social changes were largely the result of fuel and food subsidies and a distorted currency market. The subsequent oil price collapse and financial sanctions that were implemented by the US government in 2017, as a means of destabilizing the increasingly authoritarian regime amid rising social protests, had further aggravated the abrupt economic downfall in the country. In response, different economic sectors in Venezuela had shielded from the sanctions, 'by protecting themselves in the shadows of informality, meaning the ad hoc adoption of the US dollar, the use of backchannel and unofficial sales, and the under-declaration of profits for the sake of avoiding tax payments' (Bull and Rosales 2020, 8).

Our conversation was too overwhelming to take in at once. Feeling full, I had unthinkingly left the bacon and turkey aside on my plate. Guillermo noticed my peccadillo. 'Can I have it? Food should not be left untouched, you know.' I took in Guillermo's moral concern and gave him what he had asked for. The bill appeared more troublesome: 78,000 bolívares soberanos (the former national currency) was at least five times the official minimum monthly wage. Guillermo paid without surprise or complaint and, being familiar with his sweet tooth, we went for another coffee with sweet pastry at Danubio, one of the most famous bakeries in Caracas, just across the street. Although for months the online newspapers and reports had announced the huge lack in basic products, like flour and sugar,[5] there seemed to be no shortages of any kind in Danubio. The wooden shelves and glass counters were stuffed with bread, cookies, croissants, pastries with ham and cheese, and lavish pies with dots of cream and chocolate.

To get a bit more familiarized with the highly unstable food prices in Caracas, I asked one of the bakers how much the *cachito* (a croissant-like sandwich filled with ham) cost. '9,800', the young baker replied. In normal circumstances, *Cachitos* were considered a popular and inexpensive snack, but these cost nearly the same as my fancy plate of scrambled eggs. Guillermo perceived my bafflement and explained how at Danubio they had already adjusted their prices this morning, while the bistro was running late to accommodate theirs to the latest inflationary flare-up. Such price adjustments were apparently now routine in Venezuela. The hustle and bustle at the bakery reminded me of Caracas a decade ago, and together with my incompetence at grasping the disparate price adjustments and the ambiguous taste of the sugariness of the cheesecake we had ordered, I completely forget to probe where on earth all the ingredients had come from.

I am aware that these breakfast stories may not seem the most straightforward entry points to discuss contraband cultures in Venezuela, since contraband colloquially means the illegal or prohibited traffic and possession of goods. More broadly, contraband implies 'against decree', deriving from the Latin *contrabannum* – any kind of practice that works against established orders.[6] The trouble with such classification is that it still gives lived experiences meaning only in contrast to legal classifications – but social critique and endorsement of exchange, purchase and consumption of goods may not always be concerned with its prohibited entrance, or inspired by the morality of the law (Bocarejo 2018, 58; Donovan 2021, 115). How, then, can we convey what people tell us about *how* and *where* to situate ethical being in their everyday lives? Or more precisely, how can an ethnography about rapidly changing food habits and food nostalgia help us to grasp the everyday ethics of food circulation and exchange during crisis?

I believe that looking at the ad hoc actions and deliberations around the ingress of food, whether authorized or not, enables us to look at the entry and circulation of food items in and across national borders, without juxtaposing it immediately to state law. The word ingress comes from the Latin word *ingressus*, which has myriad meanings, such as the act of entering or the permission to enter,[7] but metaphysically speaking *ingressus* also means the process by which a potentiality enters into actuality.[8] Particularly the latter ties into what I have come to see as a local ethic in how Venezuelans experience and make sense of the presence and exchange of food, which is in turn related to a powerful myth of a regional abundance of natural resources, tremendously rich soils, and the eternal availability of crops and food (Peters 2019; Socorro 2021; Strønen 2017). Such a focus on potentiality, in my view, allows for significant other moral entanglements of the trade of goods with food consumption to surface. In other words, turning our gaze towards food ingress shifts the focus from the illegality of the movement of goods to thinking more about the availability or dispossession of goods, and from theorizing state law to conjecturing the everyday workings of ethics about food purchase and consumption. I believe that such a departure, from what is lawful (or not) towards thinking about what people consider right or wrong, just and unjust, and why, can be of value, to divert recent debates on irregular or prohibited circulation and exchange of goods.

In what follows, I will therefore first expand on how food has found its way into Venezuelan commerce, homes, and stomachs, in the context of tremendous scarcity. Then I will engage with the recent ethical turn in cultural anthropology that will substantiate this pervading sense of hazard surrounding escalating contraband practices during the complex humanitarian crisis in Venezuela. This alternative approach to contraband resonates with Cromwell's (2018, 178–9) historical approach to understanding contraband in Venezuela, by looking at how ordinary and widespread contraband practices intermingle with significant other features of everyday life. To close, I will look further into the powerful myth of abundant food crops and rich soils replete with natural resources that ethically situates the recent 'illegal' economic activities amid deep moral concern around food in Venezuela.

Circulation in the land of plenty

In 2019 I met Willian, a shop owner in Pacaraima, a town just over the border in Brazil. He told me that he had recently shifted from selling tourist and Indigenous souvenirs, to retailing carefully packed bags of rice, oil, sugar, pasta and canned meat, for Venezuelan consumption. Since the food crisis had deepened in neighbouring Venezuela, almost all the local shops in Pacaraima had shifted their supplies from tourist souvenirs and hiking equipment to small-scale gold mining tools and food.[9] Willian confided that customers in his shop were mainly Venezuelan couples that researched and bargained for the best price, for personal consumption and resale in Venezuela. Their cars parked in front of his shop and were loaded with merchandise, with the help of some Venezuelan migrants that had recently arrived. Willian's sister-in-law explained from behind the counter that a kilo of beans cost approximately nine *reais* (Brazilian national currency) in Pacaraima but were resold for around thirty *reais* in Venezuela. She continued that the farther away from the border, the more expensive the products became. In recent years, the only road heading north to the towns in Venezuela had become replete with roadblocks set by both the national armed forces and ad hoc informal or 'irregular' forces that charged for the passage of persons and goods in the form of *vacunas* (vaccines). *Vacunas* are a widely accepted bribe in Venezuela, paid in return for looking the other way when paperwork is not up-to-date or is missing, or as protection money to protect your business and life against violence from other criminal groups (Morillo Ramos and Van Roekel 2022). Willian's sister-in-law furthermore reasoned that it was not so much hyperinflation, but 'hyper speculation' that made life impossible – aside from extremely high incidence of bribery, there were also no fixed or reasonable prices in Venezuela anymore.

While jotting down my fieldnotes at night, I noticed that the ethical concerns at the border, like those of Willian and his sister, seemed more focused on speculation and overpricing than on the illegality of the circulation of food.[10] The illegal movement of goods seemed routinely taken for granted or justified, considering the exceptional circumstances of the crisis.

I was eager to learn more about this different ethical standing around smuggling, but the pandemic blocked further visits to the Venezuelan border. In October 2021, in Caracas, I had a longer discussion in the kitchen with Guillermo's father (my former father-in-law), Jorge Cifuentes, about the origins of basic products, like flour and cornmeal, that were used to make bread and *arepas* (corn cakes). Jorge and I agreed that under the current situation of strict economic sanctions, preceding closed borders, COVID-19 lockdowns and widespread corruption, at some point one must hit the 'black spot' in the supply chain. I told him that I had briefly spoken with a shop owner, in the old city centre, who had told me that he just bought Venezuelan products from a wholesaler he knew. Jorge looked at me pensively, and then said:

> ... *porque todo al final llega al punto negro* [in the end everything reaches the black spot] – everyone knows that somewhere in the [supply] chain the military or Maduro [the government] will appear. Our baker will also tell you that he bought his flour at a [wholesaler], nothing else. And they established the [inflated] prices, but our baker can't denounce them for robbing him, right? Because they won't sell flour to him anymore ... [the baker] will tell you nothing else, that's as far as your investigation goes.

During my subsequent stays in Venezuela, I have tried to have conversations with several shop owners about their purchase of goods and raw materials, but I never reached discussing the 'black spot', just as Jorge had warned me. Such business information was clearly confidential or simply not intended for foreign ears. More importantly, it is argued that this kind of trade holds ample social acceptance in Venezuela, particularly at the border (Albornoz-Arias 2019, 12). In recent years, the growth in smuggling and resale of food has spread across the country, due to chronic scarcities (Vasquez Lezama 2019). Yet, preoccupation with increasing illicit circulation and purchase of food and other basic items was not really the talk of the day. Notably, the irregularities about food entering Venezuela, that worked around established tax and tariff systems and increasingly operated through irregular resale, seemed not to be the most ethically challenging for my Venezuelan interlocutors and friends – or what anthropologist Arthur Kleinman (1997, 335) has eloquently called: 'what is at stake'.

This way of trading was also not new in the country. For decades, trafficking of Venezuelan fuel over the Colombian and Brazilian border has been lucrative business, for instance – highly subsidized Venezuelan fuel was being resold in Colombia and Brazil, in times of its availability. Now Brazilian fuel was being resold, in times of scarcity of Venezuelan fuel, or being reserved exclusively for gold extraction in these areas (Morillo Ramos and Van Roekel 2022; see also Beach, Chapter 5 in this volume). Trafficking is thus not one-directional and can easily be reversed according to demand. While the smuggling and resale of subsidized fuel has its origins in the 1930s, with the first oil boom, in areas along the Venezuela–Colombia border, this practice of *bachaqueo* has gained traction across the country since the economic crisis (Caraballo-Arias et al. 2017). The name derives from an analogy of a big ant – *el bachaco* – that can transport large amounts of food (see also Allard, this volume). Many people involved in these businesses perceive trafficking as indirect ways to reclaim, to disrupt, and to partially redress the failures of the Venezuelan rentier state in delivering its promises of social justice and distribution of the wealth coming from its vast oil revenues (Schwartz 2021).

The shared notion of entitlement to such trade has been historically dominant in Venezuela and its neighbouring countries. Since colonial times, many forms of unlicensed regional trade have coloured everyday social interactions and relationships, involving almost everyone – many Venezuelans even viewed such commerce as their unbounded social and communal right (Cromwell 2018, 12–17). The moral concerns that I noticed seemed therefore to be of a different moral order to the proliferating illegality in the way the merchandise was now entering Venezuela. It had much more to do with shared ideas about the incongruity of deficiency and inaccessibility in a country that was praised for its affluence and natural abundance. A recent increase in 'irregular imports', for that matter, also disordered other aspects of life in Venezuela, to which I will turn below. What interests me here is therefore not so much how trade across economic sanctions, contraband and corruption operated in these expanding 'grey' zones, but rather how Venezuelans pondered and evaluated the relations between supply, exchange and pricing during overwhelming economic crisis, connecting these ideas to moral ideas about availability, potentiality, fairness and ultimately what it means to be moral, rather than strictly legal evaluations (see also Lemon 1998, 22).

Ethical being and wealth

Theoretically speaking, ethics are about what is right or wrong, just or unjust, and reflects moral notions of what constitutes freedom, responsibility and justice. Ethics enable us to decide how to act and how to value action. Ethics are not located in reason alone, however. In other words, ethical life is not epiphenomenal, but rather phenomenal in the sense of what is explicable in the way we encounter ethics and morality in an immediate world (Dyring et al. 2018, 17–18; Van Roekel 2020). To be able to understand ethics as immediate practice we therefore need an empirical outlook. An anthropology of ethics particularly demonstrates the centrality of ethical practice, responsibility, cultivation and concrete questioning in everyday social life (Lambek 2010a, 1).

By directing our attention to these concrete problems of action and judgement in an ordinary world, in an indirect way, we acknowledge that it is often quite difficult to judge or decide what the best course of action might be (Mattingly 2013, 308). Ethics, then, do not arise from careful contemplation alone, about what is considered just, fair, or the right or most probable thing to do or possess, but also emerge in spontaneous conversation and improvised action, and retrospectively in reflections about what was done, could have been done otherwise, and why (Lambek 2010b, 43). Ethics are thus not only or primarily a matter of rules and reasons (Keane 2010, 74). Put differently, everyday ethics should not be mistaken for prearranged social structures that simply dictate a fixed moral order (like the law). Everyday or ordinary ethics are rather about an ambiguous moral field of open deliberations, mistakes, failures and ad hoc acknowledgements or improvised justifications after the fact. I believe that such an approach to the irregular circulation and exchange of food enables us to convey what people tell us about how and where they situate ethical being in their everyday lives every time anew. Also, or perhaps especially, when living ethically is under pressure. To give some empirical depth to this notion of everyday ethics during food crisis, I wish to look briefly at some spontaneous conversation in action during what is often labelled contraband or smuggling.

Aside from local shops selling food items for resale, at the Brazil–Venezuela border in November 2019, hundreds of Venezuelans were queueing under tents belonging to the United Nations Refugee Agency and the International Organization for Migration, erected as part of a larger emergency plan for refugees and migrants coming from Venezuela. All of them were leaving Venezuela in search of a better life and, as soon as possible, to send some money home. A few hundred meters away, dozens of trucks packed with merchandise were also waiting to cross the border, not to leave but to enter Venezuela. I approached one of them. One trucker disclosed he was transporting Coca Cola to a factory in Valencia, the third largest city in Venezuela. Other truckers confided that they simply unloaded their merchandise, mostly food items, in the first village, to be resold and transported further into Venezuela. They explained that their papers and goods were being checked for contraband; not so much for the transportation of prohibited goods, but for merchandise that would enter the black market. I must admit I did not entirely grasp the legality (or illegality) of their exports to Venezuela, but, like the *bachaqueros* transporting fuel across the *trochas*, the truckers did not seem very worried. Solid and permeable borders easily co-existed alongside the local practice of charging *vacunas*.

After our brief conversation, in front of the trucks, I sat next to a young migrant and his sister. They had just arrived in Pacaraima (Brazil). His name was Edinson, and they were on their way to Buenos Aires (Argentina), as life in Caracas had become unbearable. While explaining why they left and how they had managed to cross the border, in our peripheral view, we saw some packed trucks passing by. We both knew what they were transporting (food), and Edinson gestured as if his eyes filled with tears and said, '*me hace llorar*' (it makes me cry). 'On our way to the border, we saw this kind of trade everywhere, in San Felipe, Ciudad Bolivar. Everyone was trading.'

That same trip, I met another young Venezuelan migrant who had also recently arrived in the Brazilian border town. His wife was about to give birth and he was trying to earn some money for the delivery at the nearby hospital. He felt lucky to have found an ad hoc job at a retailer in town. While chatting with me, he was loading six hundred kilos of rice into a Venezuelan Toyota Landcruiser – rice that would be resold in Venezuela. He seemed content with the future. At one point he even happily shouted: 'We are a rich country! We have everything, gold, oil, and we can have everything, pasta, rice and salad oil!' Such idiosyncrasies in seemingly similar life trajectories may rightly indicate the dangers of generalizing people's experience of migration and smuggling, as one momentarily spiralled in sadness and the other joyously praised Venezuela's so-called abundance. Strikingly, both young migrants seemed completely unpreoccupied with *how* the food entered Venezuela. I believe these considerations, or rather their absence, are an important reason why we should be sceptical about viewing these import and export practices solely in a legal sense. This arguably demonstrates why illegality has become so compelling in recent studies about the Venezuelan crisis and economic transactions, and pushes us to think of new conceptual frameworks that can also encapsulate the critical immediacy of people's own moral concerns and ethical evaluations.

Thinking about what is right or wrong from a perspective of situated experience, then, is also decisive for the politics of our knowledge productions. Defining what is of moral concern (or not) is ultimately a political act. Many state-centred approaches to contraband and smuggling, in my view, furtively or openly, reproduce the illegalization of certain economic practices over other economic activities, while ignoring or overlooking what is at stake for people involved in these (in)voluntary relationships of circulation and exchange (see also Bocarejo 2018; Galemba 2017). To some this may seem a mere act of moral relativism, but I rather see it as a call to subvert and destabilize established ideas of what is considered good or just and to cast doubt on dominant Western conceptions of the foundations and contours of ethical life (Mattingly and Throop 2018, 477–85). To put it more bluntly: why do we keep highlighting the illegal movements of goods? What would happen if we took other everyday moral concerns and concrete ethical valuations as our point of departure, to think about circulation and exchange within and across national borders?

Opulence in crisis

One night in 2021, over a simple dinner with Jorge and his wife Carmen Ibarra de Cifuentes, stories about opulence and abundance naturally came up while talking about the recent produce from their new kitchen garden. I had asked if they started to grow their own crops because of need, as many other Venezuelan households had, in response to the food crisis.[11] Jorge replied it was more to keep themselves occupied, as their lives had largely been confined to the limits of their house, due to COVID-19. The latest harvest was unexpectedly mediocre, but it did bring back memories of other crops long ago. Jorge recalled the enormous pumpkins and melons, in the delta region in Venezuela, where he used to work as a civil engineer. 'The land there, in the Orinoco basin, is so rich and so humid, [crops] simply grow, grow, and grow.' 'They turn almost obese then?', I asked. 'Yes, obese pumpkins!', Jorge laughed, and his joyous memories then moved to Guiria in the eastern coastal region, where he ordered fish for lunch, many years ago. While gesturing almost a metre between his two hands, Jorge smiled that the fisherman offered him an enormous bass with huge shrimps and an enormous plate with fried plantain. 'So much food, what to do with it? I can't eat it all!' he laughed. Then, Jorge retook his thoughtful posture, 'You can't go there anymore though. It's a liberated zone, no man's land, there is no law. There was [recently] a massacre between gangs, sixty people dead, and the state does nothing. They only come to look for merchandise.'

As many other Venezuelan friends and interlocutors had done in similar spontaneous conversations, Jorge added that they were such a rich and opulent country, but with poor people, with a poor mind, and with poor values. 'We had plenty of oil, and now we have nothing.'

It is not my interest here to evaluate if such statements are factual or reveal the wilful workings of hidden economic and political structures arising from colonial oppression and class inequalities and discriminations. Rather, I am interested in how such ontologies of opulence and stories of abundance work as important epistemological lenses to focus and refract novel happenings in people's own logics (Jacka 2015, 236). What is of interest here, I argue, is not so much the rise of smuggled merchandise and the government's questionable involvements in these practices (which seemed so at stake, ethically, for Jorge), but rather the incongruity of hunger in Venezuela. In times when bonanzas are long gone, hunger in the land of plenty seemed to be twice as troubling for many Venezuelans. A rapid transformation in the accessibility of food seemed to have caused a deep moral concern about the destabilizing effects of the protracted food crisis on the foundational origins of an ethics of abundance and opulence. Regardless of class, ideology or regional background, my interlocutors and friends in Venezuela shared a deep awareness that they lived in a potentially very rich country, which was now unavailable for so many (Coronil 1997). The rich soils and abundant waters replete with natural resources and opulent crops would never leave its people hungry.[12] Venezuelans being hungry made no sense.

Although it is hard to pinpoint when this myth of abundance appeared at the centre of *venezolanidad* (Venezuelan-ness), it is seldom disputed by any Venezuelan I have met, in the many years that I have lived there and during my recent visits. Whilst there have been endless controversies and struggles over national symbols and moral exemplars since the installation of Hugo Chavez as president in 1999, and his now successor Nicolas Maduro, the national symbol of *abundancia* seemed never to have caused much contestation or social critique (Socorro 2021).[13] Since its creation, the national shield of the Venezuelan republic has featured two intertwined cornucopias that overflow with tropical fruits and flowers. Abundance seemed somehow anchored in the national and political body, so to speak. This reference to myth and symbol is not to thoughtlessly adopt people's (like Jorge) behaviour and interpretation, but rather to engage with such ontologies and myths and refocus our discussions and theories, to be based on how people make sense of (abrupt) change in their lives, and in their own terms.

In Venezuela, social expectations arising from abundance and opulence have often translated into claims for cheap fuel, low taxes, or even opportunities for extralegal business – economic activities and benefits that are often simply reflected in immoral terms as pathological of rentier societies. I agree that it is more beneficial to understand such local expressions as 'quasi-naturalized' rights that are 'simply' acquired by living in a land of plenty and opulence (Peters 2019, 12). In times of booms and bonanzas, these social expectations are reflected in shared daily practices of conspicuous consumption and local binge economies (Peters 2019; Strønen 2017). In times when shared ideas and entitlements to opulence remain unfulfilled, ethical ideas about availability, opportunity, fairness and humanity come under moral pressure in other ways.

This social incongruity and moral outrage at hunger in Venezuela is not entirely new. Unavailability of food as a major social sin has been a recurrent national trope in significant moments in recent history. In a dramatic popular revolt in 1989, for instance, the most violently suppressed urban revolt in Venezuelan history, masses of Venezuelans took to the streets, protesting rising prices and looting shops. People's right to food appeared to fall into a different moral category to other goods (Coronil and Skurski 1991, 319). Hunger 'was regarded as a natural cause for revolt, but it was a shorthand expression referring, through the image of food, to what was regarded as unnecessary deprivation and [even] an insult in a country that had both democracy and wealth' (318).

Again, the illegal circulation and ingestion of food became morally distressing in Venezuela, not so much because it defied state law, but because it inverted other important moral categories. Declining possibilities form part of a more general disordering of people's relations with food and wealth. In one of her insightful works on the practical workings and cultural meanings of the food crisis and illegal imports in Venezuela, anthropologist Paula Vásquez Lezama (2019, 105–14), also shows how an ethics of consumption, or wanting to consume, is fundamental to produce a national and political body in Venezuela. Consumption, then, not only remits aspirations and promises of social and national belonging, but its failure also becomes an extreme and destructive process of one's own hungry body and social life in general. An inability to acquire food becomes twice as troubling. In other words, Venezuelans appear to be living a kind of 'irresolvable tension' in which a local ethic is marked by consumer values and a desire to access goods and merchandise, while daily life is marked by scarcity and deprivation (Vásquez Lezama 2019, 103). Albeit deriving from different ideals of food availability and distribution of wealth, in previous contexts of rapid social and economic change in socialist Cuba similar irresolvable tensions between good citizenship and consumption have emerged (Cearns 2023; Porter 2008). Moral disquiet with food ingress and food purchase stems from the unavailability of food, but also the corrosion of forms of autonomy, food sovereignty and hospitality as a form of popular refinement, that until recently ordered everyday ethical life. Proper and abundant – or at least sufficient – food consumption is not only fundamental for biological need, but also for moral being.

The immorality of overpricing and rotten food

In 2019, when Dayana served lunch at the Cifuentes Ibarra home, she told me that I had to eat more and leave Venezuela *gordita* (chubbier). She, herself, had lost quite a bit of weight since the last time I had seen her. But Dayana assured me that it was not because of what was sarcastically called 'the Maduro diet', referring to the average loss of weight among Venezuelans due to the food crisis. I knew Dayana well from the time I had lived with the Cifuentes Ibarra family. She had already worked for more than fifteen years for the family, mostly cleaning and cooking several times a week. After she had finished her duties, we had a brief chat in the kitchen as we used to do in earlier times.

Dayana told me she had had no running water for more than nine months. After each working day she brought home five litres for consumption. The remaining water for washing and cleaning she purchased together with 45 neighbours from a passing water truck. They filled a large tank with water that lasted for a week or so. They had no clue where the truck or the water came from. Dayana did not care, she seemed more concerned with its quality – it was very dirty water, she said. I became more interested in how she was getting by, and I asked Dayana how she was managing the food supplies for her family, at her humble home in the *barrios* of Caracas, and if she received the controversial subsidized food boxes (locally called CLAP boxes) from the government. She did, Dayana said, but distribution was too irregular and infrequent to rely on: it only came every three or four months. The box contained two packs of rice, pasta, beans and two jars of tomato ketchup and mayonnaise, and if lucky, she said, a can of tuna fish. From the way she listed the food products, I guessed the box was just a small drop in an ocean of scarcity and deprivation, and I did not probe any further.

In 2021, one night while watching television, the CLAP boxes came up again in our ad hoc conversations about the rampant food crisis in Venezuela. Jorge Cifuentes looked up from his cell phone and said: 'Look, Saab is arriving in Miami!' I was not sure who this Saab was, but knew something about one of the largest food scams in recent Venezuelan history, related to the government's subsidized food programme CLAP (*Los Comités Locales de Abastecimiento y Producción* – Local Committees for Supply and Production).[14] In the following days, the extradition to the United States of government associate Alex Saab was all over the news. Saab was alleged to have had a central role in money laundering and bribery.[15] In 2019, based on violations of the Foreign Corrupt Practices Act (FCPA), he was charged, at the federal court in Miami, of taking advantage of Venezuela's government-controlled exchange rate and laundering the gains of an illegal bribery scheme, from bank accounts located in Venezuela to and through bank accounts located in the United States.[16] He could only be extradited to Miami in 2021 after an unforeseen fuel stop at the Republic of Cabo Verde during a flight between Turkey and Venezuela.

It may seem again a trivial daily conversation about subsidized food boxes and a seemingly unconnected indictment of a crooked businessman. But behind the subsidized food boxes – and Saab's involvements in these – is another social world, of circulation and exchange, that fits within the scholarship addressed in this volume.

Aimed at taming shortages and tightening the price ceiling on basic goods, due to flaring inflation rates, the Venezuelan government passed the Fair Prices Act in 2014, to strengthen its price controls (Caraballo-Arias et al. 2017). This legislation was a framework of numerous controls on the production, distribution and commercialization of a wide range of food items, and was replaced in 2017 by the Constitutional Law on Sovereign Supply and Agreed Prices (FIDH/PROVEA 2022, 26). While offences were created, of stockpiling, speculation, resale of basic needs and smuggling, with sentences of up to fourteen years' imprisonment, these price-control attempts intensified the practice of *bachaqueo* – the trafficking of subsidized products to be resold at prices up to a hundred times, or more, their official value (Caraballo-Arias et al. 2017, 151).

In the context of strict price controls and severe shortages, the acquisition and sale of subsidized food, through the social food programme CLAP, at established market prices, ironically became another highly lucrative business for those with access to imported food products of very poor quality (FIDH/PROVEA 2022, 17–18). Although CLAP was aimed at providing a house-to-house delivery method of food boxes with nonperishable food items, local newspapers and word-of-mouth rumours have revealed that the food was often inedible, sometimes even revolting (Pico et al. 2021, 2). This was not the full story around the food boxes. *Bachaqueros*, in turn, illegally purchased, resold and redistributed the subsidized food at much higher prices (ENCOVI 2020). In plain language, those allied to the government imported perished food that had been withdrawn from the market elsewhere and sold it for a price many times higher than its actual value (similar accusations have been made by the Maduro government about humanitarian food aid from the US and Colombia). Some of the poor-quality food was distributed through complex CLAP distribution mechanisms, largely based on loyalty and clientelism, but other food items found their way into *bachaqueo*. The moral outrage around the overpricing of imported food products of very low quality added to the shared indignation around the subsequent resale of the CLAP products (Vásquez Lezama 2019, 101).[17] Overpriced and rotten food appeared to be everywhere.

Conjecturing the ethical in the circulation of food

It may seem ironic to allude to legal indictments and state laws, about price controls and subsidized food programmes, when trying to make an argument about everyday ethics.[18] But fair pricing, food availability and food quality were deeply problematic for many of my Venezuelan friends and interlocutors – sometimes everyday ethics *are* inspired by the morality of the law and vice versa. These ethical concerns around overpricing and rotten food related to the CLAP boxes, entangled with moral notions of fairness, justice and a shared sense of humanity, in a country of supposed opulence, during a rampant food crisis. Inaccessibility to sufficient edible food was a clear violation of the human right to food, which existed alongside the immoral act of purposely obstructing people's 'natural' entitlements to food and wealth, in a land of plenty.

Although one may rightly question to what extent Venezuela can still be defined as a democracy (Corrales 2020), past and present appraisals of hunger in Venezuela reveal similar ordinary ethics and everyday expectations of food availability and accessibility. Food availability in Venezuela seems, indeed, of a different moral order. Ethical being through an imaginary and material presence of natural abundance has continued to produce unintended local expectations of an unconditional availability of food, and its significance for conviviality and justice. How does focusing on abundance help us to conjecture the everyday working of ethics regarding food purchase and circulation during crisis?

Fairness, and perhaps even a notion of humanity, is not so much centred here on equal distribution of this imagined and actual wealth, since inequality in Venezuela has been notorious since colonial times. I think in this respect the lived experiences reflected in this chapter differ from experiences of food failure in other countries, with histories of socialism and post-socialism (Holbraad 2017; Mandel and Humphrey 2002). Such failure of socialism derives from a social or moral contract in which the state bears responsibility for providing and caring equally for all its citizens. The recent moral concerns about food failure in Venezuela, in my view, seem not only tied to a more recent socialist contract in the country, but also to a significantly older history of the socialization of wealth, which began much earlier than the coming of Hugo Chávez in the late 1990s. The foundational myth (and partial fact) of abundance as an enduring metaphysical process, by which potentiality turns into an actuality, has less to do with equity and more to do with availability. A befriended colleague, whom I call Enrique, phrased it much more persuasively. In 2021, when the sight of empty shelves had almost magically disappeared from many grocery stores in Caracas, Enrique confided that although most Venezuelans were still not able to purchase sufficient food, he was 100 per cent sure that many people felt less anxious, because the shelves were no longer bare. Such promises keep feeding the hopes for wealth, wellbeing, consumption, modernity and progress (Peters 2019, 14) – even if actual purchase remained inaccessible for many.

Perhaps, then, it does not matter, per se, how food or other items cross borders and if a certain amount of unlawful profit is being made within these supply chains. We could validate these claims as everyday moral confirmations of living in a mafia state or criminal hub and then move on. But why not take seriously what people themselves consider inappropriate in the way they buy and consume? I believe through this grounded practice of conjecturing how and where to situate the ethical, in emergency food ingress, our analytical work on contraband cultures becomes political. Because defining what is of concern (or not) is ultimately a political act. So, departing from perceiving the illegality of the trafficking of food within and across borders in Venezuela, towards, in this case, distinguishing the moral concerns, around food ingress during food crisis and shared myths of abundance, is part of a larger anthropological project on ethics, that seeks to subvert and destabilize established ideas of what is good, correct, just and appropriate ... and what is not. I believe such conceptual upturns are much needed, to cast necessary doubt on dominant Western and overly state-centred conceptions of the grounds and contours of ethical life in practice.

Notes

1 See https://www.unhcr.org/venezuela-emergency.html. Accessed 20 March 2024.
2 See https://www.proyectoencovi.com/informe-interactivo-2019. Accessed 20 March 2024.
3 See https://gro-intelligence.com/insights/how-deep-is-venezuelas-food-crisis. Accessed 20 March 2024.
4 See https://www.nytimes.com/2019/02/12/opinion/venezuela-hyperinflation-food-shortages.html. Accessed 20 March 2024.
5 See https://www.infobae.com/america/venezuela/2019/07/09/la-crisis-del-campo-agrava-la-caida-de-la-produccion-de-alimentos-en-venezuela-el-gobierno-decide-quien-siembra-y-quien-no/ and https://talcualdigital.com/importaciones-desmedidas-de-azucar-tumban-las-ventas-de-productores-locales/. Accessed 20 March 2024.
6 Entry 'contraband', Merriam Webster Dictionary. See https://www.merriam-webster.com/dictionary/contraband. Accessed 20 March 2024.
7 Entry 'ingress'. Merriam Webster Dictionary. See https://www.merriam-webster.com/dictionary/ingress. Accessed 20 March 2024.
8 Entry 'ingression' WordSense Online Dictionary. See https://www.wordsense.eu/ingression/. Accessed 20 March 2024.
9 Increased gold mining due to the crisis has largely replaced previous tourist activities realized mainly by Indigenous communities in the region (Angosto-Ferrández, 2013). In 2016, in response to the declining oil revenues and economic crisis, the Maduro government appointed by decree a large territory of 112,000 square kilometres, south of the river Orinoco, as Arco Minero del Orinoco (the Orinoco Mining Arc), for new mining practices, which further intensified the gold rush in southern Venezuela and Indigenous territories. The expansion of the extractive area progressed steadily further to the south in the process of 'deepening logic of extractivism' (Rosales 2017), but is beyond the scope of this chapter.
10 Local experiences and negative judgements of widespread smuggling and corruption at the border between Colombia and Venezuela were likewise more related to common imaginaries about the malfunctioning of the state, rather than these economic practices per se (Albornoz-Arias et al. 2019, 13).
11 See https://www.theguardian.com/world/2016/may/24/venezuela-crisis-basic-food-shortages. Accessed 20 March 2024.
12 Being an oil producing country since the discovery of enormous oil fields in the early twentieth century, much of the national affluence has been articulated through the abundance of oil and its incentive for development and growth, which Venezuelan writer and politician Arturo Uslar Pietri (2005) powerfully phrased as *sembrar el petroleo* – sowing of oil.
13 See https://prodavinci.com/el-emblema-de-la-abundancia/. Accessed 20 March 2024.
14 See https://edition.cnn.com/2021/10/17/americas/alex-saab-venezuela-cape-verde-extradition/index.html. Accessed 20 March 2024.

15 On 20 December 2023, Alex Saab was granted clemency by President Joe Biden as part of a prisoner swap in which Maduro's government released Venezuelan political opponents and ten detained US citizens. See https://www.reuters.com/world/americas/who-is-maduro-ally-alex-saab-who-was-granted-clemency-prisoner-swap-2023-12-20/. Accessed 20 March 2024.

16 See https://www.justice.gov/usao-sdfl/pr/colombian-businessman-charged-money-laundering-extradited-united-states-cabo-verde. Accessed 20 March 2024.

17 See https://elestimulo.com/venezuela/2019-05-05/reventa-de-cajas-clap-en-catia-un-negocio-de-alto-calibre/. Accessed 20 March 2024.

18 With the recent economic openings and de facto dollarization of the economy, this kind of *bachaqueo* has lost its meaning, due to the resale of subsidized food from the CLAP boxes, and improvement in the supply chain of merchandise through other channels, as imports have become cheaper due to exchange rate distortion and smuggling (FIDH/PROVEA 2022).

References

Albornoz-Arias, Neida, Rina Mazuera-Arias, Genoveva Millán Vázquez de la Torre and Roberto Briceño León. 2019. 'Los pactos sociales y el contrabando en la frontera colombo-venezolana', *Convergencia Revista de Ciencias Sociales* 81: 1–16.

Angosto-Ferrández, Luis Fernando. 2013. 'Mundo perdido, paraíso encontrado: Lugar, identidad y producción en la Gran Sabana, Venezuela', *Revista Colombiana de Antropología* 49(1): 11–43.

Ayuso, Anna. 2018. 'Violence, corruption, and organized crime in Venezuela', *Peace in Progress*, Drug violence in Latin America series 35: 1–5. Accessed 20 March 2024. https://www.icip.cat/perlapau/en/article/violence-corruption-and-organized-crime-in-venezuela/.

Bocarejo, Diana. 2018. 'Thinking with (il)legality: The ethics of living with bonanzas', *Current Anthropology* 59(18): 1–181.

Bozçali, Firat. 2020. 'Probabilistic borderwork: Oil smuggling, nonillegality, and techno-legal politics in the Kurdish borderlands of Turkey', *American Ethnologist* 47(1): 72–85.

Bull, Benedicte and Antulio Rosales. 2020. 'The crisis in Venezuela: Drivers, transitions, and pathways', *European Review of Latin American and Caribbean Studies* 109: 1–20.

Caraballo-Arias, Yohama, Daniel González-Dos Santos, Leonel Porta-González and Sabrina Pozzobon-Gil. 2017. 'Bachaqueros: Un trabajo del mercado negro Venezolano', *Ciencia y Trabajo* 19(60): 151–6.

Cearns, Jennifer. 2023. *Circulating Culture: Transnational Cuban networks of exchange*. Gainesville: University Press of Florida.

Coronil, Fernando. 1997. *The Magical State: Nature, money, and modernity in Venezuela*. Chicago: Chicago University Press.

Coronil, Fernando and Julie Skurski. 1991. 'Dismembering and remembering the nation: The semantics of political violence in Venezuela', *Comparative Studies in Society and History* 33(2): 288–337.

Corrales, Javier. 2020. 'Democratic backsliding through electoral irregularities: The case of Venezuela', *European Review of Latin American and Caribbean Studies* 109: 41–65.

Cromwell, Jesse. 2018. *The Smugglers' World: Illicit trade and Atlantic communities in eighteenth-century Venezuela*. Chapel Hill: University of North Carolina Press.

Donovan, Kevin P. 2021. 'MAGENDO: Arbitrage and ambiguity on an East African frontier', *Cultural Anthropology* 16(1): 110–37.

Dyring, Rasmus, Cheryl Mattingly and Maria Louw. 2018. 'The question of moral engines: Introducing a philosophical anthropological dialogue'. In *Moral Engines: Exploring the ethical drives in human life*, edited by Cheryl Mattingly, Rasmus Dyring, Maria Louw and Thomas Schwarz Wentzer, 9–36. Oxford: Berghahn.

ENCOVI. 2020. 'Encuesta Nacional de Condiciones de Vida 2019–2020', Universidad Católica Andrés Bello. Accessed 2 January 2023. https://miradorsalud.com/seguridad-alimentaria-envenezuela-comparacion-de-la-encovi-2017-2020/.

Farah, Douglas. 2020. 'The Maduro regime's illicit activities: A threat to democracy in Venezuela and security in Latin America', *Atlantic Council* August: 1–13.

FIDH/PROVEA. 2022. *Food is Not a Game: Serious violations to the human right to food in Venezuela*. Accessed 8 January 2024. https://www.fidh.org/IMG/pdf/venezuela_report_en.pdf.

Galemba, Rebecca B. 2017. *Contraband Corridor: Making a living at the Mexico–Guatemala border*. Redwood City, CA: Stanford University Press.

Holbraad, Martin. 2017. 'Money and the morality of commensuration', *Social Analysis: The International Journal of Anthropology* 61(4): 81–97.

InSight Crime. 2018. 'Venezuela: A mafia state? Venezuela has become a hub of organized crime in the region', *Investigation and Analysis of Organized Crime*. Accessed 20 March 2024. https://insightcrime.org/investigations/venezuela-mafia-state/.

Jacka, Jerry K. 2015. *Alchemy in the Rain Forest: Politics, ecology, and resilience in a New Guinea mining area*. Durham, NC: Duke University Press.

Keane, Webb. 2010. 'Minds, surfaces, and reasons in the anthropology of ethics'. In *Ordinary Ethics: Anthropology, language, and action*, edited by Michael Lambek, 64–83. New York: Fordham University Press.

Kleinman, Arthur. 1997. '"Everything that really matters": Social suffering, subjectivity, and the remaking of human experience in a disordering world', *Harvard Theological Review* 90(3): 315–35.

Lambek, Michael. 2010a. 'Introduction'. In *Ordinary Ethics: Anthropology, language, and action*, edited by Michael Lambek, 1–38. New York: Fordham University Press.

Lambek, Michael. 2010b. 'Toward an ethics of the act'. In *Ordinary Ethics: Anthropology, language, and action*, edited by Michael Lambek, 39–63. New York: Fordham University Press.

Lemon, Alaina. 1998. '"Your eyes are green like dollars": Counterfeit cash, national substance, and currency apartheid in 1990s Russia', *Cultural Anthropology* 13(1): 22–55.

Mandel, Ruth and Caroline Humphrey (eds). 2002. *Markets and Moralities: Ethnographies of post-socialism*. Oxford: Berg.

Mattingly, Cheryl. 2013. 'Moral selves and moral scenes: Narrative experiments in everyday life', *Ethnos* 78(3): 301–27.

Mattingly, Cheryl and Jason Throop. 2018. 'The anthropology of ethics and morality', *Annual Review of Anthropology* 47: 475–92.

Morillo Ramos, Morella and Eva van Roekel. 2022. 'Economías inflamables en tiempos de COVID-19: La reventa de gasolina en la frontera de Venezuela–Brasil', *Journal of Latin American and Caribbean Anthropology* 27(1–2): 37–56.

Ødegaard, Cecilie Vindal. 2019. 'Translating wealth in a globalised extractivist economy: Contrabandistas and accumulation by diversion'. In *Indigenous Life Projects and Extractivism: Ethnographies from South America*, edited by Cecilie Vindal Ødegaard and Juan Javier Rivera Andía, 119–40. Cham: Palgrave Macmillan.

Pelcastre, Julieta. 2022. 'Venezuela: Hub of regional organized crime', *Diálogo Américas*, 31 August. Accessed 20 March 2024. https://dialogo-americas.com/articles/venezuela-hub-of-regional-organized-crime/.

Peters, Stefan. 2019. 'Sociedades rentistas', *European Review of Latin American and Caribbean Studies* 108: 1–19.

Pico, Rocio, Sara del Castillo Matamoros and Jennifer Bernal. 2021. 'Food and nutrition insecurity in Venezuelan migrant families in Bogotá, Colombia', *Frontiers in Sustainable Food Systems* 5. Accessed 20 March 2024. https://doi.org/10.3389/fsufs.2021.634817.

Porter, Amy L. 2008. 'Fleeting dreams and flowing goods: Citizenship and consumption in Havana Cuba', *PoLAR: The Political and Legal Anthropology Review* 31(1): 134–49.

Rosales, Antulio. 2017. 'Venezuela's deepening logic of extraction: The Maduro government's decision to push ahead with the Orinoco Mining Arc initiative shows that extractive capitalism is alive and well in Venezuela', *NACLA Report on the Americas* 49(2): 132–5.

Schwartz, Steven. 2021. 'The politics of *Bachaqueo*: Gasoline black markets and indigeneity in Venezuela', *American Ethnologist* 48(4): 504–19.

Socorro, Milagros. 2021. 'El emblema de la abundancia', *Prodavinci* 19. Accessed 20 March 2024. https://prodavinci.com/el-emblema-de-la-abundancia/.

Strønen, Iselin Åsedotter. 2017. *Grassroots Politics and Oil Culture in Venezuela: The revolutionary petro-state*. Cham: Palgrave Macmillan.

Uslar Pietri, Arturo. 2005. 'Sembrar el petróleo', *Revista de Artes y Humanidades UNICA* 6(12): 231–3.

Van Roekel, Eva. 2020. *Phenomenal Justice: Violence and morality in Argentina*. New Brunswick, NJ: Rutgers University Press.
Vásquez Lezama, Paula. 2019. 'Cuando se consume el cuerpo del pueblo: La incertidumbre como política de supervivencia en Venezuela', *Revista Iberoamericana* 85(266): 101–18.
Yildiz, Emrah. 2020. 'Nested (in)securities: Commodity and currency circuits in an Iran under sanctions', *Cultural Anthropology* 35(2): 218–24.

7

Crush your pills: smuggling medication into Rio de Janeiro's prisons

David C. Thompson

I was late to the first meeting of a newly formed association for family members of incarcerated people in the state of Rio de Janeiro, but so was everybody else. The group was founded by a woman who had spent more than a decade denouncing various forms of violence within the prison system. But she had not conjured this organization out of nothing. *Familiares* (relatives) were already well-connected to one another, and they generally organized through social media, particularly WhatsApp. What made this group different was its status as an official, registered body, one that the founder hoped would provide a vehicle for families to advocate for better treatment of themselves and their imprisoned loved ones, without exposing themselves as individuals to retribution from correctional officers or the prison administration.

The majority of the twenty people gathered that morning were Black women. Aside from myself, two men sat in the circle, but the three of us were largely silent, and the collective 'we' that emerged in the conversation was a feminine one – *todas nós*. With so much to talk about, the meeting bounced across various issues of abuse and maltreatment. But we repeatedly came back to the question of health. So many of these women's imprisoned sons and partners were sick with illnesses that were caused or exacerbated by their confinement. Those who managed to see a doctor (itself a difficult feat) were still left without any medicine, simply because the prison's stockpile, managed separately from the rest of Rio's public healthcare system, had none. It was at this meeting that one woman, Fátima, explained that her husband, who suffered from hypertension, relied on her to buy his pills. She would request a prescription from a doctor who had never seen her husband, purchase the pills, and hand them to the guards, who inspected everything brought in by visitors. But too often, a correctional officer would confiscate them, with the justification that they did not meet official standards for packaging. These confiscated medicines would often reappear when guards tried to sell them back to the prison population.

So, to make sure that her husband could access his blood pressure medication, she crushed the pills into a fine powder, funnelled the powder carefully into bottles of fruit juice, and brought those to her prison visits. The bottles passed through inspection more easily, but the pills were not manufactured to be taken and absorbed into the bloodstream like this, and it would be impossible to guarantee a consistent dosage. Given the alternative, this was the most durable line of access that the man had to a potentially life-saving medicine, one that mitigated a well-known bodily effect of punishment itself. But it was ultimately an experiment, one strung together by various actors – the wife, the guard, the doctor, the pharmacist, the broken healthcare system – and one that redistributed both the risks and the burdens of medical treatment within a death-dealing institution.

Healthcare in Rio's prisons is largely characterized by these improvised, ad hoc solutions to the presence or threat of disease. In an overcrowded, poorly ventilated set of institutions that provide only intermittent access to drinking water, and amid a project of carceral expansion, whose funding priorities skew heavily towards security over any form of treatment, illness spreads. The forms of medical care offered within Brazil's prisons are formally part of the nation's unified public health programme, one of the largest in the world. This is to say that they should be free, universal and substantially the same as that offered to those outside prison. In practice, during my fieldwork, the few doctors employed by the prison system were overwhelmed with demand and often lacked the resources to provide a proper diagnosis, let alone prescribe treatment. In response, incarcerated people, family members and others, worked to produce and maintain alternative channels of access to medicine. These pills, creams and serums are legal, for the most part, but they move in an unregulated grey area that skirts both prison security protocols and pharmaceutical regulations.

This chapter offers a brief sketch of the contraband economy of medicine within Rio de Janeiro's prison system. It sits both within and against a longer history of academic and popular fascination with prisons as sites of smuggling and traffic, illicit economies that seem to erode the image of imprisonment as a form of containment (Sykes 2007; Skarbek 2014). Contraband draws attention to the porous nature of prison walls (Fontes and O'Neill 2019). But collectively, these studies tend to reproduce the concerns of prison wardens and administrators, both through their overwhelming emphasis on narcotics and cell phones, and their insistence that visitors, rather than correctional officers themselves, are the main channel for such objects. As such, they produce a gendered narrative around contraband in which women's agency is restricted to the figure of the drug mule.

Ivermectin, benzodiazepines and birth-control pills present an opportunity to tell other stories about these institutions. There is nothing illicit about the presence of these drugs inside the prison system; instead, it is the way they are procured and their journey into these institutions that skirt both medical regulation and prison protocol. By following them, my aim is to bring into relief the smuggling of medicine as a practice that transforms the nature of both health and confinement. This chapter makes three claims about contraband medicines. First, they produce new forms of dependence – between people and substances, doctors and families, incarcerated people and the state. Second, they redistribute the burdens and risks of healthcare away from the prison administration, and largely onto poor Black families and communities. Finally, these modes of treatment are experimental: they play with borders, bodies and blood chemistry, and introduce new hazards as they attempt to mitigate others.

In making these arguments, it is important to begin by recognizing that imprisonment is a constant assault on the physical and mental health of its captives (Farmer 2004; Massoglia 2008). Brazil's prisons are known for their violence, including the periodic massacres that break into international headlines. But those held in these institutions are far more at risk from hypertension, tuberculosis, scabies, HIV, psychotic episodes – and, more recently, coronavirus – than from riots or conflict. These are the 'ordinary' deaths and pains that do not rise to the level of an event (Medeiros 2023). On its own, medication cannot adequately treat most of them or address the cause of their spread. However, in the absence of other forms of support, it becomes the primary mode of healthcare, magnifying the broader process in Brazil that João Biehl has labelled the 'pharmaceuticalization of healthcare' (Biehl 2007). Drugs have become the primary tool at the disposal of imprisoned people and their families, to attempt to survive and alleviate the effects of punishment.

This work emerges from 24 months' fieldwork that I conducted in and around the prison system of Rio between 2014 and 2018. My focus was on two penitentiaries designated for men, but gradually expanded to include visits with family members, interviews with prison staff and supervising bodies, and activist meetings like the one outlined above.

This research highlights the scope of contraband medicine and the set of relationships that produce and sustain it. I share in the apprehension of many interlocutors, that 'exposing' contraband medicine might invite the interdiction of the prison administration itself, and have taken care with what I have chosen to describe here. However, these practices are largely known by prison staff and the administration, constituting one of many 'open secrets' of criminal justice. At the same time, what I describe here constitutes a snapshot of a constantly shifting constellation of actors, prison protocol and strategies of survival, as people constantly search for new tools to survive imprisonment.

Death and scabies in Brazil's carceral project

Rio de Janeiro was the site of Latin America's first penitentiary, the House of Corrections (*Casa de Correção*). Modelled after the new institutions developing in the United States, the project was intended to modernize punishment and was explicitly promoted to control the growing free Black population in what was, at the time, the capital of the Brazilian Empire. It was also a death trap. As the historian Martine Jean records (2017, 231), almost 25 per cent of those brought to the prison between 1850 and 1859 died there, rising to 46.8 per cent of those given sentences of 8–10 years. The same could be said for the House of Detention (*Casa de Detenção*), built soon afterwards, which quickly became known as a hotbed for fevers and beriberi (Chazkel 2009). Despite their promises of improving the physical and moral character of the imprisoned, a combination of overcrowding, poor ventilation and lack of medical care made this new project of criminal justice extraordinarily hazardous, even when compared to previous models of punishment such as convict labour or transportation to penal colonies in the interior. But the deaths only seemed to propel more prison construction, as each new unit promised to resolve the problems of the former. The early twentieth century saw an expansion of biomedicine in Brazil more broadly, as well as a far greater insertion of medical knowledge into its criminal justice system, including its prisons. In part through the activism of psychiatrist Heitor Carrilho (Dias 2011) and medical jurist Nina Rodrigues (Augusto and Ortega 2011), mortality rates gradually declined, but illness remained a constant concern among both the incarcerated and prison administrators.

Brazil's most recent transition to democracy brought with it the 1988 constitution, which enshrined a 'right to health' for all citizens.

This right was realized through the Unified Health System (*Sistema Único de Saúde*, or SUS), which today operates as the world's largest federal public health system. Democratization also marked the beginning of a period of massive carceral expansion. Since 1990, the prison population of Brazil has risen by over 800 per cent. This incredible boom constitutes a new punitive politics, one that we might call mass incarceration. But as the number of those in prison exploded, investment in health remained stagnant. In Rio de Janeiro, the total number of health professionals working within the prison system declined over the following decades. At the same time, healthcare grew more fragmented, as various services, including the provision of medicine, were contracted out through public–private partnerships.

It is important to stress that the 'problem' of health is not simply one of a lack of resources. As an architectural form, prisons are pathogenic institutions, characterized by physical immobility, lack of sunlight, social isolation, severe mental strain and close proximity among the incarcerated (De Viggiani 2007). But while the absence of medical services did not create these environmental harms, it has allowed both communicable and non-communicable diseases to flourish. It has also obscured the scale of the problem. In an institution with very little capacity to diagnose illness, death records provide the most reliable measure of a disease's spread. I say this with caution; even here, the data provided by the prison administration is often lacking, and rumours circulated during my fieldwork that courts would release the sick on compassionate grounds days or hours before their death so that they might not count among these statistics. Still, records from 2016 and 2017 indicate that those imprisoned in Rio de Janeiro were five times more likely to die of infectious disease (and fifteen times more likely to die of tuberculosis) than the general population (Sánchez et al. 2021). This contrast is particularly stark, since Rio's prison population is far younger than that of the state as a whole: 37 per cent of those imprisoned are under the age of 24 (Infopen 2017).

Deaths tell one story about the state of healthcare. But for the imprisoned, their families, and anyone who has worked within the system, the most visible and widespread evidence of broken health services is not lethal. The scabies parasite causes severe itching and rashes that, when scratched, can open up small wounds that are potential sites for further bacterial infection. On its own, scabies is not life threatening. This means that it largely falls outside the purview of doctors and nurses employed by the prison system, who direct their limited time and resources to more urgent cases. But systemic overcrowding has created an ideal environment for the parasite to proliferate. The most effective treatment is the antiparasitic drug ivermectin, and a single dose is often enough to eliminate infection for an individual. What it cannot do is rid an entire cell or penitentiary of the infection. In a context where fifty people are confined in a space designated for twenty, where there are often no opportunities to disinfect clothes and mattresses, and where access to showers and running water is highly restricted, reinfections are extremely common. But the drug still offers at least a temporary reprieve from a parasite that would otherwise likely accompany the imprisoned person for their entire sentence.

Ivermectin legally requires a prescription for purchase. This is not, on its own, a significant barrier to access, since many Brazilian pharmacies routinely sell popular prescription medications over the counter. But the prison administration requires that prescription medication brought in by visitors be accompanied by the prescription itself. So, family members often turn to doctors in their own neighbourhoods for help. During a conversation I had with one such doctor, working within the public health system, she explained that she repeatedly received requests to write ivermectin prescriptions for incarcerated people she had never seen, let alone diagnosed. 'I feel like I can't say no …', she explained. As she trailed off, she avoided clarifying how she ultimately responded to these requests, which asked her to breach professional and federal regulations on providing prescriptions.

The path that ivermectin takes into Rio's prisons, and into the bloodstreams of the infected, mirrors that of the blood pressure medication outlined in this chapter's introduction. In both cases, family members worked to ensure supply by recruiting other actors, including doctors and pharmacists. Likewise, both uses of medication offered only a partial reprieve from illnesses that were caused or aggravated by the prison environment. But the two cases diverge in one important aspect. Fátima created a supply channel that skirted the regulatory gaze of correctional officers. By contrast, family members seeking ivermectin were able to meet the demands of the prison administration, but only by recruiting doctors to break the regulations on providing a prescription. These were, essentially, the only two options available for those seeking to bring medicine into Rio's prisons, because the administration had created a set of guidelines that were incompatible with both its own limited resources and the requirements of the broader health system.

Dependence

I think this impasse between prison and medical protocols was the cause of the doctor's awkward silence, her reluctance to explain what happened when patients asked her for prescriptions for their imprisoned family members. Our brief conversation took place during a meeting on health and incarceration, one that had drawn activists, government officials, and medical staff working within and outside prisons. To speak here about how such requests tested her ethical and professional commitments was a fraught task. But the silence between us only lasted a second before a lawyer entered our conversation. 'You shouldn't feel awkward', she explained to the doctor bluntly. 'Just write the prescription. Many doctors do.' As she put it, contraband medicine was not a secret that needed to be hidden; on the contrary, it functioned as a de facto institutional policy.

During my fieldwork, the official path to a prescription was essentially a bureaucratic fantasy. Most prisons in Rio had only nurses or nurse technicians on staff; even then, they often worked only two or three days a week.[1] The few doctors employed by the prison administration, with their power to prescribe, were concentrated in the state's only penal hospital. For the imprisoned, getting to this hospital required calling the attention of a nurse or guard; having them take the complaint seriously enough to schedule transportation; and risking one of the beatings that the drivers of those black, windowless vans were known for. Federal programmes and funding to combat tuberculosis and HIV meant that staff gave these diseases priority, at least when patients had already been diagnosed. Something like scabies, on the other hand, would not suffice. Even then, there was no guarantee that a specialist would be on staff at the hospital, nor that they would have the time for an accurate diagnosis. Incarcerated people in Rio de Janeiro (Minayo and Ribeiro 2016) and other Brazilian states (Xavier 2018) have reported being given paracetamol, regardless of the nature or severity of their illness. All of this is to say that Rio's prisons required prescriptions and made them virtually impossible (and potentially hazardous) to obtain. Even if a patient managed to pass through these barriers, there was a high probability that the prison system would not have the medication in stock.[2] Within this context, as the lawyer suggested, contraband medication did not undermine penal governance or diminish its control; instead, the state had deliberately cultivated it as a basic component of penal healthcare. By offloading the responsibility and the costs of diagnosis and treatment onto incarcerated people, their families, and the outside health system, state governments and administrators could mitigate the effects of their own divestment in health in an era of penal expansion.

This process also creates a new network of dependencies between actors inside and outside prison. Both incarcerated people and prison staff depend on families to secure medication. These families then rely on the leniency of doctors and pharmacists, to procure a prescription and the treatment; or else they find ways to circumvent screening by correctional officers. This network did not operate in parallel to the official prison healthcare system; instead, it had become an integral part of it. Rather than submitting requests for transfer to the penal hospital, nurses and technicians would instead write out a list of medications, along with basic guidelines on dosages and adherence, for patients to pass onto their family members. As one nurse explained to me, without this channel for treatment she simply could not do her job.

In the case of infectious disease, families also recognize the importance of medication for their own safety. For example, Analu, who I met at a church group, regularly sent over-the-counter medication to her husband, to help with his chronic pain, without much issue. But in an interview, she also spoke of one of his cellmates:

> The state doesn't provide anything, and people end up dying. Recently a guy died from tuberculosis. My husband is in a cell with another guy with tuberculosis. I sent this strong medicine for him to take, because they don't separate him, he's in the same cell as the rest of them. I mean, look at the risk. There are so many prisoners and so many visits, my conjugal visit is inside the prison, I enter the prison and they close the door. So, imagine what could happen with me inside. I can get – I'm vulnerable to get any kind of sickness, you know?

Analu's response frames her act as a preventative action, an effort to protect her husband and herself, rather than a gesture of care or solidarity with the sick man himself. This 'strong medicine' (which I will return to below) was, for her, not just an individual treatment but a public health intervention within the pathogenic environment of the prison, an attempt to substitute pills for quarantine and proper ventilation.

Where contraband medicine forges these connections and supply channels, different actors come to depend on one another, to fill in the gaps of healthcare. At the same time, the practice can foster other forms of dependence, including addiction. One of the most commonly consumed substances inside Rio's prison system is clonazepam, a *calmante* (sedative) and anti-anxiety pill. Unlike other medications, clonazepam is generally brought in by correctional officers and sold directly to incarcerated people. For the guards, these cheap pills – easy to obtain, despite legally requiring a prescription – reduce conflict inside the institution and produce 'order' by dampening the nervous system. For the imprisoned, they offer the chance to pass the time of a sentence by sleeping through it. But the continued use of the drug can also develop into an addiction, and withdrawal symptoms include insomnia and paranoia. Those who use clonazepam during their incarceration often struggle to stop, even after their release.

Redistribution

Ruth Wilson Gilmore (2007; 2022) remarks that, in the California prison system, incarceration effectively functions as a form of wealth transfer, siphoning money from the state's urban poor, and particularly from Black and Latine communities. Regardless of whether a particular prison operates under a 'for-profit' model or not, legal fees, bail bonds, transportation to visit rural prisons, the exorbitant cost of phone calls, and transfers into a loved one's commissary account, all make the attempt to care and advocate for an imprisoned family member an extremely expensive project. In contrast to the case of Brazil, those imprisoned in the United States are one of the few groups with a legal right to state-funded healthcare (Sufrin 2017). Still, Gilmore's work spotlights the incredible financial burden that incarceration places on policed communities, and particularly onto women of colour.

Brazilian prisons place similar burdens on the families and communities of the imprisoned. In an institution where basic items like clothing and clean blankets are not provided, and where food often arrives undercooked or rotten, family members invest their limited resources on such materials. These include pharmaceuticals as well as basic hygiene materials like soap, toothpaste and sanitary pads. Costs for medication can vary wildly; many are offered for free, or heavily subsidized, through the public-health administered *farmácias populares* (popular pharmacies). But during my fieldwork, these pharmacies ran out of various drugs (Freire 2023); at the same time, private pharmacies are generally more likely to sell prescription medicine over the counter, including generics. Often more expensive than the medication itself was transportation. Rio's prisons are mostly situated in the urban peripheries and across various satellite cities; visitors would often take up to four buses to reach them. Many also paid to sleep in dormitories near the prison's front gates to secure a spot at the front of the line the next morning. These costs added up to a huge financial burden for family members, even without accounting for the cost of buying medication back from guards, if it was confiscated.

Aside from families, another source of funding came from the *facções* (factions), the collectives linked to drug trafficking that establish their own practices of governance within the prison system. One of these is the *caixa*, an emergency fund for each cell maintained both by the proceeds of drug commerce and contributions from the imprisoned. This fund has a variety of functions, including the purchase of medicine for those whose families cannot afford it, as well as those who do not receive visitors. Thus, one result of the state's disinvestment in healthcare is that it consolidates these organizations, recruiting them into the maintenance of prison order.

As this example suggests, contraband medicine redistributes not only the costs, but also the responsibilities of healthcare. Incarcerated people and prison staff turn to family members and factions, rather than prison doctors or the administration itself, for treatment. This diversion also permits the state to absolve itself from responsibility for adverse reactions or deaths resulting from improper treatment. Broadly speaking, Rio's prison administration regularly places the blame for disease onto the imprisoned themselves – for instance, during my fieldwork, officials maintained that virtually all those with tuberculosis had entered the prison system with the infection, rather than acquiring it during their sentences. By limiting access to doctors, and thus to a formal diagnosis, they also rendered various illnesses statistically invisible, while greatly reducing others. As described above, both Analu and Fátima recognized that the state was failing in its responsibility to provide healthcare. But without concrete numbers, both family members and activists were left only with rumours and anecdotes that were far more difficult to transform into accountability or legal action.

Experimentation

With the onset of the COVID-19 pandemic, and amid stories of mass deaths and collapsing hospital services, many within Brazil, including the then-health minister, Eduardo Pazuello, promoted the use of dubious treatments for the viral infection. These included the use of hydroxychloroquine and ivermectin as prophylactics. Among a scramble of competing claims and counterclaims regarding the efficacy of treatments, the case study of a single prison, called Alcaçuz, in Brazil's Northeast Region, caught national attention. In a local radio interview, the unit's doctor, Lionaldo Duarte, claimed that he had provided ivermectin, which he previously prescribed for scabies, as preventative treatment for the disease to all those held in the prison, arguing that the lack of any deaths clearly demonstrated the pill's effectiveness (Lopes 2021). The story was picked up nationally, including by the talk-show host and national icon Xuxa Meneghel, who enthusiastically defended the idea of subjecting incarcerated people to medical experiments, arguing that 'at least they can be good for something before they die' (*O Globo* 2021).

The use of incarcerated people for what amounted to a poorly designed experiment in the prevention of a potentially fatal disease is not unprecedented. Instead, it follows a longer history of medical experimentation in prisons and other sites of confinement, including a series of tests run in Philadelphia's Holmesburg penitentiary (Hornblum 1998) and US-run studies that deliberately inoculated incarcerated Guatemalans with gonorrhoea and syphilis (Spector-Bagdady and Lombardo 2019). But where these examples, and the case of Alcaçuz, all captured broader attention, imprisonment in Brazil is characterized by a set of quotidian and ongoing experiments that test the limits of pharmaceuticals, blood and brain chemistry, administrative protocols and kinship ties. The effects of crushing multiple days' supply of pills into a powder, suspending that powder in the acidic environment of a fruit juice, and taking each day's dosage by the swig, for example, were largely unknown and potentially hazardous – a fact that Fátima recognized in our meeting. This tactic was also an experiment in circumventing the surveillance of correctional officers, one that had no guarantee of lasting success. But the alternative of leaving her husband's condition untreated was also untenable.

Fátima's strategy did not emerge in isolation. Instead, she drew on, and contributed to, the collective knowledge of tens of thousands of family members, mostly women, who constantly shared their experience and insights with one another. Family members of incarcerated people most often encountered one another in the lines that formed outside penitentiaries on visiting days, and in the WhatsApp groups that grew out of them, with each specific penitentiary having at least one group chat dedicated to, and run by, visitors. There, legal, administrative and medical information flowed, creating something of a collective memory, updating members about any sudden shifts in protocol and allowing them to strategize around barriers set up by the prison administration or correctional officers. This is where many women found a doctor willing to prescribe treatment without examining the patient; or else a pharmacist who might sell the treatment without a prescription. It was also a space where I was generally not welcome as a foreign, white male researcher. Many family members are wary of reprisals, against themselves or those in prison, for speaking out against the injustices they face. As such, I did not observe whether or how a medical consensus was reached among these groups, how they might register adverse reactions to contraband medicine, and the speed with which news travelled. But this was where guidelines for treatment were constantly shaped and remade, in response to the evolving conditions of imprisonment, the changing disease profile of the institutions, and new channels for healthcare that opened while others closed.

It was far from being the only community of medical knowledge and experimentation. Incarcerated transgender women and *travestis*[3] bring into prison the shared experiences of other trans people regarding gender-affirming healthcare, and particularly the use of hormones. These forms of care are extremely limited in the outside public health system; inside prison, they are largely nonexistent.[4] But while testosterone blockers are difficult to obtain without specialist care, oestrogen (specifically, estradiol) is not. Contraceptive pills or gels, as well as hormone replacement therapy, contain estradiol; both are relatively easy to buy, although like other drugs, the prison administration requires a prescription written for the user. *Travestis* and trans women are generally sent to a specific set of prisons designated for men. The few who are supported by their families often receive the medication during visits (sometimes with gel sachets disguised as salad dressing), but they also sell them to others, producing an oestrogen economy inside these units.

It was Jéssica, a *travesti* held in one of the prisons in which I conducted fieldwork, who educated me about estradiol and its risks. Without medical supervision the drug carries severe potential side effects including thrombosis. These hazards are only amplified by patchy and inconsistent access to the hormone, caused by conflicts with family members, lack of funds, changing prison protocols, and both corrupt and diligent guards. Many switched between different medications depending on their availability, and compensated for 'dry periods' by upping their dosage afterwards. This is what Jéssica described as both dangerous and *descontrolado* (uncontrolled), as she tried to teach others in the unit about the side effects of estradiol and encouraged them to be more careful as they used it. But as she admitted, safe medical care, which would include regular consultations with an endocrinologist, was simply impossible for those in prison.

As incarcerated people and visitors experimented with medication on their own bodies, they also became test subjects for another experiment in penal governance. This was a novel form of healthcare that fused the limited resources from within the prison system with these contraband channels of medication. The aggregate result was a patchwork of treatment that relied heavily on pharmaceuticals, above all other forms of prevention and care, but outsourced most of the responsibility and cost of these drugs. Like the doctor of Alcaçuz, Rio's prison administration was continually testing the possibilities and limits of healthcare provision in an era of mass incarceration.

Conclusion

What did Analu mean by 'strong medicine'? Tuberculosis is one of the few diseases that the prison system is generally equipped to treat, thanks to federal funding to combat the disease – although drug shortages and intermittent access to treatment still occur (MEPCT 2020). The fact that her husband's cellmate was not receiving this treatment at all meant that he had, most likely, not been diagnosed. Active tuberculosis is treated in Brazil with a combination of four antibiotics, which are taken for at least six months, ideally under directly observed therapy (Farmer 2004). Given the regulations on their use, doctors would be far less likely to prescribe this medication for someone they had not seen, and pharmacists would have more reservations about selling it over the counter. Maybe Analu had figured a way around these restrictions, found a sympathetic doctor, and secured a six-month supply. But I think it's more likely that 'strong medicine' referred to just one or two of these drugs, or else another, more accessible antibiotic.

These are the limits of contraband medicine. Without a clear diagnosis, treatment is always a gamble; even then, not every medication is accessible. In particular, the sale and use of drugs marked with a *tarja preta* (black stripe) are far more regulated than other prescription medications, making them much more difficult to procure outside the standard health system. Pills cannot stand in for other therapies, a public health intervention, or even a simple doctor's consultation. More than just pills, many illnesses required a complex treatment plan that was simply unavailable for those in prison. During research in one unit, I interviewed an incarcerated man who had been diagnosed with HIV before his imprisonment, and who was receiving medication regularly through the nurse technician. He had begun to feel weak, and wondered if he might need to increase his dosage or switch treatments. But without a conversation with a specialist and a test to measure his viral load, this would be impossible. In this case, contraband could not offer any solution for a man who wasn't quite sure what was wrong. A skin or ear infection might be obvious, but incarcerated people and their families had no way to respond to vague or intermittent symptoms. In the years following the completion of my fieldwork, Rio de Janeiro belatedly began implementing a national policy for prison healthcare, which expands the presence of medical professionals in most of the state's prisons. This change has improved access to healthcare, but it still does not meet the demand of an overcrowded system, guarantee the supply of medication, provide access to specialists, or produce comprehensive treatment plans. Beyond illness itself, contraband fortifies ties of solidarity across prison walls. While incarceration tears at the binds of kinship, crushing pills allowed Fátima to maintain a caring relationship with her husband, and to protect him from some of the harms of confinement. As such, it also preserved a sense of hope – not just that his blood pressure might drop, but that he might survive his prison sentence and make it out alive. Her case is not unique to Rio or Brazil; given the intrinsic harms of confinement, as well as the explosion in incarceration rates across Latin America, individuals and communities in the region improvise solutions to illness and disease, outside formal channels of distribution. At the same time, prison administrators and governments incorporate such practices, as they build new strategies to manage life and death in a time of mass incarceration.

Notes

1 Nurses can renew some prescriptions in Brazil, but they cannot write new ones.

2 In 2016, I was given access to reports detailing expired medication across various prisons in Rio de Janeiro in the previous year. These included basic materials including sterile water and ivermectin; substances were between six months and three years past their expiry dates.

3 In Brazil, the term *travesti* refers to those who are designated male at birth, but who cultivate feminine bodies and subjectivities. While some *travestis* also identify as trans women (*mulheres trans*), many do not.

4 In 2015, Rio's prison administration published a resolution outlining standards of treatment of incarcerated LGBT people. While it guarantees the right of transgender people and *travestis* to access and use of hormones like estradiol when accompanied by a prescription, the administration does not actually supply these treatments.

References

Augusto, Cristiane Brandão and Francisco Ortega. 2011. 'Nina Rodrigues e a patologização do crime no Brasil', *Revista Direito GV* 7(1): 221–36. Accessed 21 March 2024. https://doi.org/10.1590/S1808-24322011000100011.

Biehl, João. 2007. 'Pharmaceuticalization: AIDS treatment and global health politics', *Anthropological Quarterly* 80(4): 1083–126.

Chazkel, Amy. 2009. 'Social life and civic education in the Rio de Janeiro city jail', *Journal of Social History* 42(3): 697–731.

De Viggiani, Nick. 2007. 'Unhealthy prisons: Exploring structural determinants of prison health', *Sociology of Health & Illness* 29(1): 115–35. Accessed 21 March 2024. https://doi.org/10.1111/j.1467-9566.2007.00474.x.

Dias, Allister Andrew Teixeira. 2011. 'Páginas de ciência, crime e loucura: A trajetória e o projeto médico-intelectual de Heitor Carrilho (1930–1945)', *Temporalidades* 3(2): 78–97.

Farmer, Paul. 2004. *Pathologies of Power: Health, human rights, and the new war on the poor.* Berkeley: University of California Press.

Fontes, Anthony W. and Kevin L. O'Neill. 2019. 'La visita: Prisons and survival in Guatemala', *Journal of Latin American Studies* 51(1): 85–107. Accessed 21 March 2024. https://doi.org/10.1017/S0022216X18000731.

Freire, Lucas de Magalhães. 2023. 'A "justiça" e o acesso a medicamentos em tempos de desabastecimento', *Ilha Revista de Antropologia* 25(1): 43–61. Accessed 21 March 2024. https://doi.org/10.5007/2175-8034.2023.e85571.

Gilmore, Ruth Wilson. 2007. *Golden Gulag: Prisons, surplus, crisis, and opposition in globalizing California*. Berkeley: University of California Press.

Gilmore, Ruth Wilson. 2022. *Abolition Geography: Essays towards liberation*. London: Verso Books.

Hornblum, Allen M. 1998. *Acres of Skin: Human experiments at Holmesburg Prison*. London: Routledge. https://doi.org/10.4324/9780203903957.

Infopen. 2017. *Levantamento Nacional de Informações Penitenciárias*. Brasília: Ministério da Justiça.

Jean, Martine. 2017. '"A storehouse of prisoners": Rio de Janeiro's correction house (Casa de Correção) and the birth of the penitentiary in Brazil, 1830–1906', *Atlantic Studies* 14(2): 216–42.

Lopes, Mirella. 2021. 'Médico da Penitenciária de Alcaçuz é questionado por uso de medicação sem comprovação científica para tratar covid-19 entre presos.' *Saiba Mas*, 26 March. Accessed 21 March 2024. https://saibamais.jor.br/2021/03/medico-da-penitenciaria-de-alcacuz-e-questionado-por-uso-de-medicacao-sem-comprovacao-cientifica-para-tratar-covid-19-entre-presos/.

Massoglia, Michael. 2008. 'Incarceration, health, and racial disparities in health', *Law & Society Review* 42(2): 275–306.

Medeiros, Flavia. 2023. 'Matabilidade como forma de governo: Violências, desigualdades e Estado numa perspectiva comparativa entre Florianópolis e Rio de Janeiro', *Horizontes Antropológicos* 29(65), 1–36.

MEPCT – Mecanismo Estadual de Prevenção e Combate à Tortura do Rio de Janeiro. 2020. *Relatório Anual 2020*. Rio de Janeiro: Assembleia Legislativa do Estado do Rio de Janeiro.

Minayo, Maria Cecília de Souza and Adalgisa Peixoto Ribeiro. 2016. 'Condições de saúde dos presos do estado do Rio de Janeiro', *Ciências e Saúde Coletiva* 21(7): 2031–40. Accessed 21 March 2024. https://doi.org/10.1590/1413-81232015217.08552016.

O Globo. 2021. '"Errei e peço desculpas": Diz Xuxa sobre sugestão de teste de vacina em presidários', 27 March. Accessed 21 March 2024. https://oglobo.globo.com/ela/gente/errei-peco-desculpas-diz-xuxa-sobre-sugestao-de-teste-de-vacina-em-presidarios-24944418.

Sánchez, Alejandra, Celina Roma Sánchez de Toledo, Luiz Antônio Bastos Camacho and Bernard Larouze. 2021. 'Mortalidade e causas de óbito nas prisões do Rio de Janeiro, Brasil', *Cadernos de Saúde Pública* 37(9). Accessed 21 March 2024. https://doi.org/10.1590/0102-311X00224920.

Skarbek, David. 2014. *The Social Order of the Underworld: How prison gangs govern the American penal system*. New York: Oxford University Press.

Spector-Bagdady, Kayte and Paul A. Lombardo. 2019. 'U.S. Public Health Service STD experiments in Guatemala (1946–1948) and their aftermath', *Ethics & Human Research* 41(2): 29–34. Accessed 21 March 2024. https://doi.org/10.1002/eahr.500010.

Sufrin, Carolyn. 2017. *Jailcare: Finding the safety net for women behind bars*. Oakland: University of California Press.

Sykes, Gresham M. 2007. *The Society of Captives: A study of a maximum security prison*. Rev. ed. Princeton: Princeton University Press.

Xavier, Lucia. 2018. '"As cartas não mentem jamais": Quando o direito humano à saude é negado'. In *Vozes do Cárcere: Ecos da resisência política*, edited by Thulia Pires and Felipe Freitas, 329–56. Rio de Janeiro: Kitabu.

8

Intermediaries in the Haitian *wout*: the dynamics of (im)mobilities in the Americas

Mélanie Montinard

This chapter examines the experiences and dynamics of Haitian mobility and – drawing on the narratives collected during my research – explores the different *wout* (routes/roads/ways, in Haitian Creole) that Haitians have taken across boundaries and borders, specifically from Brazil, to *chache lavi* (pursue life) in their quest for *lavi miyò* (a better life).[1] In so doing, I argue that the term *wout* becomes crucial, both as a native category constitutive of Haitian mobility, and as a way of reframing the experiences of Haitian migrants, to add more nuance to their lived experiences of mobility and identity across and between places. These *wout* might be seen as corridors of contraband by state actors, whereby migrants effectively smuggle their own bodies across borders, yet this chapter will show how, for Haitians, these migration routes across state borders become strategic paths towards *dyaspora* (diaspora), to create transnational family networks.

Since 2010, Brazil has become a place of transit for numerous Haitian migrants seeking to reach French Guiana (Joseph 2015a). The country has thus become part of the Haitian socio-geographic space, and a place of passage and residence inserted within the broader collection of landscapes that map the diverse *wout* undertaken by Haitians to *chache lavi*. It is important to consider Haitian society through the diaspora that is constitutive of it (Joseph 2015a; 2015b; Glick-Schiller 2011), recognizing there is no singular event that produced or provoked migration, but rather a historical series of departures and migratory flows. These comprise a set of different economic, social, cultural, political, and environmental factors. Around 59 per cent of the population of Haiti lives on an income below US$2.41 per day, according to a World Bank household survey conducted in 2012. The authoritarian regimes of François Duvalier and Jean-Claude Duvalier, from 1957–86, and the political crises that followed, caused a series of crises within the country (see Zolberg et al. 1989), as have natural disasters such as the earthquake of January 2010. All these factors intertwine to make Haiti a country constructed and reconstructed through departures and mobility.[2]

For more than a century, Haitians have been attempting to reach the United States (one of the preferred destinations) to escape economic and political problems at home (Anglade 1982; Joseph 2015a). This migratory flow has become more intense and complex since the end of 2015, due to an economic recession in Brazil which directly affected those Haitians living in the country who had benefitted from the high demand for workers due to international events like the World Cup in 2014 and the Olympic Games in 2016. In this context, new migratory projects have opened up, such as the *wout Miami* (Miami road, see also Cearns, Chapter 10, this volume) or *pran wout la* (to take to the road), both expressions used by Haitians to refer to someone who has set off to reach the United States, traversing the borders of diverse South American and Central American countries in order to realize the dream of becoming *dyaspora*.

As I have discussed elsewhere (Montinard 2019), *pran wout la* cannot be reduced to a single voyage from Brazil to the United States, nor to a specific decision, or a specific itinerary that incorporates representations of countries such as the United States, Haiti, Brazil, Chile, Mexico, the Dominican Republic, Canada, among many other contexts. The expression denotes both a pragmatics of mobility and a state of being and becoming within the contemporary Haitian diaspora, making the term *wout* a native or analytical category for the purposes of comprehending the dynamics of the network of mobility:

> *Pran wout la* is a becoming, a state of construction, a mode of being in movement that includes physical and symbolic dimensions and can take constitutive derivatives of mobility (like *ouvè wout la* – 'open the road,' or *kite wout la* – 'abandon the road,' among others), as a way of being in different spaces and moments of mobility. (Montinard 2019, 257)

An analysis of the native category *wout* through its own terms and contexts within individual trajectories in perpetual motion – and an exploration of the different relations and (im)balances of logics within such mobility – is as much a challenge for ethnographic study as it is a rich analytic source for an ethnographic theory of mobility. Indeed, the ethnographic study presented in this chapter unfolded in multiple places and in movement, which posed unique methodological challenges, only made possible because of my multiple insertions in the Haitian networks to which I belong in diverse ways, where I myself am implicated in Haitian networks of discussions on public policies for migration. Thus, my own research necessarily has a self-analytic or auto-ethnographic dimension, which forces me to consider the different commitments and places I occupy, and the way in which I am perceived by the different agents who form part of this analysed social landscape. In this sense, within my own ethnographic experience, the dimension of 'participatory objectification' is inseparable from that of 'observant participation' (Bourdieu 1991; 2003).

During my field research between Haiti, Brazil and the United States, I was able to observe the meanings of the word *wout*, a term used by Haitians either on the move or those preparing for a (new) departure. The word *wout* can have both physical and symbolic dimensions. When, at the end of 2015, the expression *wout Miami* appeared in the everyday life of those Haitians in Brazil who had set off for the United States, the term *wout* also became part of the vocabulary of Haitian mobility via the expression *pran wout la* (taking the road), blurring the boundaries between these separate dimensions. Inquiring into the meanings and uses of the native concept *wout* thus entails connecting the pragmatics of mobility to the pragmatics of the diaspora, as described by Joseph (2015a; 2015b) or Glick-Schiller (2011). *Pran wout la* (taking the road) is not only the journey undertaken by a person between departure and arrival, between staying and leaving again, or between individual and collective strategies in navigating the physical, symbolic and collective dimensions of the *wout*. The term also relates to a sense of privilege for those people who are on the *wout:* they construct the meanings of the word 'diaspora' as a process of forging success for oneself, despite suffering or considerable challenges (*pase mizè*). Success is not always defined by obtaining a job or making a good living. It may have other meanings: for example, when a father brings his wife and son to live with him in Brazil, when two people marry in the church or when their child is born in Brazil, when someone arrives in Miami, when another is promoted to a managerial position, when someone obtains a master's degree or publishes a book – numerous possibilities that denote something beyond the purely economic sense of success.

The notion of success within the diaspora can take many forms and vary from one individual to another. Jennifer Cearns has highlighted the role of transnational networks in the construction and recognition of success within the Cuban diaspora (2023, chapter 2). The relationships established within these networks provide opportunities for artistic collaboration, resource sharing and mutual support, contributing to the personal and professional fulfilment of individuals. Cearns's work also emphasizes that the definition of success can evolve over time and be influenced by social, economic and political dynamics. The pressures and expectations of the host society (but also by the society and family of the home country – see also Olwig 2012), as well as the connections maintained with the country of origin, can play a role in how individuals perceive and seek success within the diaspora. For some people, success may be measured by economic and financial achievements, such as establishing prosperous businesses or holding positions of power and influence in their host or transit country. For others, success may be defined by the preservation and promotion of the culture abroad, maintaining strong connections with the community and contributing to the dissemination of art, music, literature and other forms of cultural expression.

Hence, *pran wout la* corresponds above all to representations of being (in the) diaspora, being able to plan the project of bringing a relative or visiting Haiti, being able to regularly send money transfers to family (in this case, in US dollars, considered a 'strong' currency), for example. The extensive literature on remittances explores the different dimensions of money transfers by migrants, highlighting their determinants, their economic and social effects and their implications for development, migration and the diaspora (see Fouratt 2017; Burman 2006; Åkesson 2011; Levitt 2001; Levitt and Lamba-Nieves 2011; Madianou 2017; Kwon 2015; Baldassar 2015). It was these representations, this dream of becoming diaspora, that opened up the road (*ouvè wout la*) for thousands of Haitians living in Brazil.

When *pran wout la* leads to Miami

A few weeks before Pipo announced to me his intention to leave Brazil (*pran wout la*), the Brazilian government had published its decision, in the Federal Official Gazette, to regularize the legal status of nearly 44,000 Haitians, the vast majority of whom had entered across the Amazonian borders.[3] Although the economic recession had started to be felt in Brazil, most of the Haitians at the end of 2015 were formally employed (OBMigra 2016). By 2015, the Haitian population had become the largest foreign nationality in the formal labour market in Brazil, having increased from 815 immigrants in 2011, to 33,154 in 2015 – that is 26.4 per cent of the total immigrant labour force. While the end of 2015 presented a positive balance sheet, in terms of a certain willingness to integrate Haitian nationals within Brazil, new routes were already emerging within Haitian networks, in response to an imaginary where *chache lavi* was only possible in the land of Uncle Sam.

Pipo's journey reveals the physical and symbolic dimensions of the *wout Miami*, mobilizing personal and collective resources, strategies, encounters, chance and fate, the *lwa* (spirits) or the hopes in *Bondye* (God), when obstacles like mountains appear ahead, and where borders become not only physical but symbolic. On one of my trips to Florida, when I went to visit him in Margate, Pipo told me the details of his experience on the *wout Miami*. The conversation began in a rather serious tone: 'Everyone has experienced this *wout* in a different way. For me, this was a trip, you know. I'm a Rasta, I must approach each stage of life in a positive way and believe in myself, believe that I shall succeed.' Pipo had opted to turn to his Rastafarian beliefs; positivity would accompany each stage of the *wout* and provide him with the courage and strength to face even the most difficult obstacles. This decision earned him a position of leadership throughout the *wout*, becoming the head of a group that had to cross somewhat turbulent waters on makeshift boats (*lancha*) and over mountains to reach Panama.

After a few days' journey by bus from Quito (Ecuador), Pipo had set out, like thousands of other people, on the road leading to Medellin (Colombia), to obtain a 30-day pass from the Colombian migration authorities that would allow him to continue his journey, in search of the 'American dream', legally. Arriving in Turbo, a town situated on the Caribbean coast in the north of Colombia, on the shores of the Gulf of Urabá (which is the point of departure for *la lancha* to reach Capurgana, also in Colombia), Pipo met a woman whose face he recognized. She had been the owner of the house that his mother used to rent in the centre of the Gonaïves, a town in the north of Haiti, where Pipo was originally from. This sudden re-encounter transported him momentarily to Haiti. As his memories flooded back, Pipo told me how this woman had helped him, his mother and his young brother, when his father left Haiti for the United States, to *canter* (transport people by boat),[4] revealing the deep bonds of solidarity between the two families. During their reunion, they swapped news about those who still remained in Haiti, those who had died, and those who had taken the *wout* to Brazil, Chile, or the United States, each one trying their luck in search of a *lavi miyò*. But very quickly their conversation turned to the details of the organization of the *wout Miami* and the strategies that should be employed to cross the Gulf of Urabá and traverse the mountains, rivers, and dense vegetation to reach Panama: strategies that are primarily linked to the composition and choice of group. Often, Pipo told me, joining a group with children or women for a sea crossing or a trek on foot under very difficult conditions was risky, because they slowed progress and complained far more. The choice and composition of the group was, however, based on the need for women to be present to cook for the rest of the group, which should ideally be composed of strong people capable of enduring the extremely harsh conditions of the voyage. Through understanding Pipo's reconnection with this old family connection, we see how Haitian kinship structures and notions of a transnational family affect Haitians' experience of *wout*. Family relationships, gender roles and kinship relations play a central role in decision-making and the organization of migratory movements, while gender norms and social expectations can influence the migration patterns, opportunities and constraints that men and women face when they decide to migrate.

Reaching Panama from Turbo was known as the deadliest section of the *wout Miami*, passing through the green hell of Darién, a region controlled by paramilitary groups and drug traffickers. Videos and photos provoked intense discussions on the Facebook and WhatsApp groups to which I belonged, depicting and testifying to the extreme conditions involved in the crossing, showing a dense Amazonian rainforest inhabited by wildlife and vegetation unfamiliar to Haitians. This frontier, situated in a hostile tropical environment called the Darién Gap, is extremely difficult to cross, with no road enabling passage from one country to the other – it is also the only missing link on the Pan-American Highway. From Turbo, most migrants cross the Panamanian border clandestinely either by land, trekking through the Darién jungle for days, or by sea, taking a commercial boat to cross the Gulf of Urabá. According to some stories collected through social networks, many were unable to endure such extreme conditions, where risks for inexperienced and poorly equipped hikers abound, including criminal groups, wild animals, diseases, starvation or dehydration. The weakest died, abandoned on the path, to the cries and tears of their relatives, powerless to help and forced to continue their journey.

So this chance encounter undoubtedly marked the decision of Pipo and the woman to continue on the road together, as though 'God had sent this person to find me' – *se Bondye ki voye moun sa bay mwen* – Pipo said to me. While the woman saw in Pipo a young, resourceful man, with a positive spirit, whom she trusted because she had known him as a child, Pipo saw in her a strong and courageous woman (*fanm vayan*) who could take care of him, cook for him, help him, or nurse him when necessary. A group of a dozen people was formed, and the women took charge of buying useful accessories, keeping everything as simple as possible, so as not to overload the rucksacks, but including enough for everyone's basic survival needs.

Pipo and his travel companions planned the boat trip across the Gulf of Urabá, which would cost US$200 per person – a dangerous journey that would last around eight hours and would oblige them to complete the *wout* on foot, to reach Panama. Pipo smiled as he explained to me that boarding *la lancha* had taken as long as the crossing, which would take two and a half hours, because they had to weigh the baggage. Each kilo overweight had to be paid, and everyone was advised to wrap their things in trash bags to protect them. Once at sea, however, the motor of *la lancha* stopped, and then started again after a few minutes as though nothing had happened – *la lancha* had three motors that operated one after the other to save fuel. The sea journey included an overnight stopover on an island, to refuel and rest, because the slightest swell, even on a relatively calm sea, made the boat lurch, pounding violently, pitching like a walnut shell flush to the water's surface and throwing around the passengers, who screamed in fear, many of them unable to swim, and most of them seasick.

After eventually arriving at Capurgana, the group led by Pipo set out again on foot to cross the mountains and jungle, a story that he told me with a lump in his throat, revealing that *chache lavi* can also become mixed with the meanings and practices of the *mistik* (magic, mystic) when the *wout* involves confronting extreme travel conditions, inducing people to take solace in their only hopes, like their Bible, prayers or rituals. To reach Panama, the group had to march for five days across the mountains, traversing rivers in flood, wading through mud, sleeping with one eye open in the jungle to watch out for scorpions, vipers or other poisonous snakes. In Capurgana, Pipo had negotiated the voyage for US$250 per person with a Colombian guide. He told me that the small Colombian town had a vibrant market for smuggling undocumented migrants across: 'It's a market, they know that you're a foreigner and they approach you telling their price. Then you can negotiate. It's a full-blown business in the region.' Sometimes it was necessary to wait days or even weeks to negotiate with smugglers, who refused to enter the mountains on foot due to the military operations undertaken by the Panama government to combat drug trafficking in the Darién Gap region.

Then, people would say, *la selva come* – the jungle eats – meaning that the jungle can eat those who venture into it, by means of heavy rain, military operations, or the presence of paramilitary groups or drug traffickers.

Once the negotiation was done, the Colombian guide asked Pipo to organize his group. The important thing was to have water and to wear boots for walking in case of rain. They set off following the guide, who carried a machete to cut through the foliage and clear a path for the rest of the group. Pipo's account told of a trek on which it was difficult to breathe due to the heat and humidity, even though the guide had planned a break every 30 minutes for them to rest. It was important for the Colombian guides to know the composition of the group they would have to guide as far as the Panamanian frontier, since the reputation of their business could be jeopardized. Sometimes, Pipo laughed, 'when we took a break to catch our breath and rest, the *endyen* [referring to the Indigenous Colombian guide] would ask us to take photos or make videos with our mobile phones to show our families that we were fine, that they were treating us well. But it was primarily to send messages to those who were still behind, saying that so-and-so was a good guy, a good contact, and that once they arrived in Capurgana they should ask for him and make a deal to cross the border.'

But Pipo confided to me that this *raketè* (here: *endyen*, literally 'Indian', a Haitian word to define an intermediary agent, such as a Colombian guide)[5] abandoned them after a few hours of trekking – without doubt, he said, because the group was too slow owing to the presence of young children – and the group found itself alone, lost, without map or compass, with no idea which direction to take. As panic and fear set in, the children cried without understanding what was happening, the women screamed, Bible in hand, imploring *Bondye* (God) to save them from this dire situation and not to abandon them. But Pipo told me that as the group's leader, he could not let emotions run wild and allow the group to disband: it was up to him to find a solution for them all to survive and reach Panama. He quickly decided to separate them into two groups, walking in parallel, but at a certain distance so that one could communicate with the other by shouting.

Before resuming the trek, Pipo explained to me, he had spent some time talking to his female companion, asking her to persuade the rest of the group to once again back his decision, confiding to her that he had heard a kind of voice, a *ti zwazo* (little bird), singing to tell him the path to follow. It was then that Pipo told me that the woman was a *manbo* (a Vodou priestess) and so she understood and, even with few things at hand, knew how to prepare a ritual to ask for the protection of the ancestors, the *lwa* who would accompany them along the journey until they arrived safe and sound. Pipo related that she gathered up some plants (*fèy*) and boiled them in water on a fire that she made with three stones (*wòch*) at the foot of a tree (*pyebwa*) that she had carefully chosen. It was not a question simply of *fè maji* (making magic) by combining the important elements of Vodou like *fèy, wòch* or *pyebwa*, but rather of approaching the *lwa* and asking them for protection to *ouvè wout la* (open the way) and help them overcome the obstacles that presented themselves.

For five days, the song of *ti zwazo* guided Pipo and the group as far as Panama, where some spent three weeks while others had to stay three months, depending on the government's position in the management of these irregular migrants. While hearing the song of a *ti zwazo* or practising a ritual had the sense of a request for protection from the spirits or ancestors, to confront the impasses of the *wout*, reciting evangelical prayers from a Bible that someone had slipped into their backpack as an object guaranteeing their protection, was also a means of pleading for *Bondye* to save them. *Pran wout la* was thus accompanied by elements of a collective dimension at a spiritual and transcendental level, where rituals and objects were necessary for the safety of individuals over the course of their journey, some even practising this ritual before their departure (see also Richmann 2005, 152).

In his work exploring the dynamics of mobility and associated narratives in the northern Caribbean region, Jeffrey Kahn (2019) examines the cosmographies of mobility, focusing on smugglers, migrants and local beliefs. He shows how these elements are interwoven and influence the perceptions and decisions of the actors involved in migratory movements. Kahn's work explores the different representations and perceptions of smugglers, describing them as both heroes and demons, depending on the points of view of the different social actors, and highlights how stories and legends of demons and evil spirits are often used to explain the difficulties and dangers encountered during clandestine travel. These beliefs influence the perceptions of migrants and smugglers (or *raketè*), as well as the decisions they make throughout the migration process. In a similar vein, Pipo's narrative as recounted here invokes networks and activities that many states or other academic disciplines would call 'people smuggling', but which, when considered through an ethnographic lens, should arguably also be understood as part of a deep, cultural understanding of life: of 'becoming' *through* mobility.

Reaching Panama is not easy for Haitian migrants, and the declaration of the Panamanian government on 9 May 2016, banning the entry of Haitian and Cuban nationals coming from Colombia, further complicated the *wout* for thousands of individuals who wanted to cross the country to subsequently reach the United States. This was a new impasse on the *wout Miami*, that led to the invention of new strategies to reach the border at the expense of negotiating a higher price. When Pipo arrived in Panama in the small and impoverished village of Yaviza, they were welcomed by the Indigenous community who had little to offer them. They negotiated crossing the border with police officers for US$100 each. Pipo then took a bus to Paso Canoas, on the frontier with Costa Rica, where he split from the group. Pipo waited a few days while his father sent him US$500 by international transfer, an amount that enabled him to negotiate the services of another *raketè* to reach the Nicaraguan border at Peñas Blancas, a journey known by the name of *la ruta del tráfico* – the trafficking route – due to the circulation of drugs, illegal merchandise, and even human trafficking. Located near the Pacific coast, permitting entry into Nicaragua via a narrow strip of land, Peñas Blancas is the sole point of passage by land between the two countries. The waiting time might last between three to four months for some people, while others opt for one of the various clandestine means of crossing the border: on foot over the mountains (for a sum of US$1,000 to US$1,200), by truck or bus (for a sum of US$1,500 to US$1,800), or by boat via Los Chiles (for a sum of US$900),[6] often putting their own lives at risk.

While some gave up their jobs and used the money from their redundancy pay or their unemployment benefit to purchase an air ticket from Rio de Janeiro to Rio Branco and then finance their *wout* from the Peruvian border to Quito (Ecuador), others bought their air ticket using a loan from their bank account, or borrowed from their friends living in Brazil. But embarking on the *wout* and travelling up through various countries to get to Miami demands a certain guarantee that the individuals have opportunities to receive money from relatives already living in the diaspora, to fund each stage where the money transfer market has taken off, especially in Quito (Ecuador), Peñas Blancas (Costa Rica) and Tijuana (Mexico). Thus, the clandestine *rakèt* market fuels the negotiations between the *raketè* and the people on the *wout*, who must appeal to family members living in the diaspora to raise the money to obtain papers, or pay to cross the border from one country to another. The more people wishing to cross a border, like the case of Peñas Blancas between May and September 2016, the higher the price demanded by the *raketè*, in this instance increasing to US$1,800 per person. In general, the *wout Miami* lasts between three and six months and costs around US$7,500 per person on average, according to the information I obtained from lengthy conversations in the WhatsApp groups that marked the everyday life of Haitians in Brazil during the first half of 2016, as well as from the stories that people told me personally, both in Miami and in Haiti. The duration of the journey and the cost of funding it – evoked by individuals through the expression *fanmi-m ap ede-m* (my family will help me) – vary according to the intensity of the flows over time: the stronger the demand, the higher the price asked for by the local *raketè* and the shorter the length of the voyage.

While Pipo cited Peru as a *vye peyi, peyi lèd*, to say that the country is ugly, unattractive, and not a good place to live or even transit through, he defined Honduras and Guatemala as countries where it was easy to transit illegally for around US$150, although he was quick to recall scenes of violence too. His story narrated, with an air of resignation, the attempts of the local border authorities or the *raketè* to negotiate cash for a pass from Peru to Guatemala, and once he arrived on Mexican soil, a certain relief took over as a new *wout* loomed, this time administrative in kind, organized between the Mexican and US immigration authorities. Once he was registered as a Haitian national by the Mexican Federal Police services and had obtained a 20-day pass, Pipo undertook a new trip of a few days by bus to arrive at the Tijuana–San Diego border, where the local humanitarian services were deployed to receive and shelter migrants while they awaited the hearing at the immigration court that would rule on their application for asylum or refuge. In the meantime, they would wait, a tracking device on their ankle.

At the foot of the wire mesh fence that marks the border between Tijuana and San Diego, many were hesitant to cross the border after the US government declared, on 22 September 2016, the resumption of deportations for Haitians living irregularly in the United States.[7] The messages sent by the US authorities to these migrants and asylum seekers, who they allowed to enter while promising to expel them, plunged them into uncertainty. On the verge of reaching the end of their *wout*, an epic crossing of half of the American continent, from Brazil to Baja California, they were left standing at the San Ysidro border post, on the US side, where they applied to live in the United States, despite the high risk of being sent back to Haiti. Some were discouraged from attempting to cross the border, and saw their hopes turn to dust as they decided to remain in Tijuana, at the foot of the fence, trapped between the sea and the desert. They had never imagined staying in Mexico, far from the idea they had of the American dream, the dream of becoming successful diaspora.

Like most of those on the *wout Miami* and who were heard by the US immigration officials in San Diego, Pipo spent four months in a detention centre, before being released in November 2016. Once out, he joined his father, in Margate, Florida, with whom he has lived ever since. He waited close to six months before obtaining his work permit, a period he used to take an English course. During those few months, he attended three court interviews, accompanied by a lawyer hired by his father for US$500, where he was asked to provide proof of his asylum request or his request for family reunion. It was in January 2018 that the courts granted him temporary US residence (for two years) based on family reunion.

Ultimately, being (in the) diaspora does not just entail sending money or goods to those still living in Haiti, or realizing a social project or organizing the voyage of a family member. It also means showing the fact publicly on social media, revealing the behavioural, moral, social and symbolic value of the success of the *wout*, so many characteristics definitive of the diaspora person in the Haitian imaginary, where the idea of *gwo dyaspora* (grand diaspora) is only possible when living in *gwo peyi* (economically wealthy countries) like the United States. *Chache lavi* is only truly possible, therefore, outside the terrestrial borders of Haiti, making mobility a resource cultivated to achieve the individual's social, economic and cultural progress.

Intermediaries in Haitians' *wout*

Based on an ethnography of the experiences of mobility of people on the *wout Miami*, my aim here has been to detail the different strategies used by Haitian nationals to cross borders increasingly regulated by the different nation states of the Americas. The *wout* may be long, fragmented, dangerous, and perhaps even redefined throughout the process; the destination may change en route. The processes of mobility are then interrupted by regimes of immobility that prevent migrants from moving in the desired directions, effectively creating an involuntary immobility (Carling 2001) that becomes the reality for many people who venture on the *wout*. This impossibility of continuing the journey, added to the shame of returning to the country of origin without having succeeded in becoming *dyaspora*, has led to a reconfiguration of border towns and the dynamic of internal migrations on the American continent. In this context, as in the lived contexts of migration and refugee groups in many other parts of the region and the wider world, intermediaries become fundamental agents of mobility.[8] Intermediaries are central in the classic anthropological literature on migration and mobility, when considering political and economic relations at a local level, and are generally defined as 'brokers' (see Gluckman et al. 1949; Fallers 1955; Wolf 1956; Geertz 1960). The *raketè*, therefore, occupies a prominent place in these mobility narratives, not only as what many would consider an illegal agent, but also for being a facilitator of people's mobility in the *wout*, to overcome the legal or material restrictions that generate situations of immobility. *Raketè*, Colombian guides, illegal agents, coyotes, smugglers, intermediaries, facilitators, people who help, experts; there are many interchangeable terms in the narratives of Haitian people on the *wout*, regarding the context and the success rate of a paid service. This ethnographic emphasis contributes to a more nuanced reflection of how people navigate life and physical journeys (*wout*). This figure, that my interlocutors generally called a *raketè*, is usually simplified within academic literature and by agents of international organizations and governments as a mere 'coyote' or people smuggler, and, for this reason, the figure of the *raketè* has been the object of denunciation in the context of combating international trafficking or smuggling. However, this criminalizing bias has obstructed a more accurate perception of the complexity of the *raketè* in the dynamics of (im)mobilities. In certain contexts, for example, these people make mobility possible, intermediating routes, documents, tickets and information, whether acting as individuals (*kontak, m konn moun, m gen moun* – contact, I know people, I have people), or as institutions (*ajans* or *ajans vwayaj* – travel agency) (Montinard 2019, 205–10). In this way, I argue, these are crucial terms for a better understanding of the dynamics of Haitian mobility, both originating in Haiti and abroad, and revive discussions around 'governmentality', defined by Michel Foucault as:

> The set formed by institutions, procedures, analyses and reflections, the calculations and tactics that allow the exercise of that quite specific, though very complex, form of power which has as its main object the population, as its major form of knowledge the political economy, as its essential instrument the security devices. (Foucault 2004, 111–12)

Raketè operate in parallel to the state, and have formed their own sort of institutionalized procedures and strategies, informally, to enable mobility across what I call 'impasses'. The use of the category *raketè* is not restricted to the fields of Haitian migration or mobility, but serves more to designate an individual who charges money in return for their services, which generally requires them to carry out various stages of intermediate transactions to achieve the goal of the initial negotiation. The *raketè* is therefore seen by my interlocutors as an expert, who takes economic benefit from his ability to control various mechanisms and tricks in a context of informality. In Haiti, the figure of the *raketè* is very often associated with a category of accusation, synonymous with the thief (*volè*), where mistrust is important in the eyes of the people who negotiate his services. For example, people say that the *raketè 'manje tout sa m te posede'* – ate everything I owned – meaning that he has taken everything, that he has 'eaten' all the money or possessions that a person may have, without actually providing the service for which he was paid. The choice to contract or negotiate the services of a *raketè* also often reveals a feeling of resignation (*rezinye*) for many people, who face a formal system that is restrictive and not fit for purpose.

In this sense, an issue that stands out in the ethnographic narrative of this research is the constant relationship of Haitians with the most distinct processes of migratory governmentality underway throughout the American continent, most particularly in Brazil. In the different physical *wout* they travel along, unusual routes are used, and practices are constructed in constant reaction to attempts at state regulation and intervention. As pointed out in the introduction to this volume, the informal and the formal mutually inform one another. This contact with control structures appears in the choice of extremely dangerous and expensive routes, as well as in the use of the services of the *raketè*, increasingly disseminated in the migratory routine of different groups and individuals. Regimes of (im)mobility emerge, for example, detention centres for foreigners, and announcements of deportation in the United States (Montinard 2019, 223–33), and the actions of international agencies in modulating the control of populations, such as the role of the International Organization for Migration (IOM) in Haiti (Montinard 2019, 297–315). These regimes of (im)mobility arguably result from the practical consequences of the distinct prohibitions of Haitian mobility in Central America, the Brazilian government's actions in restricting the mobility of people requesting refugee status, as well as a set of strategies by Haitian nationals to counteract the control practices engendered by state devices.

These regimes of immobility can also refer to the return to Haiti. This return remains an almost impossible option, however, as returnees are considered a failure in the eyes of those who stayed in Haiti or in the transition country such as Brazil: they have failed in the search for *chache lavi* for themselves and their families. When deportation caught up with them, some of my interlocutors took different decisions: some chose not to stay in the United States and went to Canada, as a *chimen dekoupe* (shortcut route), while others, illegally in the United States, launched themselves into a *rezistans* (resistance) movement, referring to an ideal of individual and collective change, and others returned to Brazil. Once they had arrived in the United States, some went in search of their first job, to send money to Haiti, others worked for a few months and tried to save enough money to finance a new *wout*, which might take them to Canada, and many were deported back to Haiti. Deportation (or its threat) diverts the *wout* of many people, some of them preferring to wait on the Mexican border at Tijuana, others (in prison or released on bail) waiting for their appointment at the US court, to appear before the judge who will rule on their application for asylum or refugee status. Finally, others are provisionally released on US soil, fear in their stomach that they will be deported before even obtaining a court ruling, and undertake the *wout* to the north of New York State to enter Canada, a border country offering a more favourable immigration policy and where the risks of deportation are lower.

In the ethnographic narrative of my research, the departure from, or even the return to Brazil, shows how strategies for crossing physical, symbolic, or technological borders almost always resort to the *raketè*, a constitutive element of Haitian mobility, deeply anchored in networks and cultural practices. Although these forms may refer, for some, to a criminal and sometimes even violent organization, the *raketè* is a figure that has always existed in the history of Haitian migration. Its contemporary practices can take different forms, such as a *kontak* (contact), a *rezo* (network), people or institutions facilitating the diffusion of information that will be stitched together along a confusing discourse, which makes people continue to believe that *chache lavi* is only possible outside Haiti's borders.

The ambiguities surrounding the figure of the intermediaries, in particular the *raketè*, are revealed in the complex relations that individuals and families may have with them, sometimes being a friend, a neighbour, a family member or someone recommended by someone else, a representative of a public authority or from civil society, among others. This multiplicity of relations between intermediaries and migrants raises issues of loyalty, obligation, reputation and secrecy, which go far beyond a simple market relation in which people pay for a service. The ambiguities surrounding the forms potentially taken by the *raketè* become meaningful insofar as they also represent an alternative to increasingly rigid legal procedures, an opportunity to access and open new *wout*, linked to negotiations with people on the move, to the economic and emotional projections of a migration project for *chache lavi* and to the pressures of migration control institutions.

Migration controls, national variations and constantly changing policies force migrants to deal with intermediaries and 'experts' such as *raketè*. It is necessary not only to describe the public policies related to migration issues in each country through which Haitians migrating via Brazil move, but also to understand the subjective experiences and representations that individuals have towards these policies while on the move. It is necessary to observe the relationships between people who circulate in the *wout*, sometimes in groups, the *raketè* that facilitate crossing borders or obtain a document, the strategies developed by individuals to pass from one border to another, the state agencies and security bodies, border police or immigration officers and other government agents.

This chapter has not only revealed the complexity of the modes of organization that Haitians must navigate to migrate, but also raised questions concerning the national and transnational circulations that may characterize such dispersions, giving rise to strategies in which spatial extension is itself used as a resource (Ma Mung 1999). Through description and ethnographic analysis of the dynamics of mobility articulated across such networks, told through the stories of people who were leaving or had left Haiti, we see how activities often termed as 'people smuggling' also energize discourses of a search for a better life. The mobility of those who leave can contribute to the immobility of those who stay, and vice versa, especially when those who embark on the *wout* participate by sending money for the maintenance of those remaining behind, or when those who stay behind or who already live abroad participate in financing those who leave to embark on a new *wout*. Exploring the *wout* on which people set out means talking about the search for a full life, about the individual and collective mechanisms and strategies that are reinvented and developed over time within networks and spaces in which creativity, hopes and uncertainties coexist, sometimes generating strong tensions and frustrations. These strategies and mechanisms define the dynamics of mobility, forcing us to (re)think territories, relations and people.

A hierarchy thus exists between the different physical and symbolic *wout*, forming an economic and geopolitical hierarchy, both for people living in Haiti and for those Haitians living abroad. From one individual to another, a *wout* may assume different dimensions and be modified over its course, making it a mobile category – not static, associated with a territory in a dichotomous manner as though a clear separation existed between the places of origin and the places of destination. The return to a known or original territory is the story of many Haitians who have taken *wout* filled with obstacles, some ending up deported while others have become *dyaspora*. *Pran wout la* is indeed a becoming, a state of construction, a mode of being in movement, which can assume derivations constitutive of mobility (like *ouvè wout la, kite wout la*, among others) as a way of being in different spaces and moments of mobility (Biehl and Locke 2017, 6).

Chache lavi means knowing how to live well (*byen viv*) in the new country of residence and can thus take the form of a search for a better life, a quest to realize one's dream of becoming *dyaspora* one day, where individual and collective strategies are constantly reinvented and rethought around new *wout*. Moreover, while many of the strategies employed by Haitians to pursue a better life might be considered illegal by states and formal institutions, the ethnographic material in this chapter also points to an alternative perspective, whereby navigating the *wout* becomes a strategy to live one's life, drawing on socio-economic networks of kinship and relatedness to follow the path.

Notes

1 This research formed part of my PhD in Social Anthropology at the Museu Nacional of the Federal University of Rio de Janeiro (PPGAS/MN/UFRJ).
2 The first Black republic in the world to be born from the revolt of slaves, Haiti is today considered the poorest country in the Americas.
3 Brazil responded to the 'problem' of the flows of Haitian migrants through government decisions like Normative Resolution n. 97 of 2012, Ministry of Labour and Employment (MTE 2012) which 'provides for the granting of a permanent visa as stipulated under Article 16 of Law n. 6.815, of August 19, 1980, for Haitian nationals' or the interministerial decree of 2015 (section 1, p. 48) granting residence to nearly 44,000 people. Also see Vieira (2014 and 2017).
4 '*Li te pran dlo*', Pipo would say to me, an expression meaning that a person has ventured on a *wout* by sea.
5 The *raketè* occupy a dominant place in the tales of mobility, less because of their potential status as 'illegal agents', and more because of their role as actors and facilitators of the mobility of people on the *wout* who may face legal or material restrictions, thereby leading to situations of immobility. The *raketè* is an integral element of Haitian mobility, deeply rooted in social networks and cultural practices.
6 A three-day trip if the smuggler carries out his mission honestly, since many would abandon the group halfway, forcing its members to turn back and pay for the services of another *raketè*.
7 Article from the *Miami Herald*, 22 September 2016 (Charles 2016).
8 See the documentary by Carlos Sandoval Garcia, 'Casa en Tierra Ajena' (2017), which tells of the life stories and dreams of Nicaraguans forced to emigrate to North America. https://www.youtube.com/watch?v=AkrZIumTRjI&fbclid=IwAR377JOnVTqlIraDeT4yhbGgToljPplXwc5cbk7-E9wxv9ZlOwXhX3iMlHY. Accessed 22 March 2024.

References

Åkesson, Lisa. 2011. 'Remittances and relationships: Exchange in Cape Verdean transnational families', *Ethnos* 76: 326–47.

Anglade, Georges. 1982. *Espace et liberté en Haïti*. Montreal: ERCE & CRC.

Baldassar, Loretta. 2015. 'Guilty feelings and the guilt trip: Emotions and motivation in migration and transnational caregiving', *Emotion, Space and Society* 16: 81–9.

Biehl, João and Peter Locke. 2017. *Unfinished: The anthropology of becoming*. Durham, NC: Duke University Press.

Bourdieu, Pierre. 1991. 'Introduction à la socioanalyse', *Actes de la recherche en sciences sociales* 90: 3–5.

Bourdieu, Pierre. 2003. 'L'objectivation participante', *Actes de la recherche en sciences sociales* 150: 43–58.

Burman, Jenny. 2006. 'Migrant remittances as diasporic communication', *Journal of International Communication* 12: 7–18.

Carling, Jørgen. 2001. 'Aspiration and Ability in International Migration: Cape Verdean experiences of mobility and immobility'. MS thesis, Department of Sociology and Human Geography, University of Oslo.

Cearns, Jennifer. 2023. *Circulating Culture: Transnational Cuban networks of exchange*. Gainesville: University Press of Florida.

Charles, Jacqueline. 2016. 'US shifts Haiti deportation policy and gives a warning', *Miami Herald*, 22 September. Accessed 9 April 2024. https://www.virginislandsdailynews.com/ap/u-s-shifts-haiti-deportation-policy-and-gives-a-warning/article_f44f3852-a6e6-5b01-9ab7-df56351df14b.html.

Fallers, I. 1955. 'The predicament of the modern African chief: An instance from Uganda', *American Anthropologist* 57: 290–305.

Foucault, Michel. 2004. *Sécurité, Territoire, Population*. Paris: Seuil.

Fouratt, Caitlin. 2017. 'Love for the land: Remittances and care in a Nicaraguan transnational community', *Latin American Research Review* 52: 792–806.

Geertz, Clifford. 1960. 'The Javanese kijaji: The changing role of a cultural broker', *Comparative Studies in Society and History* 2(2): 228–49.

Glick-Schiller, Nina. 2011. 'Locality, globality and the popularization of a diasporic consciousness: Learning from the Haitian case'. In *Geographies of the Haitian Diaspora*, edited by Regine O. Jackson, xxi–xxix. New York: Routledge.

Gluckman, Max, J. C. Mitchell and J. A. Barnes. 1949. 'The village headman in British Central Africa', *Africa* 19: 89–106.

Joseph, Handerson. 2015a. 'Diáspora: As dinâmicas da mobilidade haitiana no Brasil, no Suriname e na Guiana Francesa'. PhD thesis, Museu Nacional, Federal University of Rio de Janeiro.

Joseph, Handerson. 2015b. 'Diáspora: Sentidos sociais e mobilidades haitianas', *Horizontes Antropológicos* 21: 51–78.

Kahn, Jeffrey S. 2019. 'Smugglers, migrants, and demons: Cosmographies of mobility in the Northern Caribbean', *American Ethnologist* 46: 470–81.

Kwon, June H. 2015. 'The work of waiting: Love and money in Korean Chinese transnational migration', *Cultural Anthropology* 30: 477–500.

Levitt, Peggy. 2001. *The Transnational Villagers*. Berkeley: University of California Press.

Levitt, Peggy and Deepak Lamba-Nieves. 2011. 'Social remittances revisited', *Journal of Ethnic and Migration Studies* 37: 1–22.

Madianou, Mirca. 2017. '"Doing family" at a distance: Transnational family practices in polymedia environments'. In *The Routledge Companion to Digital Ethnography*, edited by L. Hjorth, H. Horst, A. Galloway and G. Bell. 102–12. London: Routledge.

Ma Mung, Emmanuel. 1999. 'La dispersion comme ressource', *Cultures et Conflits* 33–4: 89–103.

Montinard, Mélanie. 2019. 'Pran wout la: Dinâmicas da mobilidade e das redes haitianas'. PhD Thesis, Museu Nacional da Universidade Federal do Rio de Janeiro.

MTE (Ministèrio do Trabalho e Emprego). 2012. *Resolução Normativa n. 97. Diário Oficial da União*, 13 January, (1)19: 'dispõe sobre a concessão do visto permanente previsto no art. 16 da Lei no 6.815, de 19 de agosto de 1980, a nacionais do Haiti'.

OBMigra (International Migration Observatory). 2016. 'Relatorio anual. Observatório das Migrações Internacionais; Ministério do Trabalho/Conselho Nacional de Imigração e Coordenação Geral de Imigração'. Brasília, DF: OBMigra. Accessed 22 March 2024. https://portaldeimigracao.mj.gov.br/pt/dados/relatorios-a.

Olwig, Karen F. 2012. 'The "successful" return: Caribbean narratives of migration, family, and gender', *Journal of the Royal Anthropological Institute* 18: 828–45.

Richmann, Karen E. 2005. *Migration and Voodoo*. Gainesville: University Press of Florida.

Sandoval Garcia, Carlos. 2017. *Casa en Tierra Ajena* (video). Accessed 22 March 2024. https://www.youtube.com/watch?v=AkrZIumTRjI&fbclid=IwAR377JOnVTqlIraDeT4yhbGgToljPplXwc5cbk7-E9wxv9ZlOwXhX3iMlHY.

Vieira, Rosa. 2014. 'Itinerâncias e governo: A mobilidade haitiana no Brasil'. Master's dissertation in Sociology and Anthropology, Federal University of Rio de Janeiro.

Vieira, Rosa. 2017. 'O governo da mobilidade haitiana no Brasil', *Mana: Estudos de Antropologia Social* 23(1): 229–54.

Wolf, Eric. 1956. 'Aspects of group relations in a complex society: Mexico', *American Anthropologist* 58: 1065–78.

World Bank. 2012. 'Living Standards Measurement Study (LSMS)'. Washington, DC: World Bank.

Zolberg, Aristide, Astri Suhrke and Sergio Aguayo. 1989. *Escape from Violence: Conflict and the refugee crisis in the developing world.* Oxford: Oxford University Press.

9

'We don't produce anything in Bolivia': subordinate financialization and contraband economies in the Bolivia–Argentina borderlands

Charles Dolph

Introduction

In a 2018 report, Bolivia's Ministry of Economy and Public Finances noted the depreciation of currencies in neighbouring countries – Argentina, Brazil, Chile, Paraguay and Peru – against its national currency, the boliviano, as a key factor in promoting a contraband boom. While Bolivia adopted a fixed exchange rate against the US dollar in 2011, the progressive devaluation of its neighbours' currencies was generating profit margins for smugglers operating in a range of items – foodstuffs entering from Peru, against the outflow of Bolivia's heavily subsidized fuel; the bustling trade in used cars (so-called *autos chutos*) arriving from Chile; food, wine, agricultural products and more, pouring in from Argentina, while hard currency (dollars, but also bolivianos) flowed out; Bolivian cocaine entering Paraguay and Brazil, against beer from the latter inundating Bolivia's lowlands (see the contributions to Rabossi 2021 for recent case studies of many of these regional commercial networks).

The report's author notes, furthermore, that this monetary dynamic was particularly acute vis-à-vis Argentina, where the peso was experiencing more severe devaluationary pressure than other currencies (Pérez Trejo 2018, 18, 39). Since then, this monetary asymmetry has only intensified. Argentina has been mired in an ongoing monetary crisis, with the peso losing value precipitously, parallel dollar markets offering rates around double the official one and inflation among the highest in the world. Meanwhile, the administration of Bolivian President Luis Arce remains committed to the fixed exchange rate policy as a pillar of its macroeconomic programme, despite growing strain on this in the global context of renewed inflation.

Bolivia's monetary asymmetries with its neighbours, Argentina most starkly, are indeed fuelling a contraband boom. A recent report by the National Chamber of Industries – *Cámara Nacional de Industrias* – estimates that since 2013, when the currencies of its neighbours began to depreciate against the boliviano, through 2022 the amount of contraband entering Bolivia grew 44 per cent, to over US$3 billion annually, totalling nearly US$27 billion over that period (*La Razón* 2023).

As I discuss below, Bolivia's thriving contraband economies, and the monetary dynamics which fuel them, highlight a fundamental tension within the economic model of the governing *Movimiento al Socialismo* (Movement Towards Socialism, or MAS). This is premised on a productive transformation of the national economy. Yet, as state monetary policies encourage and are, in turn, reinforced by the contraband boom, the resulting influx of cheap goods from neighbouring countries contributes to the undermining of this goal.

This tension within Bolivia's economic model, between state monetary policies and productive transformation, which the contraband boom lays bare, is characteristic of what scholars have called 'subordinate financialization'. Central to this is a monetary dynamic whereby developing countries are compelled to acquire US dollars, as world money used to settle international trade transactions and debt obligations, as well as to back the value of their national currencies (Lapavitsas 2014). So, while Bolivia and Argentina represent monetary extremes, this is in fact the result of their common attempts to grapple with subordinate financialization.

In linking Bolivia's contraband boom to these dynamics of subordinate financialization, I add to a growing body of literature exploring similar themes in other contexts. As scholars have documented from Africa's Chad Basin (Roitman 2005) to the Southern Cone of South America (Schuster 2015), resurgent practices of smuggling and contraband are enmeshed with regional and global processes of financialization in various ways. Bolivians' commercial networks are similarly linked to wider economic forces. Indigenous traders, for example, have long articulated their commercial practices to the movements of the global economy (Tassi 2016). Drawing on fieldwork in the Bolivia–Argentina borderlands – principally Potosí department in southern Bolivia – as well as with state officials and functionaries in the capital of

La Paz, I thus place Bolivia's contraband boom against the wider sweep of financialized capitalism.

Subordinate financialization and the commodities boom-bust in Latin America

To appreciate how Bolivia's contraband boom is entangled with subordinate financialization, it is necessary to first unpack this concept and sketch its features in contemporary Latin America. The term 'financialization' can be conceptually vague and empirically slippery.[1] Historically, the financialization of capitalism since the 1970s can be linked to swings in cycles of accumulation between productive and financial channels as relative sources of profit (Arrighi 2010; Krippner 2011). Following this, I engage here with Lapavitsas (2014) in theorizing and analysing the current wave of financialization on the basis of Marx's monetary writings. In this political economy perspective, 'money is the initial category, while credit and finance derive from the further unfolding of the category of money (and capital). Marxist theory of credit and finance is inherently monetary in the sense that it rests analytically on the theory of money' (Lapavitsas 2014, 69).

Crucial to the underpinnings of financialization, therefore, is control over world money. Marx characterized world money as the key coordinating mechanism of the otherwise anarchic world market. As such, it performs crucial roles as international means of payment and hoarding, and vehicle for the transfer of value (Marx 1976, 240–4; Lapavitsas 2014, 101–5). Giovanni Arrighi similarly extended this perspective in highlighting command of world money as 'the crucial instrument of capitalist power' (2010, 28). While this brings power relations to the fore in apprehending money and finance, Arrighi's overriding concern was with the ascent and decline of successive world hegemonies of historical capitalism under the United Provinces (Netherlands), United Kingdom, and the United States (and potentially China). The idea of subordinate financialization, meanwhile, foregrounds the hierarchical and uneven character of contemporary financialization (Lapavitsas 2014); attention to its specific historical and empirical features can thus help us better understand how money power operates in – and on – developing economies in regions like Latin America (see also Bonizzi et al. 2020).

In this regard, an important peculiarity of the current historical cycle of financialization is that it is no longer an impersonal commodity such as gold which performs the coordinating role of world money but a state-backed fiat currency: the US dollar. This is vital to the monetary compulsions of subordinate financialization, as world money has 'become even more clearly an instrument of state power, particularly of hierarchical, imperial power in the world market' (Lapavitsas 2014, 104).

This power relation is expressed in how central banks in developing countries contrive to assemble the dollar hoards needed to participate in international trade, mitigate the destabilizing effects of financial flows, and back the value of domestic currencies. One strategy has been to purchase US public debt, especially in the form of Treasury securities. China has become a major holder of these, accruing a third of dollar reserves among developing countries (Lapavitsas 2014, 249). Such accumulation of dollar hoards in the form of US securities amounts to what Lapavitsas characterizes as a form of 'informal tribute', which developing countries pay to developed ones (mainly the US) (2014, 246, 253). This compulsion to hoard dollars is the monetary hallmark of the 'subordinate' character of financialization in developing countries. As Lapavitsas explains:

> Increasing hoards of quasi-world-money [the US dollar] by developing countries, therefore, represent a form of official lending by developing countries to the US state undertaken with funds that could have been potentially invested domestically to support development. Consequently, international capital flows and reserves of world money have created a source of gain for the US economy under conditions of financialized capitalism. Developing countries have been implicitly subsidizing the hegemonic power in the world market purely to gain access to the dominant form of (valueless) world money. (2014, 252)

In arguing thus that subordinate financialization entails a reversal of capital flows from developing to developed countries, Lapavitsas's main point is to distinguish it from what Lenin had identified as the hallmark of classical imperialism, whereby the formation of monopolies spurred the export of capital from metropolitan centres across the globe in search of profits.

Another implication, which Lapavitsas suggests but does not draw out, is that subordinate financialization attenuates the productive capacities of developing countries. That is, the exigencies which it exerts on them to accumulate dollar hoards divert a portion of their resources away from investment in domestic industries. As I discuss below, in fuelling deindustrialization and thwarting the development of productive capacities, subordinate financialization helps drive the formation and expansion of contraband economies in areas such as the Bolivia–Argentina borderlands.

First, some regional dynamics bear further scrutiny. While purchasing US Treasury securities has been one means whereby developing countries amass dollar hoards, in early twenty-first century Latin America another was via the pursuit of comparative advantage in the export of primary commodities such as oil, natural gas, and soybeans (Coronil 2011).[2] Largely on the back of a global commodities boom, every country in Latin America accumulated substantial dollar reserves, which collectively rose from US$163 billion in 2001 (ECLAC 2010, 272) to US$833 billion by 2014 (ECLAC 2014, 191). Bolivia and Argentina followed this pattern. Both countries, albeit for somewhat different reasons, distanced themselves from global financial markets and lending institutions, like the International Monetary Fund (IMF), while still accumulating large dollar reserves.[3]

A global boom in prices of natural gas, which became Bolivia's key export sustaining the MAS under successive Evo Morales administrations, filled central bank coffers, whose reserves rose from barely US$1 billion in 2001 to over US$15 billion by 2014 (Banco Central de Bolivia 2016). Similarly, Argentina emerged during this time as the third-largest global producer of soybeans, the export of which during the upswing of the boom swelled its central bank reserves. Despite the country remaining effectively shut out from global credit markets, in the wake of its 2002 sovereign debt default, reserves jumped from a low of barely US$9 billion, at the depths of its 2001–2 crisis, to over US$50 billion by 2008, at a moment when the onset of the global financial crisis sent soybean prices spiking (Banco Central de la República Argentina 2015, 9).

Rather than an alternative to financialization per se, however, Latin America's commodities boom entailed significant continuities with the Washington Consensus which preceded it (Svampa 2015). Indeed, the strategy of state monetary authorities in Latin America to accumulate dollar hoards through primary commodity exports has been thoroughly bound up with financialization. For example, while Argentina and Brazil have emerged as two of the three largest global producers and exporters of soybeans (along with the US), animating this process has been the financialization of global agriculture and associated land rush (Fairbairn 2020). Similarly, the financialization of the Bolivian economy and its institutional arrangements over recent decades has circumscribed the

MAS's ability to channel hydrocarbon revenues towards transforming the country's productive structures (Macías Vázquez and García-Arias 2019).

Contemporary Latin America thus presents crucial variations *within* subordinate financialization, whereby the formation of central bank dollar hoards has been deeply linked to the swings of global commodities markets and contests over the distribution of surplus value between capitalists and landlords, the latter sometimes including organs of the state.

The slowing of the commodities boom since 2011 has intensified the exigencies of the US dollar on Latin American economies, and so on state monetary policymaking. Pressure on central bank reserves has sharpened a contradiction within the world money-form, which is called upon to perform simultaneously as means of *international* payment and as store of value backing *domestic* currencies (Marx 1976, 243). Monetary policymaking in contexts of subordinate financialization is riven by this contradiction and, as I discuss below, specific policies attempting to grapple with it generate conditions on which smuggling and contraband thrive.

Bolivia and Argentina: subordinate financialization, monetary extremes

This contradiction at the heart of world money plays out through the movement of exchange rates, which express the hierarchy between the US dollar as de facto world money and so many specific national currencies. This raises basic questions about state monetary policymaking in contexts of subordinate financialization. How do policymakers navigate the contradictory demands of world money in international trade and finance, on the one hand, and domestic currency stability on the other? Do they devalue national currency, thereby prioritizing the international dimension of world money? Or try to resist this, instead privileging the stability of national currency? What are the political calculations, constituencies and forces involved? What do such policies look like in practice?

In Bolivia and Argentina alike, domestic political considerations about the damaging effects of currency devaluation have informed monetary policies seeking to defend exchange rates and govern access to dollars. But the results have been drastically different. These uneven monetary dynamics shape, in turn, contraband economies traversing their respective national territories.

Bolivia

In Bolivia, the waning of the global gas boom beginning in 2014 has had relatively slow-moving effects. This largely reflects the approach to grappling with subordinate financialization since Evo Morales and the MAS came to power in 2006.[4] The linchpin has been the programme to 'bolivianize' savings and credit. Bolivia experienced a traumatic hyperinflation and debt crisis in 1985, when the boliviano to dollar exchange rate skyrocketed to 1,900,000-to-one. This resulted in the dollarization of savings practices and credit formation, with just 3 per cent of deposits in Bolivia's financial system denominated in national currency and the rest in dollars, by the early 2000s (Molina 2019, 8). As Economy Minister, Luis Arce devised the programme of 'bolivianization' that sought to reverse this. Flush with dollars from the gas boom, the central bank accrued sufficient reserves to revalue the boliviano. Together with a series of measures such as a tax on financial transactions which incentivize the formation of savings and credit in national currency, 'bolivianization' has been a success: by 2015, 94 per cent of deposits were in bolivianos and just 6 per cent in US dollars (Molina 2019, 8).

A second, and closely related, measure is the adoption of a fixed exchange rate against the US dollar, since 2011, which monetary authorities pegged at 6.96 bolivianos.[5] At the time, this was considered central to both 'bolivianization' and achieving a productive transformation of the national economy, the former by preempting recourse to the dollar for savings and credit and the latter by enabling the import of capital goods for Bolivia's manufacturing and industrial sectors.

Both 'bolivianization' and the fixed exchange rate have thus been central to what the MAS defines as its 'Economic Social Communitarian Productive Model' (*Modelo Económico Social Comunitario Productivo*), which Arce first articulated in 2006. Its overarching goals are defined in terms of transition, whereby the state will direct the development of Bolivia's productive forces in manufacturing and industry, tourism and agriculture, so as to move the country beyond its position in the international division of labour as a primary commodity exporter and lay the foundations for a future socialist society (see Arce Catacora 2014).

Monetary stability is increasingly taking precedence over productive transformation, however. Beginning in early 2023, the pressures of the US dollar began to weigh on Bolivia's macroeconomy. Central bank reserves have steadily eroded with the slowing of the global gas boom. This, combined with the generalized lack of dollar liquidity in the banking system, due to rising US interest rates, has placed increased strain on the fixed exchange-rate policy. This precipitated a series of stopgap measures regulating access to the US currency and seeking to bolster central bank reserves amid swirling rumours of currency devaluation (Dolph 2023). Nevertheless, the Arce administration remains committed to the fixed exchange rate as the cornerstone of Bolivia's macroeconomic stability.

Anchored by this policy, Arce's administration touts Bolivia's 'lowest inflation in the region' as its major achievement. Indeed, when walking off a plane upon arriving in Bolivia, or strolling down the Prado in the capital city of La Paz, one encounters prominent banners and billboards touting this indicator of hard-won macroeconomic stability. True, the government similarly continues to promote its efforts towards industrialization, especially of Bolivia's lithium deposits, as advancing. But as I discuss below, these two objectives – monetary stability and productive transformation – are increasingly at odds.

Argentina

In contrast, the waning of a boom in global prices for soybeans, beginning during 2011, had immediate and dramatic effects on monetary policymaking in Argentina. Since devaluation in early 2002, with the demise of the Convertibility regime which had pegged the Argentine peso at parity with the US dollar, the exchange rate had hovered around 4:1. As the soy boom showed signs of slowing, monetary authorities within the Cristina Fernández de Kirchner administration faced swift and intense pressure from powerful agribusiness interests for currency devaluation. Authorities instead implemented a series of currency controls, limiting access to US dollars to defend central bank reserves and avoid devaluation. As I have discussed at length elsewhere, central to this policy turn was a calculation, borne of Argentina's traumatic experience with hyperinflation in 1989, that another devaluation and its inflationary effects would be too politically damaging (Dolph 2022).

A key effect of currency controls was the rapid expansion of parallel dollar markets and multiple exchange rates, most importantly the so-called 'blue' dollar market which has operated more or less openly despite controls (Ferradás 2013). Wealthy businessman Mauricio Macri made eliminating exchange controls a centrepiece of his successful 2015 presidential bid, a promise he fulfilled immediately after taking office. However, Wall Street's eschewal of taking on yet more Argentine debt over early 2018 sparked a run on central bank reserves, pushing the Macri administration to seek the largest ever Stand-By Arrangement with the IMF and reinstitute controls (Dolph 2018). Since then, and exacerbated by the COVID-19 pandemic and rise in US interest rates, Argentine currency has been in a prolonged devaluationary spiral. By December 2023, when ultra right-wing Javier Milei took office as Argentine president after running on a platform of abolishing the central bank entirely and dollarizing the national economy, the official peso to dollar exchange rate plummeted to around 800:1, with the 'blue' rate hovering around 1000:1 and annual inflation running at the third highest in the world, at over 100 per cent.

The upshot of these respective attempts to grapple with subordinate financialization is two monetary extremes: Bolivia is committed to a fixed exchange rate and boasts the lowest inflation in Latin America; Argentina is marked by severe devaluation, multiple exchange rates with large breaches between them and soaring inflation. As state monetary policies engender radically uneven regimes of value side-by-side, this generates profit margins upon which contraband economies flourish.

In the rest of this chapter, I turn to ethnographic data from fieldwork in southern Bolivia and with government officials and functionaries in the capital, La Paz, to draw out the entanglements of state policies and contraband economies.

Continuities of 'contraband' and 'imports' in the Bolivia–Argentina borderlands

Bolivia and Argentina share a 773-kilometre-long border, ranging across the Bolivian departments of Potosí and Tarija and the Argentine provinces of Jujuy and Salta (see Figure 9.1). There are three major border conurbations: the towns of Villazón and La Quiaca in Potosí–Jujuy, and Bermejo–Aguas Blancas and Yacuiba–Salvador Mazza in Tarija–Salta. These borderlands have long had a consistent flow of contraband, mainly in food and textiles. Traditionally, this has taken the form of small scale *hormiga* (literally 'ant', comparable to '*el bachaco*' discussed in Allard, Beach, and Van Roekel, this volume) contraband carried on by petty smugglers known as *bagalleros*.

Common in South American borderlands, these types of contraband economies can become bound up with global financial flows in myriad ways. For example, Caroline Schuster (2015) details how in Ciudad del Este, on the Paraguayan side of the so-called Triple Frontier the country shares with Brazil and Argentina, 'ant' contraband sometimes diverts microloans extended to women entrepreneurs. As one of multiple forms of flexible, non-waged work which women may engage

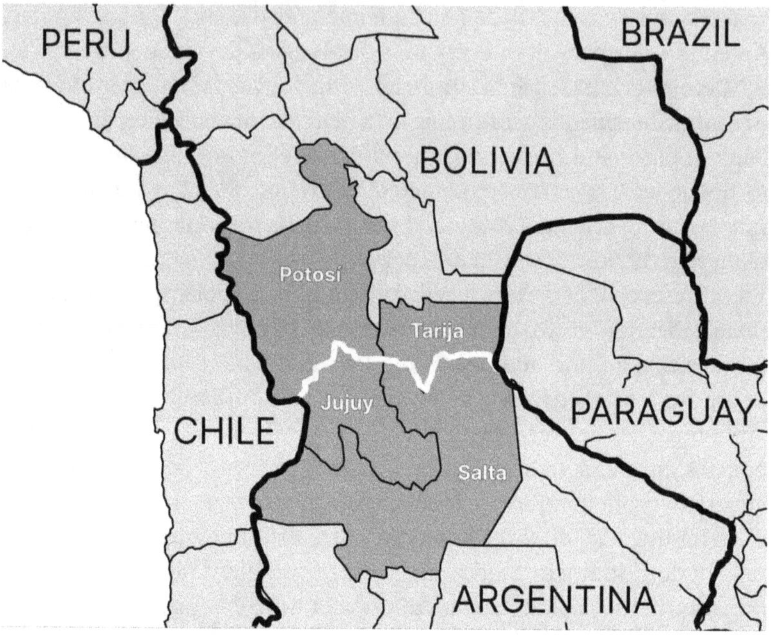

Figure 9.1 Map showing the 773 km border (in white) between Argentina and Bolivia. © Charles Dolph.

in, such smuggling can come to comprise part of the 'life cycle of loans' given by international microfinance foundations operating in the area.

Here, meanwhile, I am interested in how the circulation of currencies and contraband goods in the Bolivia–Argentina borderlands are interwoven with the dynamics of subordinate financialization discussed above.

I carried out fieldwork in Bolivia's Potosí department. This stretches from the *altiplano* (high plateau) southwards to the city of Potosí and on to the border at Villazón, across from which sit the Argentine provinces of Jujuy and Salta. Geographically and culturally, this central Andean landscape spans national borders in linking together thick networks of people, goods, labour and money. It is thus a main thoroughfare for licit and illicit trade.

Multiple national currencies – bolivianos, Argentine pesos, US dollars – now circulate unevenly through the cross-border areas connecting southern Bolivia and northern Argentina. In Jujuy and Salta, for example, daily transactions are still mainly carried out in Argentine pesos, but the boliviano is widely used as a savings currency attractive for its more stable value. Meanwhile, Bolivians with access to dollars frequently cross the border at Villazón (as well as Bermejo and Yacuiba) to exchange them on Argentina's 'blue' market with its favourable rate. This multiplicity of currencies and values facilitates circuits of contraband and smuggling in a variety of goods. For example, Bolivians converting dollars into Argentine pesos at the 'blue' rate often do so to engage in so-called 'shopping tourism' (*turismo de compras*), using their enhanced purchasing power to scoop up devalued Argentine goods and bring them back to Bolivia.

The influx of Argentine goods in Bolivia was evident when I visited the town of Santiago de Cotagaita in southern Potosí, about 100 miles north of the border at Villazón. I first arrived in this town, which sits halfway between the border and Potosí city to the north, twenty years ago to work in the development sector. It has since seen extensive transport and infrastructural developments which have increased its connections to surrounding areas in southern Bolivia and northern Argentina. The paving of the road from Potosí city, south to the border, completed about ten years ago, has halved travel times on this route, leaving Cotagaita now just a couple of hours drive from each. I was struck by the explosion of the town's transportation connections across Potosí department and north to major tourist destinations such as the Salar de Uyuni salt flats, east to the neighbouring department of Tarija (the road to which was previously considered so dangerous that my then-employer explicitly prohibited me from taking it), and south into Argentina towards Jujuy and Salta.

This growth of the transportation sector provides an important source of work for local residents. Such was the case of one *cotagaiteño* (resident of Cotagaita) friend who I first met more than a decade earlier in Buenos Aires, Argentina where he had migrated to work in the construction industry. When his work opportunities there dried up during the COVID-19 pandemic, he and his wife returned to Cotagaita, where he now works as a minibus driver making daily trips to and from Tupiza, a larger town about an hour south towards the border which acts as a regional hub for connections to southern Bolivia and northern Argentina.

Another friend from Cotagaita explained some recent changes in contraband entering the area as well as the logistics of the smuggling involved. A mother of two, about 40 years old, she is part of a network of extended family and *cotagaiteños* stretching to Salta, where she previously lived on multiple occasions for years at a time, and as far afield as Buenos Aires. She and her children, she recounted, crossed into Argentina a week before COVID-19 pandemic lockdowns began in 2020, which would be harsher in Cotagaita (and Bolivia in general).

They stayed in Salta for seven months with family before deciding to come back to Cotagaita, where her parents still live. At the time, however, lockdowns and border closings were still in place. To cross back into Bolivia, they passed through the Villazón riverbed at night.

This riverbed, she explained, is the same area which smugglers heavily traffic. Indeed, an array of Argentine goods are smuggled into Bolivia through this corridor. Argentine food and beverages including grapes, wine, meat and beer have inundated the region. For example, *Quilmes*, a popular Argentine beer brand, now dominates in Cotagaita. The abundance of high-quality Argentine beef has allowed people there to adopt the habit of Sunday *asados* (barbecues) like those common in Salta and throughout Argentina (see Figure 9.2).

Moreover, it's no longer just the small-scale 'ant' contraband, my friend explained. Especially in the last five years it has come to include televisions, washing machines and other electronics and home appliances. These require more sophisticated smuggling operations, to which the increased density of transport connections and infrastructural developments are vital. What she described as 'caravans' of ten-metre-long shipping trailers filled with merchandise come down on the Argentine side of the Villazón riverbed, where Bolivian crew meet them to unload (using wheelbarrows for larger items) and reload into vehicles for transport north. This, then, is beyond the operations of *bagalleros* engaged in small-scale 'ant' contraband.

Transport and infrastructural developments also facilitate the arrival of Argentine goods further north. A friend from Potosí city who moved to La Paz about fifteen years ago, where she now works in Bolivia's national customs agency (*Aduanas*), explained to me that the popular Uyuni market near Potosí's colonial-era centre includes a section of specifically Argentine goods. 'Just tell a taxi driver you want to go to the section of Argentine products,' she told me, 'and they'll take you right to it'. One can even place orders, she explained. For example, items like *Leche la Serenísima*, a popular Argentine dairy brand, are perishable – if nobody buys them, they go bad – so vendors do not always carry them. But you can place an order and next week, or as soon as they are able, vendors will fulfil orders for such items through *bagalleros* working in border areas. When I visited the Mercado Uyuni, my taxi driver indeed knew exactly where to take me for Argentine products. As others there explained to me in more detail, these vendors set up in the mornings on a particular street with many barber shops and in the afternoon circulate as *ambulantes* (mobile street vendors) through the square blocks which comprise the bustling open-air market.

Figure 9.2 A butcher advertises Argentine beef in Santiago de Cotagaita, Bolivia, a town in southern Potosí a few hours north of the border. Photo © Charles Dolph.

Janet Roitman (2005) has shown that rather than straightforwardly undermining state sovereignty, cross-border contraband networks in Africa's Chad Basin exist in tension with its power and regulatory authority. She documents how structural adjustment and the evaporation of wage-labour opportunities have fuelled resurgent practices of smuggling and banditry, which are now enmeshed with reconfigured networks of international trade and finance. Challenging dominant notions of the 'informal economy', she argues that this resurgence has multiplied figures of regulatory authority in ways that make these practices 'part and parcel of the political logics of the state' (Roitman 2005, 22).

Similarly, as state monetary policies generate conditions favourable to the contraband economies in the Bolivia–Argentina borderlands, sketched above, these interact in complex and contradictory ways with those same policies. On the one hand, the flow of cheap Argentine goods into Bolivia serves the Arce administration's overriding policy priority of maintaining the fixed exchange rate with the US dollar. This policy, as the anchor of Bolivia's macroeconomic stability, is essential to the MAS's legitimacy and especially Arce's, as long-time Economy Minister and now President. The wide availability of devalued Argentine goods, by boosting the purchasing power of ordinary Bolivians, eases pressure for a currency devaluation which would severely damage this legitimacy.

On the other hand, contraband and smuggling, and the fixed exchange-rate policy they serve, increasingly clash with the MAS's long-term goal of effecting a *productive* transformation of the national economy, as discussed above. For example, the saturation of southern Potosí and Tarija, where Bolivia's fledgling grape and wine industries are concentrated, with cheap Argentine competitors undermines their local production. Contraband Argentine goods fuel a sort of 'Dutch disease'[6] effect here, common in situations of a natural-resource boom, when foreign exchange inflows can cause the appreciation of domestic currency.

In other words, Bolivia's fixed exchange rate with the US dollar promotes the influx of cheap foreign competitors which progressively undercut its own national industries. As a high-level official in the Vice Ministry of Tax Policy pointed out to me, moreover, unlike their Argentine (and Chilean) counterparts, Bolivian wine producers have not yet gained a foothold in international markets which would allow them to shift towards export. Some have sought to move production towards *singani*, a grape-derived spirit which is not produced in Argentina and has a growing domestic market. Supermarkets throughout Bolivia now carry a wide variety of *singanis* of different qualities, which was not the case twenty years ago. Still, Bolivian producers complain about operating at a fraction of capacity due to the capture of the domestic market by Argentine wines.

To be sure, wine production is not the motor of Bolivia's national economy; but given that contraband is now equivalent to eight per cent of the country's GDP (Cámara Nacional de Industrias 2023), its Dutch disease effect ramifies more broadly. In its volume and effects, contraband has become a structural feature of the Bolivian economy. As such, it muddies the waters of 'policy'. Consider, for example, the comments of the director of the Bolivian Institute of Foreign Commerce on the smuggling opportunities which Argentina's 'blue' dollar market generates in border regions, as 'a very appealing market for dollars from here [Bolivia] to bring *imports and contraband products*'. Thus, referring to the practice of 'shopping tourism', whereby Bolivians cross the border to change their dollars on the 'blue' market and bring devalued Argentine goods back into the country, he added that 'those products are brought into the country *via import, as luggage or as contraband*' (*Ámbito Financiero* 2023, emphasis added).

The repeated slippage between categories of 'import' and 'contraband' here is notable; it belies that the former is commonly understood in terms of macroeconomic policy while the latter a question of (il)legality and border security (Jiménez 2023; Renoldi 2021). This translates into a disconnect between economic policymaking and the regulatory orientation of *Aduanas*, Bolivia's national customs agency. Customs operates within the Ministry of Economy and Public Finances, as part of the Vice Ministry of Tax Policy. As a functionary from the agency reminded me, as a strictly 'operational agency' it plays no active role in formulating economic policies, even though it is part of the institution which does so.

Customs hence carries out directives according to policies formulated beyond its ambit, approaching contraband and smuggling through a logic of border security. For example, it interfaces with the Vice Ministry for Combating Contraband (*Viceministerio de Lucha Contra el Contrabando*), which the Evo Morales administration created in 2018 within Bolivia's Ministry of Defence. This new agency is headed by a retired brigadier general and organized into a 'Strategic Command' (*Comando Estratégico*) populated by military personnel. In April 2023, the Ministry of Defence announced the deployment of an additional contingent of 425 military troops to fortify the Strategic Command in its fight against contraband along Bolivia's border areas (*InfoDefensa* 2023).

Contraband and smuggling often imply the transgression of national borders, such that it can be difficult to think about them otherwise. But they are also – and centrally – a matter of monetary policies which aim to grapple with subordinate financialization. As we have seen, such policies create multiple and uneven regimes of value which fuel those very contraband economies. Devalued Argentine goods entering Bolivia aid the Arce government in achieving its policy priority of maintaining the fixed exchange rate with the US dollar, but in doing so, 'contraband' – just like the 'import' of cheap foreign goods – can inflict a version of Dutch disease on national industries, to which local producers must adapt.

In this way, Bolivian monetary authorities' attempts to confront the exigencies of subordinate financialization, through the adoption of a fixed exchange rate, further entrenches the dominance of commercial activity – including in smuggling and contraband – over production. This is, again, at odds with the productive vision of the national economy which the MAS articulates. Nevertheless, the Arce government now further projects this productivist ethos through Bolivia's 'New Customs Agency' (*Nueva Aduana*), ads for which portray it as efficiently and transparently facilitating international commerce while resolutely protecting the domestic economy and national industry according to the macroeconomic policy of import-substitution industrialization. Despite such protectionist proclamations, Customs seems to be doing little to stem the inflow of contraband from neighbouring countries; it seized just US$105.9 million worth, or 2.8 per cent of the estimated US$3.6 billion of contraband goods which entered Bolivia in 2022 (*Página Siete* 2023).

Conclusion: 'We don't produce anything in Bolivia'

As we stood looking down on Cotagaita from a hill, high above town, and marvelling at its vertiginous growth over the last twenty years, my *cotagaiteña* friend, who had crossed the border back and forth between Bolivia and Argentina during the COVID-19 pandemic lockdown, summarized a common refrain I had heard in conversations about smuggling and contraband. 'We don't produce anything in Bolivia', she said. 'Everyone is a petty merchant [*pequeño comerciante*] of one sort or another.' While such absolute terms of 'not producing anything' and 'everyone' being a petty merchant are surely something of an exaggeration, her comment effectively captures a dynamic which I have been arguing is fundamental to the intertwining of contraband economies and subordinate financialization in Bolivia.

State officials and functionaries echoed variations of this oft-repeated lament time and again in our conversations, albeit in less stark terms. One instance was particularly revealing. I managed to arrange a collective interview with officials and functionaries from the Vice Ministry of Tax Policy and Customs, together with others from the central bank and the Vice Ministry of Pensions and Financial Services (*Viceministerio de Pensiones y Servicios Financieros*, VPSF). I was interested in the type of dialogue and coordination (or lack thereof) between these different areas within Bolivia's Ministry of Economy – taxation and customs on the one hand, and the monetary and financial side on the other – around issues of smuggling and contraband.

All my interviewees were keenly aware that the government's fixed exchange rate policy was fuelling Bolivia's contraband boom, especially with Argentina. One of them, a high ranking official in the Vice Ministry of Tax Policy, linked this dynamic to Bolivia's continued subordinate position in the international division of labour:

> This helps explain why Bolivia is still a country that lives off raw materials. In theory, that should change. According to the economic model, and if you listen to the president these days, he says: 'we are advancing with industrialisation'. But there is an element here that is not permitting that, which is the exchange rate. If you really want to industrialize, for firms that are trying to grow, give added value to products, you are not supporting them with your exchange rate policy. There is a real conflict there. Surely the whole economic cabinet is analysing and discussing this. But the question is not only economic, it is profoundly social. (Interview with the author)

This comment captures what has emerged as a central tension in the MAS project, between productive transformation and monetary stability. In a global context of renewed inflationary pressures, the latter has taken precedence. This further underlines how subordinate financialization works to reproduce the 'structural subordination in global production' (Bonizzi et al. 2020, 176) of countries like Bolivia as primary commodity exporters.

In pointing to the Arce government's commitment to the fixed exchange rate as fundamentally a 'social question', meanwhile, this government official and my other interlocutors in the state apparatus repeatedly invoked Bolivia's 1985 hyperinflation and debt crisis, which effectively dollarized the national economy. This event marked the consolidation of Bolivia's subordinate financialization, with the government of Victor Paz Estenssoro agreeing to Washington Consensus-style conditions imposed by the IMF, for a bailout from the debt crisis (Nash 1992). This precipitated the collapse of Bolivia's tin-mining industry, which had emerged during the twentieth century, and especially following the 1952 national revolution, as the key productive sector of the national economy and home to the most militant and organized working-class force in Bolivian politics (Nash 1993). Miners and their families were displaced en masse – or 'relocated' in the official discourse (see Gill 1997) – to various locations within the national geography and so-called 'informal economy'.[7] These included coca producing regions such as the Yungas and Chapare, the burgeoning city of El Alto and its far-flung commercial networks, and, crucially, border areas where many would come to make a living by inserting themselves into growing contraband and smuggling networks.

The importance of Bolivia's contraband economies exceeds their quantification and statistical measurement. Those 'relocated' from mining economies to border areas and their commercial networks brought political militancy and organizational capacity with them. While, as miners, their militancy formed as class consciousness rooted in the experience of exploitation within the production process (Nash 1993), their displacement into cross-border commercial networks has transformed these into sites of ongoing struggles for subsistence. Those who found livelihoods in contraband economies have reconstituted their organizational prowess into the formation of associations of *contrabandistas* and transportation workers. Working as a *bagallero* is, in practice, considered a regular occupation in Bolivia's border zones. In Yacuiba, for instance, they have established a formal organization, the *Asociación de Bagalleros*. Frequently negotiating with state authorities on both sides of the Bolivia–Argentina border, such organizations represent a 'pluralization of regulatory authority' akin to that which Roitman (2005) describes in the Chad Basin.

To be sure, organized *contrabandistas* and transporters do not comprise a form of co-government such as the miner-dominated *Central Obrera Boliviana* (Bolivian Workers' Centre) did in the decade following Bolivia's 1952 national revolution, when the union was able to effectively veto unpopular government initiatives. But they are a crucial constituency vis-à-vis a MAS project which defines itself as a 'government of social movements'. Indeed, the functionary from the VPSF recounted attending numerous meetings about contraband in border areas such as Bermejo and Yacuiba, describing local communities as deeply divided between those operating in the formal sector, who push for government crackdowns on smuggling, on the one hand, and on the other, those in contraband economies as organized social forces which assert their dependence on smuggling as a subsistence strategy for themselves and their families. At least with respect to the fixed exchange rate adopted since 2011, then, these social forces exert a similar ability to block government initiatives such as any move to devalue the boliviano. This is the deeper historical meaning of what the state official quoted above meant when describing exchange-rate policy as a 'profoundly social' question.

It is within this historical trajectory that the MAS now prioritizes monetary stability, increasingly to the detriment of its own initiative to industrialize the national economy. The irony is that, while Arce and the MAS define their economic model precisely against that introduced in the wake of Bolivia's 1985 crisis, their monetary policies now stoke the contraband boom, whose actors' political mobilization helps uphold those policies, even as they undermine the MAS's goals of productive transformation.

Janet Roitman paved the way for anthropologists to understand smuggling and contraband as intertwined with new international networks of trade and finance in ways which alternately challenge and buttress state power. However, her argument that such means of extracting wealth amount to novel forms of 'productive activity' (2005, 16–17; see also Roitman 2003) fundamentally departs from 'production' as a category of political economy. As I have been arguing, and my variously positioned interlocutors insisted, the burgeoning of Bolivia's contraband economies is directly related to its deindustrialization and lack of productive activity.

More than an abstract concept that scholars may use to make theoretical sense of changes in global capitalism, my interlocutors in the field were thus acutely conscious of how the far-reaching dynamics glossed here as 'subordinate financialization' operate in their everyday lives and in state policies. I have followed their lead in seeking to integrate their perspectives into my analysis. Grasping the resurgence of contraband economies may mean analytically decentring 'production' in places like the Bolivia–Argentina borderlands and far beyond.

Notes

1 For a succinct review of approaches to financialization see Mader et al. (2020).

2 Lapavitsas does observe that commodities exporters differ from China's path in their accumulation of dollar reserves, but only in very general terms and limited to oil exporters, principally Russia and Gulf states (Lapavitsas 2014, 249).

3 Bolivian President Evo Morales declared the country's independence from the IMF and it incurred no debt with the Fund throughout his presidency. Argentina's distancing was due to protracted litigation by vulture funds over its sovereign debt restructurings in 2005 and 2010 following its then world-record default in 2002.

4 While it is beyond my scope here, Bolivia contrasts markedly in this regard with other regional hydrocarbon exporters, such as Venezuela.
5 The official policy stipulates a narrow band, between 6.86 bolivianos to the US dollar for buying and 6.96 for selling. As this band has been fixed since October 2011, and for the sake of simplicity, I follow local norms in referring to a fixed exchange rate policy.
6 This term originated to describe the decline in Dutch manufacturing and appreciation of its currency following the discovery of a large natural gas field in the 1950s.
7 Some 30,000 Bolivian miners were forced into retirement between 1986 and 1992 with the closing of the state-owned mining corporation, COMIBOL, thereby dismantling entire regional economies and communities (Gill 1997, 293–4).

References

Ámbito Financiero. 2023. '¿Turismo de dólar? En Bolivia aseguran que los ciudadanos cambian sus billetes en Argentina', *Ámbito Financiero*, 19 March. Accessed 25 March 2024. https://www.ambito.com/finanzas/turismo-dolar-bolivia-aseguran-que-los-ciudadanos-cambian-sus-billetes-argentina-n5677499.

Arce Catacora, Luis. 2014. 'Modelo económico social comunitario productivo', *EcoPlural*. La Paz: Ministerio de Economía y Finanzas Públicas.

Arrighi, Giovanni. 2010. *The Long Twentieth Century: Money, power and the origins of our times*. London: Verso.

Banco Central de Bolivia. 2016. 'Boletín del sector externo'. La Paz: Banco Central de Bolivia.

Banco Central de la República Argentina. 2015. 'Evolución del mercado único y libre de cambios y balance cambiario: Cuarto trimestre y año 2015'. Buenos Aires: Banco Central de la República Argentina.

Bonizzi, Bruno, Annina Kaltenbrunner and Jeff Powell. 2020. 'Subordinate financialization in emerging capitalist economies'. In *Routledge International Handbook of Financialization*, edited by Philip Mader, Daniel Mertens and Natascha van der Zwan, 177–87. New York: Routledge.

Cámara Nacional de Industrias (Bolivia). 2023. 'Industriales y autoridades de Bolivia, Perú, y Chile plantean la lucha conjunta contra el contrabando'. Accessed 25 March 2024. https://www.cni.bo/noticia/96.

Coronil, Fernando. 2011. 'The future in question: History and utopia in Latin America (1989–2010)'. In *Business as Usual: The roots of the global financial meltdown*, edited by Craig Calhoun and Georgi Derluguian, 231–64. New York: New York University Press.

Dolph, Charles. 2018. 'The second time as farce? The IMF returns to Argentina', *Focaal Blog*, 20 June. Accessed 25 March 2024. https://www.focaalblog.com/2018/06/20/charles-dolph-the-second-time-as-farce-the-imf-returns-to-argentina/.

Dolph, Charles. 2022. 'The Cultural Battle against the Dollar: Struggles over hoarding and democracy in the twilight of Argentina's soy boom', PhD dissertation, City University of New York.

Dolph, Charles. 2023. '¿Estamos saliendo adelante? Assessing Bolivia's macroeconomic stability'. North American Congress on Latin America. 16 March. Accessed 25 March 2024. https://nacla.org/estamos-saliendo-adelante-assessing-bolivias-macroeconomic-stability.

ECLAC. 2010. 'Economic survey of Latin America and the Caribbean 2009–2010: The distributive impact of public policies'. Santiago: Economic Commission on Latin America and the Caribbean.

ECLAC. 2014. 'Economic survey of Latin America and the Caribbean 2014: Challenges to sustainable growth in a new external context'. Santiago: Economic Commission on Latin America and the Caribbean.

Fairbairn, Madeleine. 2020. *Fields of Gold: Financing the global land rush*. Ithaca, NY: Cornell University Press.

Ferradás, Carmen. 2013. 'The nature of illegality under neoliberalism and post-neoliberalism', *PoLAR: Political and Legal Anthropology Review* 36(2): 266–73. Accessed 25 March 2024. https://doi.org/10.1111/plar.12026.

Gill, Lesley. 1997. 'Relocating class: Ex-miners and neoliberalism in Bolivia', *Critique of Anthropology* 17(2): 293–312. Accessed 25 March 2024. https://doi.org/10.1177/0308275X9701700212.

InfoDefensa. 2023. 'Bolivia fortalece su comando estratégico de lucha contra el contrabando', 2 April. Accessed 25 March 2024. https://www.infodefensa.com/texto-diario/mostrar/4235789/bolivia-fortalece-comando-estrategico-lucha-contra-contrabando.

Jiménez, José Blanes. 2023. *Bolivia's Border System: Globalization of illegal markets*. New York: Routledge.

Krippner, Greta R. 2011. *Capitalizing on Crisis: The political origins of the rise of finance*. Cambridge, MA: Harvard University Press.

Lapavitsas, Costas. 2014. *Profiting Without Producing: How finance exploits us all*. London: Verso.

Macías Vázquez, Alfredo and Jorge García-Arias. 2019. 'Financialization, institutional reform, and structural change in the Bolivian boom (2006–2014)', *Latin American Perspectives* 46(2): 47–64. Accessed 25 March 2024. https://doi.org/10.1177/0094582X18813566.

Mader, Philip, Daniel Mertens and Natascha van der Zwan. 2020. 'Financialization: An introduction'. In *The Routledge International Handbook of Financialization*, edited by Philip Mader, Daniel Mertens and Natascha van der Zwan, 1–16. New York: Routledge.

Marx, Karl. 1976. *Capital: A critique of political economy*, vol. 1. Translated by Ben Fowkes. London: Penguin Books.

Molina, Fernando. 2019. 'Bolivia: "Es la economía, estúpido"', *Nueva Sociedad* 283(October): 4–14.

Nash, June C. 1992. 'Interpreting social movements: Bolivian resistance to economic conditions imposed by the International Monetary Fund', *American Ethnologist* 19(2): 275–93.

Nash, June C. 1993. *We Eat the Mines and the Mines Eat Us: Dependency and exploitation in Bolivian tin mines*. New York: Columbia University Press.

Página Siete. 2023. 'Decomisos de la Aduana de 2022 representan solo el 2,8% de todo lo que mueve el contrabando', 7 February. Accessed 11 September 2023. https://www.paginasiete.bo/economia/decomisos-de-la-aduana-de-2022-representan-solo-el-28-de-todo-lo-que-mueve-el-contrabando-AI6318442.

Pérez Trejo, Carlos Armando. 2018. 'Cuantificación del contrabando en Bolivia: Impactos y propuestas de política pública'. La Paz: Ministerio de Economía y Finanzas Públicas.

Rabossi, Fernando (ed.). 2021. '(Trans)fronteriza: Fronteras y circuitos económicos populares', special issue of *Boletín del Grupo de Trabajo Fronteras: Movilidades, identidades y comercios* 5 (April).

La Razón. 2023. 'En una década, el contrabando movió $US 26.764 MM', *La Razón*, 2 June. Accessed 25 March 2024. https://www.la-razon.com/economia/2023/07/02/en-una-decada-el-contrabando-movio-us-26-764-mm/.

Renoldi, Brígida. 2021. 'Temporary autonomous zones, control and security simulations: With regard to the Aguas Blancas (Argentina)–Bermejo (Bolivia) Border', *Journal of Illicit Economies and Development* 3(2): 242–60. Accessed 25 March 2024. https://doi.org/10.31389/jied.118.

Roitman, Janet. 2003. 'Unsanctioned wealth: Or, the productivity of debt in northern Cameroon', *Public Culture* 15(2): 211–37.

Roitman, Janet. 2005. *Fiscal Disobedience: An anthropology of economic regulation in Central Africa*. Princeton: Princeton University Press.

Schuster, Caroline E. 2015. *Social Collateral: Women and microfinance in Paraguay's smuggling economy*. Illustrated ed. Oakland: University of California Press.

Svampa, Maristella. 2015. 'Commodities consensus: Neoextractivism and enclosure of the commons in Latin America', *South Atlantic Quarterly* 114(1): 65–82.

Tassi, Nico. 2016. *The Native World-System: An ethnography of Bolivian Aymara traders in the global economy*. Oxford: Oxford University Press.

10

'Los piratas del Caribe': disrupting capitalism through digital piracy in Cuba

Jennifer Cearns

While the US and Cuba have had a long and complex history of migration and trade, the relationship changed most dramatically in response to the social, economic and political restructuring of Cuban society in the late 1950s and early 1960s. More than one-tenth of Cuba's present-day population migrated to the US in response to the Revolution, with several further waves of migration in the decades that followed. Sixty years on, the Cuban diaspora in Greater Miami is now around two million strong (and growing). As of 2019, over 30 per cent of all Caribbean immigrants to the US had migrated from Cuba (Lorenzi and Batalova 2022), making the Cuban diaspora in Greater Miami the largest Caribbean diaspora in the United States.

Despite such obvious interconnection between Miami and Havana (which are just a 45-minute flight apart), few borders in the world could feel more finite, or reified. Since 1962, the US government has applied full economic sanctions ('the Embargo') upon Cuba, meaning that – with a few exceptions – very little can 'legitimately' move back and forth between the two places. To circumnavigate these restrictions, there is a vast informal network of circulation connecting the two places, with all sorts of everyday items being moved by *mulas* (or mules), who effectively smuggle items across the border despite the embargo (Cearns 2023). As has been documented in many comparable cases across Latin America and the Caribbean (Ulysse 1999), such cross-border contraband is frequently innocuous stuff: trousers, washing powder, shampoo, packets of salt and pepper. In the case of Cuba at the time of my fieldwork (2016–19), this also included digital content, in large part because, at that time, Cuba had very limited internet access.

This chapter explores the consumption practices and power dynamics within an emerging digital transnational network of circulation which punctures the political boundaries at the heart of one of the longest diplomatic conflicts of the past century. In so doing, it explores the permeability of what is arguably one of the most politicized and reified borders in the world: that between the US and Cuba. Drawing on fifteen months of ethnographic research, following the flows of people, material items and digital content, between Miami (US) and Havana (Cuba), the chapter traces these circuits to understand how Cubans negotiate extraordinary economic and political circumstances on a daily basis, to maintain their cultural identity across borders. In so doing, they also disrupt the binaries and borders erected between socialism and capitalism, state and individual, public and private.

The internet in Cuba

The Cuban internet has long been characterized by government censorship, self-censorship, high costs and slow speeds, along with a frail infrastructure of access. More recent transformations have provided internet access to some of Cuba's population, but this has been inadequate for the needs (and wants) of most citizens, and so numerous workarounds have been created, which are the main topic of discussion in this chapter. Nonetheless, internet access does exist, and it is worth briefly tracing the genesis of that and positioning it within the official political framework of legal or 'licit' internet access that citizens must operate within and navigate on the island.

Cuba adopted a limited-access internet policy in 1996, but this was not widely accessible to the public, and it relied on slow and expensive technology. In 2013, an undersea cable connected Cuba to Venezuela, facilitating public access to the internet and to email within cybercafes and at limited wi-fi hotspots. In December 2018, the government launched a 3G internet service for mobile phones, which in 2019 was upgraded to 4G in some areas, although this mobile data was prohibitively expensive for most Cubans, with prices starting from US$30 for 4 Gigabytes. As of January 2021, a Cuban would have to pay nearly ten times the monthly official minimum wage (adjusted to 2,100 Cuban pesos or US$84) for full-time internet access at home. Since 2014, it has also been possible for people abroad to pay for internet access for Cubans on the island, and in practice this is how many of my interlocutors were able to fund their internet access, via relatives in the diaspora.

The internet in Cuba remains 'arguably the worst in Latin America and the Caribbean – minimal, slow, and unfree' (Press 2021), and in 2018 *Freedom House* ranked it sixty-first (of sixty-five) in the world, with only China, Iran, Ethiopia and Syria ranking lower. As of 2019, internet penetration in Cuba was estimated at 68 per cent (according to figures from the International Telecommunication Union), and the country still has the lowest mobile-phone penetration rate in Latin America, at 53 per cent of the population (*Freedom House* 2021). Devices that use GPS or satellite technologies to pick up signals from nearby Miami are explicitly prohibited in Cuba, and there are still restrictions on owning modems, wireless faxes and satellite dishes.

Until 2019 (by which time I had finished my fieldwork) the Cuban government largely tolerated the existence of alternative methods of accessing digital content, such as *el paquete semanal* (the main subject of discussion in this chapter) and the SNET (street) networks that I have described at length elsewhere (Cearns 2021a; 2021b; 2021c), although all these networks were subject to significant self-censorship (Escobar 2017). Since 2019 government officials have increasingly taken over the services and much of the content offered by these informal networks, permitting access to the content only from the Computing and Electronic Youth Clubs located in all Cuban cities, or through the government-run equivalent to *el paquete semanal,* known as *La Mochila* (Farrell 2021). In so doing, the administrative autonomy is gradually being removed from these previously non-political and community-based networks of content distribution, and some have interpreted this as an increase on censorship of digital content in the country (Cimpanu 2021). A new law, introduced in July 2019, explicitly prohibits the hosting of a website on a foreign server, or the circulation of 'information contrary to the social interest, morals, good customs, and integrity of people' (*Gaceta Oficial de la República de Cuba* 2019).

Contraband content

Cuba's peer-to-peer digital file-sharing network *el paquete* (the package) has gained global attention (Helft 2015; San Pedro 2015; García Martínez 2017; Parish 2018), viewed as a domestic response to this widespread scarcity of internet access, and even an inventive answer to Netflix (Ayuso 2015), from an island which remains officially prohibited from consuming any more than a very limited amount of international online content. The network has grown and consolidated itself, since around 2014, to become the primary source of online information and entertainment for most Cubans across the island. Indeed, some even consider it to be the island's largest (unofficial) employer (Press 2015; Fazekas and Marshall 2016).

This curated database of digital content circulates hand-to-hand across the island, on USB sticks and hard drives, and includes thousands of hours of international TV shows and movies, video games, music and music videos, sports matches, e-books and magazines, cell phone applications, antivirus updates and classified advertisements. Altogether the content amounts to up to one terabyte per week, although few Cubans purchase all of it. The popularity and ubiquity of this network is such that, while in 2015 it was distributed on a weekly basis, crossing the island every Monday morning with bus drivers and pilots, by 2017 it had already become a daily phenomenon, with content copied, recopied and sold on, across networks of *paqueteros* (packagers), who in turn were distributing the material for a profit in their local area. The cost of subscribing to the *paquete* varied from neighbourhood to neighbourhood, and dealer to dealer, but prices could be as low as 2 Cuban pesos (10 cents US) for an episode of a show, thus allowing Cubans to 'transform their offline digital devices and television set into the equivalent of cloud-enabled, data-rich smart phones and TVs' (Henken 2017).

For the most part, compilers of this digital content have been tracing a delicate line of legality, and the unwritten rule for participation without unpleasant consequences has been that no politics or pornography can be included. Meanwhile, revenue comes back through two avenues: payments from subscribers on the one hand, and paid advertisements from local private businesses on the other. Most compilers operate legally under a set of licences for self-employed work (Ritter 2014), although many of these licences were frozen in 2017, and private advertising remains illegal on the socialist island.

While *el paquete* has been largely fetishized by the wider world, as a surprising digital quirk in an otherwise 'analogue' place, characterized as being stuck in the past (Nelson 2016), it in fact does not represent anything drastically new to Cuban societal organization. Indeed, *el paquete* is arguably the archetypal Cuban response to a scarcity of digital content, and in this regard it is the latest iteration of what has long been a local approach to obtaining both material and digital goods on the island. Informal networks have been crucial to most aspects of Cuban consumption for decades, becoming the definitive manner in which the problems of everyday life are resolved (Fernández 2000; Henken 2005).

The acquisition of goods through informal means is entirely standard practice to Cubans, who consider it 'normal or even admirable behaviour that is not necessarily a disavowal of the Cuban state or of the socialist economy' (Pertierra 2012). This attitude of resourcefulness (which is commonly referred to in Cuba as 'inventiveness' – *invento*) dominates a myriad of aspects in Cuban everyday life, from sourcing groceries to getting from place to place, as has been typical in many post-Soviet economies (Morris and Polese 2014). Such practices of informal music circulation are common in many lower-income countries and communities the world over (Manuel 2014; Stern 2014; Steingo 2015; Schoon 2016; Boudreault-Fournier 2017). In this chapter I argue that *el paquete* can best be understood as an informal network that observes local practices of gender, power and kinship to circulate valued digital-media materials across transnational Cuban communities, similar, perhaps, to some of the informal networks described by Mélanie Montinard in Chapter 8 of this volume. While this may at first appear an 'underground' informal economy at odds with the Cuban state, this chapter argues that such networks do not necessarily indicate a wholehearted acceptance of foreign (or 'American') capitalist consumption practices either, as might readily be assumed from some of the ethnographic material presented.

Contraband capitalism?

El paquete's genesis goes back several decades to the 1970s and 80s, when Cubans first started to find ways to circulate foreign films, magazines and music that didn't air on state-run TV. My friend Nestor has vivid childhood memories of helping his grandfather, who had a side-business of renting out books and movies:

> He had this great passion for cinema … so as an alternative means of income he started renting out magazines, books, and films in the 70s. The earliest memory that I have of that part of the business was a big wooden trunk he had for all the magazines. And I remember another person would come from another city to swap with my grandfather. The thing was, you'd have a hundred or a hundred and fifty books and a group of customers, so when your customers had read everything, you had to do something, so to get round that problem my grandfather would circulate materials with someone in another city. They used to communicate between themselves, like networks, and like that it grew … a network to distribute and

> interchange materials … At that time, the other way of getting hold of magazines and so forth was the ones left behind by tourists or visiting relatives in hotels. People would laminate them so they lasted longer and rent them out … At the same time cassette tapes started to circulate, and my grandfather exchanged all 200 of his books for 8 VHS tapes. People loved that you could watch something more than once, and from that moment the business started to grow. (Interview, Havana, February 2018)

Throughout the 1980s, ship workers, touring musicians and plane pilots would bring in Betamax-format videos, from abroad, either to sell or rent out: word would go around as to who had what, and people would copy their own versions. In 1991 the Cuban government installed an aerial on the roof of the Hotel Havana Libre so that tourists and diplomats could watch ten American channels, and locals quickly found a way to catch and (illegally) repeat the signal in the neighbourhood and record shows to (illegally) sell on to others. So, content sharing became a sort of 'side hustle', or a way of quietly making some extra income outside of the formal (state socialist) economy.

The Cuban diaspora in Miami also made the most of this development and started broadcasting radio and television programmes through satellite dishes facing out across the sea, in the hope of transmitting alternative sources of news to the island. This was explicitly a strategy of the American state, to counter socialist discourses on the island (Harney 2021). To this day, many of the more affluent Havana households own a parabolic antenna to catch the signal from Spanish-speaking channels in nearby South Florida. Some also repeat the signal to their neighbours and make a profit in the process by charging a monthly fee. As of 2021, the import or ownership of parabolic antennas remains illegal in Cuba, and the authorities regularly pursue individuals that utilize this equipment (Rodríguez 2021). Nonetheless, much of this equipment makes its way into Cuba, in travellers' suitcases, and nowadays it is also easier to get hold of a computer, a smartphone, or an antenna within Cuba, via various classified advertisement groups and networks, often paid for with the support of remittances from overseas.

Some households in Havana are in fact more connected with American media networks than those in the Miami diaspora itself. In November 2017 I was asked to give a lecture about *el paquete* at Florida International University in Miami, and the event resulted in several short interviews on various local Spanish-language television stations afterwards. As my Miami household couldn't afford cable TV, I never saw the footage but, to my surprise, a friend's grandmother in Havana saw the coverage later that night on the 'local' news and convinced a neighbour to send me some of the clips she had recorded, via his workplace email address (which had a greater bandwidth for sending images). And so, ironically, I was ultimately able to see coverage of my own Miami lecture about *el paquete* courtesy of an older lady in Havana and her deftness at hiding foreign content within an encrypted *archivo* (folder) on her *memoria* (USB stick).

While most of *el paquete*'s content originally came from abroad, nowadays most of the content is actually downloaded in Havana itself. Some is downloaded through special internet accounts, granted to university staff and Socialist Party members, which are less restricted, while the rest is downloaded on hotel computers through the night, when the available bandwidth is typically greater (Fowler 2019). The *matrices* (headquarters) of the major producers and distributors of *el paquete* have sufficient technical equipment to be able to copy multiple files at the same time, enabling them to reproduce *el paquete* on a mass scale that was impossible even just a few years before my fieldwork began.

Notably, this emerging arena of circulation is also largely dominated by demographics that traditionally have not occupied primary positions in Cuban cultural production: many of the *paqueteros* I encountered were young, not university educated, and of Afro-Cuban descent, essentially those often excluded from any more lucrative possibilities within the more formal or 'licit' economy (Hansing and Hoffmann 2020). Those developing and distributing their own digital content also frequently came from more marginalized groups, including young Afro-Cuban men and women, and communities of queer or trans activists (Whynacht 2009; Stout 2014; Levine 2020; Speakman 2021).

Yet the enthusiasm for foreign digital content does not necessarily signal an ideological shift towards aligning with consumption practices abroad. Nor is the foreign content consumed through *el paquete* solely American; in fact, Asian programmes (such as Korean *dorama*, Turkish soap opera and Japanese *manga* and *anime*) are becoming increasingly popular (Concepción 2021), as are other Latin American genres such as Mexican and Brazilian *telenovelas*. Most of this content is available with Spanish subtitles or dubbed sound (Köhn 2019), and some viewers even consume language-learning materials through *el paquete*, so as better to follow their favourite foreign show (Humphreys 2017; Humphreys 2021). This can arguably be seen as a legacy of socialist cosmopolitan cultural policies that encouraged the consumption of world cinema and distribution (Iordanova 2003), resulting in a contemporary audience across Cuba that is well versed in a variety of filmic genres. The most successful *paqueteros* are those culturally fluent enough in various social idioms and genres, both domestic and foreign, to be able to tailor packages to their clientele, as is common to informal traders in multicultural settings (Rhys-Taylor 2013). While there is certainly a clear and growing appetite to consume foreign digital media within Cuba, therefore, this need not necessarily map onto equivalent cross-border discourses in the political sphere.

Contraband and common good(s)

While *el paquete* has attracted considerable attention from across the world for being an ingenious response to limited internet access, it has also become a trope of the increasing stereotyping of Cuba as an analogue or 'digital detox' destination, 'where Wi-Fi is both slow and terrible, you will be an emissary from the future, a hint of the degeneracy to come' (García Martínez 2017). To Cubans, however, *el paquete* is distinct from the internet as the wider world might know it. The internet (in the sense of the World Wide Web, provided in Cuba by the state-owned company ETECSA) is slow, expensive, and is used primarily for communication purposes, such as sending emails or conducting internet calls to friends and relatives overseas. *El paquete,* meanwhile, is a source of information, entertainment, and most importantly, a network of social relations, where USB sticks assume the role of 'social portable libraries of Cuban identity, where librarians are a latticework of social networks of friends and trusted colleagues' (Astley 2016).

As Daniel Miller and Heather Horst point out: 'the importance of cultural relativism and the global nature of our encounter with the digital' is to negate 'assumptions that the digital is necessarily homogenizing', and thus a digital anthropological lens onto such phenomena as *el paquete* might allow us to explore 'the illusions we retain of a non-mediated, noncultural, predigital world' (2012, 12). Digital technology exists within wider social networks that include analogue and other media technologies, and Cuba's *paquete* is a prime example of how digital practices are extensions of pre-existing social and material worlds, constructed by agents who are situated in cultural specificities. Vincente Morin Aguado (2015) has seen USBs in Cuba as 'the people's Internet', but *el paquete* would perhaps be better understood as a parallel internet which has developed in its own unique techno-social and economic setting. In this network of 'contraband content', notions of ownership and property are distinct (as will be discussed later), as are conceptualizations of authentic or 'original' content, and the interface of state and citizen through mutual surveillance. In this regard, the network is conceived of as more a mutual creative project of common ownership (*bienes en común*), curated by each of its participants as it moves from hand to hand. *El paquete* is a response to a particular moment in time, where private business licences are obtainable on the island, and yet material (and digital) things still often circulate locally through older networks of distribution consolidated under socialism. *El paquete* has rendered visible an emerging public space in the Cuban landscape (Duong 2013): information and material exchange has always been mediated through social relationships in Cuba and beyond, but this process has manifested itself through new digital channels of circulation in the public domain.

'Los piratas del Caribe'

Despite the oft-celebrated, decentralizing, 'do-it-yourself' aspect of content production in the digital era, at the same time there is a contradictory tendency 'toward a certain form of concentration in the industry', as has been evident in various music scenes, globally (Azenha 2006; Manuel 2014). While *el paquete* has created a new public space within Cuba, this is not to say that this public space operates as a democracy, just as internet access in no way predetermines democratic organization. Perhaps one of the most dynamic aspects of the consolidation of *el paquete*, as a material and digital network spanning the entire island, has been its increasing commoditization and centralization under the emerging hegemonic powers of cultural representation in Cuba: the *matrices.* In a few short years, two *matrices*, both based in Havana, became the major portals through which most digital content consumed in Cuba, both domestic and international, flowed.

The increasing importance of such branding (which is watermarked at the bottom of a significant proportion of digital audiovisual content seen in Cuba) also trickled down to the *paqueteros*, who, in a bid to maintain their territories of distribution, competed for customer loyalty. Some individuals have achieved both national and international renown (along with a prized visa to visit the US) due to a combination of their roles in the circulation of *el paquete*, and their ability to market themselves as gatekeepers to this world. This cultivation of personal brand has repeated itself along the *paquete* food chain, with many adverts placed in the classifieds section on *el paquete* trying to undercut others' business, by promoting a uniquely personal service, highlighting individual experience, competitive pricing, selection of content, and willingness to deliver to customers at home.

While this consolidation of *el paquete* as the primary source of digital content in Cuba has fomented an increasing commoditization of digital content associated with personal brand, it also simultaneously invokes parallel movements across Latin America, the Global South and beyond, towards decommoditization, as consumers find ways to share content among themselves. Heather Horst's ethnographic work (2011) has revealed how open-source software and 'free culture' in Brazil is more broadly tied to a culture of resistance to hegemonic global culture and traditional patterns of production and ownership. In Brazil, pirated products are almost everywhere, and carry a 'particular urgency' as a critique of the injustice of the international market (Dent 2012; Pinheiro-Machado 2017; Dent 2020).

The case of *el paquete* in Cuba has similarly opened these forms of media piracy to a wider demographic, making digital products available to a broad swath of citizens while also, paradoxically, providing them with lucrative business opportunities which often simultaneously seek to deconstruct this democratization of assets. Henry Stobart has shown how media piracy in Bolivia might be 'seen to serve the interests of the many traders of contraband goods on both sides of the frontier ... [and this] might be seen as a symptom of Bolivia's exceptionally informal economy, where money is to be made, even if in very small quantities, from the circulation of goods along trajectories shaped by national imaginaries' (2010). Likewise, the common perception of Cuba as a somehow exceptional analogue or digitally illiterate place has arguably allowed this informal digital marketplace to quietly grow, fomenting local possibilities for ingenuity.

Discussion of music 'piracy' has often polarized characterizations as, on the one hand, insidious criminal activity that threatens musical creativity and musicians' livelihoods alongside the production of culture, or, on the other, as a legitimate and democratic struggle against hegemonizing corporatism and industry (Lessig 2004; Knopper 2009). In Cuba, *el paquete* seems to bridge this chasm, both in its capacity to foment public creative production and exchange, and in its disavowal of international notions of ownership and copyright. The complexity of lived social relations surrounding and flowing through such networks as *el paquete* defies polarizing discourses of capitalism versus socialism, for in reality, actors have their own multiple agendas for participation, which at times can appear contradictory to outsiders.

When I asked Nestor, for example, if he saw the rise of *el paquete* as signalling a nascent American-style imported capitalism in Cuba, he responded:

> the problem is, what is capitalism? I imagine it has to do with the idea of consumption. I live in a country where, if I want to find a brand of perfume, or shampoo, it's impossible to consume it, because six months can go by without being able to find it. Everything can disappear in Cuba … but if it's about ownership, well then maybe we have it right after all. I can buy a *paquete* this week and gift it to my friends, that doesn't happen in other places. If you bought a cell phone app or a song, your system is made so that you can't share it with other people. That's capitalism. It's complete control, and an impossibility to share. In Cuba, the *paquete* is a business, and we mustn't forget that, but it's also a business that's so open, not all the earnings are centralized. So, talking about consumption in Cuba is a delicate thing … (Interview, Havana, February 2018)

With this, Nestor highlighted two parallel conceptualizations of possession that coexist in present day Cuba. On the one hand, private ownership is now officially recognized with the introduction of the New Constitution in 2019, yet other items are considered *bienes en común* – goods in common ownership – drawing upon socialist notions of public utility and creative commons. Some of my friends viewed *el paquete* as a daring domestic challenge to American corporate hegemony; one even proudly called himself the digital 'pirate of the Caribbean', for plundering lucrative channels of material exchange monopolized by colonizing corporate powers (such as Amazon and Netflix), invoking a notion of social banditry (Hobsbawm 2000). Yet, in other instances my interlocutors seemed quick to restrict circulation networks and control the flow of material, for personal gain. My artist friend Nestor had also embraced the term 'pirate', and as part of his exhibition on Cuban digital media in Queen's Museum (New York), he wryly placed a publicly browsable copy of *The Pirate Book*, which itself contains an essay about *el paquete* (Maigret and Roszowska 2015).

Video piracy has undoubtedly enabled people across the Global South to participate in accelerated circuits of global media flows, from which they might otherwise have been excluded. Examples abound across Latin America, Asia and Africa, allowing Nigerian audiences, for example, to watch films contemporaneously with audiences in Bogotá or Bangkok (Mattelart 2009). Felicitously, the name of one of the main sites from which international digital content is downloaded in Cuba is 'eMule', which is a peer-to-peer file sharing site dating back to 2003. The 'portable homelands' – to borrow a phrase from Cuban journalist Luis Ortega (1998) – of *el paquete* thus echo the material packages carried back and forth across the US–Cuba border by *mulas* (Cearns 2023) as a means of sourcing and perpetually recreating local Cuban culture from and through its relations with another place.

Cuban anthropologist Fernando Ortiz suggested a neologism – 'transculturation' – as 'fundamental and indispensable for an understanding of Cuba' (1947), describing the process of transition from one culture to another as involving the syncretic fusion of various elements. In so doing, Ortiz cites a metaphor of a Cuban stew – *ajiaco* – which is explicitly comprised of various ingredients of European, African and Indigenous origin, all of which cooks down into one inseparable central substance (see also Palmié 2013). Inside the *olla cubana* (Cuban pot), ingredients cannot be separated out, and there is a constant process of ingredients decomposing (as they cook) and recomposing into something new, and essentially 'Cuban'. This is broadly akin to other formulations of hybridity, creolization, *mestizaje* (mixed-race) and hegemonic discourses of 'mixture', often cited across Latin America and the Caribbean as central to regional and national identity. Such discourses have also often been cited as central to the celebration of local creative responses to neoliberal policy or elitism (Dibbell 2004). It is possible to see the flow of digital media (via portable storage devices) of *el paquete* as a continuation of this transcultural practice, which posits *cubanidad* or Cuban cultural production in constant encounters and fusion with 'the other'. Participation in such networks becomes a way of participating in Cuba itself, or a shared project of inventiveness that is seen as a defining mutual feature of this shared community.

In his ethnography of media piracy in Nigeria, Brian Larkin points out that while piracy has connected Nigerians to 'the globalized world, it does so by emphasizing [their] marginalization at the same time' (2004). In Cuba, *el paquete* is more than 'just a bunch of bootleg stuff from outside Cuba' (Parish 2018), it's a media ecosystem in its own right. By participating in this transnational network of circulation, Cubans are both connected to a public font of *cubanidad* and reminded of their own liminal position within this network. A study of the informal economy of digital media reveals the often-underground channels through which cultural globalization operates. Pirated cultural products follow the paths of 'globalization from below' (Basch et al. 1994; Portes 1999) and, in this light, everyday Cubans arguably mobilize more agency than might first be thought, in shaping transnational circuits of digital media.

Copyright, copyleft

A striking characteristic of digital technology is the almost effortless capability it provides to create multiple identical copies, which in turn has fundamental implications for notions of ownership, copyright, and what it means to copy. Scholars have cited the distinction between 'original' and 'copy' as needing ethnographic development in terms of local conceptions of 'piracy' and 'originality' (Vann 2006; Aguiar 2013). While almost all of the content on *el paquete* is pirated, or copied without licence, much of it is also re-authored in the process, with the individual attributions of the *matriz* or *paquetero* attaching themselves palimpsestically to the product through the insertion of branded watermarks, advertising, and subtitles. In this way, many of my Cuban interlocutors advertised *un producto original* – an original product – despite the fact the vast majority was copied from someone else, who copied it from someone else, who copied it from the internet.

The very word 'piracy' suggests an illegal act, yet anthropological research has thematized resistance, subversion and the creation of non-hegemonic networks for the circulation and flow of culture through the infringement of copyright restrictions (Chang 2004; Bosch 2010; Miller, J. 2012). The sharing of digital assets can challenge hegemonic notions of ownership and property (Commaerts 2011), as has also become evident in a large movement towards open digital access (Coleman and Golub 2008; Kelty 2008; Coleman 2012).

This becomes even more resonant in the case of Cuba, where 'copyright' as a concept is not given the same weight as in many other parts of the world. If 'to oppose copyright is to oppose capitalism' (Söderberg 2002), Cuba has a long trajectory of either denying copyright as a concept, or not enforcing it, in a bid to undermine nearby capitalizing (and possibly colonial) projects in the US and beyond. Artistic production has long been fundamental to the Revolutionary project in Cuba, and as such was considered a communal effort and asset, as opposed to an expression of individualism or the sole property of an author. For this reason, many artists in Cuba are still considered state employees, as opposed to the self-employed or freelance nature of artist status in many other parts of the world. With the advent of electronic and digital technologies of reproduction, 'the global reach of the mass media, and the transnational circulation of mass culture, the culture industries – which rely on creative labor and a general respect for intellectual property rights – have become export industries fundamental to the expansion of capitalism and related hegemonic projects' (Hernández-Reguant 2004).

This confronts the Cuban socialist project with new challenges regarding recognition of individual property. Moreover, the rise of *el paquete* has proved problematic, insofar as it generates surplus value through further creative input (or labour) by additional parties:

> In the case of music, this value is created through its reinterpretation, in 'sampling,' 'versions,' and 'remixes'; through its circulation in broadcasting and advertising; and in some cases, through its mere consumptive use, via a jukebox or Internet downloads. This is all crucial for understanding the intersections of Cuban late socialist structures and capitalist practices, for under neoliberal capitalism, capital is created not only through productive labor, but also through the circulation, use, and consumption of products as well as through speculation – in this case, with mass-cultural products that are also copyrights. (Hernández-Reguant 2004)

Nonetheless, networks like *el paquete* also present some advantages to the Cuban state project. On the one hand, they facilitate the marketing of Cuban cultural production, both across the island and abroad through transnational commercial networks. Moreover, the consumption and circulation of digital content through new public spaces arguably undermines the hegemonic status of international and capitalizing 'intellectual property'; in this regard, the flow of digital products as *bienes en común* (to borrow Nestor's earlier phrase), is arguably entirely in line with the Cuban Revolutionary project, which seeks to disrupt the progression of capitalist power structures (Cearns 2021c). While the *paquetero* pirates of *el paquete* may operate at the margins of state-sanctioned trade, they also actively unsettle the power hierarchies common to hegemonic corporate structures elsewhere in the world. Counter to what many might expect, some *paqueteros* have even started to informally export their content to the nearby diaspora audience in Miami, actively enabling Cubans abroad to evade participation in capitalistic consumerism (Cearns 2023).

Ariana Hernández-Reguant argues for the Cuban culture industries as a sort of border zone, 'structured by the interests of a new array of stakeholders, both state and corporate' (2004, 2). *El paquete*, as the latest iteration of a Cuban culture industry, can be and has been mobilized in multiple directions: both as a litmus test for the existence of imported neoliberal capitalist practices, and as evidence of resistance to global hegemonic patterns of top-down ownership, on both sides of the Florida Straits, simultaneously. If *el paquete* is a border zone, it bridges not only formulations of international and domestic, capitalist and socialist, but also confronts conceptualizations of what it is to be Cuban.

State-sanctioned piracy

Some of these debates, surrounding the role of copyright in Cuba (*el derecho del autor* – author's rights) came to a dramatic head in the summer of 2023. With financial assistance from the ICAIC (*Instituto Cubano del Arte e Industria Cinematográficos*), independent Cuban film director Juan Pin Vilar made a documentary about the Argentinian musician Fito Páez, whose musical output is owned and distributed by the international music company Sony. While final permissions for the copyright of the music featured in the film were being arranged, the Cuban director secured permission from Páez and Sony to show a draft version to a small audience at a theatre in Havana. No sooner had this 'first showing' been announced on social media, the Cuban Ministry for Culture decided to shut down the event.

Word went around that this was because the film included footage of Páez making some comments about Cuba that might be deemed 'political', and that the director had been asked to edit two such moments out of the film. Vilar had refused to do so. The international press and interested parties on social media began to talk of censorship (Reyes 2023), and tensions rapidly grew. Suddenly, a few days later, the rough cut of the film was broadcast on national Cuban television, without the permission of the director, Fito Páez, or any other parties that might hold copyright over any of the content, and a furore erupted among filmmakers in Cuba. By way of rebuking any claims regarding censorship within Cuba, the state-owned TV channel had committed a volte-face of quite some degree and simply broadcast the film to the whole nation.

'The state has violated their rights as artist and creatives', through this 'improvised and dirty solution to the censorship problem', fumed a friend of mine, a senior academic in Film Studies in Havana, who I'll here call Pablo. In a private communication with me later on, through an encrypted chat forum, he explained that Cuban artists can, and do, exercise their copyrights within Cuba, and that the actions of the Cuban Ministry of Culture itself to deny this was what had caused such consternation among his colleagues. These actions had not only breached international copyright (at the time of writing, Sony Music is now pursuing this in court), but had also effectively ensured that Vilar, the filmmaker, would not be able to premiere his work at international festivals. 'There's always some value, some money to be made' (*hay siempre un dinero que es invertido o un fruto que viene de esto*), my friend told me, 'and now in this case he [Vilar] has lost control [*autonomia*] over it ... anyone can copy it onto *el paquete* or even put it on YouTube, and he won't be able to derive benefit from it'. He continued:

> In Cuba since the outset of the revolution, the government decided that any artistic product, or products of any kind realized by North American companies, would be subject to piracy in Cuba because there was no agreement in place about ownership [*derecho de propriedad*] across the Embargo. So that started to generate a legitimization of piracy, a mentality whereby anything can be copied, reproduced, pirated, shared, whatever you want to call it, within Cuban territories ... but that's not written into law anywhere, it's more an informal truth everybody understands. (Interview by phone, 13 June 2023)

This status quo stretches back to the 1960s, but times have of course changed in the decades since. Up until the 1990s (when Cuba entered a period of economic difficulty following the collapse of its ally, the Soviet Union), while copyright did technically exist within Cuba, very few artists would ever seek to assert such rights, but this is gradually changing. Pablo explained:

> for the longest time everyone knew not to complain about copyright, because the Revolution came above all else, and if an individual artist tried to assert their rights over their work, the government apparatus might consider that individualistic, or bourgeois, and up until the 1990s it was really taboo in Cuba to talk about making a profit ... but when the economy deteriorated in the 90s and people struggled to make ends meet [*el dinero no alcanzaba*] things changed and artists started to demand payment for use of their work. A new law appeared, which has continued to be modified in

> the twenty-first century, as we've entered the age of digitalization, and that's been broken here for political ends, for the government to save face, which is what makes this violation so egregious [*descarada*]. (Interview by phone, 13 June 2023)

In fact, the latest modification to the Cuban law on copyright was in December 2022 (*Gaceta Oficial* 2022). Complaints regarding breach of copyright must be put to the Ministry for Culture, as the 'national competent authority' on the matter, and in this case, of course, the party considered to have breached authorial copyright is that same Ministry of Culture. There are several ambiguities in the most recent decree which enable a wider interpretation as to how content can be shared without requiring remuneration. Three such exceptions include when the content is used in any 'act' coordinated by an 'institution of the State' (Article 86.1.c), when the artistic creation draws, in any part, from resources financially supported by the state (such as a scholarship) (Article 86.1.n), or any public reproduction realized with 'cultural diffusion' as its objective (Article 86.2.b). Additionally, the use of any artistic content for 'educational' purposes also enables content sharing without abiding by copyright restrictions.

This latest (and, at the time of writing, ongoing) debacle highlights the complexities surrounding legality, ownership, the challenges of defining 'piracy' within the Cuban context, and the ambiguities that pervade even seemingly simple distinctions such as state/individual or public/private in such a setting. Ironically perhaps, it is the state itself which here has pirated audiovisual content created by an individual. And as my friend Pablo pointed out to me, while the state originally did so ostensibly to revoke international criticism for censorship, the state continues to maintain its position – including in an international lawsuit against Sony Music – as a politicized stance against the American Embargo and all its associated ills to do with bourgeois notions of private ownership.

Conclusion

This chapter has shown how nascent digital networks in Cuba and its diaspora are providing an emerging transnational public space, which both encourages social participation and yet is centralizing itself into an increasingly commoditized platform of fewer voices. The media piracy network known as *el paquete* reveals a potential clash between the emerging capitalistic practices and latent socialist ideologies that coexist in Cuban society; something which, to most Cubans, is not problematic, but simply a normal aspect of everyday life. Notions of ownership flex according to context, and these informal networks of digital circulation build upon longstanding pragmatism and flexibility when it comes to acquisition through participation in social networks.

With the arrival of digital content, Cuba clearly is not morphing into a pseudo-American model of media consumption, as had been anticipated (Venegas 2007). The recent debacle over Juan Pin Vilar's documentary and the Cuban Ministry of Culture's decision to breach Vilar's copyright, by sharing a pirated copy on national television, points vividly to the tensions that arise as content-sharing in an increasingly transnational setting takes form. Such cases force us to re-examine our own notions of where the boundary lies, between public and private, state (or corporation) and citizen (consumer), authorship, and 'authenticity' or originality. Cuba's *paqueteros* continue to navigate their course as digital 'pirates' of the Caribbean, perhaps mirroring wider policies taken by the state itself, as they trace the borders between capitalism and socialism, Cuba and the US, participation in a system, and resistance to it.

References

Aguiar, José Carlos G. 2013. 'Smugglers, fayuqueros, piratas: Transitory commodities and illegality in the trade of pirated CDs in Mexico', *PoLAR: Political and Legal Anthropology Review* 36(2): 249–65.

Astley, Tom. 2016. 'The people's mixtape: Peer-to-peer file sharing without the internet in contemporary Cuba'. In *Networked Music Cultures: Contemporary approaches, emerging issues*, edited by R. Nowak and A. Whelan, 13–30. London: Palgrave Macmillan.

Ayuso, Silvia. 2015. 'Netflix contra el "paquete" cubano', *El País*, 15 February. Accessed 27 March 2024. https://elpais.com/internacional/2015/02/15/actualidad/1423981072_014165.html.

Azenha, Gustavo S. 2006. 'The internet and the decentralisation of the popular music industry: Reflections on technology, concentration and diversification', *Radical Musicology* 1(1). http://www.radical-musicology.org.uk/2006/Azenha.htm.

Basch, Linda G., Nina Glick Schiller and Cristina Blanc-Szanton (eds). 1994. *Nations Unbound: Transnational projects, post-colonial predicaments, and de-territorialized nation states*. London and New York: Routledge.

Bosch, Tanja. 2010. 'Piracy as counter-hegemony', *Communicare* 29(2): 99–116.

Boudreault-Fournier, Alexandrine. 2017. 'The fortune of scarcity: Digital music in circulation'. In *The Routledge Companion to Digital Ethnography*, edited by L. Hjorth, H. Horst, A. Galloway and G. Bell, 344–53. London: Routledge.

Cearns, Jennifer. 2021a. 'Connecting (to) Cuba: Transnational digital flows between Havana and the Cuban diaspora', *Cuban Studies* 50(1): 161–85.

Cearns, Jennifer. 2021b. 'Packaging Cuban media: Communities of digital sharing in Cuba and its diaspora', *Cuban Studies* 50(1): 99–110.

Cearns, Jennifer. 2021c. '"A una Cuba alternativa": Digital millennials, social influencing and cuentapropismo in Havana'. In *Cuba's Digital Revolution: Citizen innovation and state policy,* edited by T. A. Henken and S. Garcia Santamaría, 262–81. Gainesville: University Press of Florida.
Cearns, Jennifer. 2023. *Circulating Culture: Transnational Cuban networks of exchange*. Gainesville: University Press of Florida.
Chang, Hsiao-Hung. 2004. 'Fake logos, fake theory, fake globalization', *Inter-Asia Cultural Studies* 5(2): 222–36.
Cimpanu, Catalin. 2021. 'Cuba passes internet censorship and cybersecurity law', *The Record.* Accessed 27 March 2024. https://therecord.media/cuba-passes-internet-censorship-and-cybersecurity-law/.
Coleman, Gabriella E. 2012. *Coding Freedom: The ethics and aesthetics of hacking*. Princeton: Princeton University Press.
Coleman, Gabriella E. and Alex Golub. 2008. 'Hacker practice: Moral genres and the cultural articulation of liberalism', *Anthropological Theory* 8(3): 255–77.
Commaerts, Bart. 2011. 'Disruptive sharing in a digital age: Rejecting neoliberalism?', *Continuum* 25(1): 47–62.
Concepción, Sunamis Fabelo. 2021. 'Japón en Cuba: El fenómeno del manga y otros espacios de cooperación en materia cultural', *Mirai: Estudios Japoneses* 5: 77–89.
Dent, Alexander Sebastian. 2012. 'Piracy, circulatory legitimacy, and neoliberal subjectivity in Brazil', *Cultural Anthropology* 27(1): 28–49.
Dent, Alexander Sebastian. 2020. *Digital Pirates: Policing intellectual property in Brazil.* Redwood City, CA: Stanford University Press.
Dibbell, Julian. 2004. 'We pledge allegiance to the penguin', *Wired.* Accessed 27 March 2024. https://www.wired.com/2004/11/linux-6/.
Duong, Paloma. 2013. 'Bloggers unplugged: Amateur citizens, cultural discourse, and public sphere in Cuba', *Journal of Latin American Cultural Studies* 22(4): 375–97.
Escobar, Luz. 2017. 'El "paketito", un rival clandestino para el "paquete" – 14ymedio', *14ymedio.* Accessed 27 March 2024. https://www.14ymedio.com/cienciaytecnologia/paketito-rival-clandestino-paquete_0_2211978784.html.
Farrell, Michelle Leigh. 2021. 'Disrupting the algorithm: The streaming platforms in the Cuban audiovisual landscape: El paquete semanal, Netflix, and Mi Mochila', *Cuban Studies* 50(1): 186–204.
Fazekas, David and Serena Marshall. 2016. 'The Package (El Paquete) is illegal but it's Cuba's no. 1 employer', *ABC News*, 21 March. Accessed 27 March 2024. https://abcnews.go.com/International/package-el-paquete-illegal-cubas-number-employer/story?id=33279812.
Fernández, Damián J. 2000. *Cuba and the Politics of Passion*. Austin: University of Texas Press.
Fowler, Víctor. 2019. '"El Paquete": Internet in Cuba'. In *The Cuba Reader: History, culture, politics*, edited by A. Chomsky, B. Carr, A. Prieto and P. M. Smorkaloff, 667–71. Durham, NC: Duke University Press.
Freedom House. 2021. 'Cuba: Freedom on the net. Country report'. Accessed 27 March 2024. https://freedomhouse.org/country/cuba/freedom-net/2021.
Gaceta Oficial de la República de Cuba. 2019. 'Sobre la Informatización de la sociedad en Cuba', *Gaceta Oficial* 45. Accessed 31 March 2024. https://www.gacetaoficial.gob.cu/es/gaceta-oficial-no-45-ordinaria-de-2019.
Gaceta Oficial de la República de Cuba. 2022. 'Aprueba el reglamento de las organizaciones de gestión colectiva de derechos sobre creaciones literarias y artísticas', 122. Accessed 27 March 2024. https://www.gacetaoficial.gob.cu/es/gaceta-oficial-no-122-ordinaria-de-2022.
García Martínez, Antonio. 2017. 'Inside Cuba's DIY internet revolution', *Wired*, 26 July. Accessed 27 March 2024. https://www.wired.com/2017/07/inside-cubas-diy-internet-revolution/.
Hansing, Katrin and Bert Hoffmann. 2020. 'When racial inequalities return: Assessing the restratification of Cuban society 60 years after revolution', *Latin American Politics and Society* 62(2): 29–52.
Harney, Connor. 2021. 'Radio Free Cuba: From détente to re-escalation in Havana and Miami', *International Journal of Cuban Studies* 13(1): 67–85.
Helft, Miguel. 2015. 'No internet? No problem: Inside Cuba's tech revolution', *Forbes*, 1 July. Accessed 27 March 2024. https://www.forbes.com/sites/miguelhelft/2015/07/01/no-internet-no-problem-inside-cubas-tech-revolution/.

Henken, Ted A. 2005. 'Entrepreneurship, Informality, and the Second Economy: Cuba's underground economy in comparative perspective'. Papers and proceedings of the fifteenth annual meeting of the Association for the Study of the Cuban Economy, 360–75. Accessed 27 March 2024. https://citeseerx.ist.psu.edu/document?repid=rep1&type=pdf&doi=8bcd7ba355a9d9823eb11a9c6208efd5555d2d7d.

Henken, Ted A. 2017. 'Cuba's digital millennials: Independent digital media and civil society on the island of the disconnected', *Social Research* 84(2): 429–56.

Hernández-Reguant, Ariana. 2004. 'Copyrighting Che: Art and authorship under Cuban late socialism', *Public Culture* 16(1): 1–29.

Hobsbawm, Eric J. 2000. *Bandits*. London: Weidenfeld & Nicolson.

Horst, Heather A. 2011. 'Free, social and inclusive: Appropriation and resistance of new media technologies in Brazil', *International Journal of Communication* 5: 437–62.

Humphreys, Laura-Zoë. 2017. 'Utopia in a package? Digital media piracy and the politics of entertainment in Cuba', *Cultural Anthropology*, Hot Spots, 27 March. Accessed 27 March 2024. https://culanth.org/fieldsights/utopia-in-a-package-digital-media-piracy-and-the-politics-of-entertainment-in-cuba.

Humphreys, Laura-Zoë. 2021. 'Loving idols: K-pop and the limits of neoliberal solidarity in Cuba', *International Journal of Cultural Studies* 24(6): 1009–26.

Iordanova, Dina. 2003. *Cinema of the Other Europe: The industry and artistry of East Central European film*. New York: Wallflower Press.

Kelty, Christopher. 2008. *Two Bits: The cultural significance of free software*. Durham, NC: Duke University Press.

Knopper, Steve. 2009. *Appetite for Self-Destruction: The spectacular crash of the record industry in the digital age*. London: Simon & Schuster.

Köhn, Steffen. 2019. 'Unpacking El Paquete: The poetics and politics of Cuba's offline data-sharing network', *Digital Culture & Society* 5(1): 105–24.

Larkin, Brian. 2004. 'Degraded images, distorted sounds: Nigerian video and the infrastructure of piracy', *Public Culture* 16(2): 289–314.

Lessig, Lawrence. 2004. *Free Culture: How big media uses technology and the law to lock down culture and control creativity*. New York: Penguin.

Levine, Mike. 2020. 'Sounding El Paquete: The local and transnational routes of an Afro-Cuban repartero', *Cuban Studies* 50: 139–60.

Lorenzi, Jane and Jeanne Batalova. 2022. 'Caribbean immigrants in the United States'. Migration Policy Institute. Accessed 27 March 2024. https://www.migrationpolicy.org/article/caribbean-immigrants-united-states.

Maigret, Nicolas and Maria Roszowska (eds). 2015. *The Pirate Book*. Ljubljana: Aksioma Institute for Contemporary Art.

Manuel, Peter. 2014. 'The regional North Indian popular music industry in 2014: From cassette culture to cyberculture', *Popular Music* 33(3): 389–412.

Mattelart, Tristan. 2009. 'Audio-visual piracy: Towards a study of the underground networks of cultural globalization', *Global Media and Communication* 5(3): 308–26.

Miller, Daniel and Heather A. Horst (eds). 2012. *Digital Anthropology*. New York: Berg.

Miller, Jade. 2012. 'Global Nollywood: The Nigerian movie industry and alternative global networks in production and distribution', *Global Media and Communication* 8(2): 117–33.

Morin Aguado, Vincente. 2015. 'The strange case of Cuba's Gilbert Man', *Havana Times*, 14 February. Accessed 27 March 2024. https://havanatimes.org/features/the-strange-case-of-cubas-gilbert-man/.

Morris, Jeremy and Abel Polese (eds). 2014. *The Informal Post-Socialist Economy: Embedded practices and livelihoods*. London: Routledge.

Nelson, Anne. 2016. *Cuba's Parallel Worlds: Digital media crosses the divide*. Washington, DC: Center for International Media Assistance.

Ortega, Luís. 1998. *Cubanos en Miami*. La Habana: Editorial de Ciencias Sociales.

Ortiz, Fernando. 1947. *Cuban Counterpoint: Tobacco and sugar*. New York: Knopf.

Palmié, Stephan. 2013. *The Cooking of History: How not to study Afro-Cuban religion*. Chicago: University of Chicago Press.

Parish, Nick. 2018. 'Inside El Paquete: Cuba's social network'. Accessed 27 March 2024. https://withintent.uncorkedstudios.com/inside-el-paquete-cubas-social-network-2fa6c99660ee.

Pertierra, Anna Cristina. 2012. 'If they show Prison Break in the United States on a Wednesday, by Thursday it is here: Mobile media networks in twenty-first century Cuba', *Television and New Media* 13(5): 399–414.

Pinheiro-Machado, Rosana. 2017. *Counterfeit Itineraries in the Global South: The human consequences of piracy in China and Brazil*. Abingdon: Routledge.

Portes, Alejandro. 1999. 'Globalization from below: The emergence of transnational communities', *Actes de la recherche en sciences sociales* 129: 15–25.

Press, Larry. 2015. 'El paquete update: Cuba's largest private employer?', *The Internet in Cuba*, 14 September. Accessed 27 March 2024. http://laredcubana.blogspot.com/2015/09/el-paquete-update-cubas-largest-private.html.

Press, Larry. 2021. 'The past, present, and future of the Cuban internet'. In *Cuba's Digital Revolution: Citizen innovation and state policy*, edited by T. Henken and S. García Santamaria, 29–49. Gainesville: University Press of Florida.

Reyes, José Luis. 2023. 'La televisión cubana exhibe un documental censurado de Juan Pin Vilar sin su autorización'. Accessed 27 March 2024. https://diariodecuba.com/cultura/1686486398_47754.html.

Rhys-Taylor, Alex. 2013. 'The essences of multiculture: A sensory exploration of an inner-city street market', *Ethnography, Diversity and Urban Space* 20(4): 393–406.

Ritter, Archibald R. M. 2014. 'Economic illegalities and the underground economy in Cuba'. In *A Contemporary Cuba Reader: The revolution under Raúl Castro*, edited by P. Brenner, M. R. Jiménez, J. M. Kirk and W. M. LeoGrande, 203–30. Lanham, MD: Rowman & Littlefield.

Rodríguez, Juan Diego. 2021. 'Cuba increases police raids to confiscate satellite dishes', *14ymedio*, 12 August. Accessed 27 March 2024. https://translatingcuba.com/cuba-increases-police-raids-to-confiscate-satellite-dishes/.

San Pedro, Emilio. 2015. 'Cuban internet delivered weekly by hand', *BBC News*, 10 August. Accessed 27 March 2024. https://www.bbc.co.uk/news/technology-33816655.

Schoon, Allette. 2016. 'Distributing hip-hop in a South African town: From the digital backyard studio to the translocal ghetto internet', proceedings of the First African Conference on Human Computer Interaction, 104–13. Accessed 27 March 2024. https://dl.acm.org/doi/pdf/10.1145/2998581.2998592.

Söderberg, Johan. 2002. 'Copyleft vs. copyright: A Marxist critique', *First Monday* 7(3). Accessed 27 March 2024. https://doi.org/10.5210/fm.v7i3.938.

Speakman, Maile. 2021. '"Hay muchísimo poder en la oscuridad": Black cuir cinema clubs in contemporary Havana', *Revista Periódicus* 1(15): 40–62.

Steingo, Gavin. 2015. 'Sound and circulation: Immobility and obduracy in South African electronic music', *Ethnomusicology Forum* 24(1): 102–23.

Stern, Monika. 2014. 'Mi wantem musik blong mi hemi blong evriwan ['I want my music to be for everyone']: Digital developments, copyright and music circulation in Port Vila, Vanuatu', *First Monday* 19(10). Accessed 27 March 2024. https://doi.org/10.5210/fm.v19i10.5551.

Stobart, Henry. 2010. 'Rampant reproduction and digital democracy: Shifting landscapes of music production and "piracy" in Bolivia', *Ethnomusicology Forum* 19(1): 27–56.

Stout, Noelle. 2014. 'Bootlegged: Unauthorized circulation and dilemmas of collaboration in the digital age', *Visual Anthropology Review* 30(2): 177–87.

Ulysse, Gina. 1999. *Uptown Ladies and Downtown Women: Informal commercial importing and the social/symbolic politics of identities in Jamaica*. Ann Arbor: University of Michigan Press.

Vann, Elizabeth F. 2006. 'The limits of authenticity in Vietnamese consumer markets', *American Anthropologist* 108(2): 286–96.

Venegas, Cristina. 2007. 'Shared dreams and red cockroaches: Cuba and digital culture', *Hispanic Review* 75(4): 399–414.

Whynacht, Ardath. 2009. 'Raperas of the NeoRevolución: Young women, capitalism and Cuban hip hop culture', *Girlhood Studies* 2(2): 119–38.

11

Counterfeit: disruption and creation in the files of transnational adoptions from Guatemala to Europe

Silvia Posocco and Sophie Villérs

Transnational adoption flows from Guatemala grew steadily over the second part of the twentieth century up until 2007, when legislative reforms in the country brought the practice formally to a halt. Adoptions from Guatemala attracted the attention of journalists, academic researchers and adoption experts, who from different perspectives raised questions about the ethics of the practice, alongside noting concerns over the increasingly marketized aspects of these transnational movements and the displacement of children. Tenuous legal provisions governed the adoption process from 1977 through to the years of expansion in the 1990s and 2000s. In practice, national legislation geared towards framing the role of notaries (*notarios*) within the Guatemalan legal system also consolidated and regularized notaries' position as the key intermediaries in the transaction between birth mothers and adoptive families. Legal provisions issued in 1977 determined that notaries could finalize the adoption process without the involvement of the country's judicial system. The extra- or para-judicial character of the process to all intents and purposes privatized adoptions, turning them into arrangements between individuals engaged in the transfer of the *patria potestad* (right of custody) over the children. In practice, the adoption process did mobilize the courts – and judges' interventions more specifically. The involvement of judges was sometimes important, notably in cases where the children were placed in state-run orphanages, or children's homes run by religious orders and private providers (Casa Alianza et al. 2007; Posocco 2011; 2019). Whether fully dejudicialized, or partly judicialized, transnational adoptions grew exponentially in the latter decades of the twentieth century.

The growth and consolidation of transnational adoption networks and flows over time did not, however, take place in a vacuum. Rather, all of this coincided with the bloodiest years of the Guatemalan conflict (1960–96) – one of the many so-called 'dirty wars' in Latin America in the twentieth century. The Guatemalan conflict began officially in 1960, with an attempted coup d'état by a group of disaffected military officers who rose up against the regime of General Ydígoras Fuentes. The roots of the conflict can be traced back to the United States' Central Intelligence Agency (CIA)-sponsored coup d'état that took place in 1954 against the democratically elected government of Juan Jacobo Árbenz Guzmán (1951–4), whose commitment to agrarian reforms and land redistribution encroached on the commercial interests of the United Fruit Company (Schlesinger and Kinzer 1982). The internal displacement of population and widespread political violence intensified during the 1980s, when the assaults against Indigenous populations through 'scorched earth' military actions tore communities apart. The Commission for Historical Clarification declared the violence genocidal for the particular way in which Maya communities in the highlands of the country were targeted in army operations (CEH 1999; see also Oglesby and Nelson 2019). The conflict severely impacted communities in the rural areas and in the urban centres, creating internal displacement as well as migration across the borders, as those fleeing the violence sought refuge in Mexico and other neighbouring countries. As many international and local civil society organizations have argued, children were severely affected by the violence (CEH 1999; ODHA 2005).

Against this background, transnational adoptions networks began to consolidate and expand, aided by the legislation of 1977 which placed the adoption process firmly in the hands of notaries whose legal counsel could be directly mobilized by those seeking to adopt, or by adoption agencies and brokers. In view of this, transnational adoptions from Guatemala over the course of the twentieth century and early twenty-first century ought to be understood as part of larger geopolitical processes which fuelled political violence and genocide, greatly impacting the lives of ordinary Guatemalans. Indigenous populations bore the brunt of the onslaught, while those who were active in guerrilla organizations, popular grassroots movements and social justice groups sought to resist state violence, and were met by brutal state repression (CEH 1999; ODHA 2005). Campaigns to identify and locate the disappeared, to oppose forced displacement and dispossession, and to organize and bring to justice those responsible for crimes against humanity, flourished in the years of the conflict and in the immediate aftermath of the peace accords that were signed in 1996 by the representatives of the guerrilla organizations and the Guatemalan government. Transnational adoptions appeared in the post-conflict discussions and settlements, but did so very rarely, and until recently continued to be relatively marginal in public debate and public consciousness. Since the mid-noughties, researchers and human rights activists in Guatemala and the Global North have progressively worked to shed light on the operations of transnational adoptions networks. Associations of adopted persons from Guatemala have also become increasingly vocal and have demanded institutional accountability and clarification over the adoption process, with leading public activist campaigns in Belgium, Canada and France.

This chapter aims to contribute to the growing literature on the appropriation of children, including child abduction and irregular adoption, specifically in the context of violence and dispossession brought on by colonial domination and imperialism. As Briggs has noted, practices of taking children (2020) – *somebody's* children (2012) – are embedded in complex terror formations that have in places been tied to explicit genocidal strategies. Whilst this has been the case across the Americas – as many scholars have carefully charted (Briggs 2012; 2020; Gesteira 2019; Gesteira et al. 2021; Salvo Agoglia and Marre 2019; Salvo Agoglia and Alfaro Monsalve 2019; Villalta 2010) – the nexus between spectacular violence, structural violence, and genocidal violence is particularly evident in Guatemala, where transnational adoptions flourished at the intersections between transnational family-making and state practices of politically motivated and institutionally sanctioned forced disappearance and 'scorched earth' campaigns against Indigenous communities, the poor and those organizing for social justice. Adoptions relied on elaborate paper regimes alongside intricate extrajudicial bureaucracies that have in practice regularized appropriative kinship practices, enabled by child abduction but also, most fundamentally, by the everyday dispossession of birth mothers.

Against this background, counterfeiting as a practice and method was part of legal and paralegal processes tied to the documentality of administrative apparatuses and state institutions. Counterfeiting documents that would be included in the adoption files (*expedientes*) and would thus enable the transnational movement of children, was in some instances specifically connected to managing the aftermath of genocidal military operations, tying adoptions to the counterinsurgency that fomented disruption in the urban areas and the countryside in the wake of military coups, terror campaigns and political repression (Posocco, forthcoming). More broadly, and as we illustrate in detail below, counterfeiting and forgeries were multifarious, uneven and diffused. They engaged individuals closely connected to those in the high offices of the state (Fanon 2022), while also inciting state officials, members of the judiciary and civil servants into counterfeiting identities and kinship relations, repositioning kinning as contraband, and transnational adoption as an implicit national foreign policy that mobilized embassies and plurality of legal jurisdictions internationally. From this perspective, counterfeiting displaces understandings of transnational adoption as a form of making family, to re-signify relatedness in terms of both 'genocide kinning' (Posocco 2011) and 'contraband kinning' – as relations emerge in and out of genocidal violence and counterfeiting practices.

In this chapter, we specifically focus on adopted persons' search for origins in the context of adoptions tied to the forced removal of children and child abduction in Guatemala. We draw on our respective work on the transnational adoption files that ordered the movement of children from Guatemala to Europe in the latter part of the twentieth century and up until 2007, to consider strategies to detect and understand the irregularities that underpinned these transnational adoption flows. We intersect approaches to deciphering the files drawn from research conducted in Guatemala – including in judicial archives – and in Europe in the context of anthropological research on the aftermaths of the Guatemalan conflict, and work to support adoptees' individual and collective search for origins. As our individual and joint research shows, what are conventionally understood to be transnational adoptions from Guatemala entail many complex possible scenarios: children stolen at birth, children declared dead, children who disappeared during village massacres, children resulting from systematic rape of the population, children also sold or given away by their parents. Real adoption opportunities also exist. But then, there are the adoption papers: change of identity of the mother, disappearance of fathers on paper, change of dates of birth or other biographical information. And worst of all: mixing the files between the children put up for adoption to prevent everyone from finding each other. As Sophie Villérs explains:

> I knew that traffic required organization, but at this point, everything needs to be reviewed in the adoption records: the dates, the signatures, the names. And several people both in Guatemala and in Belgium can be found in the records. I was adopted in Belgium via the association Hacer Puente. My Belgian mother trusted them in the proper handling of the adoption process and the adoption file, as she received information about them from the official bodies in Belgium. However, at the time there was still no legislation on

> international adoptions, no formal approval or oversight for associations that could make the link with Belgium and the country of origin. Everything could be done without any transparency or accountability. The Hacer Puente association claims to have only made the link, not to have a copy of our files, nor to know how many children were adopted. I know this because I telephoned the person in charge of my file within this association. On what basis, then, can we rely, to find one's true history and one's true identity? (Posocco and Villérs 2023, 384, translated by the authors)

The course of Villérs' quest for information and clarification changed significantly over time. As Villérs notes:

> When I met Silvia Posocco again in August 2022, a lot of things had changed in relation to my story. DNA and ancestry testing have been beneficial in uncovering the truth. But not just for me. Over three years, I discovered the existence of two sisters and one brother. One of them was adopted and now lives in Canada. I found her on Facebook. We made contact and, very quickly, we were able to establish an incredible bond. We were supposed to have the same mother, but we had some doubts because there appeared to be no resemblance between us. We decided to take a DNA test, via the commercial service provided by 23&Me. The result emerged without the possibility of an appeal: we are cousins in the fourth degree, not sisters. One of us noticed that two of us have no connection with the person who is listed in our files as our mother. So, we went on a quest. The public circulation of the media report, 'Duties of investigation: Trafficker of souls', by Malika Attar of the RTBF media channel in 2020[1] highlighted the extent of the traffic and the forgery. The report was seen by a large number of people and reached beyond the Belgian borders. Canada in particular is starting to take an interest in these stories, but mainly my vicissitudes and those of my sister. Further to a report on our story, we met the person who should be the nephew of one of us. Again, we took a DNA test. Again, disappointment followed. There is no link between us, but he found someone from his family in connection with our paper mother – the person named as our mother in our files. This therefore confirms that the woman in our adoption files is neither the mother of my 'sister', nor mine. Those who did not want us to find our families did a good job. But what they did not suspect at the time was that technologies are changing. People are able to find each other even

> thousands of miles away. People are talking. People exchange their information and then one can discover similarities in the inconsistencies. These exchanges are necessary and important. My story is not representative of all the stories that may exist. The importance of these DNA tests – both recreational and via the Guatemalan Forensic Anthropology Foundation, FAFG – and the support of qualified people, notably by the Liga Guatemalteca de Higiene Mental (LGHM), were essential in my research journey. Finding one's origins is definitely not easy. It comes to upset a life, beliefs, families. What we learn may not be what we wanted to hear. But we must be able to continue to move forward with this information to be able to build on the basis of the truth. With two kinds of roots: that of our family from Guatemala. And that of our adoptive family. (Posocco and Villérs 2023, 384–5, translated by the authors)

Aiming to share insights drawing on our respective work on the adoption process and the adoption files, we initiated this writing collaboration, following our meeting in August 2022. The overview of the historical and political context, as well as the legal arrangements that led to the rise of transnational adoption flows in Guatemala (1977–2007), provides the background against which transnational adoption processes from Guatemala can be understood. In what follows, we consider how adoption files operate as entry points into individuals' searches for origins and the process of their adoption. When read against the grain and not taken at face value, adoption files simultaneously reveal and occlude individual histories and bureaucratic practices. They evidence entrenched, varied and sometimes haphazard practices of forgery, omission and creation, in order to move children as contraband across borders, with a face of legitimacy. Anomaly and incongruity in the files emerge as structuring devices that partially reveal the operations of transnational adoption shadow circuits. For those searching for origins and historical clarification, deciphering forgeries and irregularities entails developing interpretative exertions over their adoption papers.

Our aim is to contribute to individual and collective quests for origins, historical clarification and justice. We hope to show that while the adoption papers can tell us something – if not by assertion, then by omission – about the past and how individual lives were marked by momentous events in the history of the country, we are also equally committed to showing that what is being revealed in the paperwork cannot be fully anticipated. Documents that were supposed to be records of the origins of persons might in fact have little to say in that regard – if anything at all, in some instances – and might instead become evidence of something else entirely, namely, extrajudicial and illicit operations. Persons who were adopted continue to be protagonists of their own lives and of myriad, diverse personal trajectories and experiences. An awareness of the larger geopolitical dynamics and micropolitics that underpinned adoptions from Guatemala, then, entails both disruption and creation. Persons who were adopted are leading the search for *esclarecimento* (clarification) and historical reckoning – and in this context, the development of interpretative strategies, which are also exertions over the meanings of their adoption files, is a critical step in the process. Coming to terms with the past and what might have happened is part of moving forward with this history. From this perspective, the adoption files contain facts, fictions and errors, and it is in such files that personal histories are created and the forgeries that underpin smuggling identities across time and borders can be recursively undone.

Repetitions, irregularities and forgeries as method: 'What are you going to look for? What do you want to know?'

The adoption files that enabled the transnational movement of adoptees from Guatemala to Europe and North America are complex artefacts. They are records of judicial and extrajudicial bureaucracies that were established over decades, as the adoption circuits became increasingly commercialized, sophisticated in their operations, and highly profitable. Academic researchers, activists and adopted persons concur that, in many instances, the adoption files are records of the irregularities at the heart of the practice (see Crespo and Escalón 2015; Fanon 2022; Posocco 2011), but their meaning is by no means fixed, and forgeries themselves can hold different resonances and implications, depending on the questions that are being asked of them: 'What are you looking for in the files? What do you want to know?' Guatemalans who have been adopted transnationally in Europe are increasingly raising these questions, as they reflect on their life experiences – including, but not exclusively, on their adoption process – in a range of practices and accounts which take varied genres and aesthetic registers (see, for example, Calito 2020; Fanon 2022; Vega 2019; Villérs 2022; Tagen-Dye and Givens 2022).

While academic researchers and journalists have largely accessed the adoption paperwork in judicial archives, adopted persons have engaged in systematic analysis of their personal adoption files. They are therefore expert custodians and interpreters, who have developed a range of strategies for deciphering the files in their search for origins and a greater understanding of their personal journeys. In the context of this work, assumptions that the adoption files might contain errors are not uncommon, as associations are made between bureaucratic systems' errors and the social, political and – presumably – administrative disruption in Guatemala in the late 1970s, 1980s and early 1990s. For adopted persons and their families, when errors emerged and became legible as such, they were initially regarded with particular concern and were understood to amount to inconsistencies that might be the result of human error. Regularities and irregularities became more prominent when meeting other adopted persons, whose files also featured similar inaccuracies, patterns and sometimes reproduced the same dubious information across files.

By way of an example, the file of more than one person might contain the same address, or the name of the same *comadrona* – the midwife present at the birth – or the same social worker. Sometimes the address given in one *expediente* for the biological mother, appeared in someone else's file as the address of a *comadrona*. The repetition of information across files introduced the possibility that this might not be a unique, isolated human error. Rather, the repetitions indicated a possible systematic inputting of information whose accuracy and veracity appeared increasingly in question. On closer inspection, files revealed other recurrent elements that could only become apparent when comparing the adoption files of different individuals. The same persons appeared across files – the lawyers, the same notary, the same midwife, the same social worker. The same name featured in some files in one capacity, and in other files in another role – the roles of social worker, midwife and witness could be, seemingly, interchangeable. Most importantly, the names of the same notaries and lawyers reappeared in the files. Notaries are more prominent figures, as some files do not list any lawyers at all, just the notary underwriting the *acta notarial* (affidavit) that performatively brought the adoption into being under Guatemalan law.

Through knowledge practices of juxtaposition and comparison, irregularities appear as constitutive features of the adoption files, with omission or misattribution a regular occurrence, amounting to a norm and a method. Discrepancies – that appeared initially as errors – suggest that one has to keep an open mind, when one engages in the act of deciphering the files. It might not be possible to match names to persons, or persons to roles, or names to addresses, or street addresses to actual places, and so forth. Far from simple mistakes due to administrative oversight, the adoption files suggest the contours of a system of conceiving and inscribing omission and deflection in the paperwork. They point to bureaucratic practices of occlusion *through* record keeping and the making of records. In other words, documents here seem to be made not to record, but to create impediment, false impression and diversion to produce a blurring of the lines, a muddying of the waters, a calculated erasure of the traces.

In addition to tracking persons and their roles across the documents, a detailed consideration of the dates that appear on the files have been fundamental in deciphering forgery. The adoption papers often feature contradictory statements concerning where and when the documents were issued. Dates do not always follow logical sequences, for instance, a linear timeline from birth certificate to social worker's report, to notary's *acta notarial* sealing the process of adoption of individual children. Sometimes, dates do not align in this way. In some instances, the documents issued by embassies to enable the adoption and the onward travel of the child have dates that are chronologically later than the dates of the arrival of the child in the country of destination. The documents appear to have been issued retrospectively, despite the fact that they were handed over with the child at destination. Chronologies are not linear. Adoptive parents explain that they received the paperwork with the child at the airport in their own home country, and that the papers were handed over to them directly by the non-governmental organization that brokered the adoption on their behalf. When they noticed inconsistencies in the paperwork, they attributed them to errors or inefficient administration. Interestingly, when comparing and juxtaposing multiple records, the same dates recur across the adoption files of different individuals. Persons adopted in Belgium, for instance, appear to have their birthdays in the month of November. Putting files together for analysis is a relational exercise and different elements come to the fore, depending on which records are being brought within the analytical frame. What appears when examining the files of persons adopted in Belgium, might not be as prominent when comparing files of persons adopted in Belgium and France, for example, though the names of the same lawyers and notaries are common across the adoption archives, across sites and temporalities.

The recurrent feature might not be the name of the same social worker, or the name of the same biological mother. The repetition might lie in the story, as the files often offer the same account of poverty, inability to care for the infant, assent to give the child up for adoption (Posocco 2011). Formulaic narratives unfold alongside notable contradictions, as those that emerge in the reports of the social workers. A child appears as having siblings in one report; in other documents they appear as an only child. There are sisters who turn out to be not biologically related to one another, though in the paperwork they appear to be offspring of the same mother. They are recorded as having the same mother, the same name and the same adoptive parents, making the sibling relation a constant feature of their documentary histories, but one that is not borne out in the regime of legibility of genetic relations.

In a context where siblings might not be siblings in the sense of sharing a biogenetic origin, adoptive persons reach out to others with a view to ascertain whether – and how – they might be related to one another. Communities of adopted persons from the same country are relatively small. Connections with those sharing parts of one's adoption history have been facilitated by the associations that have emerged since about 2010. These associations are adoptee-led and have been at the forefront of the work of making sense of the transnational adoption processes and related practices. In this context, cross-referencing records is important in the identification of forgery, and access to digitized information in ancestry archives has proved particularly useful for the task. The Latter-day Saints Online Genealogy Records, for example, have yielded notable results, as these archives hold digital copies of the Guatemalan national identity register, and of some Guatemalan local birth registers too. This has enabled the identification of some of the individuals who appear with different roles and responsibilities in adoptees' files. By searching for the names of birth mothers in the Latter-day Saint Online Genealogy Records,[2] for example, adopted persons have located birth mothers' identity records, taking them as proof that these individuals in Guatemala exist and are related to them. Cross-referencing their individual files, persons adopted by different families were found to have the same birth mother, so assumed they were siblings who might one day be able to locate their birth mother – as a real living person in Guatemala. Extending the cross-referencing to include other adoptees who had the same woman named as the mother in their files, they located yet another sibling. In this case, the sibling turned out to be slightly older. Having been adopted as an older child, they remembered their mother well and recognized the name and the face of the woman who appeared in the online genealogy records, and in their respective adoption files. Three siblings, however, were eventually reduced to two in the register of biogenetic relations, as DNA tests revealed one of them not to share a DNA profile with the other two. Different registers of legibility of relations in the adoption files vary from case to case. Documents that relate or do not relate to individuals, and the new technologies of relatedness production such as genetic and ancestry testing, make and remake adoptee sibling relations, biogenetic relations, and more generalized and more difficult to pin down affinities. These, in turn, are understood anew, as people, paperwork and genetic substance align and misalign in searches.

Davidson (2009) has argued that the availability of digital records through commercial providers such as Ancestry.com and the Latter-day Saint Online Genealogy Records has given ground to 'speed-relating', a novel practice of relating that has arisen out of new possibilities for cross-referencing of public, private and DNA biorepositories. Davidson raises important ethical questions about intellectual property as well as personal privacy, as digital tools change the way people engage with their family history. For adopted persons who are perusing their files for clues, ascertaining that a living woman in Guatemala might have given two of her children up for adoption is a very significant finding. The existence of a third adopted child, whose papers list the same woman as the biological mother, alongside the certainty that this cannot be the case, generates more questions still. Whilst the finding suggests forgery a constitutive element of the adoption file, what is the actual meaning of the counterfeit narrative? Could the woman be at once the birth mother of two siblings, and a *jaladora*, a procurer of children – thus turning the 'sibling' who is biogenetically unrelated to the other two into a trafficked or kidnapped child – and the woman into someone who might have played an active role in their abduction? Documents in the ancestry digital records repositories can be used to corroborate or invalidate information in the adoption files, but the fuller picture often remains elusive. The capacity to establish overlaps and echoes in the archives emerges out of the prolonged experience of handling the files and inhabiting the information and stories in them. On occasions, the story told in one adoption file (*expediente de adopción*) might not be reconciled with the person it is attributed to, but it might resonate with the details known about another individual. This might even be the case with adopted persons residing in different countries, but who share an adoption broker or agency in their personal trajectory. Here, then, another practice of the adoption circuits is gradually foregrounded: substituting one *expediente* with another, muddling the histories further and making it more arduous still for individuals to make sense of things.

Shadow archives, DNA legibility and new forms of kinship

The law of 1977 that regulated the role of notaries in the adoption process stipulated that with the conclusion of the adoption, a copy of the adoption files should be deposited in judicial archives in Guatemala City. Not all legal practitioners did so, but those that did effectively established adoption records which can now be accessed following the presentation of a formal request. Records are kept in storage, so civil servants retrieve the documents, which can then be inspected in situ. No copies can be made, but readers are allowed to take notes and study the files in the building. These judicial archives are by definition partial, and their fragmentariness specifically evidences how the duty to deposit records was not universally adhered to in practice; neither was it enforced in any meaningful way. In turn, the personal archives held by adoptive persons and their families constitute a powerful, dispersed counter-archive, as no institution or gatekeeper has to be mobilized to gain access to the materials. Adoptive persons are in possession of their files and as discussed above, academic researchers and adopted persons have sought institutional archives to compare files side-by-side. Through these knowledge practices of juxtaposition and comparison, they have conjured up the contours of practices of systematic forgery of records. They have also pointed to the challenges that emerge when entrusting documents with qualities such as transparency or truth. In the process, what has been brought into stark relief is the capacity of archives to multiply and reproduce, as copies are made, openly or through subterfuge, as notes are taken and photographs or digital scans are generated through people's interactions with the records. Reproduction and plasticity are therefore also important qualities of the adoption archives.

The inception and expansion of commercial and ancestry databases such as the Latter-day Saints Online Genealogy Records, or FamilySearch, provides some way of corroborating or invalidating the information contained in the adoption files of individuals. These repositories are not stable, and materials appear and disappear, as they are made available for access. They can be easily withdrawn from view, without any explanation. The databases are held by private institutions who do not have a specific remit for public accountability or clear-cut processes of ethics governance or clear jurisdiction. In 2021, the Guatemalan Government announced that it would facilitate adopted persons' access to their records, as part of the National Adoption Council's set of responsibilities and public duty (O'Dwyer 2021), thus in principle bypassing the reliance on commercial ancestry dataset searches, and giving adopted persons access to the records of the National Registry of Persons (RENAP). The promise of institutional transparency presents the prospect of possible collaboration with state institutions, but contradictions exist when institutional transparency engages the very structures that have historically operated transnational adoption shadow circuits and shadow archives, and which continue to remain elusively out of view. The multiplication of records – paper records and digital files – alongside the emergence of a multiplicity of archival sites and diverse materialities of records entail the duplication and doubling of documents. The haphazard reproduction and doubling of documents and files – their very replicability – can be mobilized for oblique readings and in the service of the detection of forgeries. By way of an example, an individual's *acta de nacimiento* (birth certificate) can be found in the local Civil Register, or *Registro Civil*. A copy of the same document for the same individual can also be located on one of the commercial ancestry databases. However, there are instances in which the copy of the document in the commercial repository features the signature of the assumed birth mother, while the paper copy of the *acta de nacimiento* in the adopted person's possession does not bear any signature of the birth mother. When comparing signatures across documents, the signature is consistent in places – sometimes, it appears different. Who signed the documents as the biological mother? Why are signatures not consistent? And why are there no signatures in some iterations of the *acta de nacimiento*? What is in a signature? How can a signature be tied to a person – and be proof of identity in any case? How have paper regimes and bureaucracies come to rely on signatures as markers of individuality and as proof of identity?

The validity of signatures as markers and verifications of identity depends on social, cultural and bureaucratic conventions. Signatures occlude the fundamental fictions about the congruity between person, name and signature. Philosopher Jacques Derrida (1977) conceived of claims of stability between the signature and the referent as one of presence – about writing and the metaphysics of presence. The adoption files expose the brittle status of such a claim, accentuating not only the structural, but more fundamentally the political dimensions of the claim, against a context in which signatures – false signatures – for birth mothers can be traced back, for instance, to the writing of the social worker whose entitlement to sign the name of the birth mother is never questioned. Social workers signed documents on behalf of, for example, the birth mother, adding notes as an aside stating that it was not possible to obtain a statement from the birth mother on account of a spell of bad weather, difficulties in reaching the woman's village to obtain their statement, so that the paperwork could be complete for the notary. In the arbitrariness of power that has some individuals appear repeatedly through their signatures, issued on their and on others' behalf, others are erased – notably birth mothers – unable to appear at all. Those at the centre of transnational adoption circuits cannot hide, as their marks – their signatures – recur in the records: notaries, social workers, lawyers. Sometimes their names appear, without their clear role being specified. Lawyers are not always named in the paperwork. The weight of visibility through signatures falls squarely on the notaries, as the legal executors who operationalized the adoption process. Lawyers assisting the process are more elusive and are not always named. On occasion, the signature of the person who was present at the birth – a witness – and registering the birth, is not the same as the signature of the *comadrona* (the midwife) suggesting a blurring of the figure of the midwife with the ringleader, but also compromising the figure of the witness, turning witness into accomplice. With access to commercial repositories of records, it is now possible to conjure up some of these figures, though pinpointing exactly where they fit, in what role and if they fit at all, remain open questions.

The shifting meanings of continuities and incongruities in the adoption records pose challenges to the legibility of adoption files. This instability endures in a terrain that now also features increasingly widely available devices and infrastructures for deciphering biogenetic origins. Genetic and ancestry testing systems, like 23&Me, are growing in popularity and are widely used. They are direct-to-consumer technologies whose cost is not prohibitive and that do not require the mediation of experts or public institutions. As with the paper and digital files, adoptive persons have strategies for interpreting the findings, or 'matches'. The great majority of 'matches' are deemed irrelevant, in the sense that they are understood to mark relations that are simply too distant to register as socially meaningful and as kin. Dealing with such newly legible biogenetic relations is a complex task that entails the negotiation of notions of proximity and distance, in a fast-multiplying relationality whose implications are not fully known. Where files could be swapped, counterfeited in whole or in part, from the minutiae of a signature to whole birth certificates, the transnational adoption paperwork illustrates that things are not as they seem. Yet, it is in this context that adopted persons ask: What is one left with to understand one's story? What can one do, when six months in one's early life trajectory seem to be unaccounted for, when names do not correspond to persons, or street addresses to actual places? When one's name, date of birth and place of origin all remain elusive, or when they seem – as they appear in the files – to belong to someone else?

Through practices of deciphering, the minutiae of the files and the method of counterfeiting are reducible to one, streamlined narrative: a child given up as an act of love, because the birth mother was not able to look after them. This compressed, abridged and generalized story is often found in the files, in the formulaic declarations of birth mothers (Posocco 2011). It is in practice also a very good origin story to grow up with, especially when set against the confusion that arises with the swapping of files. In a context where it is possible on occasions to ascertain that the person who appears as the birth mother, once located, is not actually genetically linked to the adopted person, the adopted person is turned into a ghost, as they have no date of birth, no exact place of origin, no name. All certainties can be removed and those in this predicament must find other routes through the files, other interpretative strategies. In practice, and as a direct result of the activism of adopted persons, there are now cases whose details are in the public domain and that can help other individuals understand some of the practices and processes in play in their adoption trajectories. These accounts are all in themselves partial. Even though some detail might not be fully accurate and might seem fictionalized, as in the case of *Ixcanul*, the award-winning film by Guatemalan filmmaker Jayro Bustamante (2015), whose plot includes the abduction, through deception in a hospital, of a newborn child from a young Maya Kaqchikel woman, the reality of the disappearance of the child and the helplessness of the birth mother and community continue to resonate and make even the most elaborate, unlikely narratives seem possible. These narratives are possible because there are so many other cases that make seemingly incredible and improbable stories seem plausible.

Detailing the similarities and inconsistencies in the files, as we have done here, might convey the impression of chaotic paperwork and a haphazard system. The haphazard character of the transnational adoption circuits from Guatemala to Europe relates to the sheer plurality and complexity of practices of documentality and counterfeiting that enabled the transnational movement of children over time. We have to stress that this account is the result of the slow, painstaking study of the files by researchers and adopted persons and processes of analysis and reflection on what could be understood as a recurrence, a discrepancy, a contradiction, a pattern, a forgery. Knowledge practices of juxtaposition and comparison reveal forgery – and counterfeiting as method – in the paperwork, and both patterns and haphazardness acquire significance, in terms of enabling strategies to begin to address the question: 'What are you looking for in the file?' The question requires an opening towards registering that which might appear implausible – a hyperbole, a fantasy, an unnecessarily baroque and unwieldy plot. Or a totality of counterfeiting, which leaves one with no more clues.

Yet, there are always more clues. One might focus on a photograph (cf. Clemente-Martínez 2022), perhaps the photograph of the woman presumed to be the birth mother, that is visible in the copy of the identity document included in the adoption file. It might be possible to locate a copy of the same image in one of the commercial depositories of records noted earlier and attribute the file not to the person the records are said to belong to, but someone else whose personal story seems a better fit with the narrative in the file. It might be possible to locate the person in Guatemala and ascertain to whom, if anyone, they are biogenetically related. The legibility enabled by newly accessible DNA tests might yield extended family beyond what is a socially meaningful relation, including kinship among adoptees, which even if distant, acquires renewed significance. In this multiplication of relations across countries, borders, communities, then, one is not alone. When a closer relation appears, the more distant, extended ones recede into the background. This biogenetic hyper-relationality and the ability to navigate shifting proximities and distancing occur in contexts where it is not always easy to discuss transnational adoption and its nexus to violent histories, as is still the case in Canada and Italy, or where there are considerable barriers to investigation, as is the case in France, where legislation on privacy precludes and even criminalizes the querying of adoption paperwork.

Conclusion

Transnational adoptions from Guatemala are not a homogeneous phenomenon. Many diverse histories and perspectives exist among adopted persons and their families in the adopted country and Guatemala. Whilst it is important to continuously reflect on the heterogeneity of personal stories and meanings assigned to the adoption process, it is equally pressing to connect transnational adoptions to the history of violence, conflict and genocide that marked Guatemala from the mid-twentieth century. Spectacular violence such as the 'scorched earth' campaigns of the early 1980s and the internal displacements that targeted Indigenous communities in different areas of the country and that continue in different form to the present day, all took place alongside the routine everyday violence and wearing out of populations in rural and urban areas through harsh social and economic structural adjustment, extractivism and predatory capitalism (AVANCSO 2016; 2020).

Guatemalans have consistently resisted and have continued to organize and respond to these dynamics through social mobilization, the crafting of new political forms, cultural mobilization and intervention. The emergence of transnational adoption in public discourse in the country and internationally is therefore part of a broader process of reckoning with histories of violence and resistance and a reminder of the *longue durée* of any aftermath in the post genocide period. The removal of children from families and communities during the armed conflict makes personal histories recede into the background in the interest of a larger narrative concerned with marking violence and dispossession. The transnational adoption files give an insight into the personal dimensions of the broader historical arc.

In this chapter, we have been specifically concerned with the researchers' and adopted persons' approaches to the adoption files and their commitment to understanding the widespread practices of forgery of documents that led to their creation. The partiality of any archive has not been a hindrance to this project. Knowledge practices of juxtaposition and comparison have however been instrumental to eliciting repetitions and discrepancies which could be framed not as isolated mistakes due to human error, but as practices tied to counterfeiting as a method. The mixing of files, that is, the exchange of one person's file with another person's file, to prevent any of those involved ever tracing one another, is the practice we are particularly keen to highlight here, as a crucial mechanism of disorder and disorganization that retrospectively appears to constitute a considerable obstacle in adopted persons' searches for origins. The substitution of entire files, the interchangeable nature of names, the repetition of dates and the disconnection between information in the file and referents in the world are the elements that conjure up the sense that counterfeiting as method entailed rupture, invention and creation. Forgery of documents at a state level, and their movement with children across borders, facilitated by intermediaries akin to the *raketè* of Chapter 8 and the *mulas* of Chapter 10 in this volume, reveals how acts of contraband were in fact mobilized by state actors as part of a wider process of repositioning the nation in relation to its own history.

Incoherence and disjointedness are a rich terrain that elicits new strategies of meaning-making and the framing of new questions.

As academic researchers and adopted persons have found, there are always alternative perspectives and registers of legibility that can be fashioned and mobilized to make sense of the counterfeited files. Transnational adoptees' activism has focused on enabling adopted persons to generate new insights through knowledge practices of juxtaposition and comparison of the documents. Recent developments in DNA analysis and the availability of direct-to-consumer DNA testing have opened other relationalities. Biogenetic hyper-relationality poses challenges, as persons negotiate what might count as socially meaningful proximity and distance. They do so alongside creative interrogations of the inconsistencies and occlusions in the adoption files. Through these practices, the adoption files are no longer strictly markers of relations – or of performative acts that instantiate and sever relations, such as the declaration of birth mothers. In the new register of legibility, established by these engagements with the files, the documents come to refer to something else, that is: they become records of counterfeiting as method. Counterfeiting thus appears as constitutive of the very bureaucracies of adoption – or 'contraband kinning' – in Guatemala, though the meanings and implications of forgeries are open challenges. In the ruptured interstices between signature and hand, name and person, identities and relations, the creation of new meanings and new relations thrive.

Acknowledgements

We wish to thank Marco Antonio Garavito and colleagues at the Liga Guatemalteca de Higiene Mental, for their work, collaboration and friendship over many years. We also thank Sebastián Escalón and Alejandra Colom, for their important research and support. We acknowledge the work of associations of Guatemalan adoptees in Europe, as well as many individuals in Guatemala who have generously shared with us, over many years, their ideas and knowledge of the adoption circuits. Parts of this chapter were originally published in Spanish, and can be read at Posocco and Villérs 2023.

Notes

1 See https://www.rtbf.be/article/enquete-sur-les-enfants-voles-du-guatemala-tout-est-parti-d-un-post-facebook-10402456. Accessed 30 March 2024.

2 'FamilySearch', the database of the Church of Jesus Christ of Latter-day Saints, is the largest genealogical archive in the world – it strives to capture all the genealogical records of the world in the interest of posthumous baptism and other religious ordinances. As of the second decade of the twentieth century, the church has amassed in the vicinity of four billion genealogical images, approximately one-quarter of the world's records. The genealogical project of the church fostered the conditions for the emergence of the industry of genealogy as a republican enterprise that disguises its moral roots (see Creet 2020, 5).

References

AVANCSO (Asociación para el Avance de las Ciencias Sociales en Guatemala). 2016. *Despojos y resistencias Una mirada a la Región Extractiva Norte desde Tezulutlán-Verapaz*. Guatemala City: AVANCSO. Accessed 5 April 2024. https://avancso.org.gt/wp-content/uploads/2022/02/C.I.-28-DESPOJOS-Y-RESISTENCIA.pdf.

AVANCSO (Asociación para el Avance de las Ciencias Sociales en Guatemala). 2020. *Espirales de despojos y violencias en Tezulutlan Verapaz*. Guatemala City: AVANCSO. Accessed 5 April 2024. https://avancso.org.gt/wp-content/uploads/2022/02/C.I.-30-Espirales-de-despojos-y-violencia.pdf.

Briggs, L. 2012. *Somebody's Children: The politics of transracial and transnational adoption*. Durham, NC: Duke University Press.

Briggs, L. 2020. *Taking Children: A history of American terror*. Berkeley: University of California Press.

Bustamante, Jayro (director). 2015. *Ixcanul* (film). Accessed 30 March 2024. https://www.youtube.com/watch?v=EJfvKnLPqFM.

Calito, J. A. E. 2020. *La Nuit des Nahuatl: Nouvelles Guatémaltèques*. Paris: Editions Amalthee.

Casa Alianza, COPREDEH, Fundación Myrna Mack, Fundación Sobrevivientes, Movimiento social por la Niñez y la Adolescencia, ODHAG and Secretaría de Bienestar Social de la Presidencia de la República. 2007. *¿Adopciones en Guatemala: Protección o mercado?* Guatemala: Tipografía Nacional.

Clemente-Martínez, C. K. 2022. *Volver a los Origenes: Una etnografía de la adopción transnacional*. Barcelona: Ediciones Bellaterra.

CEH (Comisión para Comisión para el Esclarecimiento Histórico). 1999. *Guatemala. Memory of Silence, Tz'inil Na'tab'al: Report of the Commission for Historical Clarification. Conclusions and recommendations*. Guatemala City: United Nations.

Creet, J. 2020. *The Genealogical Sublime*. Amherst, MA: University of Massachusetts Press.

Crespo, P. and S. Escalón 2015. 'La increíble historia de Edmond Mulet y los niños que 'exportaba', *Plaza Pública*, 30 January. Accessed 30 March 2024. http://www.plazapublica.com.gt/content/la-increible-historia-de-edmond-mulet-y-los-ninos-que-exportaba.

Davidson, G. 2009. 'Speed-relating: Family history in a digital age', *History Australia* 6(2): 1–43.

Derrida, J. 1977. 'Signature event context'. In *Limited Inc*, translated by Samuel Weber and Jeffrey Mehlman, 1–24. Evanston, IL: Northwestern University Press.

Fanon, C. (Mariela SR). 2022. *Mamá, No Estoy Muerta: La increíble historia de Mariela, secuestrada al nacer*. Guatemala: Piedrasanta.

Gesteira, S. 2019. 'Activismo por el derecho a conocer los orígenes en Argentina', *Nuevo Mundo Mundos Nuevos*. Accessed 30 March 2024. https://doi.org/10.4000/nuevomundo.77902.

Gesteira, S., I. Salvo Agoglia, C. Villalta and K. Alfaro Monsalve. 2021. 'Child appropriations and irregular adoptions: Activism for the "right to identity", justice, and reparation in Argentina and Chile', *Childhood* 28(4): 585–99.

ODHA (Oficina de Derechos Humanos del Arzobispado de Guatemala). 2005. *Hasta Encontrarte: Niñez desaparecida por el conflicto armado interno en Guatemala*. Guatemala: ODHA.

O'Dwyer, J. 2021. 'Guatemala launches new program to help adoptees access records', *Newswires*, 17 September. Accessed 30 March 2024. https://www.einnews.com/pr_news/551478929/guatemala-launches-new-program-to-help-adoptees-access-records.

Oglesby, E. A. and D. M. Nelson (eds). 2019. *Guatemala, the Question of Genocide*. London and New York: Routledge.

Posocco, S. 2011. 'Expedientes: Fissured legality and affective states in the transnational adoption archives in Guatemala', *Law, Culture and the Humanities* 7(3): 434–56.

Posocco, S. 2015. 'Substance, sign, and trace: Performative analogies and technologies of enfleshment in the transnational adoption archives in Guatemala', *Social & Cultural Geography* 16(5): 567–84.

Posocco, S. 2019. 'Postplurality: An ethnographic tableau'. In *Queering Knowledge: Analytics, devices and investments after Marilyn Strathern*, edited by P. Boyce, E. J. Gonzalez-Polledo and Silvia Posocco, 131–47. Abingdon: Routledge.

Posocco, S. (forthcoming). 'The shadow circuits: Transnational adoption, forced disappearance and genocide in Guatemala'. In *Genocide and Resistance in Guatemala*, edited by V. Sanford and W. Gruner. New York: Rutgers University Press.

Posocco, S. and Villérs, S. 2023. 'Falsificaciones: creación y disrupción en los archivos de adopciones transnacionales de Guatemala a Europa', *Revista del Museo de Antropología de la Universidad Nacional de Córdoba, Argentina* 16(2): 381–94.

Salvo Agoglia, I. and K. Alfaro Monsalve. 2019. '"Irregular adoptions" in Chile: New political narratives about the right to know one's origins', *Children & Society* 33(2): 201–12.

Salvo Agoglia, I. and D. Marre. 2019. 'Children forever: The search for origins among Chilean adults who were adopted', *Child and Family Social Work* 27(3): 127–34.

Schlesinger, S. and S. Kinzer. 1982. *Bitter Fruit: The story of the American coup in Guatemala*. New York: Doubleday and Anchor Books.

Tagen-Dye, C. and G. Givens. 2022. 'Between two worlds: Entre dos mundos', *Maya America* 4(1). Accessed 30 March 2024. https://digitalcommons.kennesaw.edu/cgi/viewcontent.cgi?article=1089&context=mayaamerica.

Vega, C. M. 2019. *Le Chant du Bouc: La quête de vérité d'une enfant adoptée*. Paris: Editions Flamarrion.

Villalta, C. 2010. 'De los derechos de los adoptantes al derecho a la identidad: Los procedimientos de adopción y la apropiación criminal de niños en la Argentina', *Journal of Latin American and Caribbean Anthropology* 15(2): 338–62.

Villérs, S. 2022. 'I, volcano: of earth and fire…', *Maya America* 4(1): 47–53. Accessed 30 March 2024. https://digitalcommons.kennesaw.edu/cgi/viewcontent.cgi?article=1089&context=mayaamerica.

Conclusion: beyond contraband

Rebecca Galemba

'Isn't [what you're describing] just trade?' I recall someone asking me, one time I gave a lecture on the smuggling of corn across an unmonitored pathway from Mexico into Guatemala. Indeed, the title of the article that emerged, 'Corn is food, not contraband' (see Galemba 2012), came directly from residents along the Mexico–Guatemala border, who saw this corn trade not as contraband, but as critical to peasant subsistence and livelihoods in the wake of the decimation of the Mexican countryside, the state's support of small farmers, and the lack of alternative options. Yet designations of contraband and smuggling were polysemous and slippery, shifting depending on the direction of the commerce, the products traded, the particular individuals involved and their roles, the nature of the prohibition and degree of state enforcement, and changing political and economic dynamics. The geopolitical division at once made this corn trade technically contraband; it involved the unauthorized entry of a product from one country into another, while evading required sanitary inspections and tariffs. However, until the corn arrived at the border, and even after crossing into Guatemalan territory, it mostly proceeded through legal trading and purchasing channels, informal exchanges in marketplaces, and into the homes and bodies of consumers.

The contributors to this volume unsettle the term contraband, as they do the very nature of the borders and nation-states that sanction and prohibit particular commodities, bodies, and even technologies and ideas that cross them. Despite a growing body of literature on critical smuggling studies, existing volumes focus heavily on migration, or privilege 'the logistics of movement' and border crossing over other dynamics involved in wider landscapes of contraband – such as financing (Dolph, Chapter 9 this volume), production, consumption

(Van Roekel, Chapter 6), bureaucracy and paperwork (Posocco and Villérs, in Chapter 11) social organization and integration with everyday life (Allard, Chapter 3 this volume), and other forms of class and identity formation and political agitation (Beach, Chapter 5), land ownership and dispossession (Tusing, Chapter 4) (Gallien and Weigand 2022, 5; Cearns and Beach, Introduction, this volume). The contributors point to broader, as well as more intimate, spaces of surveillance, governance, and contests over legitimacy and value by critically engaging the term contraband and highlighting its social, cultural and historical embeddedness in daily life. They ask broader questions about resources, land, politics, socialities, identities, kinship and livelihoods, that take us beyond narrow concerns with mobility across geopolitical divisions. In doing so, they thus help us rethink a theoretical sticking point: how do we critique the impacts of national borders and controls without reifying them in the very process? This volume raises the task of reclaiming contraband from its negative and criminalizing connotations, as articulated by states and international organizations, to instead posit, as Cearns and Beach offer, the 'valence of contraband as a lens onto local strategies of cultural expansion, economic survival and political resistance'. Contraband can perhaps orient insight into larger questions about inequality, power and identity in the region; both as a response to historical and ongoing processes of colonial racial capitalism that generate dispossession, criminalization and exclusion, as well as a tactic of subversion and mode of organizing social, political and economic relations differently.

In this conclusion, I raise the following questions: aspects of examining contraband that are specific to the context of Latin America, the Caribbean and its diasporas; the strength of ethnography in dismantling a false impasse between contraband as resistance versus reinforcing of hegemonic systems; and exploring contraband beyond nation-states and their geopolitical borders to comment on wider historical and postcolonial global assemblages of accumulation, extraction and dispossession, as well as everyday, localized resistances to them.

Contraband in Latin America, the Caribbean, and its diasporas

High levels of informality, porous yet contested borderlands, diverse colonial histories, uneven transitions to democracy amid neoliberal structural adjustment policies, the presence of drug trafficking and criminal gangs, and the rise and fall of the commodities boom amid sharp political realignments make Latin America and the Caribbean region the frequent subject of studies of smuggling, contraband, and different forms of piracy, counterfeiting and other illegalities (see Aguiar 2012; 2013; Thomas 2016; Jusionyte 2015; Galemba 2017; Dent 2020; Dewey and Thomas 2022). In response to characterizations that depict the region's democracies as fragile, weak, failed, violent, or at risk of becoming criminal states, scholars have been careful to document the complexity of plural forms of violence and regulatory authorities, including how it is difficult to separate the state from the violence and criminalities it ostensibly targets (for example Arias and Goldstein 2010; Heyman and Smart 1999).

In the context of state violence, corruption and the presence of diverse criminal entities, scholars have analysed how marginalized groups across the region have taken matters into their own hands, via both forms of collective organizing and sometimes more violent means, to assert sovereignty, demand the rights of citizenship (Lazar 2008; Holston 2007), 'the right to smuggle' (Allard, Beach, this volume), punish criminals and exact justice (Godoy 2004; Goldstein 2004), levy their own taxes (Galemba 2017), or participate in petty informal and illegal activities, street vending, small-scale smuggling, counterfeiting and copying, to survive systemic state exclusion, abuse and neglect (Goldstein 2016). As Mathews, Ribeiro and Vega's (2012) edited volume describes, these everyday-level illegalities, in contrast to larger-scale criminal enterprises generally requiring a level of state complicity, often enjoy a level of social legitimacy and, in fact, constitute how the majority of the world, excluded from top-down hegemonic forms of globalization, experience global integration from below.

Much existing scholarship in Latin America focuses on how marginalized groups rely on such illegal, yet frequently socially legitimate (Van Schendel and Abraham 2005) activities in the context of the selective violent presence – in terms of militarized policing and repression of poor and racialized subjects – and absence of the state – in terms of satisfying basic needs, upholding citizen rights, and the promises of democracy (Leeds 1996). Despite frustration with the state, Dewey and Thomas (2022, 2) note that 'in Latin America ... structures of social domination depend on the effective promotion of certain expectations' or 'hope' for the state to fulfil its promises (also see Auyero 2012; Nuijten and Anders 2007). With the dearth of opportunities for formal employment and substantive participation, such 'aspirations' may motivate marginalized populations to select 'forms of economic exchange that take place outside the bounds of state law' (Dewey and Thomas 2022, 2; Dewey 2020).

In these contexts, whether or not there exists a 'culture of contraband' per se, contraband often becomes a normalized and necessary survival strategy, even if local perceptions of its legitimacy are contingent, shifting and contested (Dewey and Thomas 2022). A type of moral economy (Galemba 2012; Thompson 1971) may develop whereby contraband activities become embedded in social life, forming modes of expected, ethical behaviour and notions of fairness. This is not to say that exploitation, dispute and inequality do not exist, as the contributors to this volume describe, but instead indexes a generally understood ethos around what people are willing to accept. In other works, E. P. Thompson (1975; 1967) was also concerned with crime and criminalization, including how colonizers marshalled law and criminalization to control colonial subjects (Schneider and Schneider 2008; Merry 1998). Writing about anti-poaching in eighteenth-century England, E. P. Thompson explained how the concept of crime becomes possible 'when we simply take over the definition of those who own property, control the state, and pass the laws which "name" what shall be crimes' (Thompson 1975, 193–4, cited in Schneider and Schneider 2008, 355). Yet, Van Roekel (this volume) raises important questions regarding how well such ethical frameworks travel from their Eurocentric origins, highlighting the need to take 'people's own moral concerns and ethical evaluations seriously' from situated experience. She insists that defining what is of moral concern and what people consider to be right and wrong can thus constitute a 'political act' in its own right. By focusing on illegalities or ethical frameworks imported from Euro-American logics, scholars may miss not only what is actually important to people, but risk reinforcing depictions that resemble what Eric Wolf (1982) famously termed 'people without history', de-historicizing, decontextualizing and depoliticizing contraband from larger social, economic and political forces, as well as from its local meanings, ethics and contestations.

Various contributors to this volume focus on Venezuela, including its relationship with neighbouring countries, in light of the collapse of the state's Bolivarian promises, with economic crisis and hyperinflation. Yet a focus on illegality and contraband can mask what most concerns people, reinforcing both criminalizing narratives and deflecting from local needs. Indeed, Van Roekel demonstrates how Venezuelans were less ethically concerned with smuggling or even official corruption, but instead were contending with a profound disconnect between a long-held national myth of abundance and the realities of scarcity and hunger in a wealthy country (also Allard, this volume). Similarly, in the case of contraband medications smuggled into Rio de Janeiro's prison system, Thompson (Chapter 7) identifies contraband as a red herring, but simultaneously a productive lens to examine how contraband deflects attention from the state failing in its responsibility to provision universal healthcare, unsafe prison conditions and mass incarceration. He astutely observes that while contraband created ways to access necessary medications and fortified ties between prisoners, their family members, and providers, it nonetheless fostered new dependences and hazards, creating a 'patchwork of treatment that relied heavily on pharmaceuticals above all other forms of prevention and care, but outsourced most of the responsibility and cost of these drugs'. Tusing's chapter, in contrast, reveals the reverse – how her initial attempts to *not* focus on illegalities could miss how drug trafficking in Northern Paraguay is not easily disentangled from larger conflicts over land agglomeration, social and economic ties, cattle ranching and peasant dispossession.

Contraband inheres within the existing social and economic structure, while also reflecting its very exclusions. Several contributors, for example, reference contraband as a 'resource for the poor' (Allard this volume) that provides an avenue to access resources the state has failed to deliver, which is an especially prominent discourse in post-collapse Venezuela. Yet discursive justifications shift even in close proximity; the same claim to the state's patrimony holds less weight, for example, in neighbouring Guyana (Allard). In my own work, petrol smugglers in Mexico also insisted on their right to petrol as a national resource, which at the time was nationalized in Mexico, to smuggle to Guatemala (Galemba 2017). In contrast, this discourse was absent in Guatemala, where the gasoline industry was controlled by transnational companies and also infused with various criminal elements.

Whether contraband economies nurture particular kinds of alternative ethical sensibilities is shifting and contingent; in many contexts, as Roitman (2006) demonstrates in her work in the Chad Basin, the semblance of an 'ethics of illegality' is instead consonant with a larger shared ethos around appropriate forms of accumulation and extraction, which involves various powerful players including military personnel and elite. In this volume, for example, Dolph connects the circulation of contraband between Argentina and Bolivia to wider dynamics of 'subordinate financialization', which not only creates a conducive climate for contraband, but does so in ways that 'paradoxically, further entrench dynamics of such financialization'.

Understanding how contraband can be co-constitutive of, rather than a threat to, the current order demonstrates why efforts to transition participants into the formal economy without addressing larger inequities and systemic forms of oppression frequently fail. When they do, it becomes facile to fall back on stigmatizing tropes of the poor and marginalized as undeserving, unruly, backwards, ungovernable and difficult, which frequently carry racialized and colonial connotations (see Beach's descriptions of Colombian petrol smugglers in this volume). For example, Rus and Vigil (2007) have noted how anxieties around urbanization, neoliberalism, insecurity and state corruption in the city of San Cristóbal in Chiapas, Mexico, were displaced onto indigenous youth as suspected 'delinquents' out of place in the largely *ladino* city. The figure of the *marero* (gang member) in post-war Guatemala similarly stands in for growing unease around pervasive inequality, corruption, impunity and neoliberal dispossession (Burrell 2013; also see O'Neill and Thomas 2011). In Brazil, 'the liberalization of the … economy, shift to democratic rule, and spread of drug use and trafficking … [were also deflected to stigmatize] poor *favela* dwellers, recent immigrants from the Northeast, youth, and women of dark complexion', justifying increased police repression and assaults on urban slums in the name of crime prevention (Schneider and Schneider 2008, 357; Caldeira 2000). These descriptions closely echo colonial depictions of 'dangerous classes' and 'outlaws', used to justify colonial rule and subjugation (Schneider and Schneider 2008, 356). Or, as Clark highlights in Chapter 1, inquisitorial investigations of witchcraft – which largely targeted a 'multiethnic, economically independent group of unmarried women' – in colonial Caribbean ports, proceeded alongside efforts to suppress smuggling and buttress imperial commercial empires.

Gallien and Weigand (2022, 2; and citing Koram 2019; and Schuster 2022) note that the 'colonial and imperial history of the making of smuggling both through border-making and the making of global rules of trade and consumption have often been embedded deeply in unequal power structures and consequently have been racialized and gendered starkly'. The implication is that policies targeting contraband often disproportionately punish those at the political margins of the state (Gallien and Weigand 2022). Yet, contraband and anti-contraband accusations have been critical not only to taming the political margins, but also establishing order within interiors, extended to groups placed at the margins of society according to race, gender, class, religions and sexuality (see Chapter 1, this volume). In Latin America, derogatory descriptions around criminality, unruliness and lawlessness are more recently extended to similar groups that historically threatened racial colonial and modern-nation-state building projects – poor youth, indigenous, creole, migrant and Black populations. Contributors thus importantly link accusations of, reliance on, and reclamations around contraband, not only to nation-states and their bordering practices, but wider historical, as well as more locally contingent, forms of rule-making and social ordering.

In response to mainstream analyses of illegalities in Latin America that have tended to obscure larger forms of corruption, complicity and illegality, scholars have begun to show the ways that illegality is fused into the political system through its more violent manifestations, as well as through mundane administrative and bureaucratic processes (see Chapter 11, this volume). In many contexts, contraband enjoys social legitimacy not only when it is one of the few means of earning a living, but also because, as Allard notes, the lines between legality/illegality, taxation/extortion, predation/rule, have unravelled: 'there is little difference between officials and criminals, between racket and tax'. For example, Michael Taussig (2003) viscerally reveals the repercussions for the most marginalized in the Colombian conflict, where law and lawlessness became violent mirages of one another. Charles Tilly (1985, 169) famously places 'banditry, piracy, gangland rivalry, policing, and war-making on the same continuum … [with states being] quintessential protection rackets with the advantage of legitimacy' (cited in Schneider and Schneider 2008, 359).

Contraband as resistance?

Despite its formal definitions, in practice, contraband does not exist outside of, or contra society and norms, laws and rules, but is instead a 'structural feature of the international order' (Keshavarz and Khosravi 2022, 16) that is interwoven with the social reproduction of daily life. The volume's ethnographic focus demonstrates how the meanings of contraband are socially reproduced, contested, but also empirically and historically contingent, and often improvised within particular contexts. Much ink has already been expended questioning whether contraband offers a form of resistance to oppressive neoliberal abandonment and colonial racial capitalism, or if it instead shores up corrupt authorities and reinforces the hegemony of the rule of law, through its very existence (Andreas 1999; Roitman 2006; Galemba 2017). Peter Andreas's body of work (1999; 2011; 2013; also Heyman and Smart 1999), in particular, has guided scholars to consider the structural symbiosis between the state and smuggling: by formalizing one official way for commerce, or restricting the mobilities of particular gendered and racialized peoples, states produce illegality and guarantee a niche for smugglers, whose existence in turn keeps law enforcement in business (Andreas 1999). As Montinard (Chapter 8) reveals in her chapter on Haitians' use of intermediaries as a way of joining the diaspora amid formidable challenges, smuggling becomes a critical service, but one simultaneously open to abuse and unpredictability.

The very designation of smuggling and contraband reflects dominant arrangements of power, which shift over time and place; 'one state's pirate was another state's privateer' (or a pirate with state permission/papers) (Gallant 1999, 28; also see Chapter 1 this volume; Andreas 2013), and what may be criminalized in one time and place may not hold in another. Indeed, many of the contributions in this volume show how marginalized groups advocate for their 'right to smuggle' and participate in contraband economies as legitimate work in contexts of extreme marginalization or to insist on 'insurgent claims' (Holston 2007; Keshavarz and Khosravi 2022, 5; Allard, and Chapter 5, this volume) for citizenship, sovereignty, and recognition when states have failed to deliver their promises (Introduction, this volume; Galemba 2012; Schwartz 2021; Allard, and Chapter 6, this volume).

As historians remind us: 'states helped make states and states made bandits', with those on the winning side becoming part of the security forces of emerging nation-states and competing alternatives branded as outlaws (Nugent 1999, 25). States, as well as colonial imperial powers, have also strategically used smugglers both indirectly and directly (see Chapter 1 this volume), or selectively targeted some over others, to benefit their own political and economic interests (Andreas 1999; 2011; 2013; Parsa 2022; Keshavarz and Khosravi 2022; Galemba 2017). In a striking example, Posocco and Villérs (in Chapter 11) reveal the Guatemalan state as smuggler, through tracing massive, repetitive errors and irregularities (some of which were found to be deliberate counterfeiting and forgery) in international adoption files during the country's counterinsurgency conflict that facilitated illegal adoptions abroad.

Yet there remains a tendency towards reinforcing the criminalizing gaze of the state and romanticizing smuggling as 'social banditry' (Hobsbawm 2000). Alternatively, others remind us how contraband can operate to preserve the status quo in ways that deflect public discontent from deeper forms of inequality and oppression

(Keshavarz and Khosravi 2022; Galemba 2017; Chapter 7; Roitman 2006). Because contraband is tied in with colonial racial structures of rule, capital accumulation and state-making, accusations tend to target the most marginalized. Contraband activities that many rely on to survive may thus inadvertently 'produce new, or reproduce existing, structures of patriarchy, race, and class' (Keshavarz and Khosravi 2022, 12).

The volume's ethnographic focus helps dismantle binaries between resistance and preservation, demonstrating the complexities of everyday life, as well as ways to move beyond state-centric assumptions even when critiquing them. The contributors unsettle boundaries between formality, informality and illegality that assume a stark division between these domains and morally stigmatize informality and illegality as a vestige of the past, or the result of the 'naiveté' of the marginalized and poor populations (Chapter 1). Attempts to 'formalize' illegal activities and cultivate a culture around the 'rule of law' not only mask historical contexts where law and order have been used to repress and extract land, labour and wealth, but also inflict epistemic violence on populations that have adopted contraband as legitimate modes of work, sociality, and being in-the-world in the context of exclusion (chapters 3 and 5, this volume). They miss informality not only as a response to, or even a rejection of (see Millar 2018), modern conditions of uneven neoliberal globalization, but also how it is bound up in other social processes of identity formation, sociality and politics.

Ethnographic encounters reveal nuance, as contraband practices can be at once a rejection of the state, as well as a tactic to simultaneously assert demands for recognition and belonging, much as Daniel Goldstein's (2004) work on lynchings in Bolivia constituted a violent demand for security and state inclusion. In Beach's chapter (this volume), Venezuelan petrol smugglers who petitioned the state for entrepreneurship programmes used illegality to garner concessions from the state, but in doing so, they faced risks of further criminalization and lack of substantive alternatives. Contraband practices may also constitute ways of building social and kinship relationships, accessing goods, and maintaining cultural identities that make state-centric concerns less relevant. For example, Cearns's contribution (Chapter 10) on *el paquete* informal networks of digital peer-to-peer pirated media across the Cuban diaspora shows how these circuits were less about defying the Cuban state or US imperialism, or capitalism versus socialism, but instead indexed 'how Cubans negotiate extraordinary economic and political circumstances on a daily basis to maintain their cultural identity across borders'. Similarly, Van Roekel notes how ordinary Venezuelans were less concerned with the extralegal movement of food and petrol into the country, but weighed more the ethics of consumption and scarcity, which were at odds with their longstanding 'relations with wealth and food', based on a narrative of national abundance that had been fundamentally disrupted.

In this volume, Beach also ties contraband associations to identity, by showing how petrol smugglers (*pimpineros*) along the Colombian border with Venezuela cultivated a sense of 'working class solidarity' from their smuggling economic activities. Petrol smugglers drew on their collective identity and militancy to unite and negotiate, from the state, training programmes and a place for themselves in the 'legitimate economy'. However, these opportunities fizzled, and the state failed to provide substantive means for smugglers to surmount conditions of continuing economic precarity, social marginalization and stigma. In Beach's chapter, converting smugglers into entrepreneurs involved attempting to change their very identities, which had congealed around being *pimpineros*, by attempting to give them a 'new culture'. Instilling values of entrepreneurship, or what Beach calls 'forced entrepreneurs', foists an ideal of what citizenship should look like, which is warranted by paternalistic assumptions that the poor and marginalized are premodern, or 'people without history'. In this fashion, entrepreneurship 'is linked with histories of colonists conquering the internal frontiers of the early colonies and viceroyalties' and 'ideas of whiteness, masculinity, colonization, development and the creation of a modern nation' (Chapter 5). Moving beyond binaries of legality–illegality, margins–centres, state–non-state, and resistance–status quo, the contributors use the lens of contraband to open wider conversations about value, identity and social relations amid profound inequality and disruption, where contraband can form a mode of connection among limited options for mobility and access to goods and livelihoods. Yet, as Thompson (Chapter 7) reminds us, it can also generate new forms of dependencies and aggravate existing inequalities.

In the concluding chapter to Keshavarz and Khosravi's *Seeing Like a Smuggler* (2022) volume, Nandita Sharma (2022, 172) reveals the ways that 'seeing like a smuggler [rather than from a state-centric view] … tells us that capitalism is reliant on states to create categories of people who fall outside the law' as a crucial technique of 'labor discipline and social division'. Smuggling does not mean the absence of law, but quite to the contrary it indexes its very presence – even as smuggling activities may 'fill in the gaps created' by the law's exclusions and restrictions

(Sharma 2022, 174). Contraband can thus offer a form of resistance, survival, or even signal a political stance (Chapter 5).

Sharma (2020) has historically traced how the development of documentary mobility controls emerged in the wake of the abolition of slavery, as the 'coolie' labour recruitment scheme was devised to maintain imperial powers' dependence on cheap, docile labour, while avoiding accusations of 'unfree labour'. As such, the 'coolie' system of indentured labour deployed documentary controls to recruit the populations subject to, and dispossessed by, slavery, colonialism and the introduction of capitalism, and disciplined their labour by controlling their mobility rights (Sharma 2020, 41). With the rise of nationalism and nation-states, Sharma (2020) traces how the racialized legacies of colonialism and slavery informed the emergence of the immigrant as a negatively racialized and gendered figure. As she argues, 'without national immigration policies, there would be no such group as those we know of as immigrants who could be subordinated, scapegoated, and abused or rescued' (Sharma 2020, 48; also see Walia 2021). Sharma (2022, 169) similarly situates the figure of the 'smuggler' and the problematization of smuggling within this national-racial order that 'makes sovereignty sacrosanct'. The criminalization of smuggling and smugglers, she argues, operates not only to insulate and 'nationalize the capitalist wage' by suppressing mobility and labour power, but also 'mutes' resistance and masks what laws against smuggling harbour – 'the fact that states and capital are responsible for the harms ascribed to smugglers' (Sharma 2022, 173).

A parallel argument can be extended beyond migration to apply to other forms of contraband and illegalities. It is well-known that criminalization guarantees a price premium for narcotics (Andreas 1999; Gootenberg 2012), but official trade policies that exclude small businesses, entrepreneurs or peasants, may make contraband more expensive (through bribes and the need for multiple intermediaries) than legal commercial avenues (Galemba 2017). Or, as Alexander Dent (2012, 32, emphasis in original) notes in his work on digital media piracy in Brazil: 'the presence of the pirated in informal economies ... [is] used to *keep* the informal informal' (also cited in Galemba 2017, 20). As I have argued elsewhere (Galemba 2017, 20): 'The criminalization of contraband moralizes the limited options of the poor by blaming them for their own plight while allowing more powerful entities to claim and protect legitimate profits and determine who can sell and have access to goods'.

Contributors to this volume take the conversation not only beyond its well-travelled articulations in migration and smuggling studies, but to intervene in debates about how we think about nation-states, borders and other spaces of socio-political regulation and contestation. As Cearns and Beach note, ethnographic accounts 'muddy the waters', whether it be between the state–individual, capitalism–socialism (Chapter 10), formality–informality (Chapter 5), and resistance–oppression. Specifically, Cearns and Beach (Introduction) situate contraband in terms of how 'the region was (re)invented through specifically capitalistic concerns which centred around discourses of freedom to profit and trade without limit'. Early on, concerns with contraband were intimately connected with the desire of colonial powers to control the mobility and activities of local populations, with borderlines themselves playing only a small part (see Introduction, citing Piliavsky 2013).

A growing body of critical smuggling studies has emerged to show how states and the expansion of bordering practices criminalize everyday livelihood strategies and mobilities (for example, Keshavarz and Khosravi 2022; Gallien and Weigand 2022; Zhang et al. 2018; Sánchez 2017). Rather than accept state-devised categories, critical voices point to how smuggling and smugglers are convenient scapegoats for what is being concealed – or more broadly – what is truly at stake. As Sharma (2022, 176) argues, smuggling may detract attention from what should most concern us: 'the criminalization of mobility and the commodification of life'. Although existing work recognizes dynamics of contraband beyond borders, the focus tends to be on nation-state borders, perhaps because that is often where the contrast between statist designations and local perceptions of legitimacy are most starkly visible (see Van Schendel and Abraham 2005). For example, Gallien and Weigand (2022, 2) define smuggling as the 'purposeful movement across a border in contravention to the relevant legal frameworks', noting how the definition of smuggling is closely tied to histories of imperialism, colonial rule and the construction and maintenance of national boundaries. As Cearns and Beach demonstrate in the Latin America context, the very term 'contraband' is a colonial one, referring to undesirable economic activity that is intimately interwoven with imperial projects of territorial expansion, racial subjugation, rule, taxation and capital accumulation, and border-making across porous territory with competitive imperial claims. Thus, there is a tendency to see smuggling as a form of resistance, even when it is not overtly political and rarely interrupts capitalism (Sharma 2022; Mathews et al. 2012). Instead, contraband activities may appropriate the logics of capitalism, or fill in its spaces of organized abandonment, or what Gilmore (2008, 31–2) describes as the 'forgotten places' that 'accompan[y] globalization's large-scale movements of capital and labor'.

Beyond states and illegal practices?

Much existing critical analysis of contraband and illegal practices remains largely state centric, focusing on their symbiotic relationship with states and their legal-definitional, regulatory powers and enforcement (Andreas 1999; Heyman 1999; Van Schendel and Abraham 2005). However, it is important to situate contraband and its associated accusations within transnational configurations of power, within, between and across states, that congeal to advance particular moral, economic and political agendas of prohibition and condemnation, pressure weaker states into compliance, and rely on criminalization as a tactic of dispossession and organized abandonment (Andreas and Nadelmann 2008; Gilmore 2008). For example, the ability of the United States to marshal international support for the War on Drugs, criminalize Black inner-city communities, and dispossess small growers from their land and livelihoods (Schneider and Schneider 2008; Gootenberg 2012). Similarly, wealthy Western countries and powerful corporations and foundations formulate and steer the agenda around intellectual property protections, even when it is not in the interests of other countries, such as Guatemala (see Thomas 2016) to fully comply. The confluence of neoliberal policies, free-trade agreements, privatization and deregulation, and transnational corporate interests, also motivates states to generate climates conducive to extractive development schemes that rely on criminalization through racialized dispossession of Black and Indigenous inhabitants, their land and livelihoods (for example, see Nolin and Stephens 2010; Loperena 2016). The analytic thus must expand to consider the symbiosis between states and illegal practices within broader colonial and global assemblages of il/legitimacy, plunder and racialized violence and dispossession (Mattei and Nader 2008), that position contraband as both threat and necessity. A particular strength of this volume is to problematize the socio-political construction of borders and states to broaden the analysis to internal and regional frontiers 'asserted along lines of topography, ethnicity, religion, language, colonial history, political ideology and so on', that contraband also moves across, resists, constitutes and weaves together (Introduction).

There is a limit in focusing in on the state, which can risk reinforcing pathologizing archetypes of Latin American states while not excusing the behaviour of their elites. States, elites, and extralegal activities also respond to colonial and neocolonial forms of domination, with intellectual property regime standards and punishments designed to protect corporate profits, neoliberal structural adjustment policies, devised by international financial institutions, that particularly decimated the livelihood opportunities and social supports for the marginalized, and free trade agreements intended to facilitate transnational forms of extraction and capital accumulation and criminalize alternative forms of trade long practised across borders (Grimson 2002; Jusionyte 2015; Galemba 2017). Contraband and illegality are thus not only re/produced by states in their attempts to regulate their borders, sovereignty and national identity, but also by global regimes that preserve colonial racial hierarchies that conceal dynamics of accumulation and dispossession. Clark's chapter expertly demonstrates historical, colonial antecedents, in how contraband and smuggling accusations were used to broker particular arrangements of power and control in the region, careful to note specificities across different colonial powers, locations and time periods. Balancing the ethnographic particular with broader patterns, it is important to note that: 'from the beginning of colonial racial capitalist modernity, criminalizing processes and repertoires have sorted people, geographies, and socialities' (Cacho and Melamed 2022, 167). Cacho and Melamed (2022, 166) suggest an examination of the ways that 'criminalization operationalizes racial capitalism' by making violent forms of accumulation, enclosure, deprivation and extraction appear natural. The framework of colonial racial capitalism makes visible the role of race in providing the logic for the kinds of differential value that capitalism requires to empty out, expand and accumulate (Koshy et al. 2022). In the Latin American and Caribbean context, rather than focusing on crime and illegalities, we might instead ask how dynamics of underdevelopment, land dispossession for development and resource extraction, or the criminalization of contraband and petty illegalities, might be recast in terms of the ongoing legacy of slavery, forced assimilation and genocide of Indigenous peoples and land expropriation, colonial imposition and ongoing militarization of borders, and settler colonialism.

Despite critiques of top-down and state-centred analyses, existing studies of contraband, including my own, tend to focus on activities defying nation-state borders, which can inadvertently reify them and narrow our concerns. We risk becoming seduced by illegalities and national borders versus, as Van Roekel suggests, attuning to what people consider to be truly 'at stake'. Or, as Dolph (Chapter 9) demonstrates, contraband is not just about the border, the margins, or even illegality, but instead can highlight more central dilemmas around monetary policymaking, which he argues can also be seen as a 'type of border-making practice that generates grounds on which contraband economies flourish'. Cearns's study of digital piracy across the Cuban diaspora further demonstrates how binaries of legality–illegality, state–individual, and even capitalism–socialism, are too rigid for understanding what are more complex processes of circulation, identity formation, social relations and exchange. Rigid terminologies, as she notes, do little to explain how 'Cubans negotiate extraordinary economic and political circumstances on a daily basis, to maintain their cultural identity across borders'.

Following the contributors, I suggest the need to move beyond the constraints of a nation-state frame, to examine contraband's imbrication with ongoing, evolving processes of colonial racial capitalism. An ethnographic approach is critical to contextualizing contraband within, rather than outside of, the contours of social, political and economic life. A repoliticization of contraband (see Van Roekel) may attune us to not only how marginalized populations survive in contexts of precarity and criminalization, but also to the larger social and political problems from which accusations and practices of contraband so frequently deflect. These contestations go beyond national borders, implicating the international property regimes, rulemaking and border policies often set by countries in the Global North and international financial institutions. Political debates over mass incarceration and universal healthcare become recast as concern over smuggling medications, the impact of US sanctions and state corruption become debates about food and petrol smuggling and scarcity, and fears over drug trafficking are divorced from struggles around land agglomeration (Tusing, this volume). As Van Roekel writes about Venezuela: 'illegality [has] been so compelling in recent studies about the … crisis and economic transactions', rather than engaging what is worrying most Venezuelans – the irony of being hungry in a country founded on and sustained by a myth of abundance.

Kate Meagher (2014), in her study of African clandestine economies, notes how scholars have been frequently blinded by 'smuggling ideologies', tending to interpret empirical findings in light of the prevailing theories or economic logic and failing to capture important empirical distinctions and change over time and place. Some of the contributions to this volume raise important questions about focusing on contraband when it may mask wider 'harms done by state laws … [and] capitalist markets … depoliticizing the [violent] ruling relations' upheld by and naturalized by borders, such that illegality in itself constitutes a way for states to extract more value by criminalizing, suppressing and silencing alternative mobilities (Sharma 2022, 173; Walia 2021).

This volume, while including contraband arrangements across borders more recently and historically, shifts the analytical frame to other regulatory regimes and spaces of contested legitimacy, from that of the Brazilian prison (Chapter 7), the digital mediascape of the Cuban diaspora (Chapter 10), Guatemalan adoption archival records (Chapter 11), to even the body consuming food in a context of scarcity in Venezuela (Chapter 6). As such, they encourage a broader, yet deeply empirical engagement with particular activities, peoples involved, and their own perceptions. The Introduction by Cearns and Beach thus invites scholars to reclaim the term contraband from its criminalizing roots, to explore it as a 'fabric of communal life' that can also illuminate oft-hidden debates around personhood, morality, politics, statehood, political (dis)connection and economic value. Returning to the opening invitation, to rethink what constitutes mundane trade versus smuggling, should motivate deeper political questions around value and legitimacy, as well as more intimate engagements with how people attribute meaning to their lives and activities within contexts of deep exclusion.

References

Aguiar, José Carlos G. 2012. 'Cities on edge: Smuggling and neoliberal policies at the Iguazú triangle', *Singapore Journal of Tropical Geography* 33(2): 171–83.

Aguiar, José Carlos G. 2013. 'Smugglers, fayuqueros, piratas: Transitory commodities and illegality in the trade of pirated CDs in Mexico', *PoLAR: Political and Legal Anthropology Review* 36(2): 249–65.

Andreas, Peter. 1999. 'Smuggling wars: Law enforcement and law evasion in a changing world'. In *Transnational Crime in the Americas,* edited by Tom Farer, 85–98. New York and London: Routledge.

Andreas, Peter. 2011. 'Illicit globalization: Myths, misconceptions, and historical lessons', *Political Science Quarterly* 126(3): 403–25.

Andreas, Peter. 2013. *Smuggler Nation: How illicit trade made America*. Oxford: Oxford University Press.

Andreas, Peter and Ethan Nadelmann. 2008. *Policing the Globe: Criminalization and crime control in international relations*. Oxford: Oxford University Press.

Arias, Enrique Desmond and Daniel M. Goldstein (eds). 2010. *Violent Democracies in Latin America.* Durham, NC: Duke University Press.

Auyero, Javier. 2012. *Patients of the State: The politics of waiting in Argentina*. Durham, NC: Duke University Press.

Burrell, Jennifer. 2013. *Maya after War: Conflict, power, and politics in Guatemala*. Austin: University of Texas Press.

Cacho, Lisa Marie and Jodi Melamed. 2022. '"Don't arrest me, arrest the police": Policing as the street administration of colonial racial capitalist orders'. In *Colonial Racial Capitalism,* edited by Susan Koshy, Lisa Marie Cacho, Jodi A. Byrd and Brian Jordan Jefferson, 159–205. Durham, NC: Duke University Press.

Caldeira, Teresa P. R. 2000. *City of Walls: Crime, segregation, and citizenship in São Paulo*. Berkeley: University of California Press.

Dent, Alexander S. 2012. 'Piracy, circulatory legitimacy, and neoliberal subjectivity in Brazil', *Cultural Anthropology* 27(1): 28–49.

Dent, Alexander S. 2020. *Digital Pirates: Policing intellectual property in Brazil*. Redwood City, CA: Stanford University Press.
Dewey, Matías. 2020. *Making It At Any Cost: Aspirations and politics in a counterfeit clothing marketplace*. Austin: University of Texas Press.
Dewey, Matías and Kedron Thomas. 2022. 'Futurity beyond the state: Illegal markets and imagined futures in Latin America', *Latin American Politics and Society* 64(4): 1–23.
Galemba, Rebecca B. 2012. '"Corn is food, not contraband": The right to "free trade" at the Mexico–Guatemala border', *American Ethnologist* 39(4): 716–34.
Galemba, Rebecca B. 2017. *Contraband Corridor: Making a living at the Mexico–Guatemala border*. Redwood City, CA: Stanford University Press.
Gallant, Thomas. 1999. 'Brigandage, piracy, capitalism and state formation: Transnational crime from a historical world systems perspective'. In *States and Illegal Practices*, edited by Josiah M. Heyman, 25–62. New York: Berg Press.
Gallien, Max and Florian Weigand. 2022. 'Studying smuggling'. In *The Routledge Handbook of Smuggling*, edited by Max Gallien and Florian Weigand, 1–15. Abingdon: Routledge.
Gilmore, Ruth Wilson. 2008. 'Forgotten places and the seeds of grassroots planning'. In *Engaging Contradictions: Theory, politics, and methods of activist scholarship*, edited by Charles R. Hale, 31–61. Berkeley: University of California Press.
Godoy, Angelina Snodgrass. 2004. 'When "justice" is criminal: Lynchings in contemporary Latin America', *Theory and Society* 33: 621–51.
Goldstein, Daniel M. 2004. *The Spectacular City: Violence and performance in urban Bolivia*. Durham, NC: Duke University Press.
Goldstein, Daniel M. 2016. *Owners of the Sidewalk: Security and survival in the informal city*. Durham, NC: Duke University Press.
Gootenberg, Paul. 2012. 'Cocaine's long march north, 1900–2010', *Latin American Politics and Society* 54(1): 159–80.
Grimson, Alejandro. 2002. 'Hygiene wars on the Mercosur border: Local and national agency in Uruguaiana (Brazil) and Paso de los Libres (Argentina)', *Identities: Global Studies in Culture and Power* 9(2): 151–72.
Heyman, Josiah M. (ed.). 1999. *States and Illegal Practices*. New York: Berg Press.
Heyman, Josiah M. and Alan Smart. 1999. 'States and illegal practices: An overview'. In *States and Illegal Practices*, edited by Josiah M. Heyman, 1–24. New York: Berg Press.
Hobsbawm, Eric. 2000. *Bandits*. Rev. ed. New York: The New Press.
Holston, James. 2007. *Insurgent Citizenship: Disjunctions of democracy and modernity in Brazil*. Princeton: Princeton University Press.
Jusionyte, Ieva. 2015. *Savage Frontier: Making news and security on the Argentine border*. Oakland: University of California Press.
Keshavarz, Mahmoud and Shahram Khosravi. 2022. 'Introduction: To see like a smuggler'. In *Seeing Like a Smuggler: Borders from below*, edited by Mahmoud Keshavarz and Shahram Khosravi, 1–18. London: Pluto Press.
Koram, Kojo (ed.). 2019. *The War on Drugs and the Global Colour Line*. London: Pluto Press.
Koshy, Susan, Lisa Marie Cacho, Jodi A. Byrd and Brian Jordan Jefferson. 2022. 'Introduction'. In *Colonial Racial Capitalism*, edited by Susan Koshy, Lisa Marie Cacho, Jodi A. Byrd and Brian Jordan Jefferson, 1–32. Durham, NC: Duke University Press.
Lazar, Sian. 2008. *El Alto, Rebel City: Self and citizenship in Andean Bolivia*. Durham, NC: Duke University Press.
Leeds, Elizabeth. 1996. 'Cocaine and parallel polities in the Brazilian urban periphery: Constraints on local-level democratization', *Latin American Research Review* 31(3): 47–83.
Loperena, Christopher A. 2016. 'Conservation by racialized dispossession: The making of an eco-destination on Honduras's north coast', *Geoforum* 69: 184–93.
Mathews, Gordon, Gustavo Lins Ribeiro and Carlos Alba Vega (eds). 2012. *Globalization from Below: The world's other economy*. Abingdon: Routledge.
Mattei, Ugo and Laura Nader. 2008. *Plunder: When the rule of law is illegal*. Malden: John Wiley & Sons.
Meagher, Kate. 2014. 'Smuggling ideologies: From criminalization to hybrid governance in African clandestine economies', *African Affairs* 113(453): 497–517.
Merry, Sally Engle. 1998. 'The criminalization of everyday life'. In *Everyday Practices and Trouble Cases*, edited by Austin Sarat, Marianne Constable, David Engel, Valeria Hans and Susan Lawrence, 14–40. Evanston, IL: Northwestern University Press.

Millar, Kathleen M. 2018. *Reclaiming the Discarded: Life and labor on Rio's garbage dump*. Durham, NC: Duke University Press.
Nolin, Catherine and Jacqui Stephens. 2010. '"We Have to Protect the Investors": "Development" & Canadian mining companies in Guatemala', *Journal of Rural and Community Development* 5(3): 37–70.
Nugent, David. 1999. 'State and shadow state in northern Peru circa 1900: Illegal political networks and the problem of state boundaries'. In *States and Illegal Practices*, edited by Josiah M. Heyman, 63–98. New York: Berg Press.
Nuijten, Monique and Gerhard Anders (eds). 2007. *Corruption and the Secret of Law: A legal anthropological perspective*. Aldershot: Ashgate.
O'Neill, Kevin Lewis and Kedron Thomas (eds). 2011. *Securing the City: Neoliberalism, space, and insecurity in postwar Guatemala*. Durham, NC: Duke University Press.
Parsa, Amin. 2022. 'Kolbari: Workers not smugglers'. In *Seeing Like a Smuggler: Borders from below*, edited by Mahmoud Keshavarz and Shahram Khosravi, 80–91. London: Pluto Press.
Piliavsky, Anastasia. 2013. 'Borders without borderlands: On the social reproduction of state demarcation in Rajasthan'. In *Borderland Lives in Northern South Asia: Non-state perspectives*, edited by David N. Gellner, 24–46. Durham, NC: Duke University Press.
Roitman, Janet. 2006. 'The ethics of illegality in the Chad Basin'. In *Law and Disorder in the Postcolony*, edited by Jean Comaroff and John Comaroff, 247–72. Chicago: University of Chicago Press.
Rus, Jan and Diego Vigil. 2007. 'Rapid urbanization and migrant indigenous youth in San Cristóbal de las Casas, Chiapas, Mexico'. In *Gangs in the Global City: Alternatives to traditional criminology*, edited by John Hagedorn, 152–84. Champaign: University of Illinois Press.
Sánchez, Gabriella. 2017. 'Critical perspectives on clandestine migration facilitation: An overview of migrant smuggling research', *Journal on Migration and Human Security* 5(1): 9–27.
Schneider, Jane and Peter Schneider. 2008. 'The anthropology of crime and criminalization', *Annual Review of Anthropology* 37: 351–73.
Schuster, Caroline E. 2022. 'Gender and smuggling'. In *The Routledge Handbook of Smuggling*, edited by Max Gallien and Florian Weigand, 168–79. Abingdon: Routledge.
Schwartz, Steven. 2021. 'The politics of bachaqueo: Gasoline black markets and indigeneity in Venezuela', *American Ethnologist* 48(4): 504–19.
Sharma, Nandita. 2020. 'The "people out of place": State limits on free mobility and the making of im(migrants)'. In *Paper Trails*, edited by Sarah B. Horton and Josiah M. Heyman, 31–52. Durham, NC: Duke University Press.
Sharma, Nandita. 2022. 'Afterword: Seeing freedom'. In *Seeing Like a Smuggler: Borders from below*, edited by Mahmoud Keshavarz and Shahram Khosravi, 169–77. London: Pluto Press.
Taussig, Michael. 2003. *Law in a Lawless Land: Diary of a limpieza in Colombia*. Chicago: University of Chicago Press.
Thomas, Kedron 2016. *Regulating Style: Intellectual property law and the business of fashion in Guatemala*. Oakland: University of California Press.
Thompson, Edward P. 1967. 'Time, work-discipline, and industrial capitalism', *Past & Present* 38: 56–97.
Thompson, Edward P. 1971. 'The moral economy of the English crowd in the eighteenth century', *Past & Present* 50: 76–136.
Thompson, Edward P. 1975. *Whigs and Hunters: The origin of the Black Act*. London: Penguin.
Tilly, Charles. 1985. 'The state as organized crime'. In *Bringing the State Back In*, edited by Peter Evans, Dietrich Rueschemeyer and Theda Skocpol, 169–91. Cambridge: Cambridge University Press.
Van Schendel, Willem and Itty Abraham (eds). 2005. *Illicit Flows and Criminal Things: States, borders, and the other side of globalization*. Bloomington: University of Indiana Press.
Walia, Harsha. 2021. *Border and Rule: Global migration, capitalism, and the rise of racist nationalism*. Chicago: Haymarket Books.
Wolf, Eric R. 1982. *Europe and the People without History*. Berkeley: University of California Press.
Zhang, Sheldon X., Gabriella E. Sanchez and Luigi Achilli. 2018. 'Crimes of solidarity in mobility: Alternative views on migrant smuggling', *The ANNALS of the American Academy of Political and Social Science* 676(1): 6–15.

Index

www.ingramcontent.com/pod-product-compliance
Lightning Source LLC
LaVergne TN
LVHW020130270926
848888LV00003B/12